THE EDUCATION
OF A CHRISTIAN WOMAN:
A SIXTEENTH-CENTURY
MANUAL

THE OTHER VOICE IN EARLY MODERN EUROPE

A Series Edited by Margaret L. King and Albert Rabil Jr.

OTHER BOOKS IN THE SERIES

Juan Luis Vives

THE EDUCATION
OF A CHRISTIAN WOMAN:
A SIXTEENTH-CENTURY
MANUAL

Edited and Translated
by
Charles Fantazzi

THE UNIVERSITY OF CHICAGO PRESS
Chicago & London

Charles Fantazzi is Distinguished Visiting Professor of Humanities at
East Carolina University and professor of classics at the University of Windsor.
He has translated several volumes for the *Collected Works of Erasmus*
(University of Toronto Press) and has published critical editions
and translations of works of Juan Luis Vives
(Brill Academic Publishers).

The University of Chicago Press, Chicago 60637
The University of Chicago Press, Ltd., London
© 2000 by The University of Chicago
All rights reserved. Published 2000
Printed in the United States of America
09 08 07 06 05 04 03 02 01 00   1 2 3 4 5

ISBN: 0-226-85814-6 (cloth)
ISBN: 0-226-85815-4 (paper)

Permission for the separate publication of the English translation has been
kindly granted to the translator by Koninklijke Brill NV, Leiden, The Netherlands.

Library of Congress Cataloging-in-Publication Data

Vives, Juan Luis, 1492–1540.
   [De institutione feminae Christianae. English]
   The education of a Christian woman : a sixteenth-century manual /
Juan Luis Vives ; edited and translated by Charles Fantazzi.
      p.   cm. — (The other voice in early modern Europe)
   Includes bibliographical references and index.
   ISBN 0-226-85814-6 (cl. : alk. paper). — ISBN 0-226-85815-4 (pbk.)
   1. Christian women—Conduct of life—Early works to 1800.
   2. Christian women—Education—Early works to 1800.   I. Fantazzi,
Charles. II. Title. III. Series.
B785.V63D4713 2000
371.822—dc21   99-30671
                                                                      CIP

Nous employons toutes sortes de moyens pour leur abattre le courage;
les forces seroient égales, si l'éducation l'étoit aussi.

[We use every sort of stratagem to demoralize them (i.e., women);
their powers would be equal to ours if their education were also.]

—MONTESQUIEU, *LETTRES PERSANES*

WITHDRAWN

CONTENTS

THE OTHER VOICE
IN EARLY MODERN EUROPE:
INTRODUCTION TO THE SERIES
Margaret L. King and Albert Rabil Jr.

THE OLD VOICE AND THE OTHER VOICE

In western Europe and the United States women are nearing equality in the professions, in business, and in politics. Most enjoy access to education, reproductive rights, and autonomy in financial affairs. Issues vital to women are on the public agenda: equal pay, child care, domestic abuse, breast cancer research, and curricular revision with an eye to the inclusion of women.

These recent achievements have their origins in things women (and some male supporters) said for the first time about six hundred years ago. Theirs is the "other voice," in contradistinction to the "first voice," the voice of the educated men who created Western culture. Coincident with a general reshaping of European culture in the period 1300–1700 (called the Renaissance or early modern period), questions of female equality and opportunity were raised that still resound and are still unresolved.

The "other voice" emerged against the backdrop of a three-thousand-year history of the derogation of women rooted in the civilizations related to Western culture: Hebrew, Greek, Roman, and Christian. Negative attitudes toward women inherited from these traditions pervaded the intellectual, medical, legal, religious, and social systems that developed during the European Middle Ages.

The following pages describe the traditional, overwhelmingly male views of women's nature inherited by early modern Europeans, and the new tradition that the "other voice" called into being to challenge reigning assumptions. This review should serve as a framework for understanding the texts published in the series "The Other Voice in Early Modern Europe." Introductions specific to each text and author follow this essay in all the volumes of the series.

TRADITIONAL VIEWS OF WOMEN, 500 B.C.E.–1500 C.E.

Embedded in the philosophical and medical theories of the ancient Greeks were perceptions of the female as inferior to the male in both mind and body. Similarly, the structure of civil legislation inherited from the ancient Romans was biased against women, and the views on women developed by Christian thinkers out of the Hebrew Bible and the Christian New Testament were negative and disabling. Literary works composed in the vernacular of ordinary people, and widely recited or read, conveyed these negative assumptions. The social networks within which most women lived—those of the family and the institutions of the Roman Catholic Church—were shaped by this negative tradition and sharply limited the areas in which women might act in and upon the world.

GREEK PHILOSOPHY AND FEMALE NATURE. Greek biology assumed that women were inferior to men and defined them as merely as childbearers and housekeepers. This view was authoritatively expressed in the works of the philosopher Aristotle.

Aristotle thought in dualities. He considered action superior to inaction, form (the inner design or structure of any object) superior to matter, completion to incompletion, possession to deprivation. In each of these dualities he associated the male principle with the superior quality and the female with the inferior. "The male principle in nature," he argued, "is associated with active, formative and perfected characteristics, while the female is passive, material and deprived, desiring the male in order to become complete."[1] Men are always identified with virile qualities, such as judgment, courage, and stamina, and women with their opposites—irrationality, cowardice, and weakness.

The masculine principle was considered to be superior even in the womb. The man's semen, Aristotle believed, created the form of a new human creature, while the female body contributed only matter. (The existence of the ovum, and the other facts of human embryology, was not established until the seventeenth century.) Although the later Greek physician Galen believed there was a female component in generation, contributed by "female semen," the followers of both Aristotle and Galen saw the male role in human generation as more active and more important.

In the Aristotelian view, the male principle sought to reproduce itself. The creation of a female was always a mistake, therefore, resulting from

---

1. Aristotle, *Physics* 1.9 192a20–24 (*The Complete Works of Aristotle*, ed. Jonathan Barnes, rev. Oxford translation, 2 vols. [Princeton, 1984], 1.328).

an imperfect act of generation. Every female born was considered a "defective" or "mutilated" male (as Aristotle's terminology has variously been translated), a "monstrosity" of nature.[2]

For Greek theorists, the biology of males and females was the key to their psychology. The female was softer and more docile, more apt to be despondent, querulous, and deceitful. Being incomplete, moreover, she craved sexual fulfillment in intercourse with a male. The male was intellectual, active, and in control of his passions.

These psychological polarities derived from the theory that the universe consisted of four elements (earth, fire, air, and water), expressed in human bodies as four "humors" (black bile, yellow bile, blood, and phlegm) considered respectively dry, hot, damp, and cold, and corresponding to mental states ("melancholic," "choleric," "sanguine," "phlegmatic"). In this scheme, the male, sharing the principles of earth and fire, was dry and hot; the female, sharing the principles of air and water, was damp and cold.

Woman's psychology was further affected by her dominant organ, the uterus (womb), *hystera* in Greek. The passions generated by the womb made women lustful, deceitful, talkative, irrational, indeed—when these affects were in excess—"hysterical."

Aristotle's biology also had social and political consequences. If the male principle was superior and the female inferior, then in the household, as in the state, men should rule and women must be subordinate. That hierarchy did not rule out the companionship of husband and wife, whose cooperation was necessary for the welfare of children and the preservation of property. Such mutuality supported male preeminence.

Aristotle's teacher Plato suggested a different possibility: that men and women might possess the same virtues. The setting for this proposal is the imaginary and ideal Republic that Plato sketches in his dialogue of that name. Here for a privileged elite capable of leading wisely, all distinctions of class and wealth dissolve, as consequently do those of gender. Without households or property, as Plato constructs his ideal society, there is no need for the subordination of women. Women may therefore be educated to the same level as men to assume leadership. Plato's Republic remained imaginary, however. In real societies, the subordination of women remained the norm and the prescription.

The views of women inherited from the Greek philosophical tradition became the basis for medieval thought. In the thirteenth century the

2. Aristotle, *Generation of Animals* 2.3 737a27–28 (Barnes, 1.1144).

supreme Scholastic philosopher Thomas Aquinas, among others, still echoed Aristotle's views of human reproduction, of male and female personalities, and of the preeminent role of the male in the social hierarchy.

ROMAN LAW AND THE FEMALE CONDITION. Roman law, like Greek philosophy, underlay medieval thought and shaped medieval society. The ancient belief that adult, property-owning men should administer households and make decisions affecting the community at large is the very fulcrum of Roman law.

Around 450 B.C.E., during Rome's republican era, the community's customary law was recorded (legendarily) on twelve tables erected in the city's central forum. It was later elaborated by professional jurists whose activity increased in the imperial era, when much new legislation was passed, especially on issues affecting family and inheritance. This growing, changing body of laws was eventually codified in the *Corpus of Civil Law* under the direction of the emperor Justinian, generations after the empire ceased to be ruled from Rome. That *Corpus*, read and commented upon by medieval scholars from the eleventh century on, inspired the legal systems of most of the cities and kingdoms of Europe.

Laws regarding dowries, divorce, and inheritance mostly pertain to women. Since those laws aimed to maintain and preserve property, the women concerned were those from the property-owning minority. Their subordination to male family members points to the even greater subordination of lower-class and slave women, about whom the laws speak little.

In the early republic the *paterfamilias*, "father of the family," possessed *patria potestas*, "paternal power." The term *pater*, "father," in both these cases does not necessarily mean biological father but denotes a householder. The father was the person who owned the household's property and, indeed, its human members. The *paterfamilias* had absolute power—including the power, rarely exercised, of life or death—over his wife, his children, and his slaves as much as his cattle.

Male children could be "emancipated," an act that granted them legal autonomy and the right to own property. Those over fourteen could be emancipated by a special grant from the father, or automatically by the father's death. But females could never be emancipated; instead, they passed from the authority of the father to that of a husband or, if widowed or orphaned while still unmarried, a guardian or tutor.

Marriage in its traditional form placed the woman under her husband's authority, or *manus*. He could divorce her on grounds of adultery, drinking wine, or stealing from the household, but she could not divorce him. She could possess no property in her own right, nor could she bequeath any to her children upon her death. When her husband died the household property passed not to her but to his male heirs. And when her father died she had no claim to any family inheritance, which was directed to her brothers or more remote male relatives. The effect of these laws was to exclude women from civil society, itself based on property ownership.

In the later republican and imperial periods these rules were significantly modified, and women rarely married according to the traditional form. The practice of "free" marriage allowed a woman to remain under her father's authority, to possess property given her by her father (most frequently the "dowry," recoverable from the husband's household on his death), and to inherit from her father. She could also bequeath property to her own children and divorce her husband, just as he could divorce her.

Despite this greater freedom, women still suffered enormous disability under Roman law. Heirs could belong only to the father's side, never the mother's. Moreover, although she could bequeath her property to her children, she could not establish a line of succession in doing so. A woman was "the beginning and end of her own family," said the jurist Ulpian. Moreover, women could play no public role. They could not hold public office, represent anyone in a legal case, or even witness a will. Women had only a private existence and no public personality.

The dowry system, the guardian, women's limited ability to transmit wealth, and their total political disability are all features of Roman law adopted by the medieval communities of western Europe, although modified according to local customary laws.

CHRISTIAN DOCTRINE AND WOMEN'S PLACE. The Hebrew Bible and the Christian New Testament authorized later writers to limit women to the realm of the family and to burden them with the guilt of original sin. The passages most fruitful for this purpose were the creation narratives in Genesis and sentences from the Epistles defining women's role within the Christian family and community.

Each of the first two chapters of Genesis contains a creation narrative. In the first "God created man in his own image, in the image of God he created him; male and female he created them" (Gen. 1:27). In the second, God created Eve from Adam's rib (2:21–23). Christian theologians relied principally on Genesis 2 for their understanding of the relationship between man and woman, interpreting the creation of Eve from Adam as proof of her subordination to him.

The creation story in Genesis 2 leads to that of the temptations in Genesis 3: of Eve by the wily serpent and of Adam by Eve. As read by Christian theologians from Tertullian to Thomas Aquinas, the narrative made Eve responsible for the Fall and its consequences. She instigated the act; she deceived her husband; she suffered the greater punishment. Her disobedience made it necessary for Jesus to be incarnated and to die on the cross. From the pulpit, moralists and preachers for centuries conveyed to women the guilt they bore for original sin.

The Epistles offered advice to early Christians on building communities of the faithful. Among the matters to be regulated was the place of women. Paul offered views favorable to women in Gal. 3:28: "There is neither Jew nor Greek, there is neither slave nor free, there is neither male nor female; for you are all one in Christ Jesus." Paul also referred to women as his coworkers and placed them on a par with himself and his male coworkers (Phil. 4:2–3; Rom. 16:1–3; 1 Cor. 16:19). Elsewhere Paul limited women's possibilities: "But I want you to understand that the head of every man is Christ, the head of a woman is her husband, and the head of Christ is God" (1 Cor. 11:3).

Biblical passages by later writers (though attributed to Paul) enjoined women to forgo jewels, expensive clothes, and elaborate coiffures; and they forbade women to "teach or have authority over men," telling them to "learn in silence with all submissiveness" as is proper for one responsible for sin, consoling them however with the thought that they will be saved through childbearing (1 Tim. 2:9–15). Other texts among the later Epistles defined women as the weaker sex and emphasized their subordination to their husbands (1 Peter 3:7; Col. 3:18; Eph. 5:22–23).

These passages from the New Testament became the arsenal employed by theologians of the early church to transmit negative attitudes toward women to medieval Christian culture—above all, Tertullian ("On the Apparel of Women"), Jerome (*Against Jovinian*), and Augustine (*The Literal Meaning of Genesis*).

THE IMAGE OF WOMEN IN MEDIEVAL LITERATURE. The philosophical, legal, and religious traditions born in antiquity formed the basis of the medieval intellectual synthesis wrought by trained thinkers, mostly clerics, writing in Latin and based largely in universities. The vernacular literary tradition that developed alongside the learned tradition also spoke about female nature and women's roles. Medieval stories, poems, and epics also portrayed women negatively—as lustful and deceitful—while praising good housekeepers and loyal wives as replicas of the Virgin Mary or the female saints and martyrs.

There is an exception in the movement of "courtly love" that evolved in southern France from the twelfth century. Courtly love was erotic love between a nobleman and noblewoman, the latter usually superior in social rank. It was always adulterous. From the conventions of courtly love derive modern Western notions of romantic love. The tradition has had an impact disproportionate to its size, for it affected only a tiny elite, and very few women. The exaltation of the female lover probably does not reflect a higher evaluation of women, or a step toward their sexual liberation. More likely it gives expression to the social and sexual tensions besetting the knightly class at a specific historical juncture.

The literary fashion of courtly love was on the wane by the thirteenth century, when the widely read *Romance of the Rose* was composed in French by two authors of significantly different dispositions. Guillaume de Lorris composed the initial four thousand verses about 1235, and Jean de Meun added about seventeen thousand verses—more than four times the original—about 1265.

The fragment composed by Guillaume de Lorris stands squarely in the tradition of courtly love. Here the poet, in a dream, is admitted into a walled garden where he finds a magic fountain in which a rosebush is reflected. He longs to pick one rose, but the thorns prevent it, even as he is wounded by arrows from the god of love, whose commands he agrees to obey. The rest of this part of the poem recounts the poet's unsuccessful efforts to pluck the rose.

The longer part of the *Romance* by Jean de Meun also describes a dream. But here allegorical characters give long didactic speeches, providing a social satire on a variety of themes, some pertaining to women. Love is an anxious and tormented state, the poem explains; women are greedy and manipulative, marriage is miserable, beautiful women are lustful, ugly ones cease to please, and a chaste woman is as rare as a black swan.

Shortly after Jean de Meun completed *The Romance of the Rose*, Mathéolus penned his *Lamentations*, a long Latin diatribe against marriage translated into French about a century later. The *Lamentations* summed up medieval attitudes toward women and provoked the important response by Christine de Pizan in her *Book of the City of Ladies*.

In 1355 Giovanni Boccaccio wrote *Il Corbaccio*, another antifeminist manifesto, though ironically by an author whose other works pioneered new directions in Renaissance thought. The former husband of his lover appears to Boccaccio, condemning his unmoderated lust and detailing the defects of women. Boccaccio concedes at the end "how much men naturally surpass women in nobility"[3] and is cured of his desires.

---

3. Giovanni Boccaccio, *The Corbaccio or The Labyrinth of Love*, trans. and ed. Anthony K. Cassell (Binghamton, N.Y., rev. paper ed., 1993), 71.

WOMEN'S ROLES: THE FAMILY. The negative perception of women expressed in the intellectual tradition is also implicit in the actual roles women played in European society. Assigned to subordinate positions in the household and the church, they were barred from significant participation in public life.

Medieval European households, like those in antiquity and in non-Western civilizations, were headed by males. It was the male serf, peasant, feudal lord, town merchant, or citizen who was polled or taxed or who succeeded to an inheritance or had any acknowledged public role, although his wife or widow could stand as a temporary surrogate for him. From about 1100, the position of property-holding males was further enhanced. Inheritance was confined to the male, or agnate, line—with depressing consequences for women.

A wife never fully belonged to her husband's family nor a daughter to her father's. She left her father's house young to marry whomever her parents chose. Her dowry was managed by her husband, and at her death it normally passed to her children by him.

A married woman's life was occupied nearly constantly with cycles of pregnancy, childbearing, and lactation. Women bore children through all the years of their fertility, and many died in childbirth. They also were responsible for raising young children up to six or seven. In the propertied classes that responsibility was shared, since it was common for a wet nurse to take over breast-feeding, and servants performed other chores.

Women trained their daughters in the household duties appropriate to their status, nearly always tasks associated with textiles: spinning, weaving, sewing, embroidering. Their sons were sent out of the house as apprentices or students, or their fathers assumed their training in later childhood and adolescence. On the death of her husband, a woman's children became the responsibility of his family. She generally did not take "his" children with her to a new marriage or back to her father's house, except sometimes in artisan classes.

Women also worked. Peasants performed farm chores, merchant wives often practiced their husbands' trades, the unmarried daughters of the urban poor worked as servants or prostitutes. All wives produced or embellished textiles and did the housekeeping, and wealthy ones managed servants. These labors were unpaid or poorly paid but often contributed substantially to family wealth.

WOMEN'S ROLES: THE CHURCH. Membership in a household, whether a father's or a husband's, meant for women a lifelong subordination to others. In western Europe the Roman Catholic Church offered an alternative to the

career of wife and mother. A woman could enter a convent parallel in function to the monasteries for men that evolved in the early Christian centuries.

In the convent, a woman pledged herself to a celibate life, lived according to strict community rules, and worshiped daily. Often the convent
offered training in Latin, allowing some women to become considerable
scholars and authors as well as scribes, artists, and musicians. For women
who chose the conventual life the benefits could be enormous, but for numerous others placed in convents by paternal choice, the life could be re-
strictive and burdensome.

The conventual life declined as an alternative for women as the modern
age approached. Reformed monastic institutions resisted responsibility for
related female orders. The church increasingly restricted female institutional
life by insisting on closer male supervision.

Women often sought other options. Some joined the communities of
laywomen that sprang up spontaneously in the thirteenth century in the urban zones of western Europe, especially in Flanders and Italy. Some joined
the heretical movements that flourished in late medieval Christendom, whose
anticlerical and often antifamily positions particularly appealed to women.
In these communities, some women were acclaimed as "holy women" or
"saints," whereas others often were condemned as frauds or heretics.

Though the options offered to women by the church were sometimes
less than satisfactory, they were sometimes richly rewarding. After 1520 the
convent remained an option only in Roman Catholic territories. Protestant-
ism engendered an ideal of marriage as a heroic endeavor and appeared to
place husband and wife on a more equal footing. Sermons and treatises,
however, still called for female subordination and obedience.

THE OTHER VOICE, 1300–1700

When the modern era opened, European culture was so firmly structured by
a framework of negative attitudes toward women that to dismantle it was a
monumental labor. The process began as part of a larger cultural movement
that entailed the critical reexamination of ideas inherited from the ancient
and medieval past. The humanists launched that critical reexamination.

THE HUMANIST FOUNDATION. Originating in Italy in the fourteenth
century, humanism quickly became the dominant intellectual movement in
Europe. Spreading in the sixteenth century from Italy to the rest of Europe,
it fueled the literary, scientific, and philosophical movements of the era and
laid the basis for the eighteenth-century Enlightenment.

Humanists regarded the Scholastic philosophy of medieval universities as out of touch with the realities of urban life. They found in the rhetorical discourse of classical Rome a language adapted to civic life and public speech. They learned to read, speak, and write classical Latin, and eventually classical Greek. They founded schools to teach others to do so, establishing the pattern for elementary and secondary education for the next three hundred years.

In the service of complex government bureaucracies, humanists employed their skills to write eloquent letters, deliver public orations, and formulate public policy. They developed new scripts for copying manuscripts and used the new printing press to disseminate texts, for which they created methods of critical editing.

Humanism was a movement led by males who accepted the evaluation of women in ancient texts and generally shared the misogynist perceptions of their culture. (Female humanists, as we will see, did not.) Yet humanism also opened the door to a reevaluation of the nature and capacity of women. By calling authors, texts, and ideas into question, it made possible the fundamental rereading of the whole intellectual tradition that was required in order to free women from cultural prejudice and social subordination.

A DIFFERENT CITY. The other voice first appeared when, after so many centuries, the accumulation of misogynist concepts evoked a response from a capable female defender: Christine de Pizan (1365–1431). Introducing her *Book of the City of Ladies* (1405), she described how she was affected by reading Mathéolus's *Lamentations:* "Just the sight of this book . . . made me wonder how it happened that so many different men . . . are so inclined to express both in speaking and in their treatises and writings so many wicked insults about women and their behavior."[4] These statements impelled her to detest herself "and the entire feminine sex, as though we were monstrosities in nature."[5]

The rest of the *Book of the City of Ladies* presents a justification of the female sex and a vision of an ideal community of women. A pioneer, she has received the message of female inferiority and rejected it. From the fourteenth to the seventeenth century, a huge body of literature accumulated that responded to the dominant tradition.

The result was a literary explosion consisting of works by both men and women, in Latin and in the vernaculars: works enumerating the achievements of notable women; works rebutting the main accusations made against

4. Christine de Pizan, *Book of the City of Ladies,* trans. Earl Jeffrey Richards, foreword Marina Warner (New York, 1982), 1.1.1., pp. 3–4.
5. Ibid., 1.1.1–2, p. 5.

women; works arguing for the equal education of men and women; works defining and redefining women's proper role in the family, at court, and in public; works describing women's lives and experiences. Recent monographs and articles have begun to hint at the great range of this movement, involving probably several thousand titles. The protofeminism of these "other voices" constitutes a significant fraction of the literary product of the early modern era.

THE CATALOGS. About 1365, the same Boccaccio whose *Corbaccio* rehearses the usual charges against female nature wrote another work, *Concerning Famous Women*. A humanist treatise drawing on classical texts, it praised 106 notable women from pagan Greek and Roman antiquity, from the Bible (Eve), and from the medieval religious and cultural tradition; his book helped make all readers aware of a sex normally condemned or forgotten. Boccaccio's outlook nevertheless was unfriendly to women, for it singled out for praise those women who possessed the traditional virtues of chastity, silence, and obedience. Women who were active in the public realm—for example, rulers and warriors—were depicted as usually being lascivious and as suffering terrible punishments for entering the masculine sphere. Women were his subject, but Boccaccio's standard remained male.

Christine de Pizan's *Book of the City of Ladies* contains a second catalog, one responding specifically to Boccaccio's. Where Boccaccio portrays female virtue as exceptional, she depicts it as universal. Many women in history were leaders, or remained chaste despite the lascivious approaches of men, or were visionaries and brave martyrs.

The work of Boccaccio inspired a series of catalogs of illustrious women of the biblical, classical, Christian, and local pasts, among them Filippo da Bergamo's *Of Illustrious Women*, Pierre de Brantôme's *Lives of Illustrious Women*, Pierre Le Moyne's *Gallerie of Heroic Women*, and Pietro Paolo de Ribera's *Immortal Triumphs and Heroic Enterprises of 845 Women*. Whatever their embedded prejudices, these works drove home to the public the possibility of female excellence.

THE DEBATE. Yet many questions remained: Could a woman be virtuous? Could she perform noteworthy deeds? Was she even, strictly speaking, of the same human species as men? These questions were debated over four centuries, in French, German, Italian, Spanish, and English, by authors male and female, among Catholics, Protestants, and Jews, in ponderous volumes and breezy pamphlets. The whole literary genre has been called the *querelle des femmes*, the "woman question."

The opening volley of this battle occurred in the first years of the fifteenth century, in a literary debate sparked by Christine de Pizan. She exchanged letters critical of Jean de Meun's contribution to *The Romance of the Rose* with two French royal secretaries, Jean de Montreuil and Gontier Col. When the matter became public, Jean Gerson, one of Europe's leading theologians, supported her arguments against Jean de Meun, for the moment silencing the opposition.

The debate surfaced repeatedly over the next two hundred years. *The Triumph of Women* (1438) by Juan Rodríguez de la Camara (or Juan Rodríguez del Padron) struck a new note by presenting arguments for the superiority of women to men. *The Champion of Women* (1440–42) by Martin Le Franc addresses once again the negative views of women presented in *The Romance of the Rose*, and offers counterevidence of female virtue and achievement.

A cameo of the debate on women is included in *The Courtier*, one of the most widely read books of the era, published by the Italian Baldassare Castiglione in 1528 and immediately translated into other European languages. The *Courtier* depicts a series of evenings at the court of the duke of Urbino in which many men and some women of the highest social stratum amuse themselves by discussing a range of literary and social issues. The "woman question" is a pervasive theme throughout, and the third of its four books is devoted entirely to that issue.

In a verbal duel, Gasparo Pallavicino and Giuliano de' Medici present the main claims of the two traditions. Gasparo argues the innate inferiority of women and their inclination to vice. Only in bearing children do they profit the world. Giuliano counters that women share the same spiritual and mental capacities as men and may excel in wisdom and action. Men and women are of the same essence: just as no stone can be more perfectly a stone than another, so no human being can be more perfectly human than others, whether male or female. It was an astonishing assertion, boldly made to an audience as large as all Europe.

THE TREATISES. Humanism provided the materials for a positive counterconcept to the misogyny embedded in Scholastic philosophy and law and inherited from the Greek, Roman, and Christian pasts. A series of humanist treatises on marriage and family, education and deportment, and the nature of women helped construct these new perspectives.

The works by Francesco Barbaro and Leon Battista Alberti, respectively *On Marriage* (1415) and *On the Family* (1434–37), far from defending female equality, reasserted women's responsibility for rearing children and managing the housekeeping while being obedient, chaste, and silent. Nevertheless, they served the cause of reexamining the issue of women's nature by placing domestic issues at the center of scholarly concern and reopening the pertinent classical texts. In addition, Barbaro emphasized the companionate nature of marriage and the importance of a wife's spiritual and mental qualities for the well-being of the family.

These themes reappear in later humanist works on marriage and the education of women by Juan Luis Vives and Erasmus. Both were moderately sympathetic to the condition of women without reaching beyond the usual masculine prescriptions for female behavior.

An outlook more favorable to women characterizes the nearly unknown work *In Praise of Women* (ca. 1487) by the Italian humanist Bartolommeo Goggio. In addition to providing a catalog of illustrious women, Goggio argued that male and female are the same in essence, but that women (reworking the Adam and Eve narrative) are actually superior. In the same vein, the Italian humanist Maria Equicola asserted the spiritual equality of men and women in *On Women* (1501). In 1525 Galeazzo Flavio Capra (or Capella) published his work *On the Excellence and Dignity of Women*. This humanist tradition of treatises defending the worthiness of women culminates in the work of Henricus Cornelius Agrippa *On the Nobility and Preeminence of the Female Sex*. No work by a male humanist more succinctly or explicitly presents the case for female dignity.

THE WITCH BOOKS. While humanists grappled with the issues pertaining to women and family, other learned men turned their attention to what they perceived as a very great problem: witches. Witch-hunting manuals, explorations of the witch phenomenon, and even defenses of witches are not at first glance pertinent to the tradition of the other voice. But they do relate in this way: most accused witches were women. The hostility aroused by supposed witch activity is comparable to the hostility aroused by women. The evil deeds the victims of the hunt were charged with were exaggerations of the vices to which, many believed, all women were prone.

The connection between the witch accusation and the hatred of women is explicit in the notorious witch-hunting manual *The Hammer of Witches* (1486), by two Dominican inquisitors, Heinrich Krämer and Jacob Sprenger. Here the inconstancy, deceitfulness, and lust traditionally associated with women are depicted in exaggerated form as the core features of witch behavior. These inclined women to make a bargain with the devil—sealed by sexual intercourse—by which they acquired unholy powers. Such bizarre claims, far from being rejected by rational men, were broadcast by intellectuals. The German Ulrich Molitur, the Frenchman Nicolas Rémy, and the Italian Stefano Guazzo coolly informed the public of sinister orgies and midnight pacts with the devil. The celebrated French jurist, historian, and political philosopher Jean Bodin argued that because women were especially prone to diabolism, regular legal procedures could properly be suspended in order to try those accused of this "exceptional crime."

A few experts, such as the physician Johann Weyer, a student of Agrippa's, raised their voices in protest. In 1563 Weyer explained the witch phenomenon thus, without discarding belief in diabolism: the devil deluded foolish old women afflicted by melancholia, causing them to believe they had magical powers. His rational skepticism, which had good credibility in the community of the learned, worked to revise the conventional views of women and witchcraft.

WOMEN'S WORKS. To the many categories of works produced on the question of women's worth must be added nearly all works written by women. A woman writing was in herself a statement of women's claim to dignity.

Only a few women wrote anything before the dawn of the modern era, for three reasons. First, they rarely received the education that would enable them to write. Second, they were not admitted to the public roles—as administrator, bureaucrat, lawyer or notary, university professor—in which they might gain knowledge of the kinds of things the literate public thought worth writing about. Third, the culture imposed silence upon women, considering speaking out a form of unchastity. Given these conditions, it is remarkable that any women wrote. Those who did so before the fourteenth century were almost always nuns or religious women whose isolation made their pronouncements more acceptable.

From the fourteenth century on, the volume of women's writings rose. Women continued to write devotional literature, although not always as cloistered nuns. They also wrote diaries, often intended as keepsakes for their children; books of advice to their sons and daughters; letters to family members and friends; and family memoirs, in a few cases elaborate enough to be considered histories.

A few women wrote works directly concerning the "woman question," and some of these, such as the humanists Isotta Nogarola, Cassandra Fedele, Laura Cereta, and Olympia Morata, were highly trained. A few were professional writers, living by the income of their pens: the very first among them was Christine de Pizan, noteworthy in this context as in so many others. In addition to *Book of the City of Ladies* and her critiques of *The Romance of the Rose*, she wrote *The Treasure of the City of Ladies* (a guide to social decorum for women), an advice book for her son, much courtly verse, and a full-scale history of the reign of King Charles V of France.

WOMEN PATRONS. Women who did not themselves write but encouraged others to do so boosted the development of an alternative tradition. Highly placed women patrons supported authors, artists, musicians, poets, and learned men. Such patrons, drawn mostly from the Italian elites and the courts of northern Europe, figure disproportionately as the dedicatees of the important works of early feminism.

For a start, it might be noted that the catalogs of Boccaccio and Alvaro de Luna were dedicated to the Florentine noblewoman Andrea Acciaiuoli and to Doña María, first wife of King Juan II of Castile, while the French translation of Boccaccio's work was commissioned by Anne of Brittany, wife of King Charles VIII of France. The humanist treatises of Goggio, Equicola, Vives, and Agrippa were dedicated, respectively, to Eleanora of Aragon, wife of Ercole I d'Este, duke of Ferrara; to Margherita Cantelma of Mantua; to Catherine of Aragon, wife of King Henry VIII of England; and to Margaret, duchess of Austria and regent of the Netherlands. As late as 1696, Mary Astell's *Serious Proposal to the Ladies, for the Advancement of Their True and Greatest Interest* was dedicated to Princess Anne of Denmark.

These authors presumed that their efforts would be welcome to female patrons, or they may have written at the bidding of those patrons. Silent themselves, perhaps even unresponsive, these loftily placed women helped shape the tradition of the other voice.

THE ISSUES. The literary forms and patterns in which the tradition of the other voice presented itself have now been sketched. It remains to highlight the major issues around which this tradition crystallizes. In brief, there are four problems to which our authors return again and again, in plays and catalogs, in verse and letters, in treatises and dialogues, in every language: the problem of chastity, the problem of power, the problem of speech, and the problem of knowledge. Of these the greatest, preconditioning the others, is the problem of chastity.

THE PROBLEM OF CHASTITY. In traditional European culture, as in the cultures of antiquity and others around the globe, chastity was perceived as woman's quintessential virtue—in contrast to courage, or generosity, or leadership, or rationality, seen as virtues characteristic of men. Opponents of women charged them with insatiable lust. Women themselves and their defenders—without disputing the validity of the standard—responded that women were capable of chastity.

The requirement of chastity kept women at home, silenced them, isolated them, left them in ignorance. It was the source of all other impediments. Why was it so important to the society of men, of whom chastity was not required, and who more often than not considered it their right to violate the chastity of any woman they encountered?

Female chastity ensured the continuity of the male-headed household. If a man's wife was not chaste, he could not be sure of the legitimacy of his offspring. If children who were not his acquired his property, it was not his household, but some other man's, that had endured. If his daughter was not chaste, she could not be transferred to another man's household as his wife, and he was dishonored.

The whole system of the integrity of the household and the transmission of property was bound up in female chastity. Such a requirement pertained only to property-owning classes, of course. Poor women could not expect to maintain their chastity, least of all if they were in contact with high-status men to whom all women but those of their own household were prey.

In Catholic Europe, the requirement of chastity was further buttressed by moral and religious imperatives. Original sin was inextricably linked with the sexual act. Virginity was seen as heroic virtue, far more impressive than, say, the avoidance of idleness or greed. Monasticism, the cultural institution that dominated medieval Europe for centuries, was grounded in the renunciation of the flesh. The Catholic reform of the eleventh century imposed a similar standard on all the clergy and a heightened awareness of sexual requirements on all the laity. Although men were asked to be chaste, female unchastity was much worse: it led to the devil, as Eve had led mankind to sin.

To such requirements, women and their defenders protested their innocence. Following the example of holy women who had escaped the requirements of family and sought the religious life, some women began to conceive of female communities as alternatives both to family and to the cloister. Christine de Pizan's city of ladies was such a community. Moderata Fonte and Mary Astell envisioned others. The luxurious salons of the French *précieuses* of the seventeenth century, or the comfortable English drawing rooms of the next, may have been born of the same impulse. Here women not only might escape, if briefly, the subordinate position that life in the family entailed but might make claims to power, exercise their capacity for speech, and display their knowledge.

THE PROBLEM OF POWER. Women were excluded from power: the whole cultural tradition insisted on it. Only men were citizens, only men bore arms, only men could be chiefs or lords or kings. There were exceptions that did not disprove the rule, when wives or widows or mothers took the place of men, awaiting their return or the maturation of a male heir. A woman who attempted to rule in her own right was perceived as an anomaly, a monster, at once a deformed woman and an inadequate male, sexually confused and consequently unsafe.

The association of such images with women who held or sought power explains some otherwise odd features of early modern culture. Queen Elizabeth I of England, one of the few women to hold full regal authority in European history, played with such male/female images—positive ones, of course—in representing herself to her subjects. She was a prince, and manly, even though she was female. She was also (she claimed) virginal, a condition absolutely essential if she was to avoid the attacks of her opponents. Catherine de' Medici, who ruled France as widow and as regent for her sons, also adopted such imagery in defining her position. She chose as one symbol the figure of Artemisia, an androgynous ancient warrior-heroine who combined a female persona with masculine powers.

Power in a woman, without such sexual imagery, seems to have been indigestible by the culture. A rare note was struck by the Englishman Sir Thomas Elyot in his *Defence of Good Women* (1540), justifying both women's participation in civic life and their prowess in arms. The old tune was sung by the Scots reformer John Knox in his *First Blast of the Trumpet against the Monstrous Regiment of Women* (1558); for him rule by women, defects in nature, was a hideous contradiction in terms.

The confused sexuality of the imagery of female potency was not reserved for rulers. Any woman who excelled was likely to be called an Amazon, recalling the self-mutilated warrior women of antiquity who repudiated all men, gave up their sons, and raised only their daughters. She was often said to have "exceeded her sex," or to have possessed "masculine virtue"— since the very fact of conspicuous excellence conferred masculinity even on the female subject. The catalogs of notable women often showed those female heroes dressed in armor and armed to the teeth, like men. Amazonian heroines romp through the epics of the age—Ariosto's *Orlando Furioso* (1532), Spenser's *Faerie Queene* (1590–1609). Excellence in a woman was perceived as a claim for power, and power was reserved for the masculine realm. A woman who possessed either was masculinized, and lost title to her own female identity.

THE PROBLEM OF SPEECH. Just as power had a sexual dimension when it was claimed by women, so did speech. A good woman spoke little. Excessive speech was an indication of unchastity. By speech, women seduced men. Eve had lured Adam into sin by her speech. Accused witches were commonly accused of having spoken abusively, or irrationally, or simply too much. As enlightened a figure as Francesco Barbaro insisted on silence in a woman, which he linked to her perfect unanimity with her husband's will and her unblemished virtue (her chastity). Another Italian humanist, Leonardo Bruni, in advising a noblewoman on her studies, barred her not from speech, but from public speaking. That was reserved for men.

Related to the problem of speech was that of costume, another, if silent, form of self-expression. Assigned the task of pleasing men as their primary occupation, elite women often tended toward elaborate costume, hairdressing, and the use of cosmetics. Clergy and secular moralists alike condemned these practices. The appropriate function of costume and adornment was to announce the status of a woman's husband or father. Any further indulgence in adornment was akin to unchastity.

THE PROBLEM OF KNOWLEDGE. When the Italian noblewoman Isotta Nogarola had begun to attain a reputation as a humanist, she was accused of incest—a telling instance of the association of learning in women with unchastity. That chilling association inclined any woman who was educated to deny that she was, or to make exaggerated claims of heroic chastity.

If educated women were pursued with suspicions of sexual misconduct, women seeking an education faced an even more daunting obstacle: the assumption that women were by nature incapable of learning, that reasoning was a particularly masculine ability. Just as they proclaimed their chastity, women and their defenders insisted upon their capacity for learning. The major work by a male writer on female education—*The Education of a Christian Woman: A Sixteenth-Century Manual*—granted female capacity for intellection but argued still that a woman's whole education was to be shaped around the requirement of chastity and a future within the household. Female writers of the following generations—Marie de Gournay in France, Anna Maria van Schurman in Holland, Mary Astell in England—began to envision other possibilities.

The pioneers of female education were the Italian women humanists who managed to attain a literacy in Latin and a knowledge of classical and Christian literature equivalent to that of prominent men. Their works implicitly and explicitly raise questions about women's social roles, defining problems that beset women attempting to break out of the cultural limits that had bound them. Like Christine de Pizan, who achieved an advanced education through her father's tutoring and her own devices, their bold questioning makes clear the importance of training. Only when women were educated to the same standard as male leaders would they be able to raise that other voice and insist on their dignity as human beings morally, intellectually, and legally equal to men.

THE OTHER VOICE. The other voice, a voice of protest, was mostly female, but also male. It spoke in the vernaculars and in Latin, in treatises and dialogues, plays and poetry, letters and diaries, and pamphlets. It battered at the wall of prejudice that encircled women and raised a banner announcing its claims. The female was equal (or even superior) to the male in essential nature—moral, spiritual, intellectual. Women were capable of higher education, of holding positions of power and influence in the public realm, and of speaking and writing persuasively. The last bastion of masculine supremacy, centered on the notions of a woman's primary domestic responsibility and the requirement of female chastity, had not as yet been assaulted—although visions of productive female communities as alternatives to the family indicated an awareness of the problem.

During the period 1300–1700, the other voice remained only a voice, and one dimly heard. It did not result—yet—in an alteration of social patterns. Indeed, to this day they have not been completely altered. Yet the call for justice issued as long as six centuries ago by those writing in the tradition of the other voice must be recognized as the source and origin of the mature feminist tradition and of the realignment of social institutions accomplished in the modern age.

We thank the volume editors in this series, who responded with many suggestions to an earlier draft of this introduction, making it a collaborative enterprise. Many of their recommendations and criticisms have resulted in revisions, though we remain responsible for the final product.

PROJECTED TITLES IN THE SERIES

Giuseppa Eleonora Barbapiccola and Diamante Medaglia Faini, *The Education of Women*, edited and translated by Paula Findlen and Rebecca Messbarger

Marie Dentière, *Prefaces, Epistles, and History of the Deliverance of Geneva by the Protestants*, edited and translated by Mary B. McKinley

Isabella d'Este, *Selected Letters*, edited and translated by Deanna Shemek

Cassandra Fedele, *Letters and Orations*, edited and translated by Diana Robin

Marie de Gournay, *The Equality of Men and Women and Other Writings*, edited and translated by Richard Hillman and Colette Quesnel

Annibale Guasco, *Discussion with D. Lavinia, His Daughter, concerning the Manner of Conducting Oneself at Court*, edited and translated by Peggy Osborn

Olympia Morata, *Complete Writings*, edited and translated by Holt N. Parker

Isotta Nogarola, *Selected Letters*, edited by Margaret King and Albert Rabil Jr. and translated by Diana Robin, with an introduction by Margaret L. King

Christine de Pizan, *Debate over the "Romance of the Rose,"* edited and translated by Tom Conley

François Poulain de la Barre, *The Equality of the Sexes and the Education of Women*, edited and translated by Albert Rabil Jr.

Olivia Sabuco, *The New Philosophy: True Medicine*, edited and translated by Gianna Pomata

Maria de San Jose, *Book of Recreations*, edited and translated by Alison Weber and Amanda Powell

Madeleine de Scudéry, *Orations and Rhetorical Dialogues*, edited and translated by Lillian Doherty and Jane Donawerth

Sara Copio Sullam, *Apologia and Other Writings*, edited and translated by Laura Stortoni

Arcangela Tarabotti, *Paternal Tyranny*, edited and translated by Letizia Panizza

Lucrezia Tornabuoni, *Sacred Narratives*, edited and translated by Jane Tylus

ACKNOWLEDGMENTS

I should like gratefully to acknowledge the assistance of various individuals and organizations on both sides of the Atlantic: my fellow editors of the Selected Works of J. L. Vives, Marcus de Schepper, Edward George, the late, lamented Jozef Ijsewijn, founder of neo-Latin studies of the present day, and particularly my collaborator in the Latin edition of the *De institutione*, Constant Matheeussen, whose expert knowledge of the art of textual criticism and the nuances of the Latin language contributed greatly to this version. To Diane Lane and her daughter, Wendy Curtis, I owe a debt of gratitude for their careful preparation of both the Latin and English texts, and to Margie Prytulak for her patient typing of the notes. In editorial matters I have been saved from numerous aberrations by the scrupulous vigilance of Philippa Matheson of Toronto and Sandy Hazel of the University of Chicago Press. I wish to thank Margaret Mikesell for the many valuable insights into the reception of Vives in England that she communicated to me in various conversations. For financial support and other facilitations of my work I should like to acknowledge the University of Windsor, East Carolina University, the Katholieke Universiteit Brussel, the Ministerie van de Vlaamse Gemeenschap, the National Endowment for the Humanities, and the Social Sciences and Humanities Research Council of Canada.

Charles Fantazzi

KEY TO ABBREVIATIONS

Allen — P. S. Allen, H. M. Allen, and H. W. Garrod, eds., *Opus epistolarum Des. Erasmi Roterodami.* 11 vols. Oxford, 1906–47.

Barnes — Jonathan Barnes, ed. *The Complete Works of Aristotle: The Revised Oxford Translation.* 2 vols. Princeton, 1984.

CWE — James K. McConica, ed. *Collected Works of Erasmus.* Toronto, 1969–.

LCL — Loeb Classical Library, Cambridge, Mass. References are made by volume number of a particular author (if there is more than one volume) followed by page numbers.

Majansius — Gregorio Mayáns y Siscar, ed., *Ioannis Ludovici Vivis Valentini opera omnia.* 8 vols. Valencia: Montfort, 1782–90. Reprint, London: Gregg Press, 1964.

NPNF — *A Select Library of Nicene and Post-Nicene Fathers.* 14 vols. Originally published in the 1880s, often reprinted in the United States by William Eerdmans.

PG — Jacques Paul Migne. *Patrologiae cursus completus . . . omnium SS. Patrum. Series Graeca.* 161 vols. Paris, 1857–66. Cited when there is no English translation.

PL — ———. *Patrologiae cursus completus . . . omnium SS. patrum. Series Latina.* 221 vols. plus 5 supplementary vols. Paris, 1844–64. Cited when there is no English translation.

INTRODUCTION:
PRELUDE TO THE OTHER
VOICE IN VIVES

Education, both in theory and in practice, was a principal concern of the great Spanish humanist Juan Luis Vives, from his early years as a private tutor and lecturer in Louvain—a city in the Netherlands duchy of Brabant—to his completion of the monumental *De disciplinis*, a twenty-one-volume synthesis of all the arts and sciences. He first challenged the prevailing system of learning in 1520 with his spirited attack against the logicians of Paris, *In pseudodialecticos* (*Against the Pseudodialecticians*), and was lauded for his eloquence and erudition by Erasmus and Sir Thomas More. Through his appointment by Cardinal Thomas Wolsey as lecturer in Greek, Latin, and Rhetoric at the new Cardinal College at Oxford, he introduced revolutionary reforms into the curriculum. But before leaving for England in 1523, Vives wrote two short manuals outlining programs of study for younger students: the one for girls he dedicated to Princess Mary, daughter of Henry VIII and Catherine of Aragon; and the other for boys he addressed to William Blount, fourth baron Mountjoy, chamberlain of the queen. At the baron's behest Vives wrote *De institutione feminae Christianae* (*The Education of a Christian Woman*) in 1523, ostensibly for Princess Mary's education but meant for a wider audience.

The first book of this work, concerning girls and young unmarried women, is of great importance in the history of education. It is the first systematic study to address explicitly and exclusively the universal education of women, even those who show no natural aptitude for learning. In his prefatory letter to Queen Catherine of Aragon, Vives alludes to the social ramifications of the treatise's theme: women are men's inseparable companions, and their proper education is essential to the well-being of the state. The main focus of this book is the spiritual formation of the woman from her early years through adolescence. Vives assigns great responsibility to the mother in teaching her daughter the native language so that the young girl may read edifying works of literature in translation. In a subsequent essay, "On the Duties of the Husband," in which he speaks of the husband's education of his spouse, he also advocates the study of Greek and Latin for women.

As for the intellectual capacity of women, Vives makes no distinction between male and female and even says that the woman often surpasses the man in this respect. This statement may strike the modern reader as trite and self-evident, but it was not so for the Renaissance mind, accustomed as it was to the Aristotelian doctrine of the inferiority of women. Vives also dispels the inveterate distrust of the learned woman, insisting, with Erasmus and More, that it is ignorance, not knowledge, that fosters evil. He even goes so far as to say that he knows of no learned woman who was evil.

Vives' progressive philosophy continues in the second book of the treatise, which concerns the married woman. Here he posits mutuality and companionship as the chief goal of marriage, contrary to the accepted dogma of the church: "Marriage was instituted not so much for the production of offspring as for community of life and indissoluble companionship" (p. 175). This observation would have far-reaching effects in subsequent treatises on the married state.

Such are some of the positive contributions of Vives' treatise. Regarding the nonintellectual qualities of the ideal woman, however, he remains staunchly traditional, even fanatically so. There are many things that the modern reader will find quite unpalatable. In his obsessive insistence on the virtue of chastity, Vives is very much influenced by Saint Jerome's polemical tract, *Against Jovinianus*, in which the exaltation of virginity over marriage turns into a diatribe against women. Vives' view of human nature was highly pessimistic, and his distrust and fear of the body almost betrays a kind of Manichaeism. As a master of the art of rhetoric, he believed that persuasive language could be a very effective weapon to combat the darkness brought on by original sin. This belief accounts for the vehement, declamatory style, full of invective and sarcasm, that characterizes this work. One can also detect the personality of the *converso* Jew anxious to find approval and give show of the most unquestionable orthodoxy.[1]

---

1. Américo Castro had noted this in 1945, before there was any documented proof of Vives' Jewish ancestry. He expresses it rather forcefully: "Su religiosidad y estoicismo ultrapasados; su mordaz agresividad; su pessimismo y su melancolía son rasgos todos ellos que adquieren sentido dentro del género 'hombre hispano-judaico'." *España en su historia*, 2d ed. (Barcelona, 1983), 684. ("His exaggerated religiosity and stoicism; his caustic aggressivity; his pessimism and his melancholy are all characteristics that make sense within the genus 'Hispano-Jewish man'."

At any rate, whatever its failings, the *De institutione* enjoyed an enormous popularity and was generally regarded as the most authoritative statement on this subject throughout the sixteenth century, especially in England, where it found favor with Catholics and Protestants alike. There can be no denying that merely by attaching such importance to the education of women, Vives laid the groundwork for the Elizabethan age of the cultured woman. The impact of his treatise, positive and negative, must be taken into account in any chronicling of the emergence of the other voice in early modern Europe.

THE LIFE AND WORKS OF JUAN LUIS VIVES

The traditional year of birth for Juan Luis Vives (or Joan Lluís Vives, to use the Catalan form of his name) is 1492, as given on his gravestone, but recently published records of the Inquisition seem to indicate early 1493.[2] He was born to a family of *converso* Jews of Valencia who were forcibly "converted" to Christianity after the uprising of 1391 in that city. His father, Lluís Vives Valeriola, was a well-to-do cloth merchant who also engaged in the trade of spices, dates, and rice with Italy and Flanders. His mother, Blanquina March Maçana, was of a family of jurists and notaries. This Jewish background is a determining factor in the life of Vives. It seems quite probable that his parents and many of his relatives secretly observed certain religious practices of Judaism, of which the young Vives could not have been unaware. Nonetheless, he never admits to any Jewish upbringing in his writings.

In 1500 inquisitorial authorities discovered a clandestine synagogue in the house of Vives' aunt Castellana Guioret, widow of Salvador Vives, and both she and her son were summarily condemned to burning at the stake.[3] His father, after a long, protracted trial, was executed on 6 September 1524.[4] Vives' mother escaped the Inquisition during her lifetime, dying of the plague in 1508, but twenty years later her remains were exhumed, and she was consigned to the flames in effigy after a macabre mock trial.[5] These terrible events and his inability to intervene in any way must have had a

2. Cf. Enrique González y González, *Joan Lluís Vives. De la escolástica al humanismo* (Valencia, 1987), 97.

3. Miguel de la Pinta y Llorente y José María de Palacio, *Procesos inquisitoriales contra la familia judía de Luis Vives* (Madrid, 1964), 96–105.

4. Ricardo García Cárcel, "Notas en torno al contexto familiar de Luis Vives," *Cuadernos de la historia de la medicina* 13 (1974): 339.

5. Pinta y Llorente, *Procesos inquisitoriales*, 85, 102.

profound effect upon Vives. His personal correspondence, especially to his good friend Frans van Cranevelt, bears this out.[6]

After his years in the gymnasium, Vives attended the Estudi General of Valencia, which had been elevated to the rank of university by the Borgia Pope Alexander VI, a Valencian himself, in 1500. There he continued his study of Latin grammar and began the study of Greek, completing the three-year arts curriculum under grammarians who were still using texts of Latin grammar and teaching methods that were far from the ideals of the new humanist learning. In 1509, a year after his mother's death, Vives set out for the University of Paris to complete his studies. He enrolled in the Faculty of Arts and the Faculty of Theology, where he joined many other students from Spain, particularly Aragon. From remarks of Vives in various works, it has usually been thought that he took up lodgings at the College of Montaigu, but recent investigations have shown that he may have attached himself at first to the college of Lisieux, where the Aragonese Juan Dolz de Castellar was teaching.[7] More probably he felt free to frequent the lessons of various professors wherever they taught, as was common practice at the Sorbonne.

Vives pays special homage in his early writings to two of his tutors, Gaspar Lax de Sariñena, also of Aragon, and Jan Dullaert of Ghent. Both had been students of the Scottish nominalist John Mair, who was regent of Montaigu during this time. Dullaert, who died very young in 1513, seems to have been Vives' first teacher;[8] after his death Vives came under the tutelage of Lax. From these two mentors Vives learned the intricacies of terminist logic.[9] In his first published work, the *Triumphus Christi* (Paris, 1514),[10] a curious piece in which the victory of Christ over the devil is celebrated in the manner of a Roman triumph on Easter Sunday, Vives reserves great praise for Lax, whom he depicts as one of the orators in the dialogue. The Latinity of the work is often shaky, showing that the young Valencian was still not practiced enough in the language (he revised it thoroughly for a second edition in Louvain, 1519). Already present in these first experiments, however, is the humanistic predilection for the form of the dialogue and the declamation. As the oratorical contest continues, another speaker, Miguel de Santángel, essays the theme in a more flamboyant, Asiatic style. Christ's

6. Henry de Vocht, *Literae virorum eruditorum ad Franciscum Craneveldium* (Louvain, 1929).

7. González y González, *Joan Lluís Vives*, 134-37.

8. Vives wrote a laconic life of Dullaert after his death. It is edited and translated in Juan Luis Vives, *Early Writings 2*, ed. Jozef IJsewijn and Angela Fritsen (Leiden, 1991), 14–15.

9. Cf. Juan Luis Vives, *In pseudodialecticos*, ed. and trans. Charles Fantazzi (Leiden, 1979), 16–20.

10. Juan Luis Vives, *Early Writings* 2 (Leiden, 1991), 40–71.

triumph is followed by an ovation (usually defined as a minor triumph) of the Blessed Virgin and a description of Christ's shield in battle (*Clipeus*),[11] modeled on Virgil's description of the shield of Aeneas in the eighth book of the *Aeneid* (vv. 626–728). These early works evince a kind of naive piety combined with an impressive demonstration of both humanistic and theological learning.

Other publications during the Parisian sojourn were more closely allied to the new learning, being *praelectiones*, or inaugural lectures, on authors whom Vives explicated in private lessons or perhaps in one of the colleges of the university. Enrique González y González has recently pointed out that Vives was probably inspired to lecture on the classical authors by attending the lessons of Nicholas Bérault,[12] who had come to Paris from Orléans around 1512 and taught at the College of La Marche. He figures as a speaker in an early dialogue of Vives written at this time, *Sapientis inquisitio (In Search of a Wise Man)*, in which, like Socrates in the *Apology*, Vives approaches various classes of men who esteem themselves to be wise but in the end finds wisdom only in an ascetic theologian living as a hermit. Several of the works taught by Bérault became the subject of Vives' lectures also, such as Cicero's *On Laws* and the *Convivia* of the Italian humanist Francesco Filelfo.[13] In the last paragraph of this latter work, Vives indulges in some mild invective against the Parisian dialecticians and their obscure sophistries, prelude to the full-scale attack he would launch against them from Louvain.

With this substantial number of publications to his credit, some published in Paris and others in Lyons, Vives made his way to the Low Countries. There was a thriving Jewish community in Bruges, where he had already made contacts with the Valdaura family, related to his own and also engaged in the textile trade. It is probable that he did some private teaching there. Little is known of Vives' life during these first years in Flanders,[14] but it is clear that he attained some position of importance at the court of Charles I, king of Spain (later the emperor Charles V). In proof of this there is extant a letter to Vives from the magistrates of the city of Valencia dated 13 November 1516, in which his intercession with the king is sought concerning the affairs of the University of Valencia. He is addressed as "most learned and dutiful gentleman and philosopher, Master Luis Vives."[15]

---

11. Ibid., *Ovatio*, 80–103; *Clipeus*, 108–25.

12. González y González, *Joan Lluís Vives*, 139.

13. Vives, *Early Writings* 2, 44–51.

14. Cf. Jozef IJsewijn, "J. L. Vives in 1512–1517," *Humanistica lovaniensia* 26 (1977): 82–100.

15. Juan Luis Vives, *Epistolario*, trans. José Jiménez Delgado (Madrid, 1978), 116–18.

In the spring of 1517, Vives was appointed tutor of Guillaume of Croy, nephew of the lord of Chièvres. Guillaume's powerful uncle had great ambitions for him and saw to it that he became successively bishop of Cambrai, cardinal-archbishop of Toledo, and primate of Spain by the age of nineteen. Through the patronage of his young ward, Vives was licensed by special privilege to give public lectures at the University of Louvain without being on the official roster. Vives dedicated to Guillaume a meditation on the seven penitential psalms that once again reflects the original thinking and exceptional learning of the Spanish humanist. He informs the reader that he has translated from the Vulgate but with reference also to the Hebrew and to a translation into Chaldean (i.e., Aramaic) made by a certain Jonathan Abenuziel. The manner of composition is more in the style of forensic speech than biblical language.

During these years in Louvain, Vives composed the *Sullan Declamations*,[16] formal speeches recreating the troubled times of the Roman dictator Lucius Sulla. They were dedicated to Archduke Ferdinand of Austria, younger brother of Charles V, and bore a prefatory epistle of Erasmus,[17] who gives them lavish praise, commending Vives for his unrivalled eloquence coupled with immense learning. Thomas More echoes this encomium, describing the compositions "as stylish and as scholarly as anything I have seen for a long time."[18] Vives also published during this period an essay on the origins of philosophy, *On the Origins, Schools and Merits of Philosophy*,[19] an introduction to the study of law, *Aedes legum (The Abode of the Laws)*,[20] and a commentary on Cicero's *Dream of Scipio*,[21] preceded by an imaginative dream of his own — a clever pedagogical device that would have captured the students' attention.

The most important work to issue from his pen at this time was the *In pseudodialecticos (Against the Pseudodialecticians)*,[22] a spirited attack against the Parisian doctors in the form of a letter to his fellow student, Juan Fort from Aragon. It is a brilliant diatribe, and, as Erasmus says of Vives in a letter to Thomas More soon after its publication, "No one is better fitted to break the serried ranks of the sophists, in whose army he has served so long."[23] As

16. Juan Luis Vives, *Sullan Declamations*, ed. and trans. Edward V. George (Leiden, 1989).

17. Ep. 1082 (*CWE* 7:227–29).

18. Ep. 1106 (*CWE* 7:290).

19. Juan Luis Vives, *Early Writings 1*, ed. and trans. Constant Matheeussen (Leiden, 1987), 8–57.

20. Ioannes Lodivicus Vives, *Praefatio in Leges Ciceronis et Aedes legum*, ed. Constant Matheeussen (Leipzig, 1984).

21. Juan Luis Vives, *Somnium et Vigilia in Somnium Scipionis* (Greenwood, S.C., 1989).

22. Vives, *In pseudodialecticos*, ed. and trans Charles Fantazzi (Leiden, 1979).

23. Ep. 1107 (*CWE* 7:295).

with Erasmus himself in *The Praise of Folly* and many of the Italian humanists, the main target of Vives' ridicule is the absurd, incomprehensible language used by the dialecticians. He accuses them of corrupting Latin into a kind of nonlanguage that only they could understand. By their manipulations of this specialized language, Vives says, they give the appearance of victory in debate by leaving their adversaries more dumbfounded than defeated. Moreover, their methods had infiltrated the sacred precinct of theology, with the result that the teachings of revelation were being obfuscated by this barbarous language. Vives insists that too much time is dedicated to the study of logic, a subject that should not be learned for its own sake but as a support to the other arts. He gives a humorous picture of these denizens of the schools, who, when they emerge into the light of day and the concourse of ordinary men, seem to have been brought up in the woods and have not a word to utter. Vives predicts the end of their tyranny and the victory of the republic of letters, and he feels an immense gratitude to God for delivering him from this "Cimmerian" darkness.

In a return visit to Paris a short time later in the company of Guillaume de Croy, Vives was pleasantly surprised to be accorded a friendly reception by some of the very "sophists" whom he had attacked.[24] Soon afterwards, however, in the midst of this newly won fame and success, Vives suffered a tragic blow when his young patron fell from his horse and was killed on 11 January 1521. This turn of events left him in a state of great depression and financial insecurity. He became ill and for several months was unable to dedicate himself to the formidable scholarly task which Erasmus had set him: a commentary on Saint Augustine's *City of God*, which would form part of the complete edition of Augustine that Erasmus was preparing. He retired to Bruges, where he gradually recuperated, and by July of 1521 he had completed six books, as we learn from a letter of his to Erasmus.[25] Vives also confides in this letter to the elder scholar that he hoped to meet with Thomas More during his impending visit to Bruges in the entourage of Cardinal Wolsey. The meeting was arranged by Vives' good friend Frans van Cranevelt, legal consultant to the city of Bruges, and would prove to be of great importance to Vives' future career. He completed the Augustine commentary in the summer of 1522 at the cost of great physical and mental effort, but Erasmus was displeased with its excessive length and poor sales at the Frankfurt fair.[26] The relations between the two humanists became strained

---

24. In a letter to Erasmus sent from Bruges 4 June 1520. Ep. 1108 (*CWE* 7:297).
25. Ep. 1222 (*CWE* 8:267).
26. Erasmus to Vives, 27 December 1524. Ep. 1531 (*CWE* 10:470).

after this publishing venture. In the meantime, Vives continued to give lectures at the University of Louvain, benefiting from the hospitality of Don Pedro Aguirre, a wealthy merchant.

In May of 1522 he was offered the prestigious chair of Latin philology at the University of Alcalá, to succeed the famous Antonio de Nebrija. We hear nothing of his response until a year later, when, according to letters written to Erasmus and Cranevelt, he announced his intention to set out for Spain by way of England.[27] The trip to Spain never materialized for various reasons, chief of which must have been Vives' fear of what might befall him there because of the Inquisition. Once in England he immediately found great favor with the king's chancellor, Cardinal Thomas Wolsey, who appointed him to a lectureship in Wolsey's own foundation, Cardinal College (then housed in Corpus Christi College at Oxford).[28] There Vives joined friendship with prominent English humanists of the day: Cuthbert Tunstall, Thomas Linacre, William Latimer, John Fisher, and, above all, Thomas More. During the tenure of this position, Vives effected various curricular reforms in the college, bringing him undying fame in the annals of Corpus Christi.[29] In homage to the cardinal, he produced translations of two famous speeches of the Greek orator Isocrates: his address to the Areopagus and his speech to Nicocles, both on the subject of government. Vives also exercised great influence at court in the role of friend and spiritual counselor to Queen Catherine. His various works composed at her behest are discussed in more detail in the next section.

Returning temporarily to Bruges in the spring of 1524, Vives contracted marriage with Margarita Valdaura, the young daughter of Bernard Valdaura, at whose home he had often stayed in his frequent visits to Bruges. By September he was back at Oxford to resume his teaching duties. In the spring of the following year, Vives returned once more to Bruges after the outbreak of the plague. Just before his departure from England, he addressed an appeal to Henry VIII concerning the capture of the French monarch Francis I by the imperial forces at the battle of Pavia.[30] He exhorts Henry to make moderate and magnanimous use of this victory and not to devastate the most flourishing realm of Christendom. From Bruges he transmitted to Henry another brief message, urging the king to use his vast authority to achieve

27. Ep. 1362 (*CWE* 10:14); de Vocht, *Literae virorum*, ep. 141.

28. Cardinal College was not built until 1525. The appointment is documented in a letter of Vives to Wolsey, 13 December 1523, in appreciation of the good reception afforded him at the university. Cf. Delgado, *Epistolario*, 332–36.

29. G. D. Duncan, "Public Lectures and Professorial Chairs," in *History of the University of Oxford*, vol. 3 (Oxford, 1986), 338.

30. Majansius VI, 449–52; Delgado, *Epistolario*, 396–400.

the goals of peace.[31] In 1526 Vives grouped these two petitions with an earlier letter he had written to Pope Adrian VI, *De Europae statu ac tumultu* (*On the Tumultuous Situation of Europe*), and added to them a new work, *De dissidiis Europae et bello Turcico* (*On Europe Divided and the Turkish War*). This dialogue of the dead set in Hades, in the manner of the Greek satirist Lucian, is a despairing commentary on the failures of Christian leaders in the face of the Turkish threat. All of these political writings were published in Bruges by Hubert de Croocke.

These attempts at conciliation only succeeded in further alienating Wolsey and Henry, with the result that Vives was abruptly dismissed from his lectureship. Notwithstanding these setbacks, he continued in his vein of political writing with his tract *De subventione pauperum* (*On the Relief of the Poor*), at the request of the magistrates of the city of Bruges; the request was communicated to him by Luis de Praet, imperial ambassador to England. As in More's *Utopia*, which may have influenced his own ideas, Vives sees war as one of the principal causes for poverty. He expresses his particular concern for the plight of victims of war and, unlike More, proposes concrete solutions for immediate action. His enlightened attitude toward the poor, imbued with the principles of Christian charity, was far in advance of his time.

In February 1526 Vives was again in England (his frequent crossings prompted Erasmus to call him an "amphibious animal" (Allen, ep. 1830), apparently still intent on persuading Henry to intervene on the side of peace. By 1527, with the intensification of Henry's divorce proceedings, Vives demonstrated his loyalty to the queen, incurring the king's strong displeasure. Through the machinations of Wolsey, he was subjected to house arrest from 25 February to 1 April 1528 in the care of the Spanish ambassador in London, Iñigo de Mendoza. Upon his release, Vives returned once more to Bruges.

From the time of his definitive departure from England until his death (1528–40), an extraordinary number of lengthy and important writings and revisions of previous works poured from Vives' pen. The royal pension from England was discontinued by Henry in 1528, leaving him in a penurious situation. Most of this time he spent in Bruges, with occasional visits to Paris, the imperial court at Brussels, and the University of Louvain. In 1532 Vives began to receive a pension from the emperor Charles V, which, he tells us, sufficed for half of his living expenses. In 1537 he became preceptor to Doña Mencía de Mendoza, the wife of the duke of Nassau, and resided for a time at the ducal castle in Breda in North Brabant.

Having failed in his mission as peacemaker with Henry, Vives turned

31. Majansius V, 175–76; Delgado, 415–17.

to Charles V in an essay written in 1529 entitled *De concordia et discordia humani generis (On the Concord and Discord of the Human Race)*. In it he voices his despair of European civilization, newly invigorated by the humanist revival but now doomed by political and social turmoil to fall victim to the Turks, who were already at the gates of Vienna. In the dedicatory epistle to the emperor dated 1 July 1529, Vives appeals to princes to rise above national interests and unite in the face of the common enemy. Like More and Erasmus, he exposes the false ideals of honor, virtue, and glory as being motivated by self-love and pride. True heroism is to be found in the struggle to achieve a lasting peace. Charles, like a new Hercules, must sustain the tottering world.

Vives joined to this long appeal a companion piece concerned with the life of Christians under Turkish rule. Like Thomas More in his *Dialogue of Comfort,* supposedly translated from an original Latin work written by a Hungarian after the defeat of the Christians at the battle of Mohacs, Vives warns of the folly of those false Christians who were ready to make terms with the infidel. As it happened, the Treaty of Cambrai of August 1529 brought a temporary armistice, enough time for Charles to prepare a vigorous campaign against the Turks.

A few months later, Vives published another political pamphlet, *De pacificatione (On the Making of Peace)*, addressed to Spanish Grand Inquisitor Alfonso Manrique, a fellow *converso*. Without pointing his finger at anyone in particular, Vives alludes to an inquisitor's grave responsibilities and the dangers of not acting justly, owing to human passions and the false testimony of accusers protected by the cloak of anonymity. With considerable daring, Vives questions the excessive authority of the Holy Tribunal and writes movingly of the plight of those who were forced to leave their countries for fears of the Inquisition.

Vives' most ambitious and perhaps most important work was an encyclopedic survey of education, the *De disciplinis*, which he published in Antwerp in 1531 and dedicated to King John III of Portugal. The first part of the work, in seven books, is entitled *On the Causes of Corrupt Learning.* Here the reader discovers that Vives' attitude toward the classical authors is quite different from that of the Italian humanists or even of Erasmus. In his view, truth was not given to any single author or generation, but is the "daughter of time" and subject to growth and evolution. He is highly critical of Aristotle, rejecting the *Ethics* as incompatible with Christian revelation, ridiculing the style of the *Organon* and the *Metaphysics,* and even accusing Aristotle of confusing dialectics and metaphysics. Following the Greek philosopher's own example, Vives reads his sources critically, which, as he says in the preface to the work, is preferable to accepting everything on authority.

While the first book in *On the Causes of Corrupt Learning* is a general criticism of the arts curriculum, in the succeeding books Vives focuses on the individual disciplines: grammar, dialectic, rhetoric, philosophy, medicine, mathematics, moral philosophy, and law. Influenced by his readings in Rudolf Agricola and Valla, he insists on the descriptive character of grammar and places rhetoric more at the service of dialectic. On the subject of language, Vives still reveres Latin as the "shrine of ancient wisdom," but he recognizes the importance of learning the vernacular languages as well— advice which he gives also in the *De institutione*.

Vives extensively discusses all these reforms in university education in the second part of the *De disciplinis, On the Transmission of Learning*. As a true humanist, he strongly emphasizes literature, history, and philosophy, but he does not neglect such practical subjects as architecture, geography, agriculture, medicine, and even the history of technology. Overall, the *De disciplinis* is a very important work in the history of education. Politically, it moves the responsibility of education and the professional training of teachers from the church to the state; Vives argues that each municipality should have its own school and each province its own university, and that properly trained teachers should be paid with public moneys.

In a book published in 1532, *De ratione dicendi* (*On the Theory of Public Speaking*), Vives expounds further on his philosophy of language. In 1535 he wrote a book of spiritual exercises and prayers, the *Exercitationes animi in Deum* (*Spiritual Exercises of the Mind*), and in 1537 an influential treatise on the writing of letters. During his stay in Breda, Vives published an allegorical interpretation of Virgil's *Bucolics*, probably for Doña Mencía de Mendoza. This was followed in 1538 by the *De Aristotelis operibus censura* (*An Appraisal of the Works of Aristotle*) and a collection of dialogues for the learning of Latin, the *Linguae latinae exercitatio* (*Exercises in the Latin Language*), lively vignettes of school life that demonstrate Vives' great gifts as a pedagogue.[32]

His next published work is one of great importance. The *De anima et vita* (*On the Soul and Life*), is a treatise in three books loosely derived from Aristotle's essay on this subject. Unlike Aristotle, who is more interested in metaphysical speculation, Vives remains always the teacher and moralist. The third book, on the passions or emotions, is the most original in the treatise; here Vives gives ample demonstration of his exceptional ability for shrewd psychological observation and analysis. The second book contains a brilliant chapter on *ingenium*, literally "inborn talent," but in Vives' wider signification, the qualitative differences of individual intellectual capacities.

---

32. These dialogues equaled or surpassed Erasmus's *Colloquies* in popularity, especially in Italy. Cf. Paul Grendler, *Schooling in Renaissance Italy* (Baltimore, 1989), 201.

He also has very interesting things to say about memory, the learning process, language, dreams, and old age.

Vives' final major work, published by his friend Frans van Cranevelt three years after his death and dedicated at Vives' express wish to Pope Paul III, is the *De veritate fidei Christiana (On the Truth of the Christian Faith)* in five books. In this work Vives sedulously avoids engaging the Reformers in theological debate, although he chooses to expound the traditional views of the church on such fundamental beliefs as the Trinity, the Incarnation, the life of Christ, and the Eucharist. He concentrates instead on proving the superiority of Christianity over Judaism and Islam, resorting once more to the form of the dialogue, here between a Christian and a Jew in Book III and a Christian and a Moslem in Book IV. As ever, Vives gives proof of the astonishing breadth of his learning, in this case his knowledge of the Old Testament and rabbinical commentaries. The last book extols Christianity as a religion of love that heals our emotional disorders and teaches us to live with others in peace and harmony.

Vives died in Bruges on 6 May 1540 from various infirmities that had plagued his last years. He was solemnly laid to rest in the Church of Saint Donatian in Bruges.

CIRCUMSTANCES SURROUNDING THE COMPOSITION OF THE *DE INSTITUTIONE*

Left destitute of his rich patron, Guillaume de Croy, at his death in January 1521, Vives set to work on the *De institutione,* a book commissioned by Queen Catherine of Aragon. It may be presumed from Vives' passing remark to Erasmus in a letter from Louvain dated 15 August 1522[33] that he had begun the work immediately after completing his commentary on Augustine's *City of God.* It was finished by 5 April 1523, Easter Sunday, as the date of the prefatory letter clearly indicates. Yet because of difficulties with the financier and bookseller, Francis Birckmann, the book would not appear until January of the following year.

On 10 May Vives informs Cranevelt and Erasmus of his decision to set sail for Spain via England. It seems quite certain that he never did return to Spain,[34] no doubt because he feared the Inquisition; but his trip to England turned out to be very auspicious indeed. Here at last, for a time, Vives

---

33. Ep. 1303 (*CWE* 9: 162).

34. This is the firm opinion of the historian Ricardo García Cárcel, "La familia de Luis Vives y la Inquisición," in *Ioannis Lodovici Vivis Valentini opera omnia,* vol. 1 (Valencia, 1992), 512.

seemed to have found the leisure for an untrammeled life of study that he so ardently desired.[35]

Concerning the *De institutione*, Vives expresses his dissatisfaction with the work and its title in a letter to Cranevelt on 25 January 1524.[36] This date must have coincided closely with the appearance of the work, since he remarks that it is now in the public domain. He blames the choice of the title on the publishers, who, he thinks, look to their own interests. Such titles, Vives complains, only serve to make him more hated by his enemies and more scorned by the average reader, who may find that the book does not live up to its title. Actually, the multifaceted treatise cannot easily be summarized in a convenient title. Not only does it discuss the education of women in the three states of life—unmarried woman, wife, and widow— but it also addresses the social status of women in general, the church's doctrine on the sacrament of matrimony, and the moral instruction of womankind.

In October of that same year, at the express wish of the queen, Vives produced the *De ratione studii puerilis* (*On a Plan of Study for Children*), a brief manual outlining a course of study to be followed by Princess Mary. The manual is composed of two letters, one for the princess and another for Charles Mountjoy, son of William Mountjoy, the queen's chamberlain. In writing this practical outline, Vives was perhaps tacitly aware that Mary, sole heir to the throne, might someday be destined to rule. The books he counsels for her study are much more oriented to government than those recommended in the *De institutione*: dialogues of Plato relating to the government of the state, More's *Utopia*, and Erasmus's *Education of a Christian Prince*. Additionally, along with the Scriptures and the church fathers, he would have her learn the secular wisdom of the *Distichs of Cato*, the *Mimes* of Publilius, and the *Sentences of the Seven Sages* collected by Erasmus. As a true pedagogue, Vives advocates also the active learning of Latin conversation in the company of three or four fellow students, under the supervision of her tutor. And from her own reading the princess should copy down sententious sayings in a notebook for memorization. Altogether, the *De ratione* is an innovative, stimulating program of studies.

At about the same time, Vives put together a collection of mottoes and devices entitled the *Satellitium animi* (*Escort of the Soul*) to serve as a 'mystical

---

35. Ep. 1222 (*CWE* 8:267). Vives had expressed this same fervent desire as early as 1521, as we learn from the newly discovered letters that have been published at the University of Louvain under the sponsorship of the former king of Belgium, *Litterae ad Craneveldium Balduinianae*. Ep. 91, *Humanistica lovaniensia* 44 (1995): 16–17.

36. de Vocht, *Literae virorum*, Ep. 90; Delgado, *Epistolario*, 341–45.

guard' over the princess. This pamphlet was followed by yet another instructional book, the *Introduction to Wisdom*.[37] Directed toward a wider audience the work attained immense popularity, with more than one hundred editions in Latin and other languages appearing before 1600.

After a long silence, which made Vives wonder about their scholarly friendship, Erasmus wrote him a brief letter from Basel on 29 May 1527 (Allen, ep. 1830). In frank response to Vives asking for his opinion of his most recent writings, Erasmus writes:

> Your writings have my enthusiastic approval, especially what you have written about marriage. But you strive after extemporaneity, which in your case, to be sure, is more successful than the most minute care exercised by most writers. If, however, you would be willing to restrain your enthusiasm and adapt yourself more to the opinion of the reader, for whom the play is being performed, then certain elements would be a little more flexible.

Erasmus then goes on to talk more specifically and more bluntly about Vives' views on marriage. He accuses him of being too hard on women, adding ironically that he hopes he is more gentle with his own wife. Vives' graphic description of the syphilitic condition of his father-in-law also elicits his criticism,[38] and he concludes with the assertion that Vives writes too much about his family.

Vives did not take kindly to the proffered criticism. In his reply of 20 July 1527 (Allen, ep. 1847), after the usual polite formalities, he reverts once again to his excuse about being worn out from his work on the Augustine commentary, but he also stresses his determination to produce something for the queen:

> Consequently, there was no time to polish the style, if indeed I could have polished it, however much I tried. Then I took into account those for whom I was writing, namely, women, and especially the one to whom I was dedicating it. I thus adopted a plainer style so that it would be understood by the one for whom I was composing the work and whose approbation I sought. . . . A good number of people have expressed their enthusiastic approval of the simple and unaffected style of the work; at least that is what they said.

---

37. *Vives' Introduction to Wisdom*, ed. Marian Leona Tobriner (New York, 1968).

38. Erasmus later wrote a colloquy exposing this kind of forced marriage between a healthy and a diseased person: "A Marriage in Name Only or the Unequal Match," *CWE* 40:844–59.

A little further on, gathering more courage, as it were, Vives exclaims: "Now that I have transgressed the bounds of modesty, may I be allowed to be well and truly shameless." He then launches into a spirited defense of his treatment of women in the book and answers all of Erasmus's critiques, especially those concerning marriage, which is the subject of the second book.

It is quite remarkable—one might even say disingenuous—that in his letter to Vives Erasmus gives no intimation that he had already published his own treatise on marriage, the *Institution of Christian Matrimony*, dedicated to the same Queen Catherine in August 1526. Actually, he had begun it two years earlier, as we learn from his letter to Thomas Lupset dated 4 October 1525,[39] in which he confides that he was prevailed upon by a person of high rank [Mountjoy] to write on the preservation of marriage. Erasmus comments that Vives had already done so in his "Virgin, Wife and Widow" (a rather disparaging manner of referring to the work) and wonders why the queen is looking for something more. One is almost led to believe that she was dissatisfied with the treatise written by her compatriot. Erasmus's work is a quite different kind of book from Vives', although it does incorporate many ideas from the *De institutione*. It is notable for its rather astonishing grasp of both Roman marriage laws and Gratian's *Decretum*, together with the voluminous commentaries of the medieval Schoolmen. In his treatment of marriage, Vives chose to avoid getting involved in theological discussions about its sacramental character.

All in all, Vives seems to have been very apprehensive for the fortunes of this book. Nevertheless, encouraged by its favorable reception, he embarked upon its sequel, *On the Duties of the Husband*. Vives wrote the treatise in response to the interests of various friends, including Álvaro de Castro, a merchant from Burgos with whom he had shared a residence in London in the latter part of 1524. He began work the following year and probably finished it quickly, for it bears the marks of hasty composition. Vives initially wrote it in Spanish, as we learn from the preface, since de Castro could not read Latin. He dedicated the work to Juan Borja, duke of Gandía, near Valencia.

In the fourth chapter of this second treatise, Vives revisits the education of women in much the same terms as he had adopted in the *De institutione*. The woman is to be denied access to those liberal arts that deal more with the man's world: dialectic, history, mathematics, and politics. Rather, she will occupy herself with those books that will improve her morals and give her

---

39. Ep. 1624 (*CWE* 11 : 308).

serenity of spirit. Once again, Vives concedes that the female sex is not wicked by nature and ridicules those who are of that opinion, but in pessimistic tones he sees all humanity as drawn toward evil, a condition that can be remedied in part by good reading. To that end, the woman should be taught to read books of piety, the Scriptures, and lives of the saints, but also works of Plato, Cicero, Seneca, and Plutarch that treat of moral conduct. On the other hand, she should not interest herself in the more abstruse regions of theology. He makes more frequent reference in this work to Xenophon's *Oeconomicus* and recommends the reading of more recent works on education by Filelfo and Pietro Paolo Vergerio.[40] The goals of marriage remain procreation and companionship (*conviventia*), but in this address to the male, Vives adds that it may also serve as a cure for concupiscence. The tone of the work is more casual and colloquial than the *De institutione*, and there is less sermonizing. It was translated into English in 1540 by Thomas Paynell as *The Office and Deuties of an Husband*.

CONTENT AND ANALYSIS OF THE *DE INSTITUTIONE*

In his courtly preface to Queen Catherine, Vives underlines the importance of his treatise for the good of all society, quoting Aristotle's *Politics* to the effect that states that do not provide for the education of women deprive themselves of a great source of their prosperity. He maintains that whereas the church fathers had written merely spiritual exhortation to virtue for virgins and widows, he will provide a practical guide for living, with the maximum of brevity. As it turns out, there is a strong tone of moral persuasion in the writing; as for brevity, Vives' rhetorical penchant often leads him into lengthy elaborations.[41]

It is noteworthy that in the 1538 revision of this prefatory letter, Vives emphasizes the importance of virtue in those who will be a man's inseparable companion in every condition of life. He may well have decided to incorporate a sentiment found in Hyrde's own preface to the queen:

---

40. Filelfo wrote the *Convivia Mediolanensia (Milanese Banquets)*, an encyclopedic work of various classical learning, sometime during his years at the court of Filippo Maria Visconti in Milan (1440–47). Vives lectured on this work in Louvain in the winter semester of 1513–14. His *Praelectio* on the work is in J. L. Vives, *Early Writings* 2 (Leiden, 1991), 144–51. Pietro Paolo Vergerio wrote his *De ingenuis moribus et liberalibus studiis (On Gentlemanly Conduct and Liberal Studies)* in 1400. It had great influence throughout the fifteenth century.

41. Cf. Janis Butler Holm, "Struggling with the Letter: Vives' Preface to *The Instruction of a Christen Woman*," in *Contending Kingdoms*, ed. Marie-Rose Logan and P. Rudnytsky (Detroit: Wayne State University Press, 1989), 265–97.

For what is more frutefull than the good education and order of women, the one halfe of all mankynd, and that halfe also whose good behaviour or evyll tatchis [i.e., taches, "defects" or "vices"] gyveth or byreveth the other halfe, almoste all the holle pleasure and commoditie of this present lyfe, byside the furtherance or hynderance forther growyng thereupon, concerning the lyfe to come?[42]

The treatise is divided into three books: on the young girl, the married woman, and the widow. In this Vives follows the plan of composition of his predecessor, Francesc Eiximenis in his *Llibre des dones (A Book on Women)*, which will be discussed later. From the first, he speaks of the preeminence of chastity in a woman's education and condemns all those writers of belles lettres who would destroy this virtue. In the opening chapter on the childhood of the young girl, Vives is much indebted to the Roman orator Quintilian, as he is in many other passages. In his revised edition, he added an excerpt from Tacitus's *Dialogue on Orators*, lauding the customs of earlier generations when boys were brought up in strict fashion under the care of stern matrons. How much more, says Vives, should this be so in the case of young girls, who are more inclined to vice? In her early education, the young maiden shall combine the skill of reading with other, more practical learning having to do with the care and management of the household. Vives quotes Jerome's letters to various Roman noblewomen to bolster his argument here and gives examples of famous women who occupied themselves with the working of wool and flax from antiquity to the present, culminating with the model daughters of Queen Isabella, "la Católica."

In the new version of the fourth chapter, Vives radically revises his earlier views on a woman's intellectual capacities. He prefaces his remarks with a pessimistic account of the proclivity of the human race to vice and the need for instruction in virtue in order to combat the purveyors of evil counsel. He refutes the inveterate prejudice against the learned woman (*femina docta*) with the assertion that men of evil disposition are just as prone as women to misuse their intelligence. The learning he proposes has no regard for gender but is directed to the whole human race. Knowledge is the greatest safeguard for chastity, just as ignorance is the cause for the loss of chastity. This belief accords well with the views and practice of Thomas More, for whom Vives expresses his admiration.

In proof of his thesis, Vives reviews the lives of famous learned women

---

42. Ruth Kuschmierz, "The Instruction of a Christen Woman: A Critical Edition of the Tudor Translation" (Ph.D. diss., University of Pittsburgh, 1961), 2.

of pagan antiquity such as Cornelia, mother of the Gracchi, a favorite paragon of his; and Porcia, wife of Brutus. To these he adds a roster of female saints and exemplary women of his own time. Such lists are common in medieval and Renaissance treatises on women, beginning with Boccaccio's *De claris mulieribus (On Famous Women)*,[43] which in turn probably owed something to Jerome's list in his *Against Jovinianus*. Vives' catalogue of women is much more interesting than the usual ones, both in scope and in detail.

Also in the fourth chapter (par. 29), Vives asserts that the young woman's early reading should be restricted to the Scriptures and the writings of philosophers that pertain to good morals. This is to be for her own spiritual betterment and edification or to be imparted to her children, but the role of teaching in school is denied her, since this would detract from her modesty and decorum. In Chapter Five, Vives specifies those authors who are to be read and those not to be read. The main object of his condemnation are the chivalrous romances of love and warfare written in the vernacular languages. Vives shows quite a thorough knowledge of this literature in Spanish, French, and Flemish. In their place he would substitute the New Testament, the church fathers, Plato, Cicero, and Seneca. If it is poetry that gives the young woman pleasure, then let her read Christian poets such as Prudentius and Paulinus of Nola.

The following chapter, "On Virginity," was subjected to a complete revision, so that it bears little resemblance to the first published version. It is obvious that Vives struggled over the proper approach to this topic. In the original version, he suddenly abandons his more discursive style for a rather personal and, one might add, paternalistic tête-à-tête with a young woman. He takes as his text, explicitly, Augustine's *De sancta virginitate (On Holy Virginity)*, with its emphasis on 2 Cor. 11:2, in which Paul compares the young girl as the spouse of Christ to the church as the spouse of Christ. Vives dramatizes the discussion by means of a dialogue between Christ and the young maiden, who is a virgin physically, but not mentally. Christ remonstrates with her and bids her to depart from him. In a successive dialogue, it is a human interlocutor who asks in a series of rhetorical questions what qualities a young woman should desire in her spouse, to which he supplies the answers himself, made up of verses taken from the Psalms.

With its mixture of scriptural quotations and declamatory rhetoric, the

---

43. As Constance Jordan maintains ("Feminism and the Humanists," in *Rewriting the Renaissance*, ed. Margaret Ferguson, Maureen Quilligan, and Nancy Vickers [Chicago, 1986], 244 and n.6), "Boccaccio instituted the humanist attitude toward famous women, but not without a vein of irony as to their 'exceptionality.' Vives goes far beyond the usual listings, adding many other examples and, in my reading, demonstrating sincere admiration for them."

style of this passage is quite strange, in some respects resembling that of Augustine, but diverging perceptibly from it in sentiment. In his revision, Vives omits this dramatic dialogue and concentrates instead on a definition of virginity that he derives from Augustine and Ambrose: "integrity of the mind which extends also to the body." From the concept of virginity of the mind, Vives reverts once again to the eulogy of chastity as the one virtue that suffices for all the others in a woman; and if that is lacking, all other virtues and natural gifts are useless.[44] It is her prized possession, which must be safeguarded most strenuously. Vives writes a long chapter on the ascetic measures that must be taken to ensure the preservation of this virtue. Fasting, cleanliness, even regulated hours of sleep are counseled as well as the avoidance of luxurious attire. A modest external appearance reflects interior modesty and integrity. Vives draws on an arsenal of passages from the Scriptures, the church fathers, and classical writers to support his affirmations, especially in his diatribe against the use of cosmetics. While continuing to insist on the preeminence of chastity, he also recommends other virtues and modes of behavior: humility, sobriety, frugality, avoidance of idle chatter, and meekness. The supreme model for imitation is the Blessed Virgin Mary, to whose example he adds those of the virgin martyrs of the church and even edifying tales of pagan heroines of chastity.

Taking his cue, as he often does, from Jerome's treatise against Jovinian, Vives instructs the young maiden on the dangers of falling in love, a predicament that may befall her from some unguarded associations with men. He warns her of the excesses to which this madness may drive her, greater than those suffered by the male lover. Vives includes some shrewd psychological advice for young women to help them avoid these pitfalls. As an antidote to the incursions of passion, Vives prescribes an attitude of mind and hierarchy of the affections that are nothing less than angelic. He directs all her love to God, the Blessed Virgin, and the saints. In her state of virginity and isolation from men, the young girl has no choice but to leave any considerations of marriage to her parents. All she can do is help them in their task by her prayers and abide by their decision. The ideal union is a *mariage de convenance.*

Toward the end of this book Vives suddenly lapses into a rhetorical outburst that is blatantly misogynistic. He imagines the kind of woman who,

44. Vives seems to be influenced here by a passage in Jerome's *Against Jovinianus:* "It is the saying of a very learned man that chastity must be preserved at all costs and that when it is lost all virtue falls to the ground. This holds the primacy of all virtues in woman." Jerome *Against Jovinianus* 1.49 (*NPNF,* 2d ser., 6:386).

like the mythical Pasiphae, would mate with men whose nature is little removed from that of the brute beast. He quotes to his purpose verses from a notorious antifeminist poet, Pere Torroella, that compare some women to she-wolves in their choice of partner. The passage is quite shocking in its unrestrained virulence.

In the 1524 version of his treatise, Vives included a general introduction to the institution of marriage in the first chapter of Book II that he suppressed in his revision. Perhaps he thought it superfluous, but he may also have excised it in response to criticism. In no other part of the book is he more profeminist. He quotes several ancient writers, including the supposed misogynist Euripides, who praise the incomparable blessings of a happy marriage. The greatest sages of the ancient world, he avers, were all married, surely because they saw that there was nothing more in accordance with nature than the union of man and woman. Then, without declaring his source, Vives paraphrases a long passage from Cicero's *On Good and Evil*, wherein he speaks of the various bonds that exist among men. He ends his encomium with the affirmation that marriage is a sacred thing that God instituted in Paradise and later sanctioned in his miracle at the wedding feast of Cana. In the last sentence, however, Vives checks himself and returns to his practical business of instructing the virtuous woman.

The primary goal of marriage, according to Vives, is not so much the production of offspring as community of life and indissoluble companionship (*communionem quandam vitae et indissociabilem societatem*). This view is in sharp contrast with the teachings of the church fathers, who consistently cite procreation as the primary goal. Erasmus in his *Christiani matrimonii institutio (The Institution of Christian Matrimony)* defines marriage in a very legalistic fashion as "a lawful and perpetual union between a man and a woman, entered into for the purpose of begetting offspring and involving an indivisible partnership of life and property."[45] In the later *On the Duty of a Husband*, Vives rectifies his statement, giving as the principal end of marriage the propagation of offspring and, as a subsidiary end, the quelling of concupiscence.

In succeeding chapters Vives gives great emphasis to the passage from Genesis: "They shall be two in one flesh." If a woman will keep this principle before her mind, she will be happy in her marriage. In addition to the indispensable virtue of chastity, the married woman must also possess great love for her husband. Against the evils of adultery, Vives delivers a vehement diatribe with great rhetorical flourishes and multiple examples from pagan

---

45. *Desiderii Erasmi Roterodami opera omnia*, ed. J. Leclerc (Leiden, 1703–1706; reprint, Hildesheim, 1961–62), vol. 5, 617D.

antiquity. The stories of heroic women—mostly from ancient writers, but some also from more recent history—are enlisted to support his hyperbolic ideals of the devoted wife. In the matter of the wife's obedience and complete subjection to the husband, no matter what his defects, Vives adheres to the usual Aristotelian teachings on the subject along with the rigid precepts of Saint Paul. To lend more credibility to his teachings, he offers an example from direct experience: the devotion showed by his mother-in-law, Clara Cervent, to her older, syphilitic husband, to whom she had been fraudulently married. Although this example was meant as a tale of edification, it will elicit in the modern reader a sense of absolute revulsion. Vives is obsessive in his insistence on obedience and respect toward the husband, whose commands should be regarded as the law of God. His bedside becomes a hallowed place, where acts of worship are to be performed! The chapter ends with a lengthy quotation from the pseudo-Aristotelian *Economics* reinforcing the authority of the husband.

On the subject of marital concord, Vives offers some good advice, although still laying chief responsibility upon the wife. As usual, he draws examples from antiquity and from more recent times, citing also the exemplary accord of his own parents, a detail that elicited Erasmus's criticism. Vives also essays the delicate matter of the more intimate relations between husband and wife, emphasizing once again the modesty and propriety of the wife. He offers some advice for the husband as well, especially that he not defile the marriage bed by acts of lust.

Separate chapters treat of the vice of jealousy and the proper adornment for a married woman. On the latter theme, Vives enlists the support of the church fathers: Ambrose, Cyprian, John Chrysostom, and Tertullian, with the last two, notorious for their severity, added in the revised edition.

Vives next takes up the matter of behavior in public and in the home. Concerning the married woman's public demeanor, he counsels great discretion and reserve. It is not good for a woman to be too well known or talked about. She should give no sign of arrogance, disdain, or affected manners, nor should she be easily swayed by worldly esteem. In a most condescending manner, Vives deigns to let women in on men's secrets, viz., that women make themselves appear foolish in men's eyes when they aspire after honors. Their place is in the home, where their skill in governing the household constitutes one of the great blessings of marital bliss.

Vives also has explicit instructions for the woman's vigilance with servants. Another duty of the mistress of the household is to look after the health of its inhabitants, for which she should be familiar with remedies for everyday illnesses. As a release from all these domestic cares, she should retire daily, if possible, to some secluded part of the house to meditate on more transcendental matters. The last part of this section is a beautiful commentary on the famous passage from the Book of Proverbs about the good woman.

The chapter on the care of children begins with a consolation to those who cannot have children, who have cause to rejoice because they have been exempted from an incredible burden. Paradoxically, the discussion turns into an attack against childbearing and all its attendant woes. From that unexpected preamble Vives passes to the early nurture of children, which should be at their mother's breast, to their formative years, when the influence of the mother is crucial. Echoing Quintilian, Vives emphasizes the importance of the mother for the proper teaching of the native language. It is the mother, too, who instills love of virtue and hatred of vice, and it is to her that children look for example. At the same time, Vives counsels rigor and discipline, as he had received from his own mother.

Vives dedicates the remaining chapters of the *De institutione* to the instruction of twice-married women and stepmothers; the behavior to be observed with in-laws; and the elderly woman's preparations for receiving her final reward. Vives does not relax his stern precepts for the state of widowhood. He goes as far as to cite the self-immolation of widows in Thrace and the Hindu practice of suttee as examples of faithfulness to one's dead husband. His view of the widow stems from the etymology of the word: empty, destitute, deserted. She is at the mercy of the winds, like a ship without a rudder, and has need of others to support her in her need. As always, Vives is preoccupied with external demeanor and has much to say about how the widow should comport herself at her husband's funeral. The preservation of chastity is still uppermost, so it is best that the widow have some good woman or an older man as the guardian of her virtue. She must avoid priests and monks, since they are not to be trusted. The widow will now have more time to pass with her immortal spouse, pray, and occupy her mind with holy thoughts.

Vives has some salutary advice for widows on how to manage their practical affairs and, in particular, how to deal with judges and lawyers when they must defend themselves in court. On the subject of second marriages, he recognizes that it would be heretical to forbid them altogether, but he shows his sympathy for the more rigid standards of Saint Jerome, citing a long passage from his rather uncompromising letter to Furia. If she wishes to remarry, the widow should leave the choice of spouse to her parents or other older relatives. In a final, sober admonition, added in the revised version, Vives counsels that this second marriage should be celebrated quietly, almost in secret, to avoid scandal. The treatise ends on this negative, austere note.

SOURCES AND CULTURAL BACKGROUND
OF VIVES' TREATISE

Although Vives professes in the opening paragraph of his address to the queen to eschew the merely exhortatory precepts of such writers as Tertullian, Cyprian, Jerome, Ambrose, Augustine, and Fulgentius of Ruspe, he paradoxically cites these very authors as the *De institutione* unfolds. The sternest of them, Tertullian and Fulgentius, he adds in the second edition to strengthen his position. Ambrose was a vehement advocate of virginity, instituting formal rituals for the public installation of virgins and exalting this state of life above all others. He was followed in this tendency by Jerome in his letters to various women followers, which Vives duly cites, especially those to Laeta, Furia, and Demetrias, all highborn ladies who had embraced a life of asceticism.

But Vives reserves a special place for Jerome's most antifeminist tract, the *Against Jovinianus*. Jovinian had taught that all baptized persons, no matter what their station in life—virgin, married, or widowed—had equal spiritual merit. In his attack, Jerome exalts virginity to the detriment of marriage, which, in this invective at least, he seems to have regarded as only slightly better than fornication. So virulent was his diatribe that his friends in Rome, especially the Christian senator Pammachius, tried to withdraw it from circulation. Jerome obliged his friends by writing a retraction (letter 48), but the piece continued to be used by antifeminist writers, thanks especially to the inclusion of an excerpt from a putative work of Theophrastus counseling the wise man not to marry.

Cyprian's ascetic views, akin to those of Tertullian, whom he much admired, form part of Vives' arsenal as well as those of the Greek fathers Gregory Nazianzen and John Chrysostom (these latter writers were added in the second edition). In addition to the fathers, he quotes liberally and appositely from the Old and New Testaments.

Of the classical writers, Vives makes good use of Quintilian for the early stages of education and shows great familiarity with other Latin writers of Spanish origin: both Senecas (although for Vives and most Renaissance writers, they were one and the same), Lucan, Martial, and Isidore. For antique legends and *exempla*, he enlists to his cause Plutarch's *Mulierum virtutes* (*The Virtues of Women*), Valerius Maximus, Pliny the Elder, and Aulus Gellius. He prefers the pseudo-Aristotelian *Economics* to Xenophon's *Oeconomicus*, which is more liberal in its attitude toward women, although the former work, especially the Third Book, defends the rights of both spouses and stresses the importance of marital fidelity in both parties. Even Ovid provides a goodly number of quotable passages, especially from the *Remedia amoris* and the *Fasti.*

Since Vives is ostensibly writing for Catherine of Aragon, daughter of Isabella the Catholic, the position of women in Spanish society must be kept in mind. Although Isabella was brought up traditionally in the countryside of Arévalo in the heartland of Castile, she wished her children to be educated in the new humanist learning, especially the knowledge of Latin. Through the instrumentality of her husband, King Fernando II of Aragon, she had two brothers, Antonio and Alessandro Geraldini, come to the court to tutor her children. Alessandro wrote a work on the education of girls, *De eruditione nobilium puellarum* (*On the Education of Well-Born Girls*), which unfortunately has not survived. It was at Isabella's request that the famous humanist Antonio de Nebrija translated his Latin grammar into Spanish so that, as he says in the preface, "religious women and young unmarried women could learn some Latin without having to rely on male teachers."[46]

Nebrija also dedicated to her his *Gramática castellana*, the first grammar of any Romance language, for instruction at court. The Castilian queen would certainly have been seconded in this initiative by her secretary, Beatriz de Galindo—"la Latina," as she was called—who had taught at the University of Salamanca. Catherine surrounded herself with learned women and insisted on reforms in education. In like manner, she was interested in the education of women, unlike Lady Margaret Beaufort, Countess of Richmond and the mother of Henry VII. A learned woman, patroness of higher education, and benefactress of the University of Cambridge, the countess made no provisions for the education of girls.

At this time in Spain and earlier in the century, a series of tracts and treatises for and against women were published, many of which must have been known, at least by name, to Vives. In 1443 the Galician writer Juan Rodríguez de la Cámara wrote *El triunfo de las donas* (*The Triumph of Women*), which attempted to prove not only the equality of women but their superiority by means of specious scholastic argumentation. He dedicated it to Doña Maria, first wife of Juan II, but was inspired by one of the ladies of her entourage, which may account for its exaggerated claims.

---

46. This was his *Introducciones latinas—contrapuesto el romance al latín* (Salamanca, 1486). Cf. Antonio de Nebrija, *Gramática de la lengua castellana*, ed. Antonio Quilis (Madrid, 1980), 14: "por que las mugeres religiosas y vírgenes dedicadas a Dios, sin participación de varones, pudiessen conocer algo de la lengua latina."

In 1446 Alvaro de Luna, also a count at the court of Juan II, wrote in praise of women *El libro de las virtuosas y claras mugeres* (*The Book of Virtuous and Famous Women*), in which he parades forth heroines from the Old Testament and Greek and Roman antiquity as well as female saints of the early centuries. He argues for the equality of women with men both in the attainment of virtue and in intellectual capacity, although this quality is less important for him than the womanly virtues of chastity, honesty, and obedience. As in later treatises, Alvaro gives the Blessed Virgin Mary as the supreme model for imitation.

Mosén Diego de Valera, Alvaro's enemy at court, wrote in the same vein a *Tratado en defensa de virtuosas mujeres* (*A Treatise in Defense of Virtuous Women*) about 1440, dedicated to Doña Maria, wife of Juan II, and directed against those who delight in calumniating women. He is less inclined than Alvaro to accept their equality of intellect.

A book that Vives placed on his forbidden list, the *Cárcel de amor* (*The Prison of Love*) of Diego de San Pedro (Seville, 1492), is a covert praise of women under the guise of a tale of unrequited love, which had much success with ladies at court. The spurned lover languishes away in his prison, refusing all nourishment save for the last two letters that he has received from his beloved, which he consumes dissolved in his tears. The letters interchanged between the lovers give a fine psychological analysis of the female sentiment of love.

There was also the *Jardín de las nobles doncellas* (*The Garden of Noble Maidens*) of Fray Martín Alonso de Córdoba (Valladolid, 1500), written for the Infanta Isabel, defending her right to the throne of Castile. It is aristocratic in tone, reserving knowledge and learning for queens and princesses. For the rest, he remains faithful to church teachings, that woman was made to be man's helpmate and for the propagation of the race.

Greater in number and influence in this debate were the detractors of womankind, chief among whom was Alfonso Martínez de Toledo, archpriest of Talavera, who entitled his work *Corbacho* after Boccaccio. It was first published in 1498 in four books, the second of which is a virulent satire against the vices and defects of perverse women. Before enumerating his catalogue of vicious women, the author attempts to shield himself from adverse criticism by claiming that the virtuous woman can only be individuated, like gold from dross, through the description of the evil woman. His book became the proverbial antifeminist tract of the period.

Another cleric from the same region, Fray Hernando de Talavera (1428–1507), professor at the University of Salamanca and confessor of Queen Isabella, wrote an essay addressed to the noblewoman Doña Maria Pacheco, concerning how a woman should spend her day in pious readings and associate only with wise persons. He wrote also on how a married woman should dress, maintaining that she should always have her head covered in sign of subjection to her husband, a practice advocated by Vives. Yet another monk, Fray Iñigo de Mendoza, favorite poet of Queen Isabella, contributed his salvoes of vituperation against evil women, *Coplas en vituperio de las malas hembras (Couplets in Vituperation of Evil Women).*

Other misogynist writers of this period are poets: Pere Torroella (whom Vives cites), who wrote *Coplas de maldezir de mugeres (Couplets on the Defamation of Women),* and his imitators Hernán Mexiá and Juan de Tapia. The Catalan poet Jaume Roig (c. 1405–78), like Vives a native of Valencia, wrote a long antifeminist poem of 16,359 verses variously entitled *Espill (The Mirror)* or *Llibre de les dones (A Book on Women).* It is in the form of an autobiography, narrating the various marital adventures of a roving *pícaro*. The tone is humorous and satirical, but a moral didacticism of a strong misogynist strain pervades the narrative: the only woman to escape censure is the Blessed Virgin. The poem was not published until 1531 in Valencia, but it certainly must have circulated in the city long before then.

Vives does not participate on one side or the other in this dispute, instead taking a middle path. The strong religious and moral impulse that informs his work has more affinity with an earlier Valencian writer. There can be little doubt that Vives was familiar with the writings of the Franciscan friar Francesc Eiximenis (c. 1340–1409), in particular his *Llibre de les dones (A Book on Women).* This tract is divided into five sections of unequal length: on girls, 9 chapters; on young unmarried women, 20; on married women, 78; on widows, 9; and on nuns, 420. Eiximenis reached the peak of his literary career during his years in Valencia from 1382 to 1408. His works were well known there, although the first printed edition of his treatise on women did not appear until 1495 in Barcelona.

While Vives draws on many other sources that became accessible to the humanists, there are many points of similarity in the two writers' citation of sources. Vives makes much more use of the classical authors, reflecting his humanist training, while Eiximenis is more dependent on medieval authorities such as John of Salisbury, Alain de Lille, Bonaventure, and Peter the Lombard. In some cases, Vives repeats passages from Eiximenis that the friar in turn had taken from a still earlier work, the *De eruditione filiorum nobilium (On the Education of Noble Sons and Daughters)* of Vincent of Beauvais,[47] written for Queen Margarida, the Catalan wife of King Louis IX of France. The last nine chapters of this work concern the education of girls and make abundant

---

47. Vincent of Beauvais, *De eruditione filiorum nobilium,* ed. A. Steiner (Cambridge, Mass., 1938).

use of the letter of Jerome to Eustochium on virginity. Its teachings are very rigorous, stressing the vigilant protection of a young girl's virtue. All three writers cite a long passage from Cyprian's *De habitu virginum* (*On the Dress of Young Women*), Jerome's letter to Demetrias, various maxims from Terence, Ovid's *Remedia amoris*, and a rather vehement harangue against female adornment from the prophet Isaiah (Isa. 3 : 16–26).

In his opening chapters, Eiximenis proclaims that God has raised up certain women, both pagan and Christian, to be models of evangelical perfection in the same way as he has done with men. When God created woman, he endowed her with goodness of nature, fortune, and grace. He warns against speaking ill of women. Some of Vives' ideas on what might be interpreted as universal education for women have a precedent in Eiximenis, as illustrated in this excerpt from the Franciscan writer: "Que tota dona sabés letra, car deys que havia major occasió de esser devota e de occupar si met exa e de informar-se en tot bé."[48] ("All women should be literate, for in that way they will have more opportunity to be devout and to occupy themselves and inform themselves of all that is good.")

During the time when Eiximenis was active in Valencia, the famous preacher Saint Vincent Ferrer (1350–1419) was the lector of theology in the city cathedral. His sermons, although delivered in the vernacular, were published in Latin while Vives was still residing in Valencia. Many of them have to do with the duties and virtues required of women. It is very probable that Vives was aware of his teachings; at any rate, he seems to share some of the more severe attitudes toward women expressed by his fellow Valencian, especially in the matter of excessive adornment.

We learn of another source used without acknowledgment by Vives through a later imitator of his work. The Venetian printer Gabriel Giolito de' Ferrari entered the *querelle des femmes* on the side of the defenders of the female sex in the mid-sixteenth century. In 1545 he published an Italian translation of Agrippa's treatise, *Della nobilità et eccellenza delle donne* (*On the Nobility and Preeminence of Women*), together with a prefatory encomium of womankind by Alessandro Piccolomini. In that same year, the Venetian writer and polymath Lodovico Dolce entrusted to Giolito his *Dialogo della*

---

48. Francesc Eiximenis, *Lo llibre de les dones*, ed. Frank Naccarato, rev. Curt Wittlin (Barcelona, 1981), 91. A Spanish adaptation of Eiximenis's treatise was written by an anonymous Franciscan at the behest of Pope Adrian VI and was published in Valladolid in 1542. In a recent article, a tentative identification of the author is given. Cf. Carmen Nácher Clausell, "El Padre Carmona, OFM, confesor de Adriano VI y probable traductor del *Llibre de les dones* de Francesc Eiximenis," *Archivum Franciscanum Historicum* 89 (1966): 287–305. This Spanish version shows a marked influence of Vives in its additions to the original text.

institution delle donne secondo li tre stati che cadono nella vita humana (Dialogue on the Instruction of Women according to the Three States of Life). Dolce's treatise is a close adaptation—almost a plagiarism—of Vives', set in a lively dialogue form. It had much more success than the literal translation of Vives' work, published in Venice in 1561. Significantly, Dolce omits the epithet *Christianae* of Vives' title and with it many of the references to sacred writings. Under the guise of the male speaker in the dialogue, Dolce assumes the role of *"spositor di parole,"* i.e., "interpreter," for a female audience of a Latin book that has just arrived from Basel. Only later in the dialogue does the *spositor* reveal who the author of the instructional book is.

As a modern analogue to the famous story of the faithful wife Camma in Plutarch (it occurs in the second book of both Vives and Dolce), Dolce recounts the tale of a Dalmatian woman named Brasilla, first related by Francesco Barbaro in his *De re uxoria (On Wifely Duties)*[49] and appropriated by Vives. The speaker remarks at this point, "I have read it in a Latin work of Barbaro, whom I mentioned above, from which Luis Vives not only took the greater part of his *Instruction of a Christian Woman*, but some other men of great renown also made use of its beginning."[50] The accusation is somewhat exaggerated, but there are many correspondences of sources and themes in both works. Vives clearly had it before him, but he differs from Barbaro in many respects, especially in his definition of marriage. Vives emphasizes the companionship of husband and wife, whereas Barbaro follows the usual church doctrine that made procreation and the avoidance of fornication the primary goals. Barbaro stresses the necessity of virtue in the wife, which suffices to make her desirable even if all else is lacking. Vives, on the other hand, is more obsessive in his insistence on the single virtue of chastity. The mother has a role in the education of the children in Barbaro's treatise, but Vives attributes more importance to her in performing this duty. Finally, Barbaro is less puritanical than Vives in talking about sexual relations in marriage (*De congressus ratione*).

Barbaro wrote the treatise for Lorenzo di Giovanni de' Medici, brother of Cosimo, at the time of his marriage to Ginevra Cavalcanti in 1416. It circulated in manuscript form for almost one hundred years and was widely known before the first printed edition appeared in Paris in 1513. A manuscript of the work existed at Valencia, and there can be no doubt that Vives did borrow heavily from it, especially in his citations of *exempla* from Greek and Roman history, taken from Plutarch and Valerius Maximus. The Vene-

---

49. Cf. note to Book I, par. 91.

50. Lodovico Dolce, *Dialogo della institution delle donne*. In Vinegia appresso Gabriele Giolito de' Ferrari, 1547, 45v.

tian writer used Xenophon's *Oeconomicus* to a much greater extent in outlining wifely duties, while Vives cites the pseudo-Aristotle *Economics* more frequently. Dolce's own work contains many new examples from Italian history and literature along with scenes from Venetian everyday life, as in an extended analogy between the education of young girls and the art of ship-building in Venice's *arsenale*. Besides Barbaro, Vives knew of the writings of other Italian humanists who wrote on education, such as Paolo Vergerio and Francesco Filelfo, whom he mentions in the *De officio mariti* (*On the Duty of a Husband*) (Majansius IV, 369).

Another important influence in Vives' moral formation was the spiritual movement of the *devotio moderna*, which spread from northern Europe to Spain. This form of spirituality emphasized contemplating the life of Christ and personal prayer. In the last decade of the fifteenth century, many works associated with this movement were translated into Catalan.[51] These include the four large volumes of the *Life of Christ* by the Carthusian monk Ludolph of Saxony, and especially the *Imitation of Christ*, at that time attributed to the famous chancellor of the University of Paris, Jean Gerson, but now usually assigned to the Flemish mystic Thomas à Kempis. Vives' habit of interspersing scriptural texts with appropriate quotations from the church fathers has much in common with the devotional books of the *devotio moderna*; they must have formed some of his early reading in Valencia.

Later on, during his stay at the College of Montaigu in Paris, where the stern discipline of Jan Standonck of Mechelen, trained in the school of the *devotio moderna*, was in force, Vives came into personal contact with this way of life. Many of his best friends in Belgium—Cranevelt, Jan van Fevyn, and Marcus Laurinus—had come under the influence of this spiritual movement. It is interesting to note that Gerard Groot, a leading figure in the northern beginnings of the movement, wrote a treatise on matrimony[52] that emphasizes the disadvantages of this state of life. The first purpose of marriage is a negative one: the avoidance of concupiscence, in the spirit of Paul's dictum "better to marry than to burn" (1 Cor. 7:9). A long chapter is devoted to the discussion of the evils inherent in the sexual act, and there is much citation of Jerome's *Against Jovinianus*. These austere teachings must have been known, at least in part, to the young Vives.

Vives may also have been acquainted with a work printed in Valencia

51. Cf. González y González, 116–18; Marcel Bataillon, *Erasmo y España* (Mexico, 1966), 44–51; Antonio Mestre, "La espiritualidad de Juan Luis Vives," in *Ioannis Lodovici Vivis Valentini opera omnia*, vol. 1 (Valencia, 1992), 409–59.

52. Groot's tract has been edited by T. A. Clarisse Groningen, "Gerardi Groet diaconi Trajectensis Ecclesiae tractatus de matrimonio," *Archief voor kerkelijke geschiedenis* 8 (1837): 159–249.

in 1497 at the express wish of Queen Isabella, the *Life of Christ* by Sister Isabel de Villena, abbess of the Convent of the Holy Trinity in Valencia. This is probably the earliest example of a feminist depiction of the life of Christ. The Blessed Virgin and Mary Magdalen are the heroes of the story, and the events of Christ's life are viewed through their eyes. For Vives also, these two figures of the New Testament are highly important examples of the holy woman.

TRANSLATIONS AND LATER INFLUENCE
OF VIVES' TREATISE

First to appear of the numerous translations of the *De institutione* into the vernacular languages was a Castilian version produced in Valencia in 1528, *Instrucción de la muger Christiana.* The translator was Giovanni Giustiniani, an Italian very well versed in the Castilian tongue who served at the court of Don Fernando of Aragon, viceroy of Valencia. He says in the preface that he wishes to make this excellent reading (*"lectura tan buena"*) available to all women of Spain, since even foreign lands have been able to enjoy it. He has heard that it has already been translated into English by the royal treasurer at the behest of the queen herself, and that a French translation already exists. From the first, the translator alerts the reader that he has taken the liberty of adding things not present in the original, such as suggested further readings more suitable for his Spanish readers: translations of the letters of Catherine of Siena, Petrarch's *On the Remedies of Good and Evil Fortune,* and the popular *Life of Christ* by the Carthusian monk Ludolphus of Saxony. He especially recommends Erasmus's *Enchiridion militis christiani (Handbook of the Christian Soldier),* which had just appeared that year in Valencia from the same printer that had issued the *Instrucción.* A year later, a corrected version by an unknown author was published in Alcalá in which many passages are re-translated and several omitted chapters are reinserted. Numerous other editions of Giustiniani, or Justiniano, as he was known, followed: Seville, 1535; Zaragoza, 1539, 1545, 1555; Zamora, 1539; and Valladolid, 1584.

It is altogether fitting that the English translation of Vives' treatise should have proceeded from the household of Sir Thomas More. It may be reasonably conjectured that Vives discussed the problem of women's education at More's estate in Chelsea, where he must have been a guest from time to time. More himself had been elaborating a version of the treatise when he learned from Richard Hyrde, who had recently entered his services as a tutor, that he had completed his own translation. Hyrde mentions in his preface to Queen Catherine that he showed his work, which he had done in secret, to his good master. More then confided that he had begun a version himself, thinking that it would have procured great pleasure to the queen in her zeal for the virtuous education of womankind in her realm.

Hyrde reserves great praise for the book, saying:

> I verily believe there was never any treatis made, either furnisshed with more goodly counsayles, or sette out with more effectuall reasons, or garnysshed with more substancial authoritees, or stored more plentuously of convenient examples, nor all these thynges together more goodly treated and hendeled, than maister Vives hath done in his boke.[53]

He does justice to the original, translating the difficult Latin of Vives into a clear and vigorous English, which he submitted to More's inspection for approval and correction. Some of Vives' more severe strictures against female adornment in the first book are omitted, and the long diatribe of Isaiah that Vives quotes in this regard is abbreviated. At other times, Hyrde adds a phrase or two for the sake of rhythm or clarity and, like the Castilian translator Justiniano, makes additions and deletions to the list of romances forbidden by Vives, inserting such English examples as Parthenope of Blois, Ipomedon, Guy of Warwick, and Bevis of Hampton.

The elaborated title of Hyrde's translation reads:

> A very frutefull and pleasant boke called the INSTRUCTION OF A CRISTEN WOMAN, made fyrst in Laten, and dedicated unto the quenes good grace, by the right famous clerke mayster Lewes Vives, and turned into Englysshe by Rycharde Hyrd. Whiche boke who so redeth diligently shal have knowledge of many thynges, wherein he shal take great pleasure, and specially women shall take great commodyte and frute towarde the encrease of vertue and good maners.[54]

The last phrase is to be interpreted in modern English as good morals, and this is indeed the primary intention of Vives' treatise. The *Instruction* went far in propagating Vives' educational ideas in England, becoming the most popular conduct book for women during the Tudor period and beyond. It went through nine known editions, most of them from the printer, Thomas Berthelet, and his successors. The last two editions, however, were from the press of Puritan printers, Robert Redgrave (1585) and John Danter (1592).[55] The first edition antedates Berthelet's appointment as *regius impressor* (king's

---

53. Kuschmierz, "The Instruction of a Christen Woman," 3.

54. Ibid., 1.

55. For various changes made in successive printings, cf. Betty Travitsky, "Reprinting Tudor History: The Case of Catherine of Aragon," *Renaissance Quarterly* 50 (1997): 164–74.

printer) on 15 February 1530. Since he opened shop in August 1528, the first undated edition must be either 1528 or 1529. In any case the work was published posthumously, for Richard Hyrde died in Italy on 25 March 1528 while on a royal mission.

In a letter to Cranevelt of 31 December 1526 (De Vocht, ep. 217, 568), Vives refers to a French translation of his work that was being prepared by a certain Clericus, who De Vocht conjectures might be either Philip de Clerck, Esquire, "Comoigne meester" of Mechelen, or Charles de Clerck, a councillor and chamberlain of Charles V. This translation may have circulated in manuscript, but no printed copy appeared. The first French translation we have is owed to Pierre de Changy and was printed together with a translation of the *De officio mariti* by Jacques Kerver in Paris, 1542: *Livre de l'institution de la femme chrestienne tant en son enfance que mariage et viduité. Aussi de l'office du mari.* The translator takes great freedom with the text, suppressing many passages, so that it almost constitutes an original work. It was reprinted many times: 1543, 1545, 1549, 1552, and 1579 in Paris, and three times in Lyons by Jean de Tournes: 1545, 1547, and 1549. Of later editions of the sixteenth century, that produced by Christopher Plantin in 1579 is of particular interest. At first he thought of publishing a reprint of the de Changy translation, but, seeing its poor quality, he sponsored a new translation by Antoine Tiron at the instigation of two Antwerp schoolmasters of a girls' finishing school, Sebastiaan Cuypers and Pieter Heyns.

The first German translation dates to 1544 and was the work of Christoph Bruno, a well-known poet and humanist from Munich. It was printed by Heinrich Steiner in Augsburg, who in 1540 had published a deluxe edition of a little book on marriage by the jurist and humanist Albrecht von Eyb. Also in 1540 the very influential book on marriage by Zwingli's successor, Heinrich Bullinger, appeared. Bruno's translation was reprinted together with the *De officio mariti (On the Duty of the Husband)* by C. Egenolffs, Frankfurt-am-Main, in 1566.

An Italian translation of the two works appeared in Venice from the presses of Vincenzo Vaugris in 1546, done by Pietro Lauro of Modena, according to the dedication. It was reprinted in Milan by Giovann' Antonio de gli Antonij in 1561.

A Dutch translation based on the French of Changy, *Die Institutie ende leeringe van een Christlijcke Vrowe*, was published in Antwerp by Jan Roelants in 1554.

The impress of Vives' treatise in Spain is seen in many sixteenth-century Spanish works on women and marriage, chief among them Alonso Gutiérrez de la Vera Cruz, *Speculum coniugiorum (The Mirror of Marriages)*, Salamanca,

1562; Antonio de Guevara, *Epístolas familiares* (Vallodolid, 1539), some of which discuss the relations between husband and wife or give advice to young lovers or old would-be lovers; and Pedro de Luján,[56] *Colóquios matrimoniales* (eleven editions between 1550 and 1589), although he draws more upon Guevara and Erasmus's marriage colloquies, especially the one entitled simply "Marriage." The famous poet Fray Luis de León wrote an essay dedicated to his niece, Maria Varela Osorio, on the occasion of her wedding, entitled *La perfecta casada* (*The Perfect Wife*), Salamanca, 1583, which became a popular book. A long section that comments on the passage on the virtuous woman from the Book of Proverbs (31:10–31) reduplicates some of Vives' exegesis.

Vives' *Instruction of a Christen Woman* enjoyed enormous popularity in England, where it continued to be printed for sixty years, with slight revisions to please each age and creed. The translator himself, Richard Hyrde, wrote a dedicatory letter commending Margaret Roper's translation of Erasmus's treatise on the Lord's Prayer to his student, Frances Staverton, granddaughter of Thomas More. In the letter he enlarges upon Vives' views on the learned woman. It is even more polemical in tone than Vives' own words, as in this excerpt:

> And where they fynde faute with lernyng bycause they say it engendreth wytte and crafte there they reprehende it for that that it is moost worthy to be commended for and the whiche is one singuler cause wherfore lernyng ought to be desyred for he that had lever have his wyfe a foole than a wyse woman I holde hym worse than twyse frantyke.[57]

In his *Defence of Good Women*, published in 1540, Sir Thomas Elyot espouses many of the ideas of Vives but is more explicit in his refutation of Aristotle's teachings on the inferiority of women, using as his paragon of womanly virtue and fortitude the Syrian Queen Zenobia, following Boccaccio and Vives. Elyot also translated Plutarch's treatise on the education of children. In its introduction he places certain strictures on what a woman should read, again following Vives in this regard. He advocates women's role in educating their children but, unlike Vives, prefers that boys be assigned to a tutor.

---

56. Pedro de Luján is one of the interlocutors in Edmund Tilney's *A Briefe and Pleasant Discourse in Mariage called the Flower of Friendshippe*, published in London in 1568, which bears many traces of Vives' work.

57. Richard De Molen, *Erasmus of Rotterdam. A Quincentennial Symposium* (New York, 1971), 100.

Also in 1540, Vives' devotional work, the *Introduction to Wisdom*, a companion piece to the *Instruction*, was translated into English by Sir Richard Morison and dedicated to the son of Thomas Cromwell. The translator is lavish in his praise of Vives: "This boke was gathered by Ludovicus Vives, a man greatly conversant in all good authours and excellentlye wel sene in all kyndes of lernyng." Vives' manual was extremely popular in the English schools, used as a textbook in the Tudor schools together with *Lily's Grammar*.[58] Before the end of the century there were one hundred editions of the work in the original Latin and in translations into other languages.

Richard Whitford, a priest at Syon Abbey in Isleworth, a women's institution favored by Queen Catherine, wrote a handbook called *Work for Householders*, a practical guide for the wife's government of the household. It reiterates many of Vives' recommendations on this subject but stresses more the mother's role in the religious education of her children.

Not much influence of Vives is to be seen in Coverdale's translation of Heinrich Bullinger's *The Christen State of Matrimonye* (1541), which is a treatise in praise of marriage and against priestly celibacy. In other Protestant works, however, Vives' insistence on the moral aims of education bolsters the Protestant belief that literacy is the key to personal salvation.[59] Richard Brathwait's *The English Gentlewoman* shows much indebtedness to Vives, especially in the matters of attire, personal adornment, and womanly accomplishments. He cites many of Vives' same sources—Jerome, Ambrose, Augustine, and Cyprian—and his list of famous women exactly reproduces that of Vives. Richard Mulcaster, headmaster of the famous Merchant Taylor School in London, makes mention of "Vives, the learned Spaniard" in his *Positions Concerning the Training up of Children* (1581). Chapter 38 of this treatise counsels "that young maidens are to be set to learning" and speaks of their "natural towardness [i.e., aptitude] for learning" as equal to that of men.[60]

Vives' influence endured through the centuries and was given new impetus by the reprinting of all his works in Valencia by Gregorio Mayáns y Siscar (1782–90). In Germany during the nineteenth century, there was great interest in his pedagogical and psychological ideas, and many books were written about him. This enthusiasm was passed on to Foster Watson, a professor of education at the University College of Wales in Aberystwyth.

58. Cf. *Vives' Introduction to Wisdom. A Renaissance Textbook*, ed. Marian Leona Tobriner (New York, 1968), 40–46.

59. Cf. Margo Todd, *Christian Humanism and the Puritan Social Order* (Cambridge, 1987).

60. Richard Mulcaster, *Positions concerning the Training up of Children*, ed. William Barker (Toronto, 1994), 172.

He reprinted parts of Hyrde's *Instruction* and translated parts of the *De disciplinis*, and in his frequent travels to Catalonia revived interest in their native son. The famous savant Menéndez y Pelayo described Vives as one of the great bulwarks of Spanish and Catalonian culture. At the present day, beginning with the quincentennial of his birth in 1992, a new edition of all his works is in progress, and in the city of Valencia the local government is sponsoring new translations of all his works into Spanish.[61] A series of Selected Works of Juan Luis Vives is being published by E. J. Brill of Leiden, edited by a group of Belgian and American scholars. *The Education of a Christian Woman* remains a very important part of his opus, especially in the area of women's studies.

BIBLIOGRAPHY

Primary Works

Alberti, Leon Battista (1404–72). *The Family in Renaissance Florence.* Trans. Renée Neu Watkins. Columbia: University of South Carolina Press, 1969

Ariosto, Ludovico (1474–1533). *Orlando Furioso.* Trans. Barbara Reynolds. 2 vols. New York: Penguin Books, 1975, 1977.

Aristotelis fragmenta selecta. Ed. W. D. Ross. Oxford: Clarendon Press, 1955.

Aristotle (384–322 B.C.). *Oeconomica.* Trans. E. S. Forster. Vol. 10 of *The Works of Aristotle,* edited by W. D. Ross. Oxford: Clarendon Press, 1921.

Astell, Mary (1666–1731). *The First English Feminist: Reflections on Marriage and Other Writings.* Ed. Bridget Hill. New York: St. Martin's Press, 1986.

Barbaro, Francesco (1390–1454). *On Wifely Duties.* Trans. Benjamin Kohl. In *The Earthly Republic,* edited by Benjamin Kohl and R. G. Witt, 179–228. Philadelphia: University of Pennsylvania Press, 1976. Translation of the Preface and Book II.

Blamires, Alcuin, ed. *Women Defamed and Women Defended. An Anthology of Medieval Texts.* Oxford: Clarendon Press, 1992.

Boccaccio, Giovanni (1313–75). *Concerning Famous Women.* Trans. Guido A. Guarino. New Brunswick, N.J.: Rutgers University Press, 1963.

———. *Corbaccio or the Labyrinth of Love.* Trans. Anthony K. Cassell. 2d rev. ed. Binghamton, N.Y.: Medieval and Renaissance Texts and Studies, 1993.

Brathwait, Richard. *The English Gentlewoman.* London, 1631.

Bruni, Leonardo (1370–1444). "On the Study of Literature (1405) to Lady Battista Malatesta of Montefeltro." In *The Humanism of Leonardo Bruni: Selected Texts,* translated by Gordon Griffiths, James Hankins, and David Thompson, 240–51. Binghamton, N.Y.: Medieval and Renaissance Texts and Studies, 1987.

Capra, Galeazzo Flavio. *Della eccellenza e dignità delle donne.* Ed. Maria Luisa Doglio. Rome: Bulzoni, 1988.

---

61. The *Institutio* was one of the first to be translated: *La formación de la mujer Cristiana,* trans. Joaquín Beltrán Serra (Valencia, 1994).

Castiglione, Baldassare (1478–1529). *The Book of the Courtier.* Trans. George Bull. New York: Penguin, 1967.

Cereta, Laura. *Collected Letters of a Renaissance Feminist.* Ed. Diana Robin. Chicago: University of Chicago Press, 1996.

Chadwick, Henry, ed. *The Sentences of Sextus.* Cambridge: University of Cambridge Press, 1959.

DeVocht, Henry. *Literae virorum eruditorum ad Franciscum Craneveldium, 1522–1528.* Louvain: Librairie universitaire, 1929.

Elyot, Thomas (1490–1546). *The Boke Named the Governour.* Ed. Henry Herbert Stephen Croft. 2 vols. New York: Burt Franklin, 1967.

———. *Defence of Good Women: The Feminist Controversy of the Renaissance.* Facsimile reproductions, ed. Diane Bornstein. New York: Delmar, 1980.

Erasmus, Desiderius (1467–1536). *Opera omnia.* Ed. J. Leclerc. Leiden: Pieter van der Aa, 1703–6. Reprint, Hildesheim: George Olms, 1961–62.

———. *Precatio dominica.* "A devout treatise upon the Pater noster." Trans. Margaret More Roper. In *Erasmus of Rotterdam. A Quincentennial Symposium,* edited by Richard De Molen. New York: Twayne Publishers, 1971.

———. *The Praise of Folly.* Trans. Clarence H. Miller. New Haven, Conn.: Yale University Press, 1979. Best edition, since it indicates additions to the text between 1511 and 1516.

———. *Erasmus on Women.* Ed. Erika Rummel. Toronto: University of Toronto Press, 1996.

IJsewijn, Jozef, and Gilbert Tournoy. *Literae ad Craneveldium Balduinianae.* Preliminary ed. Parts 1–4. Letters 1–30, *Humanistica lovaniensia* 41 (1992) 1–85; letters 31–55, *Humanistica lovaniensia* 42 (1993) 2–51; letters 56–85, *Humanistica lovaniensia* 43 (1994) 15–68; part 4, letters 86–116, *Humanistica lovaniensia* 44 (1995) 1–78.

Kempe, Margery (1373–1439). *The Book of Margery Kempe.* Trans. Barry Windeatt. New York: Viking Penguin, 1986.

King, Margaret L., and Albert Rabil Jr., eds. *Her Immaculate Hand: Selected Works by and about the Women Humanists of Quattrocento Italy.* Binghamton, N.Y.: Medieval and Renaissance Texts and Studies, 1983; 2d rev. paperback ed., 1991.

Klein, Joan Larsen, ed. *Daughters, Wives, and Widows: Writings by Men about Women and Marriage in England, 1500–1640.* Urbana: University of Illinois Press, 1992.

Knox, John (1505–1572). *The Political Writings of John Knox: The First Blast of the Trumpet against the Monstrous Regiment of Women and Other Selected Works.* Ed. Marvin A. Breslow. Washington: Folger Shakespeare Library, 1985.

Kors, Alan C., and Edward Peters, eds. *Witchcraft in Europe, 1100–1700: A Documentary History.* Philadelphia: University of Pennsylvania Press, 1972.

Krämer, Heinrich, and Jacob Sprenger. *Malleus Maleficarum* (ca. 1487). Trans. Montague Summers. London: Pushkin Press, 1928. reprint, New York: Dover, 1971. The "Hammer of Witches," a convenient source for all the misogynistic commonplaces on the eve of the sixteenth century, and an important text in the witch-hunting craze of the following centuries.

Kuschmierz, Ruth. "The Instruction of a Christen Woman: A Critical Edition of the Tudor Translation." Ph.D. diss., University of Pittsburgh, 1961.

de Lorris, William, and Jean de Meun. *The Romance of the Rose.* Trans. Charles Dahlbert. Princeton, N.J.: Princeton University Press, 1971; reprint, University Press of New England, 1983.

Marguerite d'Angoulême, Queen of Navarre (1492–1549). *The Heptameron.* Trans. P. A. Chilton. New York: Viking Penguin, 1984.

Menander. *Sententiae.* Ed. Siegfried Jaekel. Leipzig: Teubner, 1964.

Mulcaster, Richard. *Positions concerning the Training up of Children.* Ed. William Barker. Toronto: University of Toronto Press, 1994.

de Pizan, Christine (1365–1431). *The Book of the City of Ladies.* Trans. Earl Jeffrey Richards. New York: Persea Books, 1982.

———. *The Treasure of the City of Ladies.* Trans. Sarah Lawson. New York: Viking Penguin, 1985. Also trans. Charity Cannon Willard, ed. Madeleine P. Cosman. New York: Persea Books, 1989.

Rogers, Elizabeth Frances, ed. *The Correspondence of Thomas More.* Princeton, N.J.: Princeton University Press, 1947.

———, ed. *Sir Thomas More: Selected Letters.* New Haven: Yale University Press, 1961.

Spenser, Edmund (1552–1599). *The Faerie Queene.* Ed. Thomas P. Roche Jr., with the assistance of C. Patrick O'Donnell Jr. New Haven: Yale University Press, 1978.

Ioannis Stobaei Anthologium. Ed. Curtis Wachsmuth and Otto Hense. Berlin: Weidmann, 1884–1912.

Teresa of Avila, Saint (1515–1582). *The Life of Saint Teresa of Avila by Herself.* Trans. J. M. Cohen. New York: Viking Penguin, 1957.

Vives, Juan Luis (1492–1540). *Obras completas.* Trans. Lorenzo Riber. Madrid: Aguilar, 1947-48.

———. *De anima et vita libri tres.* Basel: R. Winter, 1538; reprint, Turin: Bottega d'Erasmo, 1963.

———. *Early Writings.* Ed. C. Mattheeussen, C. Fantazzi, E. George. Leiden: Brill, 1987.

———. *Early Writings 2.* Ed. J. Ijsewijn and Angela Fritsen with Charles Fantazzi. Leiden: Brill, 1991.

———. *Ioannis Ludovici Vivis Valentini opera omnia.* Ed. Gregorio Mayáns y Siscar. 8 vols. Valencia: Montfort, 1782–90; reprint, London: Gregg Press, 1964.

———. *Epistolario.* Trans. José Jiménez Delgado. Madrid: Editora Nacional, 1978.

———. *In pseudodialecticos.* Trans and ed. Charles Fantazzi. Leiden: Brill, 1979.

———. *Praefatio in Leges Ciceronis et Aedes legum.* Critical ed. Constant Matheeussen. Leipzig: Teubner, 1984.

———. *Declamationes Sullanae.* Trans. and ed. Edward George. Leiden: Brill, 1989.

———. *De conscribendis epistolis.* Trans. and ed. Charles Fantazzi. Leiden: Brill, 1989.

———. *Somnium et Vigilia in Somnium Scipionis.* Trans. and ed. Edward George. Greenwood, S.C.: Attic Press, 1989.

———. *Ioannis Lodovici Vivis Valentini opera omnia.* Vols. 1–3. Valencia: Edicions Alfons el Magnánim, 1992–93.

———. *De institutione feminae Christianae (La formación de la mujer cristiana).* Trans. Joaquín Beltrán Serra. Valencia: Ajuntament de Valencia, 1994.

———. *Instrucción de la mujer Cristiana.* Traducción de Juan Justiniano. Introducción, revisión y annotación de Elizabeth Teresa Howe. Madrid: Fundación Universitaria Española, 1995.

————. *De officio mariti (Los deberes del marido)*. Trans. Carme Bernal. Valencia: Ajuntament de Valencia, 1994.

————. *De institutione feminae Christianae*. Trans. and ed. Charles Fantazzi and Constant Matheeussen. 2 vols. Leiden: Brill, 1996–98.

Wayne, Valerie, ed. *The Flower of Friendship*, by Edmund Tilney. Ithaca, N.Y.: Cornell University Press, 1992.

West, Martin, ed. and trans. *Greek Lyric Poetry*. Oxford: Clarendon Press, 1993.

Weyer, Johann (1515–88). *Witches, Devils, and Doctors in the Renaissance: Johann Weyer, De praestigiis daemonum*. Ed. George Mora with Benjamin G. Kohl, Erik Midelfort, and Helen Bacon. Trans. John Shea. Binghamton, N.Y.: Medieval and Renaissance Texts and Studies, 1991.

Wilson, Katharina M., ed. *Medieval Women Writers*. Athens: University of Georgia Press, 1984.

————, ed. *Women Writers of the Renaissance and Reformation*. Athens: University of Georgia Press, 1987.

————, and Frank J. Warnke, eds. *Women Writers of the Seventeenth Century*. Athens: University of Georgia Press, 1989.

Women Writers in English 1350–1805: 30 volumes projected, 8 published through 1995.

Xenophon (c.431–352 B.C.). *Oeconomicus*. Ed. and trans. Sarah Pomeroy. Oxford: Clarendon Press, 1994.

Secondary Works

Barbazza, Marie-Catherine. "L'épouse chrétienne et les moralistes espagnols des XVI et XVII siècles." *Mélanges de la Casa de Velázquez* 24 (1988): 99–137.

Bataillon, Marcel. *Erasmo y España*. Segunda edición en español. Mexico: Fondo de cultura económica, 1966.

Beilin, Elaine V. *Redeeming Eve: Women Writers of the English Renaissance*. Princeton, N.J.: Princeton University Press, 1987.

Benson, Pamela Joseph. *The Invention of the Renaissance Woman: The Challenge of Female Independence in the Literature and Thought of Italy and England*. University Park: Pennsylvania State University Press, 1992.

Berriot-Salvadore, Evelyne. *Les femmes dans la société française de la Renaissance*. Geneva: Droz, 1990.

Bietenholz, Peter G., and Thomas B. Deutscher, eds. *Contemporaries of Erasmus: A Biographical Register of the Renaissance and Reformation*. 3 vols. Toronto: University of Toronto Press, 1986.

Bloch, R. Howard. *Medieval Misogyny and the Invention of Western Romantic Love*. Chicago: University of Chicago Press, 1991.

Bonilla y San Martín, Adolfo. *Luis Vives y la filosofía del Renacimiento*. 2d ed. 3 vols. Madrid: L. Rubio, 1929.

Camden, Carroll. *The Elizabethan Woman . . . 1540 to 1640*. London: Elsevier, 1952.

Cárcel, Ricardo García. "La familia de Juan Luis Vives y la Inquisición." In *Ioannis Lodovici Vivis Valentini opera omnia*, vol. 1, 489–519. Valencia: Edicions Alfons el Magnànim, 1992.

Castro, América, *España en su historia*. Barcelona: Editorial Crítica, 1983.

Clark, Elizabeth A. *Ascetic Piety and Women's Faith: Essays on Late Ancient Christianity.* Lewiston, N.Y,: Edwin Mellen Press, 1986.

Cooper, Kate. *The Virgin and the Bride.* Cambridge: Harvard University Press, 1996.

Cressy, David. *Literacy and the Social Order: Reading and Writing in Tudor and Stuart England.* Cambridge: Cambridge University Press, 1980.

Davis, Natalie Zemon. *Society and Culture in Early Modern France.* Stanford: Stanford University Press, 1975. Especially chapters 3 and 5.

Dillard, Heath. *Daughters of the Reconquest. Women in Castilian Town Society 1100–1300.* Cambridge: Cambridge University Press, 1984.

Dixon, Suzanne. *The Roman Family.* Baltimore: Johns Hopkins University Press, 1992.

Dowling, Maria. *Humanism in the Age of Henry VIII.* London: Croon Helm, 1986.

Duncan, G. D. "Public Lectures and Professorial Chairs." In *History of the University of Oxford,* edited by James McConica, 335–61. Oxford: Oxford University Press, 1986.

Estelrich, Juan. *Vives, Exposition organisée à la Bibliothèque Nationale.* Paris, 1941.

Fantazzi, Charles. "Vives, More and Erasmus." In *Juan Luis Vives. Arbeitsgespräch in der Herzog August Bibliothek Wolfenbüttel vom 6. bis zum 8. November 1980,* edited by August Buck, 165–76. Hamburg: Ernst Hauswedell & Co., 1981.

Ferguson, Margaret W, Maureen Quilligan, and Nancy J. Vickers, eds. *Rewriting the Renaissance: The Discourses of Sexual Difference in Early Modern Europe.* Chicago: University of Chicago Press, 1987.

Fox, Alistair, and John Guy. *Reassessing the Henrician Age.* Oxford: Blackwell, 1986.

Friedman, Alice T. "The Influence of Humanism on the Education of Girls and Boys in Tudor England." *History of Education Quarterly* 25 (1985): 57–70,

Gardner, Jane F. *Women in Roman Law and Society.* Bloomington: Indiana University Press, 1986.

George, Edward W. "Rhetoric in Vives." In *Ioannis Lodovici Vives Valentini opera omnia,* vol. 1, 113–77. Valencia: Edicions Alfons el Magnánim, 1992.

González y González. *Joan Lluís Vives. De la escolástica al humanismo.* Valencia: Generalitat Valenciana, 1987.

———. "La lectura de Vives, del siglo XIX a nuestros días." In *Ioannis Lodovici Vivis Valentini opera omnia,* vol. 1, 1–76. Valencia: Edicions Alfons el Magnánim, 1992.

Grafton, Anthony, and Lisa Jardine. *From Humanism to the Humanities: Education and Liberal Arts in Fifteenth and Sixteenth Century Europe.* London: Duckworth, 1986.

Grendler, Paul. *Schooling in Renaissance Italy.* Baltimore: Johns Hopkins University Press, 1989.

Haliczer, Stephen. *Inquisition and Society in the Kingdom of Valencia 1478–1834.* Berkeley: University of California Press, 1990.

Heath, Michael. "Erasmus and the Laws of Marriage." In *Acta conventus neo-Latini Hafniensis,* edited by Ann Moss et al., 477–93. Binghamton: Medieval and Renaissance Texts and Studies, 1994.

Henderson, Katherine Usher, and Barbara F. McManus, eds. *Half Humankind: Contexts and Texts of the Controversy about Women in England, 1540–1640.* Urbana: University of Illinois Press, 1985.

A History of Women in the West:

Volume 1: *From Ancient Goddesses to Christian Saints.* Ed. Pauline Schmitt Pantel. Cambridge: Harvard University Press, 1992.

Volume 2: *Silences of the Middle Ages.* Ed. Christiane Klapisch-Zuber. Cambridge: Harvard University Press, 1992.

Volume 3: *Renaissance and Enlightenment Paradoxes.* Ed. Natalie Zemon Davis and Arlette Farge. Cambridge: Harvard University Press, 1993.

Herlihy, David. "Did Women Have a Renaissance? A Reconsideration." *Medievalia et Humanistica* NS 13 (1985): 1–22.

Hogrefe, Pearl. *The Sir Thomas More Circle.* Urbana: University of Illinois Press, 1959.

Holm, Janis Butler, ed. *The Mirror of Modestie,* by Thomas Salter. New York: Garland, 1987.

———. "Struggling with the Letter: Vives' Preface to the *Instruction of a Christen Woman.*" In *Contending Kingdoms: Historical, Psychological and Feminist Approaches to the Literature of Sixteenth Century England and France,* edited by M. Logan and P. Rudnytsky. Detroit: Wayne State University Press, 1989.

Horowitz, Maryanne Cline. "Aristotle and Women." *Journal of the History of Biology* 9 (1976): 183–213.

Hufton, Olwen. *The Prospect Before Her. A History of Women in Western Europe.* Vol. 1, 1500–1800. New York: Knopf, 1996.

Hull, Suzanne W. *Chaste, Silent and Obedient: English Books for Women, 1475–1640.* San Marino, Calif.: The Huntington Library, 1982.

IJsewijn, Jozef. "J. L. Vives in 1512–1517. A Reconsideration of the Evidence." *Humanistica lovaniensia* 26 (1977): 82–100.

———, ed. *Erasmus in Hispania. Vives in Belgio. Colloquia Europalia.* Louvain: Peeters, 1986.

Jordan, Constance. *Renaissance Feminism: Literary Texts and Political Models.* Ithaca, N.Y.: Cornell University Press, 1990.

———. "Boccaccio's In-Famous Women: Gender and Civic Virtue in the *De mulieribus claris.*" In *Ambiguous Realities,* edited by Carole Levin and Jeanie Watson, 25–47. Detroit: Wayne State University Press, 1987.

Kelly, Joan. "Did Women Have a Renaissance?" In *Women, History, and Theory,* by Joan Kelly. Chicago: University of Chicago Press, 1984. Also in *Becoming Visible: Women in European History,* edited by Renate Bridenthal, Claudia Koonz, and Susan M. Stuard, 175–202. 2d ed. Boston: Houghton Mifflin, 1987.

———. "Early Feminist Theory and the *Querelle des Femmes,*" in *Women, History, and Theory,* by Joan Kelly.

Kelso, Ruth. *Doctrine for the Lady of the Renaissance.* Urbana: University of Illinois Press, 1956, 1978.

King, Margaret L. *Women of the Renaissance.* Chicago: University of Chicago Press, 1991.

Labalme, Patricia H., ed. *Beyond Their Sex: Learned Women of the European Past.* New York: New York University Press, 1980.

Laqueur, Thomas. *Making Sex: Body and Gender from the Greeks to Freud.* Cambridge: Harvard University Press, 1990.

Lerner, Gerda. *The Creation of Patriarchy.* New York: Oxford University Press, 1986.

———. *Creation of Feminist Consciousness, 1000–1870.* New York: Oxford University Press, 1994.

Lochrie, Karma. *Margery Kempe and Translations of the Flesh.* Philadelphia: University of Pennsylvania Press, 1992.

Maclean, Ian. *Woman Triumphant: Feminism in French Literature, 1610–1652.* Oxford: Clarendon Press, 1977.

———. *The Renaissance Notion of Women: A Study of the Fortunes of Scholasticism and Medical Science in European Intellectual Life.* Cambridge: Cambridge University Press, 1980.

Marshall, Sherrin, ed. *Women in Reformation and Counter-Reformation Europe: Public and Private Worlds.* Bloomington and Indianapolis: Indiana University Press, 1989.

Mateo, León Esteban. *Hombre-mujer en Vives: Itinerario para la reflexión.* Valencia: Ajuntament de Valencia, 1994.

Matter, E. Ann, and John Coakley, eds. *Creative Women in Medieval and Early Modern Italy.* Philadelphia: University of Pennsylvania Press, 1994. Sequel to the Monson collection below.

Mattingly, Garrett. *Catherine of Aragon.* London: J. Cape, 1942.

McConica, James. *English Humanists and Reformation under Henry VIII and Edward VI.* Oxford: Clarendon Press, 1968.

McLeod, Glenda. *Virtue and Venom: Catalogs of Women from Antiquity to the Renaissance.* Ann Arbor: University of Michigan Press, 1991.

McManamon, John. *Pierpaolo Vergerio the Elder.* Tempe Ariz.: Medieval and Renaissance Texts and Studies, 1996.

McMullen, Norma. "The Education of English Gentlewomen 1540–1640." *History of Education Quarterly* 6 (1977): 87–101.

Mestre, Antonio. "La espiritualidad de Juan Luis Vives." In *Ioannis Lodovici Valentini opera omnia,* vol. 1, 409–459. Valencia: Edicions Alfons el Magnánim, 1992.

Mikesell, Margaret. "Marital and Divine Love." In *Juan Luis Vives' Instruction of a Christen Woman* in *Love and Death in the Renaissance,* edited by Kenneth R. Bartlett, Konrad Eisenbichler, and Janice Liedl, 113–34. Ottawa: Dovehouse Editions, 1991.

Monson, Craig A., ed. *The Crannied Wall. Women, Religion, and the Arts in Early Modern Europe.* Ann Arbor: University of Michigan Press, 1992.

Montalvo, José Hinojosa. *The Jews of the Kingdom of Valencia.* Jerusalem: Hebrew University Press, 1993.

Netanyahu, Benzion. *The Origins of the Inquisition in Fifteenth Century Spain.* New York: Random House, 1995.

Noreña, Carlos. *Juan Luis Vives.* The Hague: Nijhoff, 1970.

———. *Juan Luis Vives.* Madrid: Ediciones Paulinas, 1978.

———. *Juan Luis Vives and the Emotions.* Carbondale and Edwardsville: Southern Illinois Press, 1989.

Okin, Susan Moller. *Women in Western Political Thought.* Princeton, N.J.: Princeton University Press, 1979.

Ornstein, Jacob. "La misoginía y el profeminismo." *Revista de filologia hispánica* 3 (1941): 219–32.

Pagels, Elaine. *Adam, Eve, and the Serpent.* New York: Harper Collins, 1988.

Pinta y Llorente, Miguel de la, y Palacio, José María de. *Procesos inquisitoriales contra la familia judía de Juan Luis Vives* (1. Proceso contra Blanquina March). Madrid: Consejo Superior de Investigaciones Científicas, 1964.

Pomeroy, Sarah B. *Goddesses, Whores, Wives, and Slaves: Women in Classical Antiquity.* New York: Schocken Books, 1976.

Powell, Chilton Latham. *English Domestic Relations 1487–1653.* New York: Russell and Russell, 1972.

Rose, Mary Beth, ed. *Women in the Middle Ages and the Renaissance: Literary and Historical Perspectives.* Syracuse, N.Y.: Syracuse University Press, 1986.

Schmitt, Charles. "Theophrastus in the Middle Ages." *Viator* 2 (1971): 251–70.

Siegel, Paul N. "Milton and the Humanist Attitude toward Women." *Journal of the History of Ideas* 11 (1950): 42–53.

Simon, Joan. *Education and Society in Tudor England.* Cambridge, Cambridge University Press, 1980.

Sinz, William. "The Elaboration of Vives' Treatises on the Arts." *Renaissance Studies* 10 (1963): 68–90.

Sommerville, Margaret R. *Sex and Subjection: Attitudes to Women in Early-Modern Society.* London: Arnold, 1995.

Sowards, J. K. "Erasmus and the Education of Women." *Sixteenth Century Journal* 13 (1982): 77–89.

Stadter, Philip. *Plutarch's Historical Method: An Analysis of the Mulierum Virtutes.* Cambridge: Harvard University Press, 1965.

Stuard, Susan M. "The Dominion of Gender: Women's Fortunes in the High Middle Ages." In *Becoming Visible: Women in European History,* edited by Renate Bridenthal, Claudia Koonz, and Susan M. Stuard, 153–72. 2d ed. Boston: Houghton Mifflin, 1987, 153–72.

Tetel, Marcel. *Marguerite de Navarre's Heptameron: Themes, Language, and Structure.* Durham, N.C.: Duke University Press, 1973.

Todd, Margo. *Christian Humanism and the Puritan Social Order.* Cambridge: Cambridge University Press, 1987.

Treggiari, Susan. *Roman Marriage: Iusti Coniuges from the Time of Cicero to the Time of Ulpian.* Oxford: Oxford University Press, 1991.

Vasoli, Cesare. *La dialettica e la retorica dell'umanesimo.* Milano: Feltrinelli, 1969.

Viera, David. "Influjó el Llibre de les dones de Francesc Eiximenis en la *De institutione feminae Christianae* de Luis Vives?" *Boletín de la Sociedad Castellonense de Cultura* 54 (1978): 145–55.

Walsh, William T. *St. Teresa of Avila: A Biography.* Rockford, Ill: TAN Books & Publications, 1987.

Warner, Marina. *Alone of All Her Sex: The Myth and Cult of the Virgin Mary.* New York: Knopf, 1976.

Watson, Foster. *Vives and the Renascence Education of Women.* London: Edward Arnold, 1912.

———. *Vives on Education: a Translation of the De tradendis disciplinis of Juan Luis Vives.* Cambridge: Cambridge University Press, 1913.

Wiesner, Merry E. *Women and Gender in Early Modern Europe.* Cambridge: Cambridge University Press, 1993.

Willard, Charity Cannon. *Christine de Pizan: Her Life and Works.* New York: Persea Books, 1984.

Wilson, Katharina, ed. *An Encyclopedia of Continental Women Writers.* New York: Garland, 1991.

Woodbridge, Linda. *Women and the English Renaissance.* Urbana: University of Illinois Press, 1984.

A NOTE ON THE TEXT

My translation is based on the following critical edition and translation. Juan Luis Vives, *De institutione feminae Christianae, Liber primus,* ed. Charles Fantazzi and Constant Matheeussen (Leiden, 1996); and *De institutione feminae Christianae, Liber secundus et Liber tertius,* ed. Fantazzi-Matheeussen (Leiden, 1998). The base text for that edition was that printed by Robert Winter (Basel, 1538), as revised by Vives himself for publication. The 1538 edition was thoroughly revised, making it much different from the original version published by Michael Hillen (Antwerp, 1524).

The English translation by Richard Hyrde, a friend of Sir Thomas More, published after Hyrde's death in 1528 or 1529, was based on the Hillen edition. It was partially reproduced—mostly its pedagogical passages—by Foster Watson in *Vives and the Renascence Education of Women* (London, 1912), which is no longer readily available. These excerpts were based on an unauthoritative edition of Hyrde's translation.

A group of scholars, under the editorship of Virginia Walcott Beauchamp, Elizabeth H. Hageman, and Margaret Mikesell, is preparing a critical edition of Hyrde's translation. This edition will be most useful for the understanding of the widespread influence of this version of Vives' text in England, but it is essential that the final, definitive text that Vives authorized for publication also be made available for the first time in English with full commentary and introduction.

PREFACE TO THE BOOKS ON THE
EDUCATION OF A CHRISTIAN WOMAN.

By Juan Luis Vives,
Addressed to Her Most Serene Majesty,
Catherine of Aragon, Queen of England, etc.

1. Moved by the holiness of your life and your ardent zeal[1] for sacred studies, I have endeavored to write something for Your Majesty on the education
of a Christian woman, a subject of paramount importance, but one that has
not been treated hitherto by anyone among the great multitude and diversity of talented writers of the past. For what is so necessary as the spiritual
formation of those who are our inseparable companions in every condition
of life? Feelings of good will are strong among good persons, but not lasting
among the wicked. With good reason Aristotle says that those states that
do not provide for the proper education of women deprive themselves of a
great part of their prosperity.[2] Obviously, there is nothing so troublesome
as sharing one's life with a person of no principles. And if this can be said
with good cause of states, all the more justly can it be said of the individual
household. Moreover, when Xenophon[3] and Aristotle[4] transmitted rules

---

1. In addition to her education in the usual womanly arts, Catherine was tutored in Latin by
Antonio and Alessandro Geraldini and was much influenced by Queen Isabella's zeal for religion. Erasmus often refers to her extraordinary learning in his letters—for example, in the
dedication of his *Paraphrase of Luke* to Henry VIII in 1523, where he speaks of the king's "most
noble consort, a unique example in our age of true religion, who with a distaste for the things
of no account that women love devotes a good part of her day to holy reading." Erasmus,
ep. 1381 (*CWE* 10:61).

2. Aristotle *Rhetoric* 1.5, 1361a (Barnes 2:2164); *Politics* 1.13, 1260b (Barnes 2:2000).

3. Chapters 7 to 10 of Xenophon's *Oeconomicus* contain a dialogue between Isomachus, a rich
property owner, and his young wife, whom he instructs in household management. The work
was much admired in the Renaissance and was translated into English in 1532 by Gentian
Hervet, a member of the household of Lady Margaret, countess of Salisbury, who was Queen
Catherine's friend and governess. *Xenophon's Treatise of Householde* was the first direct translation
of any work from Greek into English that can be dated. Cf. Xenophon, *Oeconomicus*, ed. Sarah
Pomeroy (Oxford, 1994), 80–81.

4. The pseudo-Aristotelian *Economics*, considered genuine in the Renaissance, formed with
the *Nicomachean Ethics* and the *Politics* a tripartite division of moral philosophy in the works of

for the management of domestic affairs, and Plato for the state,[5] they made some observations pertaining to the duty of the woman. Tertullian, Cyprian, Jerome, Ambrose, Augustine, and Fulgentius discussed the status of virgins and widows in such a way that they advocate a way of life rather than give instruction about it. They spend all their time singing the praises of chastity, a commendable undertaking in itself and one worthy of those minds and of the sanctity of that virtue, but they gave very few precepts or rules of life, thinking it preferable to exhort their readers to the best conduct and to point the way to the highest examples rather than give instruction about more lowly matters.

But leaving exhortation to them so that each may choose for herself a way of life based on their authority rather than on my opinion, I formulate practical rules for living. Thus, in the first book, I begin with the first stage of a woman's life and continue up to the state of matrimony; then, in the second book, I make recommendations on how time is to be passed properly and happily with one's husband from marriage to widowhood; and, in the last book, instruction is given concerning widowhood.

2. And since it could not be avoided, many things are said in the first book that pertain to wives and widows, many in the following book that pertain to the unwed, and some things in the third book that pertain to all three. I say this so that the unmarried girl will not think that she has to read only the first book or the married woman the second or the widow the third. I think all of the books should be read by every class of woman. Perhaps I have been more brief in my treatment than some would have wished, but if anyone will consider carefully the reason for my decision, he will understand that it was not done without good reason. For in giving precepts, brevity should not be among the least considerations, lest through verbosity you overwhelm the minds of the readers rather than instruct them. And the

---

Aristotle. The third book of this treatise, extensively cited by Vives, has come down to us only in two Latin versions in a large number of manuscripts, mostly from the fourteenth and fifteenth centuries. One of these, the so-called *translatio Durandi*, supposedly made by a certain Durand Paës of Spain, procurator of the University of Paris in Rome under Pope Clement IV in 1266, is the more authoritative of the two. This Latin translation enjoyed great popularity in the Middle Ages and the Renaissance for its moralizing character and its precepts on marital life, which accorded well with Christian morality. Leonardo Bruni translated all three books in 1420, changing the medieval Latin of the third book into humanist Latin. Cf. *The Humanism of Leonardo Bruni*, trans. and introduction by Gordon Griffiths, James Hankins, and David Thompson (Binghamton, 1987), chap. 7, "Moral Conduct in Business and Marriage," 300–17. The best edition of this work is Aristote, *Économique*, ed. and trans. B. A. van Groningen and André Wartelle (Paris, 1968).

5. Plato *Republic* 451D, 475E.

precepts should be such that one can learn them easily and retain them in the memory. For we must not be ignorant of the laws by which we should live. This was revealed to us by Christ and after him by the apostles—Peter, Paul, James, John, and Jude—who transmitted religious teachings to the world that, besides being divine in origin, were also few and brief. And indeed, who could observe those laws that are not even kept by those who have grown old in them? For that reason I have not extended the examples, of which I have given a great many; nor have I digressed into the commonplaces of virtues and vices, a very extensive topic on which to expatiate, and one that often presented itself throughout the work and almost invited elaboration. But I wished my book to stay within limits so that it could be read without fatigue and even reread.

3. In addition, although rules of conduct for men are numerous, the moral formation of women can be imparted with very few precepts, since men are occupied both within the home and outside it, in public and in private, and for that reason lengthy volumes are required to explain the norms to be observed in their varied duties. A woman's only care is chastity; therefore when this has been thoroughly elucidated, she may be considered to have received sufficient instruction. Wherefore all the more hateful is the crime of those who seek to corrupt this one good that women possess, as if you were set on extinguishing the sight left to a one-eyed person. There are those who write filthy and scurrilous poems, and what pretext that has even the semblance of honesty they can adduce for their intent I do not see, save that their minds, corrupted by wickedness and tainted with poison, can emit only poison, with which to destroy everything around them. They say they are lovers, and I do not doubt it, for they too are blind and insane. It is as if you cannot gain the submission of your mistress without at the same time corrupting and defiling all other women along with her. To my mind, no one was ever more justly exiled than Ovidius Naso, if indeed he was banished because of the *Art of Love*.[6] Others have sung of lewd and disgraceful things, but this supreme craftsman reduced depravity to rules and precepts—can you imagine!—a master of unchastity and public corrupter of the morals of the state.

4. I have no doubt that to some I shall seem unduly harsh and severe, but if they were to read the minute particulars that sacred writers discuss and see how meticulously they examine every detail, and with what severity

---

6. In his poems of exile, the *Tristia*, Ovid states that two things brought about his ruin: *carmen et error*, "a poem and an error," (*Tristia* 2.207). The *Art of Love* was published in A.D. 1 or 2 and Ovid was exiled to Tomis (the modern Constanza) on the Black Sea in A.D. 8.

of language and tone, they would judge me to be too mild and indulgent. But such is the nature of things that to the good the path of virtue seems very accessible and pleasant, while that of vice seems narrow and rough. For the wicked, neither the path they tread is pleasant, nor is the path of uprightness wide enough or open to them. This being the case, we must agree more with the good and believe that the wicked are more easily deceived in their judgment than the generality of good men. Pythagoras and others of his school, adopting the letter Y [upsilon] as their symbol,[7] say that after overcoming the first difficulties in the acquisition of virtue, the rest is easy. And Plato, concurring with Pythagoras, urges us to choose the best way of life, which habit will render most agreeable.[8] Our Lord in the gospel called the path to the kingdom of God narrow,[9] not because it is so in very fact, but because few enter upon it, unless one were to think that his saying is false: "My yoke is easy and my burden light";[10] along with the promise that there is no one who leaves anything for his sake who will not have much greater things, even in this life.[11] What is meant thereby but the pleasure and satisfaction that virtue brings with it.

5. Therefore, I know who will find my precepts too severe and rigid: young men, the inexperienced, the lascivious, and the depraved, who cannot bear the sight of a virtuous woman, who, like unbridled, well-fed horses, neigh at every mare. Likewise, my precepts will not appeal to stupid, vain, and foolish girls, who enjoy being looked at and courted and would like their vices to be approved by the multitudes of sinners, as if the consensus of the common crowd could change the way things are. It is nothing new that the wicked hate those that give good advice. On this same subject Theophrastus gave many stern precepts about marriage[12] and in so doing

---

7. The Greek letter Y, according to Pythagoras and his followers, symbolized the two paths of life: virtue and vice. Cf. Diogenes Laertius 8.32 and Hesiod *Works and Days* 289.

8. Plato *Republic* 331A.

9. Matt. 7:14.

10. Matt. 11:30.

11. Matt. 19:29; Luke 18:25.

12. Theophrastus (c. 370–288 B.C.E.) was a disciple of Aristotle and succeeded him as head of the Lyceum. He continued and extended Aristotle's teachings in almost every discipline, but only his work on botany is extant. In addition to the botanical studies, his *Characters* were influential in the seventeenth century. See the various volumes published by William Fortenbaugh, et al., in the series Rutgers University Studies in Classical Humanities.
Saint Jerome in his *Against Jovinianus* cites passages from a lost work of Theophrastus on marriage, which he may have derived from a lost work of Seneca. It is also possible that these fragments may have come from a work of Aristotle on marriage cited by the fifth-century lexicographer Hesychius. At any event, these passages were often cited on the authority of Jerome in the Middle Ages and the Renaissance.

incited the wrath of the courtesans against him; and Leontion, the concubine of Metrodorus,[13] rushed forward to spew out a senseless and shameless tract against a man of such learning and eloquence. The deed was seen to be so scandalous that, as if to signify there was no hope left, it gave rise to the proverb: "to choose a tree to hang yourself."[14] Saint Jerome writes to Demetrias about something that happened to him in the following manner: "About thirty years ago I wrote a book on the preservation of virginity, in which it was necessary for me to lash out against vices and expose the snares of the devil for the instruction of the young girl whom I was counseling. This language gave offense to many since each one, interpreting what I was saying as directed against himself, did not accept my words as a friendly admonition but felt aversion toward me as one who was incriminating his actions."[15] Thus says Jerome. So, what kind of persons will I offend with my pious admonitions? Those from whom if I were to please I would earn reprehension and blame.

6. On my side I will have men of sobriety and common sense, chaste virgins, virtuous matrons, prudent widows—in a word, all those who are truly Christian at heart and not only in name, all of whom know and recognize that nothing can be more mild and moderate than the precepts of our faith, from which may Christ never allow us to divert our minds and our thoughts by even a hair's breadth. To holy women I have merely given gentle advice concerning their duties. Others I have chastised, at times rather sharply, because I saw that teachings alone are of little benefit to those who resist one who guides them and must be dragged along almost against their will to their proper goal. Therefore, I have spoken rather plainly on occasion so that seeing the repulsiveness of their conduct as if it were depicted in a painting, they might feel ashamed and cease acting in a shameful manner. At the same time, good women might have reason to rejoice that they are far removed from these vices and might make all the more effort to distance themselves even further and to retreat into the innermost precincts of virtue. I have preferred, following the advice of Jerome,[16] to run the risk of offending propriety rather than undermining my argument, without, however, lapsing into indecency, the worst thing a teacher of chastity could do. As a result, sometimes more things are to be understood than are

---

13. Leontion was an Athenian courtesan who became the mistress of Metrodorus of Lampsacus (c. 331–277 B.C.E.), the most famous of Epicurus's followers.

14. Erasmus *Adages* I x 21 (*CWE* 32:242).

15. Jerome *Letters* 130.19 *NPNF*, 2d ser., 6:271. Jerome refers here to *Letter* 22 to Eustochium, a eulogy of virginity and of the monastic state, written at Rome in A.D. 384.

16. Jerome *Letters* 54.10, *NPNF*, 2d ser., 6:106.

expressed. Things that would not accord with accepted moral standards I have supported and sustained with the testimony of great authorities, lest they be nullified by the force of public opinion.

7. I dedicate this work to you, glorious Queen, just as a painter might represent your likeness with utmost skill. As you would see your physical likeness portrayed there, so in these books you will see the image of your mind, since you were both a virgin and promised spouse [17] and a widow and now wife (as, please God, you may long continue), and since you have so conducted yourself in all these various states of life that whatever you did is a model of an exemplary life to others. But you prefer that virtues be praised rather than yourself. Although no one can praise female virtues without including you in that same praise, I shall nonetheless obey you, provided that you know that under the rubric of excellent and outstanding virtues other women similar to you may be mentioned by name, but it is you always, even if tacitly, who are spoken of. For virtues cannot be extolled with praise without commending those who, though unnamed, excelled in those virtues. Your daughter Mary will read these recommendations and will reproduce them as she models herself on the example of your goodness and wisdom to be found within her own home. She will do this assuredly and, unless she alone belie all human expectations, must of necessity be virtuous and holy as the offspring of you and Henry VIII, such a noble and honored pair. Therefore, all women will have an example to follow in your life and actions, and, in this work dedicated to you, precepts and rules for the conduct of their lives. Both of these they will owe to your moral integrity, by which you have lived and through which I have been inspired to write. Farewell.

Bruges, 5 April 1523.

---

17. Beginning with the Basel edition of 1538, Vives changed his description of Catherine's marital status with Arthur, Prince of Wales, from *uxor* (wife) to *sponsa* (promised spouse), thus supporting the Queen's cause.

BOOK I

WHICH TREATS OF
UNMARRIED YOUNG
WOMEN

I

ON THE EDUCATION
OF THE YOUNG WOMAN
AS A CHILD

8. In his book on the instruction of the orator, Fabius Quintilian[18] expresses
the view that it should begin from the cradle, convinced that no time should
be wasted that could be dedicated to the attainment of those skills that we
have fixed for ourselves as our objective. How much greater care should be
expended in the case of the Christian young woman, not only in her early
formation and development but beginning with her nurturing at the breast,
which, if possible, should be with her mother's milk.[19] This is what Plutarch,
Favorinus, and other great philosophers recommended.[20] In that way, the
mutual love between mother and daughter will become greater, and the
name of mother will not be shared with another, for it is the custom to call
wet nurses mothers also. A mother thinks the daughter to be more truly her
own when she has not only borne her in her womb and given birth to her,
but carried her continually in her arms as an infant, nursed her, nourished
her with her own blood, cradled her in her arms as she slept, listened lov-
ingly to her first joyous laughter and kissed her, heard with joy her first
stammerings and helped her in her attempt to speak, and pressed her to her
bosom, praying for every blessing from heaven. These things will in turn
engender such filial devotion in the daughter toward her mother that her
mother will become much dearer to her, since she received such abundant

18. Quintilian *On the Education of the Orator* 1.1.21.

19. The fullest discussion of Renaissance views on this subject is to be found in Erasmus's
dialogue "The New Mother" (*CWE* 39:590–618).

20. Plutarch, "The Education of Children," *Moralia*, 3C–D; Aulus Gellius *Attic Nights* 12.1.1–
23. Favorinus was a second-century orator with philosophical interests. Born in Arles, he obtained his Greek training at Marseilles and rose to high office under Hadrian. His views on
breast-feeding were reported by his pupil, Aulus Gellius, from a speech he gave in Greek.

love from her in her tender years. Who can say to what degree this experience will engender and increase love in human beings when wild beasts, which are for the most part alien to any feelings of love for animals of a different species, love those who nourished and raised them and do not hesitate to face death to protect and defend them?

9. Thus it happens, I know not how, that we imbibe with our mother's milk not only love but also a disposition toward certain behavior. This is the reason, as Favorinus says in Aulus Gellius,[21] that we are often astonished when the children of virtuous women do not resemble their parents, either physically or morally. It was not without reason that the fable, known even to children, arose that he who was nurtured with the milk of a sow has rolled in the mire. For which reason the sage philosopher Chrysippus[22] taught that one must select wet nurses who are wise and of good character,[23] a precept that I too shall follow and recommend to those mothers who cannot nurture their children with their own milk. I do not require that the same care should be taken in providing a nurse for a boy as for a girl. Quintilian put it well when he said, "One must see to it that the speech of nurses is not defective, because the manner of speech that is instilled in the child is difficult to eliminate."[24] In the matter of morals he was not so concerned, since the boy learns those outside the home more often than in the home. Yet he adopted the opinion of Chrysippus concerning nurses as if he were of the same mind. But since we do not wish the young girl to be as learned as she is chaste and virtuous, care must be taken on the part of the parents that she not be defiled by anything immoral or dishonorable, and that nothing of that nature be acquired through the bodily senses or through her early upbringing. The first person she will hear and the first person she will see is the nurse, and what she will learn as an immature child she will try to reproduce when she is more practiced and experienced. In this regard, Saint Jerome in giving instruction to the daughter of Laeta says that one should not hire a nurse who is given to drink or is of loose morals or talkative.[25]

21. Aulus Gellius *Attic Nights* 12.1.19.

22. Chrysippus (c. 280–207 B.C.E.) was regarded as the most orthodox of the Stoic philosophers.

23. Quintilian 1.1.4.

24. Quintilian 1.1.4.

25. Jerome *Letters* 107.4 (*NPNF*, 2d ser., 6:191).

ON THE LATER YEARS
OF CHILDHOOD

10. When she has been weaned and has begun to speak and to walk, all her playtime must be spent with girls of her own age in the presence of her mother or nurse or a good woman of mature years, who will regulate those pastimes and the pleasures of the mind and direct them to goodness and virtue. Any male should be excluded, and the girl should not be accustomed to find pleasure in the company of men. For by nature, our affection is more lasting toward those with whom we have passed our time in childhood amusements. This attachment is even more persistent in the woman, for she is more inclined toward pleasure by her natural disposition. At that age which cannot yet distinguish between good and evil, she should not even learn about evil things, and her still immature mind should be imbued with sound opinions. Pernicious is the view of those who wish their children not to be ignorant of both good and evil. In that way, they say, in the end they will better pursue virtue and flee vice. How much more proper and useful is it not only not to do evil but not even to know it! How much more auspicious also! Who has not heard tell that the source of all our misery goes back to that moment when the first parents of the human race learned what was good and what was evil?[26]

And, of a certainty, those fathers who do not wish their sons to be ignorant and inexperienced in evil deserve that their children have knowledge of it, and when their children regret that they have done evil, let them remember that they learned to do evil at their father's instigation. The young girl should not learn obscene or indecent words or unseemly gestures when she is still innocent, since she will repeat them when she is grown up and

---

26. Gen. 3:5.

conscious of her actions. It is the experience of many people that they fall
into the same behavior to which they have been accustomed without their
being aware of it, and although at times they struggle against them and try
to control them, they slip out and burst forth against their will. This occurs
all the more frequently if they are bad things, since the human mind clings
more tenaciously to them.

11. Parents should be careful not to give approval to any unseemly action of hers either by laughing or by word or gesture, or, worst of all, welcome it with kisses and embraces. The girl will often try to repeat what she
thinks gives particular pleasure to her parents. In the early years, let everything be chaste and pure for the sake of morals, which from childhood habits take on their first features, so to speak. I would like to insert here a passage from Cornelius Tacitus on the character of the ancient Romans:

> In the good old days everyone's son, born of a chaste mother, was
> brought up not in the chamber of a hired nurse, but in his mother's lap
> and bosom, and it was her chief glory to watch over the home and
> devote herself to her children. An elderly kinswoman would be se-
> lected, of tried and true character, to whose charge all the offspring
> of that family were entrusted. In her presence no base word could be
> uttered nor any disgraceful deed done. With scrupulous piety and
> modesty she regulated not only the studies and conduct of her charges
> but also their leisure and recreation. It was in this spirit, we are told,
> that Cornelia, the mother of the Gracchi, Aurelia, the mother of Cae-
> sar, and Atia, the mother of Augustus, presided over the upbringing of
> their children and raised them up to be leaders. The object of this
> strict discipline was to ensure that the innocent and untainted natural
> disposition of the child, not yet warped by any vicious tendencies,
> would immediately seize upon honorable pursuits with all their heart.[27]

12. These are the words of Tacitus, from which it is apparent by what
method and practices men of ancient times arrived at such renown for virtue
as we can scarcely bear to behold these days. And this is what he says about
men. How much care do we think was exercised in the case of women?
Therefore, in the amusements and diversions needed at that time of life, let
anything that can harm a proper upbringing be forbidden, let nothing obscene steal into her mind, and do not let her be infected with a proclivity to
talkativeness. But even then, in the form of play, let her exercise herself in
things that will be of benefit to her later. Let her be edified by chaste tales,

27 Tacitus *Dialogue on Orators* 28.4–6.

and take dolls away from her, which are a kind of image of idolatry and teach girls the desire for adornments and finery. I would be more in favor of those toys made of tin or lead that represent household objects, which are so common here in Belgium. This is a pleasant pastime for the child, and in the meantime she learns the names and uses of various things without even being aware of it.

III

ON HER EARLY TRAINING

13. At the age when the girl seems ready to learn letters and gain some practical knowledge, let her begin by learning things that contribute to the cultivation of the mind and the care and management of the home. I do not prescribe any definite time. Some thought that this should begin at the age of seven, as did Aristotle and Eratosthenes.[28] Others preferred the fourth or fifth year of age, as Chrysippus and Quintilian.[29] I leave all this deliberation to the discretion of the parents, who will be guided by the character and qualities of the child so long as they do not spoil them through indulgence. Some parents treat their children with such delicacy and are so fearful for them that they keep them from all physical toil, lest they fall into some illness. Thinking to increase and solidify their strength, they weaken and enervate them. The indulgence of parents is very harmful to children, since it offers them free access to a thousand vices and even thrusts them in their face. But this is especially harmful for the girl, for she is held back to a great degree solely by fear. If that is not present, then all the barriers of nature are let down. If she is drawn to evil by nature, then she plunges into it headlong. She will not turn out well unless she is good of her own nature and character, which may be so in some cases. Therefore, she will learn, together with reading, how to work with wool and flax, two arts passed on to posterity from that former age of innocence, of great usefulness in domestic affairs and contributing to frugality, which should be a matter of prime concern for women. I shall not descend to particulars or I will appear to be searching

28. Eratosthenes (c. 275–194 B.C.E.), the most versatile scholar of his time, royal tutor under Ptolemy Euergetes, succeeded the famous Hellenistic poet, Apollonius of Rhodes, as head of the library in Alexandria.

29. Quintilian 1.1.16.

into matters too humble for my subject. But I should not wish any woman to be ignorant of the skills of working with the hands, not even a princess or a queen. What could she do better than this when free of all the household tasks? She will converse with men, I suppose, or other women. About what? Is she to talk forever? Will she never keep quiet? Perhaps she will think. About what? A woman's thoughts are swift and generally unsettled, roving without direction, and I know not where her instability will lead her.

14. Reading is the best occupation and I counsel it first of all, but when she is tired of reading, I cannot bear seeing her idle. Nor should she imitate those Persian women who sang and caroused amidst bands of eunuchs, immersed in unending, uninterrupted pleasures, which they varied frequently to avoid boredom, so that the end of one was the beginning of another. Yet they were not able to find any solace for their spirit through this alternation of sensual delights. There was always something missing in each one of them taken singly and in all of them together, and the first savoring of pleasure immediately brought weariness and boredom. Then they would seek again the pleasures they had found fault with and turn away in disgust and incredible anguish from the things they thought would give them most pleasure. In the end, since no one diversion satisfied them, they rejected them all. No wonder, for this is not the true nourishment of the soul. Therefore, the soul hurried eagerly after diversity as if pursuing something alien to itself. But in honorable activities engaged in by persons of good conscience, the action itself revives the spirit, what results from it gives great satisfaction, and the hours passed in this way we consider to be well spent. Nothing counsels repose so much as the fatigue caused by continuous mental effort Yet we would not wish to change even if it allowed us to do so.

15. When Saint Jerome writes to Paula, a woman of very noble family who traced her ancestry to the line of the Scipios and the Gracchi and who even displayed in her genealogy the celebrated Agamemnon, king of kings, he wishes her to learn to card wool, to hold the distaff, place a wool basket in her lap, turn the spindle, draw the thread with her fingers.[30] Writing to Demetrias, another woman of equal nobility and wealth, he bids her to have wool in her hands, and draw the thread from the distaff or turn the spindle in order to twist the yarn in the receptacles, or to gather the fibers spun by others into a ball, or arrange them for weaving.[31]

The working of wool was always the occupation and skill of a good woman. All Roman women, when they married, brought spindle and distaff

---

30. Jerome *Letters* 107.10 (*NPNF*, 2d ser., 6: 193).
31. Jerome *Letters* 130.15 (*NPNF*, 2d ser., 6: 269).

with wool to the home of their husband and wreathed the doorposts with wool,[32] which constituted a religious rite for them. Then the new bride was enjoined to sit on a skin lined with wool to learn what her household tasks were to be. Next she said these words to her husband: "Whereas thou art Gaius, I am Gaia."[33] Gaia Tanaquil[34] was an Etruscan, born of high station, a very frugal woman if ever there was one, the wife of King Tarquinius Priscus. She devoted great toil and care to the making of wool and on that account was worshipped as a goddess, and a distaff was placed on her statue as a tribute to her chastity and industry. The cry "Talassio" was often shouted out at weddings, which sounded like the word for the wool basket[35] in which wool is deposited for spinning, so that the new bride would be reminded of her task. Thus, to busy oneself in this occupation was the sign of a prudent and chaste wife.

When the king's sons rode hurriedly off to Rome after a dispute concerning their wives had arisen, they found the other daughters-in-law of the king feasting together with their ladies-in-waiting, but Lucretia[36] they found toiling at her wool late at night with her servants in her own house. The fame of her chastity endured in all people's minds.

16. After all the power and dominion of the Roman people was vested in Augustus, he wished his daughter and nieces to become accustomed to work with wool.[37] Charlemagne did the same.[38] When Terence describes a thrifty and modest maiden, he says, "With wool and the loom she seeks her livelihood."[39] Solomon in his encomium of a holy woman says that she sought out wool and flax and worked them with the skill of her hands.[40] It

---

32. Pliny *Natural History* 8.194.

33. This formula dates back to *confarreatio,* the solemn celebration of marriage practiced among the patricians, at which an offering of spelt bread was made to Jupiter. The source is Plutarch, "Roman Questions," *Moralia,* 271E.

34. Gaia Tanaquil was the wife of Tarquinius Priscus, fifth king of Rome, according to Livy 1.34.4. Vives follows Pliny the Elder *Natural History* 8.194 in identifying her with Gaia Caecilia, an honest Roman matron who busied herself with weaving. Her spindle and distaff were displayed in the temple of Sancus on the Quirinal hill.

35. Vives' explanation is probably based on Plutarch, who connects the word with *talassia,* Greek for "wool spinning" (*Moralia,* 271F). Livy 1.9.12, in his account of the rape of the Sabine women, traces this wedding cry to a certain Talassius, to whose house a gang of men was carrying off one of the fairest of the maidens. More probably the word is of Sabine or Etruscan origin.

36. Livy 1.57.9.

37. Suetonius *Augustus* 64.2.

38. Einhard *Life of Charlemagne* 19.

39. Terence *Andria* 75.

40. Prov. 31:13.

makes no difference, I think, whether it be wool or flax; both are essential to the needs of life and both are an honorable occupation of women. Hannah, the wife of Elkanah, is said to have woven a tunic every year for her son Samuel.[41] The chaste queen of Ithaca, Penelope, beguiled the twenty years of her husband Ulysses' absence by weaving. The queens of Macedonia and Epirus wove and sewed clothes for their husbands, brothers, sons, and relatives with their own hands. Some of these garments, made by his mother and sisters, Alexander the Great showed to the queens of Persia.[42]

Writers of history tell us that among the Spanish women of old, a prize was proposed in a public contest for the woman who had spun or woven more than all others, and at fixed times an award was conferred and the work exhibited publicly. It was considered a very great honor for the woman to have labored long and industriously. This same zeal for frugality still persists today in many women, and diligence in work is held up as a desirable quality. In the same way, it is dishonorable in the eyes of noble women to remain idle. Queen Isabella, wife of Ferdinand, wished her four daughters[43] to be expert in spinning, sewing, and needlepoint. Of these, two were queens of Portugal, the third we see is queen of Spain and mother of the Emperor Charles, the fourth is the saintly wife of Henry VIII of England.

17. In addition, she will learn the art of cooking, not the vulgar kind associated with low-class eating-houses that serve up immoderate amounts of food to great numbers, where hired cooks are employed, nor that which caters to self-indulgence and gluttony, but a sensible, refined, temperate, and frugal art with which, as an unmarried maiden, she prepares food for her parents and brothers, and as a married woman for her husband. She will win no small favor with the one and the other if she does not leave everything to the servants but attends to things and sets the house in order with her own hands. This will give more pleasure to her parents, husband, and children than if these duties were performed by maidservants, and all the more so if they are ill. Let no one despise the notion of cooking, for it is an art of great necessity, without which the sick cannot get well and we cannot continue in good health. Achilles, a king and son of a king and pre-eminent of heroes, did not think it beneath him when Ulysses and Ajax and Phoenix came to him to plead for his reconciliation to Agamemnon. He girded himself to prepare the tables, and cooked the food himself to welcome these

---

41. 1 Sam. 2 : 19.

42. Quintus Curtius *The History of Alexander the Great* 7.18–22.

43. Isabella, the eldest, was married first to Prince Alonso of Portugal, who died a few months later, and then to Manuel, sovereign of Portugal. Juana married Philip the Fair of Austria and was the mother of Emperor Charles V. Maria was married to Manuel after the death of Isabella; Catherine was married first at a very young age to Arthur, Prince of Wales, and then to Henry.

peerless chieftains with a pleasing and sober repast.[44] This contributes also to frugality and elegance, for when the mistress of the house or her daughters are present, everything is done with more taste and refinement, not to say with more care and less expense. What is this overconcern for their hands or aversion for the kitchen that makes some women unwilling to take part in or even inspect what those dearest to them will eat, whether it be parent, spouse, or even son? Let those who act in this way realize that the hand is more soiled if it is extended to a man other than one's husband than if it is blackened with soot, that it is more disgraceful to be seen on the dancing floor than in the kitchen, more debasing to handle dice and playing cards than food, and that it is less becoming for an honest woman to taste of a drink offered by another man at a feast than to taste an herbal decoction prepared for her husband.

Therefore, I would prescribe that a woman be practiced in this art so that she may more oblige her dear ones at every stage in her life and so that meals will come to the table prepared more properly and more naturally and at the same time in less quantity. I have personally seen here and in Spain and France men who have recovered from illness thanks to the food cooked by their wives, daughters, or daughters-in-law, whom they held much dearer afterwards than before. On the other hand, I have seen wives hated by their husbands, daughters-in-law by their fathers-in-law, and daughters by their fathers because they said they had no skill in preparing meals. And I have come to the conclusion that the principal reason why men here in Belgium spend so much time in inns and taverns is the negligence and laziness of their women in cooking meals, which forces men to avoid their own homes and seek elsewhere what they do not find there.

44. Homer *Iliad* 9.209–10.

IV

ON THE INSTRUCTION
OF YOUNG GIRLS

18. It is evident to me that the instruction of a young girl requires much more care than is commonly believed. From its very origins, the nature of the human body is inclined toward evil and is borne along on that path by its own impulse, as we are told by the sacred oracles. We are driven in that same direction by the multitude of evil people who confront us on every side, acting either as models or as catalysts for the doing of evil. Wherever you turn, evil words and evil deeds assault your eyes. We are doomed by our natural inclination, which is predisposed toward evil; we are doomed by so many bad examples, by the universal conspiracy against good, and above all by the cruel wound inflicted on us by the implacable hostility of the devil. But if there is nothing on the side of good, no admonitions, no precepts of wisdom and virtuous living, what will be left to miserable mortals but to suffer the most dire ills?

19. It would be to our advantage to have at least a knowledge of good to protect us from the constant onslaught of evil, since obviously we cannot be secure if we remain deprived and destitute of good counsel. I have said[45] that those parents act foolishly who wish that their children know good and evil, but no less in error are those who do not allow them to know either good or evil. Would that it were possible to lead our lives in the midst of so many evil people and remain ignorant of evil. If you do not pass on the knowledge of good, it cannot be known. Whereas evil, even if you conceal it, cannot be hidden; it is ubiquitous and in full view, and does not allow itself to be confined to the darkness. Learned women are suspect to many, as if the mental ability acquired by learning increased their natural wickedness and as if men should not also be suspect for the same reason if subtle

45. Cf. par. 10 above.

learning is added to a perverse mind. The learning that I should wish to be made available to the whole human race is sober and chaste; it forms our character and renders us better. It is not one that arms us or spurs us on to the wicked desires of the mind. These are the rules of life and moral principles that I recommend for the education of women. If knowledge of these is harmful, I do not see how ignorance of them will be advantageous.

20. What then? Do you wish your daughter to have knowledge of evil and be ignorant of good? Will she therefore comprehend things that lead to wickedness and be ignorant of things that lead us away from wickedness? Do you have such a prejudiced view of the knowledge of good that you deem it to be harmful while the knowledge of evil is not harmful? When she is assailed by vice, to which she has grown accustomed, what protection will be afforded by moral rectitude, which she never came to know? If we agree with this opinion, why do we take them to hear holy sermons? Why do we teach, correct, and admonish them of better things? We might as well relegate them to the countryside, if you wish my opinion, and weaken and suppress whatever natural ability they may have—in a word, turn human beings into brute beasts, since they will be so far removed from learning.

The philosopher Aristotle[46] asks why pipers and musicians hired to play at feasts and celebrations—whom the Greek populace called Dionysiacs, dedicated to the pursuit of pleasure—never attained to any virtue, but spent their whole lives in moral depravity. He answers that since they spend their lives amidst sensual pleasures and banqueting, never hear the precepts of philosophy that pertain to leading a holy life, and never see models of virtuous living, they do not know any other way to live than that which they have learned by hearing, seeing, and experiencing. Since they have heard nothing, seen nothing, and been accustomed to nothing but what is hedonistic and bestial, in the midst of discordant sounds and clamors, surrounded by people dancing, kissing, laughing, eating, drinking, vomiting, vowed to self-indulgence and oblivious of every mental or moral concern, it follows of necessity that they reproduce this same conduct in their morals and way of life.

21. You will not easily find an evil woman unless she be one who is ignorant of or at any rate gives no thought to the importance of the virtue of chastity. She is unaware of the evil she commits if she loses it, not considering the blessing she exchanges for a base, empty, and momentary illusion of pleasure and what a train of evils she ushers in with the loss of chastity. She does not consider how empty and senseless a thing physical pleasure is

46. Aristotle *Problems* 30.10, 956b (Barnes 2:1505).

and that one should not even lift a finger for its sake, let alone cast away woman's most beautiful and priceless possession; nor does she reflect on how trivial and vain it is to be so painstaking about one's hairdo, to be adorned, embellished, and richly bedecked; how dangerous it is to attract the glances and desires of others to herself. The woman who has learned to make these and similar reflections either through instinctive virtue, innate intelligence, or through her reading will never bring herself to commit any vile act, for her mind will have been strengthened and imbued with holy counsels. And if she were still to be so inclined—in spite of the many precepts of moral rectitude that would have acted as a deterrent, and in spite of so many admonishments and exhortations—one can imagine what she would be like if she had never heard anything about honorable conduct.

22. And, of course, if we wished to review past ages, we would not find any learned woman who was unchaste. On the contrary, the majority of female vices of this and previous centuries (and without a doubt they were more numerous among Christians than among any pagan or barbarian nation) sprang from ignorance, because women did not read or hear tell of those splendid exhortations of the church fathers concerning chastity, solitude, silence, and feminine adornment and attire. If they had merely known about them, it is impossible that things would have progressed to this intolerable degree of insolence. The authority of their teachings would have checked this offensive conduct at its inception and would have prevented its getting out of control.

Perhaps someone will cite one or two examples from pagan antiquity: Sappho, greatest of female poets, who did not love Phaon chastely enough;[47] Leontion,[48] the concubine of Metrodorus, who wrote against Theophrastus; Sempronia,[49] learned in Greek and Latin, who Sallust says did not hold chastity in proper esteem. As if in place of these three I could not enumerate a thousand women whom learning exalted to the heights of virtue, not only from among women of our nation but also from the ranks of the barbarians! But before doing this I must discuss these three women. There are authors of great renown who maintain that it was not Sappho, the learned poetess of Lesbos, who died of love for Phaon, but another woman who combined

47. Phaon was a mythical ferryman who plied between Lesbos and the mainland. He was made young and beautiful by Aphrodite and was loved by many women. A fable arose about a love-affair between him and Sappho, who because of her unrequited love leapt to her death from Cape Leucas, a promontory on the west coast of Greece.

48. Cf. note 13 above.

49. Sempronia is described by Sallust in *Catiline* 35 as a woman of great personal accomplishments but of profligate character, the kind of woman Catiline recruited to aid his cause.

great learning with sobriety of life.[50] As for Leontion, she was not learned before she met Metrodorus but acquired learning in his household, and it was the kind of learning that contributed very little to good morals— namely, Epicurean philosophy, which judges everything in terms of pleasure; this inspired her hatred for Theophrastus, who criticized pleasure. The learning of Sempronia was not of the kind we attribute to an honorable woman, which concerns morals and the conduct of a good life. She merely cultivated a polished form of speech, on which I do not think one should expend so much effort. The same thing could be said of Sappho.

23. But let us expand our learned field of vision. Cornelia,[51] mother of the Gracchi, will appear, who, herself a model of chastity, taught this virtue to her own children. There are women like Laelia,[52] the wife of Mucius; Porcia,[53] the wife of Brutus, who drank in great draughts of wisdom from her father, Cato; and Cleobulina, daughter of Cleobulus, one of the seven sages, who spent her life so dedicated to literature and wisdom that she abstained from all carnal pleasure and remained a virgin.[54] Her example was imitated by the daughter of Pythagoras who directed his school after his death and was in charge of a group of young maidens. From that same sect and school came Theano,[55] born in Metapontum, famous as a prophetess and distinguished for her singular chastity.

Jerome records that the Sibyls were ten in number, all virgins.[56] We read that Cassandra and Chryseis,[57] priestesses of Apollo and Juno, were also

---

50. The story of the two Sapphos is contained in Athenaeus *The Learned Banquet* 13.596, and sub voce in the lexicon called the *Suda*, compiled in the tenth century C.E.

51. Cornelia, daughter of Scipio Africanus, was the model of the Roman matron. She was admired in antiquity for her conduct during her widowhood, when she refused all offers of marriage. Instead, Cornelia devoted herself to the management of her estate and the education of her children, Tiberius and Sempronius Gracchus.

52. Laelia was the daughter of Laelius, close friend of Scipio Aemilianus and skilled orator. She was married to Quintus Mucius Scaevola, famous jurisconsult during the time of the Gracchi.

53. Porcia was the daughter of Cato Uticensis, bitter opponent of Caesar, who took his life at Thapsus in North Africa in 46 B.C.E. She shared the political views of her father and her husband.

54. Plutarch, "Dinner of the Seven Wise Men," *Moralia*, 148C–E.

55. Theano was believed to be the wife of Pythagoras, according to some accounts, or his pupil or daughter, according to others. Vives seems to have made two persons of a single historical personage. Saint Jerome, in *Against Jovinianus* 1.42 (*NPNF*, 2d ser., 6:381), speaks merely of the daughter of Pythagoras without naming her.

56. Jerome *Against Jovinianus* 1.41 (*NPNF*, 2d ser., 6:379).

57. Cassandra was the daughter of Priam and Hecuba; Chryseis the daughter of Chryses, the priest of Apollo at Troy. Both became the concubines of Agamemnon as the spoils of war. The information about their virginity is from the same passage of Jerome as in the preceding note.

virgins. This was a prerogative that was common to prophetesses as a rule. The Pythian priestess at Delphi, who gave answer to those who consulted her, always had to be a virgin. The first of these, Phemonoe, is said to be the inventor of heroic song.[58] Valerius Martial tells us that Sulpicia, wife of Calenus, wrote rules about married life, but not without having first given the example in her own life:

> Let all young brides read Sulpicia,
> Who would one husband only please;
> Husbands too should read Sulpicia,
> Who would please one bride alone.
> Chaste and holy loves she teaches,
> Amusements, grace and pleasantries.
> He who esteems her verse aright
> Will say that none is holier than she.[59]

24. It is clear that in those days there was no husband happier than Calenus, who had Sulpicia as his wife. Hortensia, daughter of the orator Hortensius,[60] so matched her father in eloquence that as a woman worthy of honor and respect, she delivered a speech in behalf of her sex before the triumvirs designated to establish the republic, that later ages read not only in admiration and appreciation of female eloquence but also for imitation, as they would the writings of Cicero or Demosthenes. Edesia of Alexandria,[61] kinswoman of the philosopher Syrianus, was the wonder of her age for her immense learning and purity of life. Corinna of Tanagra,[62] daughter of Archelodorus and a young girl of great intelligence, defeated the poet Pindar five times in poetic contests. Erinna of Telos,[63] contemporary of Plato, who

58. Diogenes Laertius 1.10; Pausanias *Guide to Greece* 10.5.7.

59. Martial *Epigrams* 10.35.1–4, 8–10, 12. Vives omits verse 11, which reads: "None is naughtier than she."

60. Hortensius was one of the greatest of the Roman orators and a rival of Cicero, who dedicated a treatise to him, now lost. Hortensia delivered her speech, in which she demanded an exemption from taxes for Roman matrons, during the time of the Second Triumvirate in 42 B.C.E. Quintilian 1.1.6.

61. Edesia, wife of the Neoplatonic philosopher Hermeias, studied in Athens with her two sons under Proclus, a philosopher of the mid–fifth century CE. Syrianus was also a Neoplatonic philosopher, the teacher of Proclus.

62. It is difficult to determine when Corinna lived. In antiquity there were many stories about her alleged victory over Pindar. In Plutarch's version, "On the Fame of the Athenians," *Moralia* 347F, she found fault with him, astonishingly enough, for neglecting myths.

63. Erinna was a poetess from the Dorian island of Telos (not Teos, as Vives states) near Rhodes, who probably lived at the end of the fourth century BCE. She is known for her poem *The Distaff* in three hundred hexameters, and is said to have been Homer's equal. *Greek Anthology* 9.190.

was the victim of fate before reaching the age of twenty, is said to have equaled Homer in the majesty of epic poetry, although he is compared to Apollo. Eunomia, a Christian virgin (as we read in Jerome),[64] the daughter of Nazarius the rhetor, is likened to her father in eloquence. Paula, trained in the teachings of her husband, Seneca, imitated him also in her morals.[65] The same Seneca regretted that his mother, Helvia,[66] in obedience to her husband's command, had only an introduction to the precepts of wisdom and was not well instructed in them. Argentaria Polla, the wife of Lucan, not only corrected the *Pharsalia* after her husband's death, but is said also to have helped him in the writing of it. She was a woman of noble lineage, substance, beauty, talent, and virtue, of whom the Muse Calliope speaks to Lucan in these terms in the poem of Statius:

> I give you not only the elegance of song
> But with the marriage torch bestow on you
> A learned woman worthy of your gifts,
> Such as sweet Venus or Juno would award,
> In beauty, purity and gentleness,
> Lineage, riches, gentility and grace.[67]

    25. Diodorus the dialectician[68] had five daughters, outstanding in letters and virtue, whose history Philo, the teacher of Carneades, has traced. Zenobia, Queen of Palmyra,[69] was skilled in both Greek and Latin and wrote history; her extraordinary continence, as well as that of certain other

64. Jerome *The Chronicle of Eusebius* 233.22.

65. Paula cut her veins, as Seneca had done, but Nero had them bound up, thereby preventing her suicide. Tacitus *Annals* 15.63–64.

66. The Latin text gives the name Albina for the mother of Seneca, but this has no precedent in ancient sources. Seneca *Consolation to Helvia* 17.5.

67. Statius *Silvae* 2.7.81–86.

68. Diodorus Cronus belonged to the philosophic school of Megara, third century B.C.E., which claimed descent from Socrates. Philon of Megara, a pupil of Diodorus, wrote a dialogue entitled *Menexenus*, in which he praises the learning and virtue of Diodorus's daughters. This Philon, however, could not have been the teacher of Carneades, founder of the New Academy, who lived from 214–129 B.C.E. Jerome *Against Jovinianus* 1.42 (*NPNF*, 2d ser. 6:381), Vives' source, is doubtless in error here.

69. Queen Zenobia was highly praised for her beauty, intelligence, and virtue, but was known also for her ruthlessness. She was defeated by the Emperor Aurelian in 274 C.E. and brought back in triumph to Rome, where she was allowed to live as a Roman matron. She figures prominently in Boccaccio's *On Famous Women* and Sir Thomas Elyot's *Defense of Good Women*, in which she is thought to represent Catherine of Aragon. The chief ancient source for her life is Trebellius Pollio, *The Thirty Pretenders*. 30, in *Scriptores Historiae Augustae*, trans. David Magee (*LCL* 3, 135–43).

women, will be recounted in the following book. Why speak of Christian women? Need I mention Thecla,[70] the disciple of Paul and a disciple worthy of such a great master? Or Barbara,[71] who was taught by Origen Adamantius, or Catherine of Alexandria,[72] daughter of Costus, who surpassed the greatest and most experienced philosophers in debate? The learned virgin of the same name, Catherine of Siena,[73] left fitting monuments of her genius in which the purity of her saintly intellect is resplendent. We need not envy the pagans their prophetesses, since we have four in the same household, the daughters of Philip. In Jerome's time all holy women were very learned. If only some aged theologians of our own day could equal this learning! Jerome writes to Paula, Laeta, Eustochium, Fabiola, Marcella, Furia, Demetrias, Salvina, Herontia. Ambrose, Augustine, and Fulgentius write to other women, all of them admirable for their talent, literary learning, and exemplary life. Valeria Proba,[74] who loved her husband to a singular degree, composed the *Vergiliocentones* about the life of our Lord, Jesus Christ. Chroniclers tell of Eudocia,[75] wife of Emperor Theodosius the Younger, who was no less renowned for her learning and virtuous life than for her rule. The *Homerocento*, which enjoys wide circulation, is attributed to her. The letters and learned books of the German maiden Hildegard[76] are in everyone's hands.

26. Our age has seen the four daughters of Isabel, whom I mentioned a little earlier, each of them well accomplished. People in various parts of

70. According to the second-century *Acts of Paul and Thecla*, she heard Paul preach in Iconium. She underwent many torments for the faith.

71. Saint Barbara was shut up in a tower by her father to keep her hidden from men's eyes. According to a Flemish version of the *Golden Legend* of Jacopo da Varagine, she sought out the Christian philosopher Origen in Alexandria by means of envoys. He sent a priest named Valentinus to instruct her in the Christian faith. This aspect of her legend may well have been known to Vives through this Flemish version, done by Jean de Wackerzeele and published in Cologne in 1495.

72. This legendary saint was martyred at Alexandria during the persecution of Maxentius (reigned 307–12). According to medieval legends, Catherine confounded the emperor with her learning. She became the patron of philosophers and theologians.

73. Caterina Benincasa (1347–80) was not a very learned woman, as Vives states. She dictated her writings in the beautiful Tuscan vernacular of Siena. Among her writings are about four hundred letters and a treatise entitled *Dialogo della divina providenza*. She was instrumental in persuading Gregory XI to return to Rome from Avignon.

74. Valeria Proba, circa 360–70 C.E., wrote a cento, or patchwork, of 694 hexameters. Composed of passages of Virgil on biblical themes, it was quite popular in the Middle Ages and was used as a school text.

75. Eudocia wrote paraphrases of certain prophetic books of the Old Testament and completed the Homeric centos begun by a bishop named Patricius.

76. Hildegard (1098–1179), abbess of Bingen, was a visionary mystic, composer, and writer of prophetic treatises and works on medicine and natural history.

the country tell me in words of praise and admiration that Queen Juana, wife of Philip and mother of our Emperor Charles, answered in Latin to the Latin ex tempore speeches that are customarily delivered in every town in the presence of new princes. The English say the same of their queen Catherine, sister of Juana. All say the same of the other two sisters, who met their death in Portugal. There were no women in human memory more chaste than these four sisters, none with a more unblemished name, and there have been no queens who were so loved and admired by their subjects. None loved their spouses more, none displayed more compliant obedience, none preserved themselves and their loved ones more blamelessly and more assiduously, none were so opposed to base behavior and lax morals, none fulfilled to such perfection the ideals expected of the virtuous woman. In my own Valencia, I see Mencía de Mendoza,[77] daughter of the marquis of Zenete, growing up, who one day, I hope, will achieve great renown. If the majesty of queens would permit that mention be made of ordinary women in the same discourse, I would add to this number Angela Zabata, my compatriot, a young woman of incredible quickness and versatility of intellect in all branches of literature and also of singular purity of morals and good sense. Then I shall mention the daughters of Thomas More—Margaret, Elizabeth, Cecilia, and their kinswoman, Margaret Giggs[78]—whose father was not content that they be chaste but also took pains that they be very learned, in the belief that in this way they would be more truly and steadfastly chaste.

27. In this that wisest of men is not deceived, nor are others who are of the same opinion, for the study of literature has these effects: first, it occupies a person's whole attention; second, it lifts the mind to the contemplation of beautiful things and rids it of lowly thoughts; and if any such thoughts creep in, the mind, fortified by precepts and counsels of good living, either dispels them immediately or does not lend an ear to vile and base things, since it has other pure, substantial, and noble pleasures to aspire after. For this reason, I think, Pallas Athena, the goddess of poetic inspiration and the arts, and all of the Muses were thought from ancient times to be virgins. Not

77. Mencía de Mendoza, Marchioness of Zenete, received an excellent education and continued her interest in humanistic studies after her marriage to Henry III, count of Nassau. She resided later at Breda and gave hospitality to Vives in his later years.

78. The last-named, Margaret Giggs, was More's adopted daughter, but she received the same education in the "school" of More, demonstrating great ability in medicine. The most learned of them was Margaret, of whom we have several writings. In ep. 1402 to John More (*CWE* 10: 130), Erasmus speaks of the letters of More's daughters written in very pure Latin, of their accurate knowledge of Greek and Latin, and their accomplishments in music.

only does the mind dedicated to wisdom shrink from lust, that is, something innocent and immaculate from filth and defilement, but likewise from those trivial and foolish pastimes that tempt the fickle minds of girls, like dancing, singing, and frivolous and insipid amusements of that sort. "Never," said Plutarch, "will a woman dedicated to literature distract herself in dancing."[79]

28. "But in what kind of literature should a woman be versed?" someone may ask, "and in what reading will she immerse herself?" I touched on this at the beginning of this discussion:[80] the study of wisdom, which forms morals in the way of virtue, the study of wisdom, which teaches the best and holiest way of life. I am not at all concerned with eloquence. A woman has no need of that; she needs rectitude and wisdom. It is not shameful for a woman to be silent; it is disgraceful and abominable for her not to have wisdom and to lead a bad life. But I would not necessarily condemn in this sex the eloquence that Quintilian,[81] followed by Saint Jerome,[82] considers worthy of praise in Cornelia, mother of the Gracchi; and in Hortensia, daughter of Quintus Hortensius; and in Eunomia, daughter of Nazarius. If it is possible to find a woman who is both pious and learned to teach the young girl, I should prefer her. If not, we should choose a man of advanced years, or at least a good man of proven virtue, not a bachelor, but one who has a wife who is not unattractive and who is dear to him. In that way he will be less inclined to conceive a passion for other men's wives. Such considerations should not be passed over lightly, since in the education of a woman the principal and, I might almost say, the only concern should be the preservation of chastity.

29. When she is taught to read, let her peruse books that impart instruction in morals; when she learns to write, do not have her imitate idle verses or vain and frivolous ditties, but rather some grave saying or a wise and holy sentiment from the holy Scriptures or the writings of philosophers, which should be copied out many times so that they will remain firmly fixed in the memory. And in speaking, I put no limit either on male or female, save that it is reasonable that the man be equipped with the knowledge of many and varied subjects, which will be of profit to himself and to the state, and that he be endowed with experience and learning, which will be diffused and transmitted to others. I wish the woman to be totally given over to that part of philosophy that has assumed as its task the formation and

79. Plutarch, "Advice to Bride and Groom," *Moralia,* 145C.

80. Cf. par. 22 above.

81. Quintilian 1.1.6.

82. Jerome *Letters* 107.4 (*NPNF,* 2d ser., 6:191).

improvement of morals. For this purpose, let her learn for herself alone or at most for her children when they are still small or for her sisters in the Lord, for it is not fitting that a woman be in charge of schools or have dealings with or speak to men, and, while teaching others, detract from her modesty and decorum either in whole or in great measure, and eventually lose these qualities little by little. If she is a good woman, it is best that she stay at home and be unknown to others. In company, it is befitting that she be retiring and silent, with her eyes cast down so that some perhaps may see her, but none will hear her.

The apostle Paul, vessel of election, imparting holy precepts to the church of Corinth, said, "Let your wives be silent in church, for it is not permitted them to speak, but to be subject, as the law commands. If they wish to learn anything, let them ask their husbands at home."[83] And writing to his disciple Timothy, he says, "Let a woman learn in silence with all subjection. I do not permit a woman to teach or to have authority over her husband, but to remain silent. For Adam was created first, then Eve, and Adam was not seduced but the woman was seduced and led astray."[84] Therefore, since woman is a weak creature and of uncertain judgment and is easily deceived (as Eve, the first parent of mankind, demonstrated, whom the devil deluded with such a slight pretext), she should not teach, lest when she has convinced herself of some false opinion, she transmit it to her listeners in her role as a teacher and easily drag others into her error, since pupils willingly follow their teacher. I am not unaware that certain women just as certain men are ill-adapted to the learning of literature. The education of such women must not be neglected. You must make known to her by word of mouth what you cannot do through the written word. She may also learn from other learned women of her own age, either when they read to her or recount the things they have read.

83. 1 Cor. 14:34–35.
84. 1 Tim. 2:11–14.

V

WHICH WRITERS
ARE TO BE READ AND WHICH
NOT TO BE READ

30. Saint Jerome, writing to Laeta about the instruction of Paula, gives this precept: "Let her not hear anything nor speak anything except what pertains to the fear of God."[85] Doubtless he would give the same advice with regard to reading. A custom has grown up, worse than any pagan usage, that books in the vernacular—written in that tongue so that they may be read by idle men and women—treat no subjects but love and war. Concerning such books, I think nothing more need be said if I am speaking to Christians. How can I describe what a pestilence this is, since it is to place straw and dry kindling wood on the fire? But these books are written for those who have nothing to do, as if idleness itself were not a strong enough aliment of all vices without laying on a torch that will set a person on fire and devour him in its flames.

What does a girl have to do with weapons, the very mention of which is unbecoming to her? They tell me that in certain places it is the custom for girls of noble birth to be avid spectators at tournaments of arms and to pass judgment on the bravery of the combatants, and that the men, for their part, respect and make more of the women's opinion than they do of the men's. But a young woman cannot easily be of chaste mind if her thoughts are occupied with the sword and sinewy muscles and virile strength. What room do these thoughts leave for chastity, which is defenseless, unwarlike, and weak? A woman who contemplates these things drinks poison into her breast, of which such interest and such words are symptoms. This is a deadly disease, which it is not only my duty to expose but to crush and suppress, lest it offend others by its odor and infect them with its contagion. When it

85. St. Jerome *Letters* 107.4 (*NPNF*, 2d ser., 6: 191). Laeta was the daughter of Paula, a patrician woman and descendant of the Gracchi as well as close friend and disciple of Jerome.

is not lawful for a Christian man to handle weapons save in dire and un-avoidable necessity, will it be lawful for a woman to be a spectator at such contests? And if she does not hold them with her own hands, she certainly participates in the spectacle with heart and mind, which is worse.

Then, tell me, why do you read about other people's loves and imper-ceptibly absorb venomous allurements and enticements little by little, and often with full consciousness of what you are doing? For there are some, who have already lost all mental equilibrium, who give themselves to this reading in order to find pleasant gratification in amorous reveries of this kind. For such girls it would have been preferable not only that they had never learned literature but that they had lost their eyes so that they could not read, and their ears so that they could not hear. How much better would it be for them to enter into life blind and deaf, as our Lord says in the gospel, rather than to be cast into the fire of hell with both eyes and both ears.[86]

31. This kind of girl is a disgrace not only to Christians but would be an object of shame and hatred even to the pagans. Wherefore I am all the more astonished that devout preachers, although often inveighing in tragic tones against petty matters, do not decry this practice in their every sermon. I marvel that wise fathers permit this to their daughters, husbands concede it to their wives, and public morals and institutions ignore the fact that women become addicted to vice through reading. It is fitting that human laws and magistrates not only concern themselves with the courts and civil disputes but also oversee public and private morals.

We would be better off if licentious and filthy songs in the mouths of the rabble were forbidden by law. Can nothing be sung in the city but what is bawdy and what no decent person can hear without embarrassment and no intelligent person without indignation? It would seem that those who compose such songs have no other purpose than to corrupt the public mor-als of youth, just like those who contaminate the public fountains with poi-son. What manner of custom is this that what is free of filth is not considered a song? This should receive the attention of the laws and the magistrates.

They should also concern themselves with pernicious books like those popular in Spain:[87] *Amadís, Esplandián, Florisando, Tirant, Tristán,* books filled

---

86. Matt. 18:9.

87. *Amadís de Gaula* is the best known of the Spanish tales of chivalry. The first published version (Zaragoza, 1508) was edited and corrected by Garci Rodríguez de Montalvo. *Esplandián* (Seville, 1510), by Garci Ordóñez de Montalvo, was a continuation of *Amadís,* in which Esplan-dián kills his father. *Florisando* was another continuation, published in the same year by Páez di Ribera. *Tirant lo Blanch* (Valencia, 1490) was the most famous Catalan chivalric romance, begun by Joanot Martorell and completed by Martí Joan de Galba. Unlike others of its kind, the romance contains adventures that are more worthy of belief. For this reason, *Tirant lo Blanch* was

with endless absurdities. New ones appear every day: *Celestina,* the brothel-keeper, begetter of wickedness, the *Prison of Love.* In France[88] there are *Lancelot du Lac, Paris and Vienna, Ponthus and Sidonia, Pierre of Provence, Maguelonne,* and *Melusine,* the heartless mistress. Here in Flanders[89] there are *Floris and Blanchefleur, Leonella and Canamoro, Turias and Floret,* and *Pyramus and Thisbe.* There are some translated from Latin into the vernacular languages, like Poggio's unfacetious *Facetiae,*[90] *Euryalus and Lucretia,*[91] and the *Decameron*[92] of Boccaccio. All these books were written by idle, unoccupied, ignorant men, the slaves of vice and filth. I wonder what it is that delights us in these books unless it be that we are attracted by indecency. Learning is not to be expected from authors who never saw even a shadow of learning. As for their storytelling, what pleasure is to be derived from the things they invent, full of lies and stupidity? One hero killed twenty single-handed, another slew

---

saved from the flames in the burning of Don Quiote's library (*Don Quijote de la Mancha,* pt. 1, chap.6).

The Celtic legend of Tristan was translated into Spanish as *Tristán de Leonís* in 1501. *La Celestina,* a dialogue novel written by the *converso* Fernando de Rojas, is the most remarkable work written in fifteenth-century Spain. The earliest surviving edition dates to Burgos, 1499. The procuress and go-between, Celestina, is a model of worldly wisdom. The *Cárcel de Amor* (*Prison of Love*) (Seville, 1492), by Diego de San Pedro is the most important Spanish novel of courtly love.

88. *Paris et Vienne* (1342) by Pierre de la Céspède tells of the love of the knight Paris and the daughter of the dauphin of Vienna. *Ponthus et la belle Sidoine* (late fourteenth century) could be regarded as a composite of all chivalric tales. Twenty editions exist, in all the languages of Europe. *Pierre de Provence et la belle Maguelonne* (anonymous, 1478) was inspired by a local legend of Languedoc; it was translated into Spanish as the *Historia de la linda Magalona y Pierres de Provenza* (1519). *Mélusine* (1387) tells of a fairy of French folklore who turns into a serpent every Saturday.

89. *Floire et Blanchefleur* is an early thirteenth-century *roman d'aventure* in which the separated lovers are reunited after many vicissitudes in the emir's seraglio. The story was well known in Flanders from a translation made in the thirteenth century by Diederic van Assende, *Floris ende Blanchefloer,* and twenty printings of the tale were produced by 1517. *Historia del rey Canamoro y de Turián su hijo,* drawn from Breton sources, appeared in 1505. Leonella is Canamoro's wife and Turián his son, whose love for Floreta forms the sequel of the story. *Turias ende Floreta* was published in 1523 in Brussels, but only the first few pages of it exist—enough to show that the story of Canamoro also existed in Flemish. The story of the ill-starred lovers, Pyramus and Thisbe, was originally told by Ovid (*Metamorphoses* 4.450–65). Many versions of it existed in various languages, beginning with the twelfth-century Old French romance, *Pyramus et Tisbe.*

90. This is a collection of anecdotes and witty sayings by the Italian humanist Poggio Bracciolini (1380–1459), first published in 1470. Contrary to what Vives says, the collection is quite facetious. *Facetiae* was translated into French in 1480 and Italian in 1483.

91. The full title of this work is *Euryalus et Lucretia: Historia de duobus amantibus* (*History of Two Lovers*). It was written by Enea Silvio Piccolomini, Pope Pius II, in 1444. This love story in the style of Boccaccio was widely translated, with the Spanish version published in Salamanca in 1496.

92. Vives seems to have thought that the *Decameron* was written in Latin. It was translated into Catalan in 1429 and Spanish about 1450.

thirty, and still another hero left for dead with six hundred gaping wounds suddenly rises to his feet and the next day, restored to health and strength, lays two giants low in a single battle; then proceeds on his way, laden with gold, silver, silks, and jewels in such quantity that even a cargo ship could not carry them.

32. What madness it is to be drawn and fascinated by these tales! There is nothing clever here except for some words taken from the secret archives of Venus that are spoken at the propitious moment to impress and arouse the woman you love if she shows some resistance. If they are read for that reason, it would be better to write books on the art of whoring (*sit venia verbi*). For on other subjects what cleverness can come of a writer who is devoid of every good skill? I never heard of anyone who liked these books except one who had never come in contact with good books. I have read some of them myself but never found any trace of good intent or superior talent. I will lend credence to those who praise such books, some of whom I know personally, if they say this after having had a taste of Cicero or Jerome or the sacred Scriptures, and if they were not completely depraved themselves. For the most part, their only reason for awarding praise is that they see their own morals reflected in them as in a mirror and are happy to find approval. Finally, even if they were very witty and pleasant, I would not want sensual pleasure that is smeared with poison or that a woman be spurred on to shameful conduct.

33. Surely one can only deride the madness of husbands who allow their wives to read these books so that they may be more clever in their depravity. What shall I say of foolish and ignorant writers when Ovid counsels that the most sagacious and learned Greek and Latin poets who sang of love should be avoided by those who shun immorality? What can be imagined more pleasant, more charming, more delightful, more clever, more cultivated and refined in every kind of learning than the poets Callimachus,[93] Philetas,[94] Anacreon,[95] Sappho, Tibullus, Propertius, Cornelius Gallus,[96]

93. Callimachus, born in Cyrene in North Africa, was the most learned poet at the Alexandrian court under Ptolemy II (285–246 B.C.E.). He wrote verse in various genres, among them erotic epigrams.

94. Philetas of Cos (born c. 340 B.C.E.) was a poet and scholar who became the tutor of Ptolemy II Philadelphus. Very few fragments of his poetry remain, but he is reputed to have written love poetry. His influence on Hellenistic and Latin poetry was very great.

95. Anacreon of Teos (born c. 570 B.C.E.) wrote both erotic (heterosexual and homosexual) and convivial verse, much of which has an epigrammatic quality.

96. These three Roman poets of love lived in the second half of the first century B.C.E. Their poems are usually referred to as elegiac love poetry, after the meter in which they are written.

whose talents and inspiration drew the admiration of all of Greece, all of Italy, and the whole world? And yet Ovid teaches that they must be repudiated by the chaste, saying in the second book of *The Remedy of Love*:

> Reluctantly I say, eschew the poets of love.
> I cast away my own poetic gift, for shame!
> Beware Callimachus, no enemy of love,
> And the Coan bard[97] can also do you harm,
> Sappho surely made me please my mistress more,
> And the Teian Muse[98] gave no stern morals.
> Who could read Tibullus with impunity
> Or the poet who sang of Cynthia[99] alone?
> Who could depart from Gallus unmoved by love?

and at the end he prohibits the reading of his own poetry:

> And my own poems, too, emit a similar ring.[100]

They have that ring indeed, and for that reason you were driven into a most deserved exile among the Getae[101] by a good ruler, an action that solicits our admiration for the strict morals either of the times or of the ruler.

34. We live in a Christian city. Who expresses even slight displeasure with an author of such poems nowadays? Did I say displeasure? Who does not embrace them with enthusiasm and commend them? Plato expels the poets Homer and Hesiod from the republic of good men that he instituted.[102] But what immorality is to be found in them in comparison with Ovid's *Art of Love*, which we read, carry about with us, wear out with use, and learn by heart? There are some teachers who lecture on it to their pupils, others who write commentaries and thus open up the path to iniquity. Are we to suppose that Augustus, who sent him into exile, would have kept these interpreters of Ovid in the Roman republic? Not unless we think it is worse to write immoral things than to expound them and sow the seeds of such "ethical" principles in the innocent minds of youth. Exile is the punishment of those who falsify weights and measurements. One who counterfeits money

---

97. Theocritus, a famous pastoral poet who dealt with themes of love (c. 300–260 B.C.E.).

98. Anacreon; see note 95.

99. i.e., Propertius.

100. Ovid *The Remedy of Love* 757–66.

101. The Getae were a Thracian tribe living by the Danube in the region where Ovid was exiled.

102. Plato *Republic* 398A.

or falsifies a document is burned at the stake. In small matters such ado! And is a corrupter of youth to be given honor in a city and regarded as a master of wisdom?

Therefore, a woman should avoid these books as she would a viper or a scorpion. And if a woman is so enthralled by the reading of these books that she will not put them down, they should not only be wrested from her hands, but if she shows unwillingness to peruse better books, her parents or friends should see to it that she read no books at all and become unaccustomed to the reading of literature—and, if possible, unlearn it altogether. For it is better to be deprived of a good thing rather than make ill use of it. A good woman will not take such books into her hands, nor will she defile her mouth with obscene songs; and, as far as she can, she will bring it about by her good actions and admonitions that others be like her, and, I should add, by direction and instruction, if that is possible.

35. As for what books should be read (for someone will ask me this), there are some on which everyone is agreed, as the Gospels of the Lord, the Acts of the Apostles and the Epistles, the historical and moral books of the Old Testament, Cyprian, Jerome, Augustine, Ambrose, Chrysostom, Hilary, Gregory, Boethius, Fulgentius, Tertullian, Plato, Cicero, Seneca, and other such authors. But in the case of certain books, the advice of learned and sensible men must be sought. A woman must not rashly follow her own judgment, lest with her slight initiation into learning and the study of letters she mistake false for true, harmful for salutary, foolish and senseless for serious and commendable. Her whole motivation for learning should be to live a more upright life, and she should be careful in her judgment. She will not give her affirmation to dubious statements, but will hold firm to what is approved by the authority of the church or the unanimous accord of good men. She will always remember and bear in mind that it was not without reason that Saint Paul forbade women the faculty of teaching or speaking in church and that they should be subject to men and silently learn what it behooves her to learn.[103] There need not be any lack of poets if a woman takes delight in the rhythm of poetry. She may read Prudentius, Arator, Prosper, Juvencus, and Paulinus,[104] who are scarcely inferior to the ancients.

---

103. 1 Cor. 14:34–35.

104. All of these are Christian poets who wrote in the meters and style of the pagan poets. The earliest of them chronologically is Juvencus, a Spaniard who composed an epic poem on the Gospels during the reign of Constantine. Prudentius (348–c. 405), also a Spaniard, was the greatest of the Christian poets and known especially for his allegorical epic, the *Psychomachia*. Paulinus of Nola (335–431) was born of a rich senatorial family in Bordeaux and studied under the poet Ausonius. He married a wealthy Spanish woman named Therasia and lived in Spain

She will find without question in authors worth reading more ingenuity, more abundance, greater and surer pleasure—in brief, a most pleasant food for the soul, all of which will be of more profit for life and will suffuse the mind and heart with infinite delight.

36. Therefore, on feast days with constant application and intermittently on ordinary working days, they must read and hear things that will elevate their minds to God, compose their feelings in a Christian tranquillity, and improve their morals. It is an excellent practice before going out to hear Mass to read the Gospel and Epistle of that day at home and a commentary, if you have one. After assisting at the holy sacrifice, when you return home and have tended to your domestic cares, if this is part of your duties, read something from the Scriptures with a calm and tranquil spirit, if you know how to read; and if not, listen. On some working days do the same thing, especially if it does not interfere with other domestic chores, and, in particular, if the books are to hand and if there is a longer interval than usual between feast days. Do not think that holy days were instituted by the church for you to amuse yourself and engage in idle conversation with your companions, but that you might turn your thoughts to God more intently and with a calmer spirit, and meditate about the brevity of this life and everlasting life in heaven.

---

for a while. After his conversion to Christianity, Paulinus later became bishop of Nola in Campania. He wrote hymns and poems in elegant classical Latin. Prosper of Aquitaine, born at the beginning of the fifth century, composed a series of epigrams on Augustinian maxims that are more didactic than poetic. Arator, a poet of the sixth century who may have been born in Milan, wrote a long poem in hexameters, in which he versified the Acts of the Apostles.

VI

ON VIRGINITY

37. Virginity is such a great and noble subject that any discussion of it neither can nor should be brief. Nevertheless, I will observe my proposed ideal brevity, bearing in mind that I am a teacher, not a panegyrist. I define virginity as integrity of the mind, which extends also to the body, an integrity free of all corruption and contamination. No way of life is more like that led in heaven. For there where the law of the flesh is abrogated we will be as angels, feeling no sexual urges, where no man or woman will be given in marriage.[105] What is there in all of creation purer, freer from sex and the carnal relations necessary for procreation and the slavery of the body than angelic minds? What expresses this more among mankind than virginity? But the essential part of this purity and integrity is situated almost entirely in the mind, which is also the source of all virtues. For the terrestrial and brute body is only the servant of the will, and God does not look to it or have any care for it, a thing totally foreign to him, but attends only to the mind, of a nature similar to his own and to some extent close to it.

Consequently, those who preserve the body intact but whose mind is defiled foolishly arrogate to themselves the name or the praise proper to virginity. The Lord calls such persons foolish virgins in his gospel,[106] who are no more like virgins than if they were dead or painted. What is meant by foolish but that it does not retain natural taste, that it is insipid? They may perhaps be virgins in the eyes of men, who see with eyes of the flesh. Certainly they will not be so to God, who is a spirit and sees with the spirit. And what of the fact that such a person is not regarded as a virgin even by men? That famous secular orator declared that she is unchaste who even without engaging in an illicit sexual act desires it.[107] If a woman who allows herself to be defiled by a man loses the honor and name of virginity, how will one who has prostituted herself to devils be called a virgin of Christ? What agreement is there between Christ and Belial?[108] What relation between the most pure God and an impure mind? Not without reason do the sacred Scriptures call fornication a separation from God,[109] because our mind has prostituted its chastity, owed to God alone, to adulterers. Fulgentius said rightly: "The devil strives to snatch away the virginity of the flesh by the aid of man, but the virginity of the heart he tries to carry off by himself."[110]

38. The strongest defenses should be moved up where the danger is greatest. The mind must be particularly fortified, lest it be defiled in a virgin body, so that all the treasures and beauty of integrity will endure there, firm and unassailable. The daughter of the king in Psalm 44, even if adorned with gold-woven robes and multicolored brocade, still directs all her glory inward.[111] This is the universal church, which Augustine said "is espoused to one man, Christ, as Paul writes to the Corinthians.[112] How worthy of honor, therefore, are her members, who preserve in their very flesh what the church preserves with absolute faith, who imitate the mother of their spouse and Lord. For the church is both virgin and mother."[113] Thus speaks Augustine. Such virgins deservedly, as Fulgentius writes, "Take their name from virtue. Of these virgins the only begotten son of God and only begotten son of a virgin is spouse, the fruit, glory and reward of holy virginity, whom holy virginity brought forth in the flesh, to whom holy virginity is spiritually wed, by whom holy virginity is made fruitful so that she may persevere intact, by whom she is given the power to remain beautiful, by whom she is crowned so that she will reign forever glorious."[114] These are the words of Fulgentius.

39. O happy condition of life, that now already in this mortal body practices what we are destined to be in eternity; that has in Christ father, spouse, and son, so that there is nothing in it that does not rightfully

107. Seneca the Elder *Controversies* 6.8.

108. 2 Cor. 6:15.

109. Eph. 5:5.

110. Fulgentius *Letters* 3.25 (*PL* 65:333).

111. Ps. 45:14–15.

112. 2 Cor. 11:2.

113. Augustine *On Holy Virginity* 2 (*NPNF*, 1st ser., 3:417).

114. Fulgentius *Letters* 3.6 (*PL* 65:326).

belong to the Virgin. But you are a spouse of Christ by virtue of integrity of the mind. See to it that you be vigilant in protecting it with greater solicitude than you would that of the body. To preserve integrity of the body, much care must be expended, but for the other much more is needed, or to put it more correctly, total vigilance. As far as you can, close your eyes and ears, which give entrance to the machinations the devil makes use of in his assaults upon us. Control your thoughts and hold them in your power, lest enticed and corrupted by some perverse attraction they betray the citadel of the mind. Corporal virginity, which all carry about in their eyes, is no small thing; it gains the respect even of immoral men, so that the poets are not wrong in imagining that Divine Majesty, descending to earth, lends its assistance to virgins in the same way it does to kings and lawmakers. Even among the pagan gods, who were in other respects foul and disgusting, they maintain that Cybele,[115] to whom they gave the title mother, was a virgin. Diana was the darling of the gods because she vowed herself to perpetual virginity. Three distinct qualities gained men's esteem for Minerva: virginity, fortitude, and wisdom, and she was imagined as having been born from the brain of Jupiter, whom they considered the greatest and foremost, father of gods and of men. Wherefore it was accounted sacrilege that anything be born of him save that which was pure, chaste, and wise, of absolute greatness and nobility. They so linked virginity with wisdom that they dedicated the same number seven to chastity and to wisdom. All of the Muses, the guardians of learning, were reputed to be virgins.

40. In the temple of Apollo at Delphi, the wise woman who was filled with divine inspiration and predicted the future to those who consulted her was always a virgin and was popularly known as the Pythia. All of the Sibyls also, whom Varro puts as ten in number,[116] were virgins, according to the testimony of Jerome. At Rome there was a temple to Vesta, served by virgins who were called Vestals. In their presence the entire Senate would rise to its feet, all the magistrates made way for them on the street, and they were held in the greatest honor by the whole Roman people. Chastity was always something sacred and venerable, especially virginity, even among thieves, men of impiety, criminals, and wicked men, and even among wild beasts it was safe and respected. "Thecla," says Saint Ambrose, "transformed the nature of beasts through the veneration they paid to her virginity."[117] So much

---

115. Cybele, the great mother-goddess of Anatolia in Asia Minor, was worshipped in wild, orgiastic rites. Her official cult was established in Rome in 205 B.C.E.

116. This citation of the Roman encyclopedic writer, Varro, is found in Lactantius *The Divine Institutes* 1.6.8–12.

117. Ambrose *On Virginity* 2.3.19 (*NPNF*, 2d ser., 10: 376).

admiration does virginity elicit that lions stand in awe of it. Of how much worth, therefore, is that quality which has so often freed and defended women from emperors, tyrants, and mighty armies?

We read that very often abducted women were released by arrogant soldiers, solely out of respect for the name of virgin, because they had declared themselves virgins. For they thought it a great crime to violate such a great good for a brief and momentary semblance of pleasure, and each one preferred that anyone but himself should be the perpetrator of such a villainous deed. O wicked girl, unworthy of life, who willingly deprives herself of that boon that soldiers, inured to every kind of crime, shrink from seizing? Even lovers blind with passion and mad with desire hesitate, for there is no lover so desperate who if he reflects that the woman who is the object of his passion is a virgin, does not bestir himself, open his eyes, exercise his judgment, consider what he is about to do, and think of changing his mind. To such an extent are all in fear of taking away a blessing of such price, which afterwards they can neither retain themselves nor give back, although they are not losing anything themselves.

41. Is a foolish girl not greatly perturbed about losing what, once lost, she cannot in any way recover afterwards, especially since it is she herself who is depriving herself of her greatest good? And if feelings have any power, as it is reasonable that just and honorable feelings should, turn wherever she will, a girl who has lost her chastity will find through her own fault everything sad, unhappy, mournful, hateful, and hostile to her. What will be the sorrow of her relatives when they sense that they are all dishonored because of the base conduct of one girl? What will be their grief? What tears will be shed by parents and those who nurtured her? Are these the joys with which you repay them in return for all their anxieties and labors? Is this the reward for your upbringing? What hatred will this arouse in the members of your houschold! What will be the talk of neighbors, friends, and acquaintances in denunciation of this wicked young girl, what derision! What gossip there will be among girls of her own age, what loathing her girl friends will have for her! How she will be avoided wherever she goes! What desolation she will find when mothers keep not only their daughters but their sons far away from the contagion of such a defiled and unclean mind? Even her wooers, if she had any, take leave of her, and those who previously simulated love for her now express their scorn openly. In the meantime, giving open expression to their feelings, they censure her misdeed so that I cannot imagine there can be any life at all, never mind enjoyable life, for a girl who is aware of such things, but that she will not rather be immediately consumed with grief.

42. Need I recount the universal hatred and wrath that caused daughters to be slaughtered by their parents, sisters by their brothers, wards by their guardians, kinsmen by kinsmen? When Hippomenes, leader of the Athenians, discovered that his daughter had been deflowered by a certain individual, he shut her in a stable with a ferocious, starving horse. When the horse had suffered starvation for a long time, driven to a frenzy by its savage nature, it tore the girl to pieces for its food.[118] When Pontius Aufedianius found out that his daughter had been delivered over to Fannius Saturninus by her slave tutor, he killed both slave and daughter.[119] Publius Attilius Filiscus butchered his daughter because she had defiled herself by losing her virginity.[120] In the same city of Rome, we encounter the centurion, Lucius Verginius, who preferred to lose his daughter, still inviolate, rather than keep her after she was defiled. Therefore, he defended his only beloved daughter, Verginia, from the lust of the decemvir in the only way he could, offering her as a sacrificial victim by his own hand.[121]

In the memory of our fathers, it is related that there were brothers in the Tarragon province of Spain who discovered that their sister, whom they believed to be a virgin, was pregnant. Concealing and restraining their sorrow until the time she would give birth, as soon as the newborn child emerged from her womb, under the eyes of the midwife, they thrust their swords into her belly and dispatched her. In that same part of Spain, when I was a boy, three young girls suffocated a companion of theirs with a large linen cloth when they caught her in an obscene act.

History is full of examples, as is the common experience of life. It is not to be marveled at that such things are done by parents and close friends and that feelings of affection are suddenly changed into the most violent hatred, since these young women themselves, victims of a detestable and savage love, casting away all filial piety from their hearts, have shown hatred for their parents, brothers, even their children, not merely friends and relatives. And I should wish that not young women alone should consider this as said to them, but also married women and widows, in a word, all women.

43. Now let the woman turn her attention upon herself and reflect

---

118. Ovid *Ibis* 335.

119. Valerius Maximus 6.1.3. Valerius Maximus wrote a handbook of illustrative examples of memorable deeds and sayings, *Factorum ac dictorum memorabilium libri IX*, during the reign of the Emperor Tiberius. It was very popular during the Middle Ages and the Renaissance, and is frequently cited by Vives in this treatise. The reference will be given simply as Valerius Maximus.

120. Valerius Maximus 6.1.6.

121. Valerius Maximus 6.1.2.

upon her crime. She will fear and be terrified of herself and will find no peace either by day or by night, constantly goaded by her conscience, inflamed as if by burning torches. She will not suffer anyone to gaze at her intently without suspecting that he knows something of her misdeed and that it now occurs to his mind. No one will speak in hushed tones without her thinking that he is speaking of her misconduct. She will not hear talk of wicked women without suspecting that it may be referring to her. She will not hear the name of her seducer even in some other regard without fearing that she is being referred to indirectly. No one will give voice to secret complaints but that she will be afraid that her crime has been discovered and that her punishment is nigh. She must be the slave of those whom she suspects as suspecting. She will have to behave humbly and abjectly for fear that if she says anything rather freely or acts a little arrogantly, her disgrace will be immediately thrown in her face. She will live always in a state of confusion, lifeless, or, rather, she will not live at all, but will be deprived of physical death while undergoing moral death many times over.

44. What kingdoms would you wish to purchase with this everlasting torment? Depraved men suffer it, but women more acutely, since their crimes are more repulsive in the eyes of all and they are more scrupulous by nature. And truly, if one weighs the matter carefully, women who take little care of their chastity are worthy of these calamities and even worse. For many things are required of a man: wisdom, eloquence, knowledge of political affairs, talent, memory, some trade to live by, justice, liberality, magnanimity, and other qualities that it would take a long time to rehearse. If some of these are lacking, he seems to have less blame as long as some are present. But in a woman, no one requires eloquence or talent or wisdom or professional skills or administration of the republic or justice or generosity; no one asks anything of her but chastity. If that one thing is missing, it is as if all were lacking to a man.

In a woman, chastity is the equivalent of all virtues. They are idle and slothful guardians who cannot guard the one thing committed to their care and enjoined upon them with many words and exhortations, especially when no one will take it from them against their will or touch it without their consent. If a woman will reflect on this, she will be a more attentive and cautious guardian of her chastity. If that is safe, everything else will be in safety; if that is lost, all things perish together with it. "What can be secure for a woman when her chastity is lost?"[122] said Lucretia; and yet she preserved a chaste mind in a defiled body. Therefore, "burying the sword in

122. Livy 1.57.7.

her entrails," as Quintilian said, "she exacted the penalty imposed by necessity so that a chaste soul would be separated as quickly as possible from a polluted body."[123] Not that I should propose this act as an example to be imitated, but her resoluteness, so that you will believe that nothing remains to a woman who has cast away her chastity. You may take away from a woman her beauty, lineage, wealth, charm, eloquence, intelligence, knowledge of the skills suited to a woman, but if you add chastity, you have given her everything in full measure. Conversely, you may lavish all those things upon her with all abundance and call her unchaste, and with this one word you have removed all. She is left naked and loathsome. There are other things both of body and of mind that help women to care for their chastity, of which I will now speak.

123. This passage comes from the pseudo-Quintilian declamations that were published under the name of Quintilian and in the Renaissance were thought to be genuine. Cf. *Declamationes XIX maiores Quintiliano falso adscriptae*, ed. L. Hakanso (Stuttgart, 1982), 3.11.

VII

HOW THE YOUNG WOMAN
WILL TREAT HER BODY

45. First of all, I should like to recommend to parents the advice that Aristotle gave in the *History of Animals:* [124] that they keep special watch over their daughters at the beginning of puberty and keep them away from all contact with men. During that period they are more inclined to lust. The young girls themselves, at this time in particular, should abstain from seeing, hearing, or even thinking of unseemly matters, a practice which they will have to maintain for the rest of their lives as well. Before marriage frequent fasts will be beneficial—not those that weaken the body, but that check and control it and extinguish the fires of youth. These are true and holy fasts. Let her nourishment be light, plain, and not highly seasoned, and it must be remembered that our first parent was expelled from paradise because of the food she ate and that many young girls who are accustomed to delicacies have sought them outside the home when they no longer had them at home, to the detriment of their chastity.

Their drink will be that provided by nature for everyone's consumption, limpid and clear water. "The use of wine," says Valerius Maximus, "was unknown to Roman women, so that they would not fall into any disgrace, because it is well known that the next step after Bacchus, father of intemperance, is that which leads to unlawful lust." [125] If the stomach does not tolerate water, then a little beer or wine shall be given, enough for digestion, but not to inflame the body. Not only is it good for restraining sexual passion, lust, and wantonness of the body, but it also promotes more robust health.

---

124. Aristotle *History of Animals* 7.1, 581b (Barnes 1:911).
125. Valerius Maximus 2.1.5.

46. In Jerome's letter to Furia we read:

Physicians and those who have written about the nature of the human body, especially Galen in his book *Hygiene,*[126] say that the bodies of young men and women and of mature men and women glow with an innate warmth, and that foods that increase bodily warmth are harmful to them; thus it is conducive to their health to consume cold food and drink. To the contrary, warm food and old wine are beneficial to old men, who suffer from catarrh and cold. Therefore our Savior said 'Take care that your hearts are not weighed down with dissipation and drunkenness and the cares of this life.'[127] And the apostle: 'Do not get drunk with wine, in which is debauchery.'[128] And it is not strange that the potter felt this way about the vessel that he had made, since even the comic writer, whose only object is to know and describe human conduct, said, 'Without Ceres and Bacchus, Venus is frigid.'[129] First of all, then, if the stomach is strong enough to take it, until after the age of puberty drink water, which by nature is very cool. But if weakness prevents this, listen to the advice given to Timothy: 'Partake of a little wine for the sake of your stomach and your frequent ailments.'[130] In solid food avoid things that are too hot. I speak not only of meat, concerning which the vessel of election makes this statement: 'It is good not to drink wine and not to eat meat.'[131] But even in the case of leguminous vegetables those that cause flatulence and are heavy should be avoided.[132]

And a little earlier on he says:

Why, therefore, must we vaunt our chastity, which without its companions and attendants, continence and frugality, carries no conviction? The apostle torments his body and makes it subject to the soul lest what he preaches to others he should not observe himself;[133] and will a mere girl, whose body is warm with food be certain of her chastity? In saying this I do not mean, of course, to condemn food, which

126. Galen *Hygiene* 5.3.5.
127. Luke 21:34.
128. Eph. 5:18.
129. Terence *The Eunuch* 732.
130. 1 Tim. 5:23.
131. Rom. 14:21.
132. Jerome *Letters* 54.9–10 (*NPNF,* 2d ser., 6:105).
133. 1 Cor. 9:27.

God has created for our use and for which we should be grateful, but I wish to remove from young men and young women the incentives to sensual pleasure. Neither the fires of Etna nor the island of Vulcan,[134] nor Vesuvius nor Olympus seethe with such fires as the marrow of youth, flushed with wine and good food.[135]

This all comes from Saint Jerome. I have introduced it to make known that master's thoughts on continence, who also in his letter to Salvina says that he prefers that the health of the body be at risk rather than that of the soul. He says, "It is preferable that the stomach be in pain rather than the mind; better to rule the body than be a slave to it, to falter in one's steps rather than in one's chastity."[136]

47. That very saintly man, Gregory Nazianzen, teacher of Jerome, wishes his ideal virgin to appease hunger with bread and thirst with water.[137] The monk Hilario, though barely sustaining his life in the desert on the most scanty diet, at times felt that his body was being stimulated by lust and would torture his body with fasts, saying, "I will tame you, concupiscence, so that you will think of food, not pleasure."[138] This is what the disciples of Christ and the companions of Paul say, dedicated to a sober and chaste religion, since they were aware that the nourishment of holy men, even when divinely sent, was meager and simple, to satisfy nature without gratifying it. Elisha nourished himself and the sons of the prophets with wild herbs and ordered the bitter food to be sweetened with flour, not honey or sugar.[139] The soldiers whose eyes he had put out in Samaria he ordered to be welcomed with a banquet of bread and water.[140] John the Baptist, the predestined precursor of Christ and the herald of the impending dawn, nurtured himself on locusts and wild honey in the desert.[141] Habakkuk at the angel's bidding brought the food of the harvesters to Daniel in Babylon.[142] Elijah was sent from heaven bread made of ashes and a cup of water to recover his strength.[143] Could not bread made from wheat-flour and

---

134. The island of Lemnos in the Aegean Sea.
135. Jerome *Letters* 54.8–9 (*NPNF*, 2d ser., 6:105).
136. Jerome *Letters* 79.10 (*NPNF*, 2d ser., 6:167).
137. Gregory Nazianzen *Precepts for Young Girls* 134 (*PG* 37:589).
138. Jerome *The Life of St. Hilarion* 5 (*NPNF*, 2d ser., 6:304).
139. 2 Kings 4:39–41.
140. 2 Kings 6:22.
141. Matt. 3:4.
142. Dan. 14:32–33.
143. 1 Kings 19:6.

partridges and capons and pheasants and marzipan have been as readily sent from heaven, or rock partridges, as formerly was done for the sons of Israel, as easily as that kind of nourishment? But obviously, holy men are in need of such nourishment to keep their soul in the body without suffocating it.

48. What of the philosophers and the teachers of worldly wisdom? They all recommend moderate and simple fare, ready to hand, so that the mind will be sober and the body continent. Socrates, the father of philosophy, followed a simple diet with the result that neither he nor his family was ever stricken by any serious or dangerous malady.[144] Seneca the Stoic, writes Tacitus,[145] amidst the greatest wealth, satisfied his nature with wild fruit and pure water. His body was so emaciated by living in that way that when he cut open his veins at the command of Nero, hardly any blood issued from them. What must we think the table of Xenocrates was like, for when the beautiful courtesan Phryne was stealthily placed in his cot by his disciples and he was fondled by her and solicited to lust in various ways, he remained unmoved.[146] Plato in his *Laws* denies the use of wine to adolescents.[147] Cicero in *On Duties* is of the opinion that all food and care of the body should be for the purpose of maintaining health and strength, not pleasure. "And moreover," he says, "if we wish to consider what is the excellence and dignity of the nature of man, we will understand how base it is to become enervated with luxury and delicate and soft living, and how noble it is to live a life of temperance, frugality, severity, and sobriety."[148] Thus speaks Cicero. Ovidius Naso, imparting the remedies of love, teaches that he who would live chastely must also be temperate and must abstain from those foods "that prepare our bodies for Venus."[149] Wine, above all, must be avoided and those courses served "that deny our bodies to Venus."[150]

49. When I speak of foods that are warm of their own efficacy, I wish this to be understood as well of every physical stimulus that excites our internal organs, such as unguents, perfumes, conversations, and the sight of men. These are all harmful to chastity, since they inflame us with shameful desires. A young woman's bed will be clean rather than luxurious so that she

---

144. Plutarch, "Advice about Keeping Well" and "Concerning Talkativeness," *Moralia,* 124E; 513D.
145. Tacitus *Annals* 15.45.
146. Valerius Maximus 4.3.3.
147. Plato *Laws* 666A–B.
148. Cicero *On Duties* 1.106.
149. Ovid *The Remedy of Love* 800.
150. Ovid *The Remedy of Love* 802.

may sleep peacefully, not sensuously. The same precepts may be applied to her clothes, which should not be luxurious or too expensive, but neat and spotless. In some way, I know not how, cleanliness of mind takes pleasure in cleanliness of the body and, conversely, a hedonistic, languid, and effeminate spirit delights in silks and fine linens and, unless it is bedecked in such finery, regards all else as harsh, coarse, and intolerable. Gregory Nazianzen forbids gold, silk, and pearls to the young girls he instructed.[151] How stupid we are if we think that those words of our Savior—"Behold those who are dressed in soft garments dwell in the house of kings"[152]— mean that those who spend their lives in the retinue of Christian kings should put on soft garments. The religion of Christ is not acquainted with courts and kings of this sort, of whom the Master said, "The kings of the Gentiles exercise lordship over them and those who have power over them are called benefactors. But not so with you; but let the greatest among you become as the least and the leader as one who serves."[153] If our Lord takes pride away from kings themselves and their kingdoms, how will he ignore the accoutrements of pride? Christ wishes that his followers remember they are Christians at every moment and not citizens of the world, for he said to them, "You are not of this world."[154] Christian piety is holy and severe and while its yoke is easy, sweet, and pleasant to the soul, which finds its rest in it, it is heavy and troublesome to the pleasures of the body, with which it is in continuous conflict. This is the world that hates Christians because they are not of the world.

50. The sleep of a virgin should not be long, but not less than what is good for her health, to safeguard which we are of the opinion that young girls are healthier if they follow the austerity we recommend rather than sensual delight, which is manifested in its devotees by weakness and pallor. To these instructions must be added some activity and occupation fitting for a young girl, several of which I have already mentioned.[155] For the devil's cunning never finds such easy access as in idleness, nor does Venus ply her skills more readily at any other time, not only in women but in the stronger and more stable male. Our minds were born and destined to perform some activity, and they thrive, grow strong, and derive enjoyment in work, whereas they are weakened by idleness, lapse into inertia, and are incapable of doing

151. Gregory Nazianzen *Precepts for Young Girls* 85–90 (PG 37:585).
152. Matt. 11:8.
153. Luke 22:25–26.
154. John 15:19.
155. Cf. above, paragraphs 15–17.

anything. Consequently, they are bound to lapse into lust and shameful conduct and worse crimes than these since they have nothing better to occupy
themselves. That master in the art of love, Ovid, asserts that the only reason
that prompted Aegisthus to corrupt Clytemnestra, the wife of Agamemnon,
and to kill Agamemnon, was that he had nothing to do.[156] Hence one of the
principal remedies against love is that Cupid's arrow does not catch us idle
and unoccupied. His words are:

> Take away idleness and Cupid's bow is dead,
> And his torches lie lifeless and unlit.[157]

51. Love grows and sends out deep roots if you think much and often
about what you love. Jerome persuades Demetrias to avoid idleness altogether. And to that end he tells her that when she has finished with her
prayers, she should take her work in hand and prepare the weaving so that
by this alternation of tasks the days will never seem long. He requires this
unceasing activity of her not because she had need of it, for she was one of
the noblest and wealthiest women of Rome; but that through this constant
activity she would think of nothing that did not have to do with the service
of God. The passage ends as follows: "I shall speak plainly. Although you
distribute all your wealth to the poor, nothing will be more precious in the
eyes of Christ than what you have done with your own hands, whether for
your own use or as an example to other virgins or as an offering to your
grandmother and mother."[158] Thus speaks Saint Jerome. And so it is in very
fact: A woman who is indolent and slothful or (if you please!) spends her
time in amusements and pleasures is unworthy of her sustenance in the
Christian church, in which Paul, Christ's chief herald, proclaims as if it were
a law: "If anyone will not work then let him not eat."[159] The penalty inflicted
by God upon the human race for that first fault is common to all men: "By
the sweat of your brow will you eat your bread."[160] Undoubtedly those who
are not subject to this general punishment, although they have sinned no
less than others, will receive another graver punishment, or at any rate one
no less lacking in severity.

Since I recommended that women's minds must be kept under control
through work or holy thoughts and conversations so that they will not lapse

156. Ovid *The Remedy of Love* 161–62.
157. Ovid *The Remedy of Love* 139–40.
158. Jerome *Letters* 130.15 (*NPNF*, 2d ser., 6:269).
159. 2 Thess. 3:10.
160. Gen. 3:19.

into shameful conduct in their idleness, to what conceivable actions will those women be driven who divert themselves in games of cards and dice? Since this pastime is disgraceful even for men, it cannot but be loathsome in women. What will a woman be able to learn or think about who gives herself to gambling? It must needs be that her mind will be weakened and she will become the victim of avarice, to which she was already inclined by nature; then she will descend to perjury for the sake of money. If there are men present at these games of hazard, she will hear many things that are offensive to a woman's ears. What a shameful thing to see a woman not with her basket of wool but at the gaming board, rolling knuckle-bones instead of the spindle, throwing dice instead of spinning the shuttle, dealing out playing cards instead of battening the wool or reading her prayer book! No person of any judgment would not prefer that she remain idle rather than occupy herself in this way, and there is no one who would not condemn with great acrimony both the woman who learned these skills and the one who taught her such vices and those who permitted it.

VIII

ON ADORNMENT

52. It is impossible to say what difference there is between the adornment and embellishment of women and that which all holy authors unanimously prescribe for the baptized woman. In this, of course, they follow the princes of the apostles and pillars of the church, Peter and Paul, whose precepts concerning the adornments of women are brief but sum up the long sermons of others. Peter has this to say: "Let women not cultivate external adornment with braided hair, gold bracelets and fine clothes; rather if her mind and conscience, which are hidden from view, are incorrupt and she is of a gentle and peaceful spirit, that is what is precious in the sight of God." [161] Paul writes, "Women should be modest and sensible in their adornment, without braided hair or gold or jewelry or costly attire; their adornment is to do good works, as befits women who profess to be religious." [162] These are the words of the apostle, and no more need be said. But some things must be explained more fully, especially for those who require many words before they are willing to listen. I will take them up one by one and attack each of these insanities.

53. First, concerning cosmetics. In this regard I should like to know for what reason a young woman smears herself with white lead [163] and purple pigment. If it is to please herself, she is mad. What is dearer or more pleasing to anyone than to be oneself just as we are. If it is to please men, she is stupid. You have one spouse, Christ; to please him, adorn your soul with virtues, and he, the most beautiful of men, will kiss you. But if you are look-

161. 1 Peter 3:3–4.

162. 1 Tim. 2:9–10.

163. Known also as cerusite, this was commonly used during this period to produce a white complexion.

ing for a husband and you wish to win him over by painting yourself, I shall first show you how foolish it is and then how impious. It seems to me that wishing to attract a man with makeup is the same as trying to do so with a mask. Just as you attracted him in this disguise, so will you drive him away when you are unmasked. You poor wretch, if you can find a husband only by the use of makeup, when you have taken it off, how will you remain attractive to him? Unless perhaps you never take off that crust but go to bed with it on, get up with it, and go around both in public and in private made up in this way. How can the constant care to ensure that the makeup remain intact not become an annoying task? And you will become a laughingstock to others if by some sprinkling of water, perspiration, or heat the white lead or the rouge melts and some of the native complexion appears. Nothing can be more hideous in a beautiful woman.

54. There was a banquet celebrated in Greece that many women attended. One of the entertainments provided for the guests among the various games that were presented was that each of the guests in turn would demand whatever he wished from all the others. The lot fell to a certain girl of singular beauty and pleasant wit who—when she noticed that there were several women present encrusted with white lead, rouge, and other pigments—to arouse shame in them said, "I shall ask something very simple, and I shall be the first to do it, that each person present wet their hands and rub them over their faces and dry them with a napkin." She followed out her order first of all, but since she was wearing no makeup, she remained lovelier than before after washing her face, whereas those that wore makeup ended up looking absurd and ridiculous; and since they were made the object of derision, from then on they did without all such cosmetics and, content with their God-given appearance, had no use for purchased beauty. Moreover, who will ever consider women beautiful when he knows they are besmeared with pigments? Even those who are beautiful lose the honor and praise owed to their beauty when it is seen that they are made up. All their comeliness and charm is attributed to art, not to nature. And what is more, young skin becomes wrinkled more quickly, the whole appearance of the face begins to look old, the breath reeks, the teeth become rotten, and a foul odor is emitted by the whole body, from the white lead, mercury, and especially from depilatories, soaps, and ointments, with which they prepare their face like a wooden tablet for the next day's painting. Ovid rightly called these substances poison,[164] and Juvenal jocosely asks:

---

164. Ovid *The Remedy of Love* 351.

> But when she's through with all those medications,
> The mud-packs and the moistened poultices,
> What shall we call it? a face, or an ulcer? [165]

55. I could pursue these topics at great length, having been born in a city whose women have a bad reputation in this regard and, in my opinion, deservedly. I choose to reproach my dear native city [166] so that, shamed by my words, it may avoid practices that are reprehensible. I may add that if you cannot marry except by painting and whitening yourself, it would be better never to marry than to marry and give offense to Christ, marrying a madman, who likes white lead more than you. What can you hope for from a man who finds more pleasure in a white encrustation than in a good woman? Who has reached that point of madness that when he is going to buy a slave or a horse he prefers that they be shown to him touched up for sale rather than in their natural state? We do this in the purchase of slaves and beasts of burden; will we not do the same with wives?

God gave you a human face in the image of his Son, but not just in outward appearance, for he breathed into it the breath of life so that a ray of that life that exists in all things might shine out in it. Why do you cover it with filth and mire? If the apostle Paul forbids a man to cover his head because it is the image of God, [167] what do you think he would say of the image of God in a woman's face befouled by that muck? In writing against Helvidius, lest anyone think this is a laughing matter, Jerome says, "She paints herself before the mirror and in defiance of her maker tries to be more beautiful than she was born." [168] And to Furia he writes, "What is rouge and white lead doing on a Christian face, the first counterfeiting the redness of the cheeks and lips, the other the whiteness of the face and neck? They are the fire of youth, the food of lust, the signs of an impure mind. How can she weep for her sins when her tears lay bare her skin and dig furrows in her face? This is not the adornment of the Lord; it is the veil of the Antichrist. What boldness to raise to heaven a face which her Creator will not recognize." [169] Thus speaks Jerome.

---

165. Juvenal *Satires* 6.471–73.

166. The women of Valencia were known for their extravagance in personal adornment. At the beginning of the fourteenth century, Vincent Ferrer had excoriated them before Vives. A German traveler named Hieronymus Münzer describes their excesses in his *Itinerarium hispanicum*, 1494: "And they all use make-up and smear themselves with perfumed oils and waters, which is bad." *Revue hispanique* 113 (1920), 30.

167. 1 Cor. 11:7.

168. Jerome *Against Helvidius* 22 (*NPNF*, 2d ser., 6:345).

169. Jerome *Letters* 54.7 (*NPNF*, 2d ser., 6:104).

56. Hear now the holy martyr Cyprian:

Outward show in adornments and clothing and the allurements of cosmetics are not fitting in any except prostitutes and shameless women,
and in general none spend more money on dress than those whose
modesty is cheap. So in the Sacred Scriptures, by which Our Lord
wished us to be instructed and admonished, a harlot city[170] is described as beautifully attired and adorned, destined to perish with its
adornments or rather because of them. Now what ignorance of the
truth and madness of the mind is it to wish for what has always done
harm and continues to do so, and to think that you will not perish
from things that you know have led to the perdition of others? God
did not make sheep scarlet or purple in color, nor did he teach us to
dye and color wool with juices from herbs or from shellfish, nor did
he make necklaces of precious stones set in gold or silk garments interwoven with pearls arranged in numerous fastenings, in this way hid-
ing the neck, which he made, so that what God fashioned in man is
covered and what the devil invented is exposed to view. Did God wish
wounds to be inflicted on the ears to torment innocent children still
ignorant of the evils of the world, so that later precious stones may
hang from these scars and holes? And if they are not heavy of themselves, they are weighted down by the price paid for them. All these
things were the invention of the evil arts of sinners and the apostate
angels when they fell to the contagion of earth and lost their heavenly
power. They also taught how to circle the eyes with black make-up
and tinge the cheeks with a counterfeit blush, and to change the color
of the hair and to destroy all semblance of truth from the face and the
head by an all-out assault of their corrupting influence.

57.

And at this point through the fear that faith inspires in me and the
love which brotherhood demands I think that not only virgins and
widows, but married women also and women in general should be
admonished that the work of God, his creation and configuration,
should in no way be adulterated by applying yellow coloring or black
powder or rouge or any other concoction that will corrupt the native
features. God says: 'Let us make man to our image and likeness,'[171] and
will anyone dare to change and transform what God has made? They

170. Apoc. 17:1.
171. Gen. 1:26.

lay hands on God when they try to remake and transform what he has made, not knowing that all that is born is the work of God, and whatever is changed is the work of the devil.

58.

If a painter represented the countenance and form and bodily appearance of someone with colors that rivaled those of nature and when his work had been completed and perfected, another applied his hand to it, thinking himself more skillful, and redid what the other had shaped and painted, this would seem to be a grievous insult to the first painter and he would be justly indignant. Do you think you can commit such an act of insolence, an offense against the divine craftsman with impunity? Though you may not be immodest and unchaste with men in the allurements of your maquillage, you will be accounted worse than an adulteress in corrupting and violating what belongs to God. What you think is adornment and embellishment is an assault upon the handiwork of God, a prevarication of the truth. Your Lord says: 'You cannot make one hair white or black.'[172] And do you think you can be more powerful by challenging the word of God? With audacious pretension and sacrilegious contempt you dye your hair, and with bad omen you make it flame-colored and sin—O horror!—with your head, the noblest part of the body.[173]

59. These are the words of Cyprian. It is embarrassing after citing Christian precepts to relate something from the pagans. I shall merely give the example of Lycurgus, a man of great wisdom, legislator of the Lacedaemonians. Since he thought the women of his country should be esteemed for their virtues and not for their dress and adornments, he forbade feminine cosmetics from the state by law and banned from Sparta all products pertaining to beauty and adornment as corrupters of virtue and good morals.[174] The Lord through Hosea the prophet teaches us that the woman who turned away from him to her lovers adorned herself with earrings and necklaces in order to follow them and not her God.[175] These ornaments are cursed, as Tertullian said, "Without them she could not be described as cursed and as a prostitute."[176] If you groom yourself for God and good men, you are beau-

---

172. Matt. 5:36.
173. Cyprian *On the Dress of Virgins* 12–16 (PG 4:450–56).
174. Plutarch, "Sayings of Spartans," *Moralia,* 228B–C; *Life of Lycurgus* 15.2.
175. Hosea 2:13.
176. Tertullian *On Female Adornment* 2.12 (PG 1:1330).

tiful enough if you are good. You will not be pleasing to the devil and evil men unless you deprive yourself of much of your natural beauty and therefore of your virtue. What good are perforated ears when nature made them of imperforate cartilage? Why doesn't she perforate her nose as well in her extravagance? This is done in barbarous nations. Why not her fingers and her lips? For a gleaming jewel holds fast every one of her fingers. What is the purpose of all this weight of gold; is it that piled up in this way it is meant to show off your strength? Do you think you are better or more beautiful or wiser, laden down with so much metal? Nothing of the sort.

60. Concerning goodness, what can be said? Can a woman who dissembles, who wishes to be thought of as something other than she is, be a good woman? And for that matter, in my opinion, those women seem more beautiful whose beauty of countenance shines out in moderate personal adornment. Fine attire obscures comeliness of form. There is nothing so grand that it is not lessened and diminished by comparison with something greater. If the adornment is so brilliant, it is inevitable that the luster of her beauty will appear to be less, and whatever is pleasing in that woman will be attributed to her adornment rather than to her beauty. That famous Roman who, though the leader of his city, dwelt in a humble abode, said wisely, "I prefer to be an ornament to my house rather than the house to me, and I want nothing to be on view in my house except myself." Similarly, those women are accounted more beautiful in whom a modest and respectable adornment commends their good character and attractiveness, not burdened down by excessive and haughty care of the self.

Gravity is the adornment of a man, honor of a woman. Do you think, perchance, there were no beautiful women who were considered such and loved by their husbands in olden days, in that pristine, unsophisticated age when vice had not yet attained such power? I think there were more beautiful women at that time and that their beauty was more lasting, since it was not merely a temporary beauty, but permanent, that is, natural, that a woman did not put on with her clothing. Since, therefore, this adornment contributes neither to their appearance nor to their virtue, of what use is it? You tell me, "I shall appear richer and for that reason more honorable." Is this the thought, are these the words of a Christian heart? Your neck is weighted down with useless gold while you refuse a pittance to so many around you who are suffering from hunger? You despoil your neighbors and perhaps also your family, your children, and even your husband so that the rays of gold and jewels will bedazzle the eyes of the onlookers? So many are divested so that you alone may be clothed? Is this Christian charity? Is this what you swore in baptism in solemn utterance, to renounce Satan and his pomps? But do you not hold on to the pomps of Satan with more tenacity and perseverance than the pagans themselves?

61. Look at yourself from head to foot. You will recognize a follower of Satan. Do you consume rich foods at home to the point of satiety, belching up capons, partridges, pheasants, delicate pastries, hors d'oeuvres, sauces, sweetmeats, all sought out and bought at great price, in the midst of those dying of hunger? Do you pass your time in idleness, games, and entertainments amidst the toils and troubles of your neighbors? Do you go about in public, clad in silk and linen, amidst the naked throngs? Do you preen yourself in gold, silver, and jewelry amidst so many beggars? With such behavior are you a disciple of the poor Christ or the rich Plutus?[177] I do not wish to see you in squalor and rags, but neither do I wish to see you in clothes whose purpose is ostentation and conceit. Imitate the one in whose name you rightly glory, Christ; imitate his humble and frugal mother, whom men now worship as their lady, before whom those below stand in trembling and those above in reverential awe. Though her outward garb was made of common and cheap material, her inner vesture is of the most beautiful gold, set and interwoven with precious stones. You cannot be golden in both parts. Which do you wish to be of gold, your body or your soul? I cannot pursue the details of this subject, which are infinite; namely, the ramifications of vice.

62. Nevertheless, I shall say something about odors. An upright and cultivated mind does not approve of uncleanliness and stench and does not reject mild perfumes, by which tired spirits are revived or roused from their languor or even cured of their ailments (for Mary Magdalen poured upon our Lord's head ointment made of precious nard, whose fragrance filled the whole house and was not displeasing to Christ).[178] In like manner it condemns excessive odors, fomentations of this body of ours, which the more it is indulged, the more it rebels insolently against the mind, claims tyranny over the whole man, and drags everything down to the basest desires, the seat of self-indulgence. This was said by Saint Jerome to the virgin Demetrias:[179] "A virgin should avoid like the plague and as poison to chastity elegantly dressed boys with their hair curled, wearing skins smelling of some exotic mousse, of whom Martial says, 'He who smells good all the time, does

177. Plutus was the Greek personification of riches, but he was not worshipped as a god. Aristophanes wrote a comedy with this title, in which Plutus is represented as a blind old man. Vives seems to identify him with Pluto, god of the underworld.

178. John 12:3.

179. Jerome *Letters* 130.19 (*NPNF,* 2d ser., 6:271).

not smell good.'" [180] There is another similar verse in Martial: "I'd rather have no smell than smell good all the time." [181] Plautus in *The Haunted House* says, "A woman smells best when she has no smell at all." [182]

63. Some supercilious woman who has acquired a reputation for wisdom through cleverness of wit will perhaps respond, "We must make some concession to ancestry, nobility, wealth, to lookers-on." Come now, what is your allegiance if you can say this? Are you a Christian or a pagan? If you are a pagan, I have no argument with you. If you are a Christian, I must inform you, haughty woman, that Christ does not know of these distinctions. These betray the devil's arrogance, not the modesty of the Christian soul. There is an old proverb that has survived because of its truth. "There is no living creature more haughty than a richly adorned woman." [183] These are not adornments of the body or of nature, but incitements to your insolence.

Tertullian said, "No one can put limits on the truth, neither a period of time, nor influence of persons, nor privilege of country, because Christ the Lord, who abides for eternity, called himself truth, [184] not convention." [185] You say, "Some concession must be made to received morals, to custom." I ask, "To whose custom?" If it is that of wise and good men, I grant it. If it is that of stupid men, why should any concession be made, except by the stupid? What of the consensus of good men, which Quintilian shrewdly said should be the only accepted custom of life? [186] A bad practice has been introduced. You should be the first to abolish it, and this glory will remain to you. Other women will follow your example, and just as a bad custom is established by bad persons, so it will be extirpated by good persons and a good one instilled. But if we must always act in compliance with and condescend to custom, the world will never improve but will grow even worse, when it will be possible to introduce bad customs, but never to do away with them.

64. Tell me, whose is this custom that you talk about so freely, and where did it originate? From pagan women. Why, then, do we not retain paganism with that custom? Or if you like the name of Christian, why do you not accept the customs appropriate to that name? She is a pagan

180. Martial *Epigrams* 2.12.4.
181. Martial *Epigrams* 6.55.5.
182. Plautus *The Haunted House* 273.
183. Juvenal *Satires* 6.460.
184. John 14:6.
185. Tertullian *On the Veiling of Young Women* 1 (PL, 2:889).
186. Quintilian 1.6.45.

woman, and she does those things because she does not know God or moderation of life. You, who know God and were baptized in his name, why do you do more than she? What is all this about your profession to renounce Satan and all his pomps if you contend with a pagan woman not merely to equal her in her pomp but outdo her? What do I mean when I say you rival pagan women? Not the matrons of the ancient world, known for their piety and severity, but those closer to our own times, frivolous, given to luxury, steeped in sinfulness and crime. Not those upright Spartan women of old, whose queen, the wife of Lysander,[187] and her daughters refused the precious stoles that Dionysius, king of Syracuse,[188] sent, with these words: "These will be more of a disgrace than an honor to us."[189] Not those women of ancient Rome, of whom when Pyrrhus,[190] king of Epirus, through his ambassador Cynea offered them gifts of gold, silver, and garments of linen and silk, not one was found so ambitious for fine apparel, so greedy, so morally depraved and shameless as to accept them.[191]

65. Quinta Claudia, a vestal virgin, aroused suspicion concerning her chastity because she was too attentive and meticulous in the care of her body.[192] There was a law in Rome called the Lex Oppia,[193] promulgated during the Second Punic War, requiring that a woman not have more than half an ounce of gold, and not dress in many-colored clothes. This law lasted until Asian luxury invaded the city. Then the women, as if in a frenzy, burst into public, demanding freedom to dress as they wished. To prevent this the consul Marcus Cato, a man of great dignity, spoke out against it in a speech full of wisdom. Two tribunes of the people also spoke against it, whose speeches are recorded in Livy,[194] but toned down, adapted more to the ears

---

187. The Spartan Lysander forced the surrender of Athens in 404 B.C.E. and established the rule of the Thirty Tyrants.

188. Dionysius I, tyrant of Syracuse, 404–376 B.C.E.

189. Plutarch, "Sayings of Kings and Commanders" and "Sayings of Spartans," *Moralia*, 190E, 229A.

190. Pyrrhus inflicted a serious defeat upon the Romans at the battle of Heraclea in 280 B.C.E. It was after this victory that he attempted this act of bribery.

191. Valerius Maximus 4.3.14.

192. Ovid *Fasti* 4.309. This occurred in 204 B.C.E. Vives tells only part of the story. Ovid goes on to relate how Quinta Claudia vindicated her chastity by using a rope to haul the vessel conveying the statue of Cybele to Rome—a feat that could only be accomplished by a chaste woman, according to the soothsayers.

193. The Lex Oppia was a wartime sumptuary measure promulgated in 215 B.C.E., the year after the disastrous battle of Cannae, in which the Romans were defeated by Hannibal. It was repealed twenty years later despite the fierce opposition of Cato.

194. Cato's speech, or a facsimile of it elaborated by the historian, is given in Livy 24.2–4. The speech of Lucius Valerius, who introduced the repeal, is reported in 24.5–7.

of the stupid populace than to those of wise men. The women won out, however, through their insistence and pertinacity, with the result that all restraints to their vainglory were relaxed and they could do as they pleased. Cato predicted what ills would follow, and, as in many other of his utterances, so in this instance he proved to be a true prophet.

Who could describe what a loss to chastity results from this competition in adornment? Shamed to be outdone by their peers in personal adornment, it is only when they consider themselves duly groomed and attired that they are impatient to issue forth in public, put themselves on display, and converse with men. That is the shipwreck of chastity. According to Plutarch, it was a national custom in Egypt that women did not wear shoes so that they could be confined to the home.[195] So, if you take away from a woman her silks, linens, gold, silver, jewels, and precious stones, you can more easily keep her in the home.

66. In this same author there are two sayings about adornment; one of Sophocles, the tragedian, and one of Crates, the philosopher.[196] The former said of rich ornamentation: "This will not be seen as adornment, you poor woman, but as dishonor and a manifest proof of your insanity." Crates said that adornment is that which adorns. But true adornment is that which makes a woman more virtuous. This does not come about with gold or emeralds or purple but by all that gives proof of dignity, moderation and chastity. Democrates[197] defined the adornment of women as economy of speech and personal adornment, and this is also the opinion of Sophocles. Among the Greeks there was a popular saying circulated in the form of a proverb that the adornment of a woman is not gold, but good morals.

Aristotle, the wisest of philosophers, bids women to make less use of luxuries, clothing, and accoutrements than is permitted by law. He urges them to reflect that it is not splendor of attire or preeminence of beauty or abundance of gold that earns praise for a woman, but modesty in her possessions and the desire to lead an honorable and respectable life.[198] This opinion is shared by all the wise men of the secular world. There is not one among them who does not declare that this cult of finery comes from vain stupidity, so that a Christian woman should be ashamed to follow the pagans—not those sage and wise men, nor those virtuous and honorable

195. Plutarch, "Advice to Bride and Groom," *Moralia,* 142C.

196. Plutarch, "Advice to Bride and Groom," *Moralia,* 141E.

197. *Opuscula graecorum veterum sententiosa et moralia,* ed. Ioannes Conradus Orellius (Leipzig, 1819), vol. 1, p. 89. These sayings are attributed in the sources to a certain Democrates but may have originated with the Greek philosopher Democritus.

198. Aristotle *Economics* 1.3, 1344a (Barnes 1 : 2132).

matrons, but the errors of stupid men and the examples of foolish women. And I confess that I cannot explain what verbal pretext women can use to excuse their adornment except that they may appear more beautiful and thereby attract men the more.

67. But even pagan women would be ashamed to acknowledge this. I shall speak to Christian women: "Is it to ensnare the souls of men more easily and more tightly?" "The desire to please by exterior embellishment does not come from a pure conscience," says Tertullian, "for we know that to be an invitation to lust."[199] Chrysostom does not include among the number of virgins those who devote themselves to preening and adorning themselves.[200] How much less would he do so if they have done it to enflame the lust of those that looked at them! Therefore, at one and the same time, you will be a slave to your vanity and will spread the nets of the devil in your body to capture the souls of those who look upon you. You are no Christian woman but the servant and accomplice of the devil! The dire threat of the wrathful Lord will be uttered against you, for God speaks thus through Isaiah:

> Because the daughters of Zion are haughty and walked with out-stretched necks and went about with wanton looks, mincing along with measured step, with scaly shoes, the Lord will lay bare the heads of the daughters of Zion and will expose their baseness and in place of adornment there will be ignominy. In that day the Lord will take away the finery of their anklets, their crescents and necklaces and pendants and bracelets and turbans and head-dress and leg-bands and amulets and perfume-boxes and earrings and rings and jewels hanging from their foreheads and capes and mantles and linens and pins and mirrors and muslins and head-bands and summer garments. And in-stead of a sweet fragrance there will be a stench and instead of a girdle a rope and instead of curly and well-kept hair baldness and instead of rich robes a haircloth.[201]

So he says of women.

68. About men who, because of women, surrendered themselves like slaves to vile and unworthy things, he says, "Your beautiful men will fall by the sword and your brave men in battle, and her gates will lament and mourn, and the city will sit desolate upon the ground."[202] These are the

199. Tertullian *On Female Adornment* 2.2 (*PL* 1:1317).
200. John Chrysostom, *Homily 8 on 1 Tim. 2* (*NPNF*, 1st ser., 13:433).
201. Isa. 3:16–24.
202. Isa. 3:25–26.

words of the Lord God, terrible when he is angered, and his holy martyr
Cyprian has this to say:

> But there are some rich women, endowed with an abundance of
> wealth, who make ostentation of their riches and claim that they are
> making use of their own resources. Let them know first of all that she
> is rich who is rich in God; she is wealthy, who is wealthy in Christ;
> true blessings are those that are spiritual, divine, heavenly, that remain
> to us with God as an eternal possession. But if you deck yourself out
> too elaborately and walk about in public in such a way as to attract
> attention and draw the glances of young men and have them sighing
> after you, encourage lustful desires, kindle the fires of sin, so that if
> you yourself do not perish you cause the perdition of others, and lend
> yourself as a sword and poison to those who see you, you cannot be
> excused from blame as if you were chaste and modest in mind. Your
> shameless apparel and immodest adornment have convicted you. You
> can no longer be numbered among the young girls and virgins of
> Christ, since you live in such a way as to be an object of sexual pas-
> sion. You say that you are rich and a virgin, but it does not become a
> virgin to boast of her riches since the divine scripture says: 'What has
> pride profited us, or what has boasting of riches brought us? All those
> things have passed away like a shadow.'[203] You say you are wealthy
> and rich, and you think you must use the things that God has wished
> you to possess. Use them, but for the good of your soul; use them, but
> for good works; use them for what God has ordained, for what the
> Lord has taught you. Let the poor feel that you are rich, let the needy
> know that you are wealthy. Invest your patrimony in God, give nour-
> ishment to Christ.[204]

Thus speaks the martyr.

69. Fulgentius elucidates further:

> Let the dress of a sacred virgin be such as to bear witness to her inte-
> rior chastity. One should not seek magnificence in the dress of the
> exterior person lest that of the interior person be sullied. The virgin
> who affects adornment of her bodily clothing despoils her soul of the
> splendor of virtue. She who rouses allurement in those who behold
> her does not possess true chastity. She who wishes to please the crowd

---

203. Wisd. of Sol. 5:8–9.
204. Cyprian *On the Dress of Young Women* 7.9–11 (PL 4:458–62).

rather than her spouse does not keep faith with Christ. Of necessity, therefore, one who sows concupiscence in the sight of humans will reap anger in the sight of God. A girl should not say when she is adorning herself: 'This dress or necklace will do no harm.' That may be. But by that path the evil-doer and the prompter of ill-will will enter.[205]

These are the words of Fulgentius. In a subject matter so foreign to my way of life and daily habits, I willingly resort to the authority of the holy fathers, so that I shall elicit greater belief from those elegant and sophisticated women who regard it as rustic and silly if one dresses in a Christian manner.

70. Nor is it enough to say as some do, "My conscience is sufficient for me, which I will prove to God." It is enough if you do not hurt your neighbor, if you are not a stumbling block to him that he will collide against. The apostle wishes that our modesty be known to all men,[206] not for our glory, but as the Lord says, "So that they may see your good works and glorify Your Father who is in heaven."[207] The same apostle says that in order not to offend his brother, he will never eat meat.[208] And will you not consent to cover your breast and refrain from putting another face over your own, so that you will not lead him into a snare? Where, then, is charity for your neighbor, to whom you prefer, I shall not say your dress, but the ostentation of your dress?

Tertullian says sternly, "It is not enough for Christian modesty that it exist, but also that it appear so."[209] Its fullness should be such that it should emanate from the soul to the external garb. Or do you not remember that your mother Eve was the cause of man's destruction? Do you wish to rival her in this? How much better it would be if you lamented the sin of your sex in clothes of mourning rather than incite the concupiscence of young men with your splendid attire! After you have enslaved some men to the devil by your snares, how will you extricate them when you want to? How will you rescue them from the servitude of the devil to the freedom of Christ? With what rites of atonement will you expiate such a nefarious deed? Are you gambling in such a critical situation, no more certain of another's skin than of your own?

205. Fulgentius *Letters* 3.22 (*PL* 65:332).
206. Phil. 4:5.
207. Matt. 5:16.
208. 1 Cor. 8:13.
209. Tertullian *On Female Adornment* 2.13 (*PL* 1.1332).

But some may object: "This is the very scandal we are trying to avoid in our dress, for others better dressed than we will interpret our mediocrity of dress as a reproof to them, since we are no less well-born than they and no less wealthy." Let them be, according to the advice of our Redeemer, because they are blind, and leaders of the blind,[210] and wish to be offended rather than challenged. If they are scandalized by your good actions, why should you not be by their evil actions? They are offended because you adorn yourselves according to the precept of the apostles. You are more greatly offended because they follow the will and precepts of the devil. That would be a fine example of zeal for your neighbor if you bring about the damnation of both you and him to avoid giving him offense! How different those fastidious girls who, even in doing good, cannot tolerate other women.

71. Someone may ask, "Do you want women to be dirty and squalid?" I certainly do not, and my teaching is not sordid, nor was uncleanliness ever a thing to my liking. I wish that the apostolic rule that I set out at the beginning of this chapter[211] be observed. It does not prescribe that women be unclean, or filthy, or unsightly in their squalor and neglect, covered with dirt and rags, but it discourages them from immoderate adornment and persuades them to dress plainly and simply. Simplicity has its own refinement, purer than that of luxury, as it is easier to protect a small vessel than elaborate furnishings. She will not dress in silk but in wool; not in lace but ordinary linen; her dress will not be resplendent, neither will it be squalid. She will not be an object of admiration, nor one of repugnance. Female cosmetics are named after the word for cleanliness,[212] not artifice or opulence of gold, silver, pearls, or precious stones. I do not see the use of this sumptuousness unless it be said that some of these stones are valued more for their power than for mere display, like corals and emeralds, if nature really did give these tiny minerals the powers they are said to possess. But how few there are who seek out these stones for that reason and not rather for the sake of vanity so that they may be thought to be richer? The use of silks is less widespread, because they become frayed in a short time; the investment is lost and the cost is too great for domestic finances.

72. Therefore, my ideal young woman will not paint her face, but clean it; she will not smear it with soap, but wash it with water. She will not bleach

210. Matt. 15:14.

211. Cf. par. 52.

212. Varro *On the Latin Language* 5.129. Both the Greek *kosmos* and the Latin word *munditia* have this meaning of cleanliness.

her hair in the sun or dye it to change its color, but at the same time she will not leave it unkempt or bristling with dandruff. She will keep her head free of perspiration and dirtiness. She will not delight in delicate perfumes, but will like malodor even less. She will look in the mirror not to preen and adorn herself painstakingly but to make sure nothing in her face and on her head appears ridiculous or repulsive, which she cannot see without looking in the mirror. Then she will groom herself in such a way that there is nothing in her countenance that would defile her chastity and modesty. Finally, she will consider the counsel that Socrates used to give his followers as addressed to her, viz., that when beholding themselves in the mirror, those who were beautiful should take care that their souls were not ugly, and if they were ugly they should compensate for their physical ugliness by their beauty of soul.[213] In all of this the chaste woman will always bear in mind that physical beauty has often driven those who possess it to great arrogance and those who behold it to foul and abominable acts of lust, which contributed to the perdition of both parties. Wherefore it came about that many holy women took pains to neglect their appearance as much as possible in order to seem less beautiful than they were and not fall into that quagmire I mentioned above.

73. These observations I have made concerning personal adornment based on the teachings of Christ are applicable to all women but especially to unmarried women, since for some reason or other the custom has prevailed that some of them are more elegantly adorned than married women. In my opinion, however, I think it more reputable that at times a wife appear in public more richly adorned, if it so pleases her husband, than an unmarried woman, whatever her station or lineage. A wife adorns herself for her husband, but the virgin belongs entirely to Christ, for whom she bedecks herself. For to ask for or seek out a husband is not a mark of true virginity, as I shall point out in the proper place. For that reason the apostle said, "The unmarried young girl thinks about what pertains to the Lord, how to be holy in body and spirit. The married woman is concerned with worldly affairs, how she may please her husband."[214]

I do not think I need to advise a woman against putting on men's clothing and attire. To do so would be a clear sign of a masculine audacity and astonishing impudence in a woman's heart. In the distinction of dress, modesty is preserved, which is the parent and guardian of chastity, and we must harken to the Lord's prohibition in these words of Deuteronomy: "A woman

213. Plutarch, "Advice to Bride and Groom," *Moralia*, 141D.
214. 1 Cor. 7:34.

shall not wear a man's clothing nor shall a man put on a woman's clothing, for whoever does this is an abomination to God."[215] Nature made a sharp distinction of sexes in the bodies of living things. If we cover the body and divert the attention of those we meet from that natural distinction by means of a suitable covering, as is proper, we must see to it that our clothes give visible sign of that distinction and do not obscure what nature has clearly marked. Therefore, one who is ambiguous in dress is justly called abominable by the Lord, since he is attempting something that is contrary to the laws of nature, which would give rise to many perils in human society. But no woman attempts such a thing unless she has already cast off her chastity together with her sense of modesty. For whom my precepts will be of no use, nor are they written for her.

215. Deut. 22:5.

IX

ON THE SOLITUDE
OF THE VIRGIN

74. So powerful is the kingdom of Satan in this world here below, so great is the conspiracy for evil that thrives in it, so obstinately do the common people defend their own vices that no one can venture forth into public without his soul being assailed immediately through all his senses by things pernicious to virtue and piety. It was wisely said by our forefathers that through all the senses as through windows, death bursts in upon the soul or stealthily penetrates its defenses. For which reason we must keep constant watch over the soul, and man's life on earth must be thought of as a warfare, as Job said.[216] Like that prophet and courageous fighter, let us be on our guard and fix our firm footing on the battlements. The young woman should seldom open these doors of the senses, fraught with danger, and when she does so, every care and precaution must be taken, lest the enemy make a sudden attack if she be lacking in strength or infiltrate themselves by cunning if she be lacking in prudence. An unmarried young woman should rarely appear in public, since she has no business there and her most precious possession, chastity, is placed in jeopardy. Not only should she be accompanied by her mother when she issues from her house but even when she is staying quietly at home, and this is enjoined upon mothers as well.

75. Jerome advises Laeta that when she has to go to her country home, she should not leave her daughter alone in her house in the city. He says, "Let her not know how or be able to live without you, and when she is alone let her have fear."[217] I understand this to mean that the mother should take her daughter with her if she is going to be away for some time. Otherwise it is not necessary that the daughter should always accompany her mother

216. Job 7:1.
217. Jerome *Letters* 107.11 (*NPNF*, 2d ser., 6:194).

every time she leaves the house, especially if the mother is going to a banquet or a wedding or a meeting at which men are present, or any similar destination where it would not be proper to take a young woman, whether she do this as part of her duty or to comply with her husband's wishes. There should be some upright woman in the home who will be a guardian of her chastity, since there is no greater or more pernicious plague than that which is nurtured at home. How can you be rid of it without expelling it altogether? What good is it to protect wood from every external harm if it is being eaten away from the inside?

76. I know a very virtuous woman who was entrusted with the care of girls and let her sons play with them in a rather free manner, because she was too fond of her children and could not bear reproving them or keeping them from offending the code of chastity. Therefore, provision must be made that the matron to whom the girl is confided does not have men, children, or brothers in her house who are inclined to licentiousness or unruliness, or persons to whom she does not dare offer resistance for the protection of the charges committed to her. She should not only be chaste but should earn respect and admiration through her facial expression and the austerity of her wisdom, morals, and conversation. Her eyes and the sternness of her brow, not to speak of her voice, should inspire esteem in everyone, even her elder brothers. She should fear no one in the fulfilling of her duties of guardian, and her presence alone should ensure that chastity be safeguarded. Anything that would invite to lasciviousness and lust by its example should be kept as far away as possible.

The woman in the pay of a lover, who encourages with words and instigates to evildoing, is not worthy to be called human, for she is something diabolical; the young girl will avoid her as if she were an asp or a viper, and she should be driven out of the city like a public scourge. There are no words to describe the evils that are caused by women such as these. Therefore, the young girl should not even tolerate the sight of them, for they are basilisks or *katoblepae*[218] that transmit a deadly poison from their eyes and annihilate you with a single glance. Let no one think that I am exaggerating. Some of these women are so skillful that they can often captivate you with their eyes with no words spoken. Others make use of spells and incantations, and would to God examples of these black arts were more rare. Why, by a mere greeting or smile or even a look, this serpent can defile a girl upon whom it has gazed, especially in the house of those who know the woman's

---

218. Literally in Greek, "that looks down." Like the fabled basilisk, it killed whatever it looked at. Cf. Pliny *Natural History* 8.32.

black art, not to mention the ineradicable dishonor that is stamped upon a house they have set foot in.

You must flee to your mother as to a sanctuary, and recount to her what the wicked woman attempted to do, or you must avoid and turn away from her in disgust to make clear to the onlookers that you fear her like the plague. In that way you will benefit yourself by your action and others by example, showing other young girls how much she is to be feared. It is up to the state to investigate haggard old women so that the official charged with public morals may know what is the source of their livelihood. If there is no visible support, they will surely become procuresses and sorceresses.

77. Concerning female companions, Jerome has this to say: "I do not wish a woman to love one servant more than another and continually whisper secrets into her ear. Whatever she says to one must be known to all. She should have a companion who is not elegantly adorned or beautiful and frivolous, who can modulate sweet songs in a clear voice, but one who is grave, pale, shabbily dressed, and somewhat melancholy."[219] He gives the same advice to Demetrias.[220] In choosing female companions, one must avoid any that may harm us by their personal adornments or by their lascivious words and amusements. Have nothing at all to do with girls who enjoy being looked at and being loved, who boast that they have a handsome or rich or elegant or noble lover and carry around with them letters written by him. From time to time they show them to girls of their own age or recount words and episodes. "He did this, he said this, he accosted me like this, he praised me like this." Out on these acquaintances, no matter if they be neighbors, wealthy close friends, relatives by blood or by marriage! And even if they are sisters, deny that they are. They have been bitten by the devil, a mad dog, and they have become rabid, in which case no name is so dear that it should lure us into their company. On the contrary, sister is smothered by sister, brother by brother, and son by mother.

78. The young woman, therefore, will amuse herself in the company of young women of her own age, sometimes in respectable and ladylike entertainments, sometimes in pious readings or conversations suggested by the reading. She should not recount stories about dancing and banquets and entertainment, lest her companions be stirred up by the false appearance of pleasure. No man should be present. Then, when she is alone in her bedroom after her companions have left, she must not remain without doing anything, for it is dangerous for her to be idle, especially when alone. "She

---

219. Jerome *Letters* 107.9 (*NPNF*, 2d ser., 6:193).
220. Jerome *Letters* 130.18 (*NPNF*, 2d ser., 6:270).

can be safer in a crowd," said Ovid of such a woman.[221] Neither is it safe for them to surrender their mind to thoughts, however honorable and pious they may be at first. A woman's thoughts are inconstant and they do not remain easily fixed in one place. She could descend from good thoughts to bad with very little trouble. Publilius Syrus, the writer of mimes, was right in saying, "When a woman thinks alone, she thinks bad thoughts."[222]

79. Mary Magdalen, sitting at the feet of the Lord listening to his words,[223] did not enjoy the contemplation of heavenly things only at that moment but while she was reading, listening, or praying. Not only should I wish my ideal young woman to do this, but any other woman, for in many passages in this book we give instructions to women in general. Therefore, she should read and pray when she is alone on feast days, and on ordinary working days as well, or be intent on manual work. Undoubtedly, the angel found Mary occupied in something of that nature when he brought his tidings. She was alarmed when the religious and habitual silence that was never interrupted was broken by a voice, which, although majestic in tone, was like that of a man. For that reason, she is called *alma* in Hebrew, which means "hidden virgin."[224] She it is of whom Isaiah speaks when he says, "Behold a hidden virgin will conceive and will bring forth God and man."[225] In the end, that virgin conceived Christ, and no one knew her but Christ.

80. Therefore, the young woman shall not admit anyone into her house except at her father's explicit command. She will begin little by little to assist her mother in domestic duties and will hold her mother and father in deep affection above all else after God himself. If they bid her to occupy herself in the working of wool or flax or some other constructive task, she will set about it not only obediently but with alacrity. She will do it with all the more diligence and skillfulness if the fruits of that labor will return to her parents as part of her daily sustenance. This will make her very happy, and she will think she is making requital for part of the great debt she owes her parents and recompensing them for the nurture she received from them.

When the young woman has acquitted herself of her household chores and can be alone to pray, let her first consecrate and dedicate herself wholly to God, venerate Christ and his mother, and ask pardon and peace from them. Then let her consider that she is a Christian virgin, the spouse of

221. Ovid *The Remedy of Love* 580.
222. Publilius Syrus 376.
223. Luke 7:38; John 11:32.
224. Jerome *Against Jovinianus* 1.32 (*NPNF*, 2d ser., 6:370).
225. Isa. 7:14.

Christ, the imitator of Mary. Virginity of body is nothing if it is not accompanied by purity of mind. If that is present, there is nothing purer, nothing more pleasing to God. As a follower of the most holy Mother of God, she must first of all reproduce in herself Mary's unrivalled virtue, her modesty and moderation of spirit, which we commonly call humility. This was so preeminent in her that when the greatest and most sublime blessing fell to her lot, nothing would exalt her in spirit and inspire arrogance in her, this noblest of women, who counted in her lineage fourteen kings and as many princes of Israel, born of rich parents, enriched by the gifts of the Magi, most beautiful, most talented, most learned, and most wise. But in the midst of all this, what equanimity of soul she displayed and lowly opinion of herself! Already conscious that she would give birth to a divine offspring and would be the mother of such a glorious Son, she did not disdain to minister to her artisan husband nor to visit her relative[226] and assist her in her pregnancy and converse with her.

To whom did she prefer herself? What woman did she look down upon despite her lineage, beauty, talent, and dignity? To whom did she not esteem herself inferior, she who surpassed even the angels, of whom she was destined to be queen? For that reason I do not approve that the divine virgin should be depicted in silk and golden garments, adorned with gems and large pearls, as if she had delighted in these things when she dwelt among mortals. In some places her image even has a set of matching articles and clothes to suit the season, if you please, when many mortals lack even everyday vesture. Nothing is of less importance to her. I would prefer that her temperateness of soul be presented more vividly before our eyes in that simple attire to which she was accustomed as a silent refutation of our pride so that the rich will be confuted and at the same time instructed, and the poor consoled. The latter would increase in courage, the former diminish in haughtiness, both brought back to a just proportion, not that the rich will despair or the poor become too confident, but that a certain equality exist between them.

81. My young woman will follow the example of the glorious Virgin, not with a feigned and simulated spirit but with true and certain intention, lest under the mask of virtue there lurk a more deadly and pernicious vice, a poison under the guise of health and a sickness concealed by a sound and healthy skin and under this cover evading cure. Let women do nothing that is counterfeit and feigned so that they may appear good, nor should they hope to change or deceive nature. Things that are simulated do not have

226. Luke 1:39.

the same validity as things that are true. That which is feigned is weak and ineffectual. In the end they give themselves away or they are exposed. Therefore, the young woman should be in very fact what she appears to be externally. She must both appear and be humble, chaste, modest, and up-right. In that way she will become more acceptable to the Blessed Virgin, of whom her life will be the true and exact reproduction, and to Christ as well, who will acknowledge in her a spouse worthy of him.

She will pray first for herself that she may grow in piety, in her com-mitment to holy chastity, and in the other virtues. Next she will pray for her parents, brothers, sisters, relatives, and others for whom it is fitting that she pray to God. Her prayers, too, will be most pleasing to God and efficacious in obtaining whatever she asks, since they proceed from a pure, unsullied spirit and one that is genuinely Christian. I wish her to understand what she is saying in her prayers, whether she prays in a language she knows or, if in Latin, that someone will tell her beforehand what it means. She is not to think that adoration consists in murmuring and movement of the lips, but in the mind and in contemplation, when she raises the soul from vile earthly concerns to the heavenly and divine. This is what we are asked to do in the holy sacrifice of the Mass when it is said, "Lift up your hearts" and we re-spond, "We have lifted them up to the Lord."[227] A great many of the faithful lie when they say this, since their heart is fixed and sunk in some lowly and sordid concern of this world, and that care which has cast them down will not allow them to raise their minds. Christ proclaims that true worshipers are those who worship the Father in spirit;[228] this worship is pleasing to him and these are the prayers most acceptable to him. Be sure, then, that your mind and spirit are not in disaccord with your words. What is said externally must correspond with what is said internally. Or she may be as silent as you please externally or speak of other things, provided that internally she cries out to the Lord and can say with the spouse: "I sleep, but my heart wakes."[229]

227. These words are spoken at the Preface just before the Canon, the central part of the Mass.
228. John 4:23.
229. Song of Sol. 5:2.

X

ON THE VIRTUES OF A WOMAN
AND THE EXAMPLES SHE
SHOULD IMITATE

82. The young woman will learn of the virtues of her sex from books she will read or hear read to her. It is fitting, certainly, that every woman should be endowed with virtues of every sort, but some are particularly necessary to her, just as while all vices are ugly, certain vices are abominable and execrable. There are some virtues that pertain more to married women and others proper to widows, but I shall speak of those that belong to every condition of women. Above all, she should be aware that the principal female virtue is chastity, and it is in itself the equal of all the others in moral worth. If this is present, one need not look for others, and if it is absent, one should disregard the others. The Stoic philosophers believed that all blessings were contained in wisdom and all misfortunes in stupidity, so that they said that only the wise man was rich, free, king, citizen, beautiful, courageous, happy, and that, conversely, the stupid man was poor, a slave, an exile, a stranger, ugly, cowardly, and unhappy. So with regard to chastity in women, we must consider that the chaste woman is beautiful, charming, gifted, noble, fertile, and possessed of every best and outstanding quality, while the unchaste woman is a sea and storehouse of all evils.

83. The inseparable companions of chastity are a sense of propriety and modest behavior. Chastity (*pudicitia*) seems to be derived from shame (*pudor*), so that one who has no sense of shame cannot be chaste. Chastity is a kind of veil placed over our face, for when nature and reason covered the corrupt body and the sinful flesh because of the shame caused by the first sin but left the face open and free of the coverings that we wear, they did not deny it its cloak, namely, shame. With this covering it could gain human approval so that no one could see it without recognizing that great virtue lay under that covering, and there was none who did not esteem one so

clothed or hate one who was without it. "He blushed," said the father of the son in the comedy, "All's well."[230] And the wise man to the young man red with blushing, "Be confident, my son, this is the color of virtue." If this is said of men, what should be thought of women and young maidens?

The Lord curses the unchaste woman, saying, "Your brow has become that of a prostitute, you have lost all shame."[231] Not only is shame considered to ennoble our face, but it is essential to it, so that the words countenance, face, and brow have become synonymous with shame and modesty. That is the origin of proverbs dating back to earliest times: "To have no face," "To have a stern face, a tender countenance,"[232] and the like, which signify shame or lack of shame. From the sense of shame come modesty and moderation, whether in thought, words, or actions, so that in all our conduct there will be nothing that is immoderate, arrogant, insolent, lascivious, offensive, unruly, boastful, or pretentious.

84. She should not think that she deserves honors, nor should she seek them. On the contrary, she shall avoid them, and if they should fall to her lot, she should feel ashamed of them as if they were unmerited. She will not grow proud of anything, neither beauty nor charm nor race nor wealth, knowing they will quickly perish, while eternal punishment is reserved for pride. Sobriety promotes continence as drunkenness impairs it. No one is ignorant of the consequences of excessive drinking. Sobriety also engenders parsimony and frugality. These qualities are the function of the woman in the management of the household, as Plato and Aristotle rightly taught: "The man acquires, the woman guards and preserves."[233] Therefore, he was given more initiative and it was taken away from her so that he would strive more energetically and she would hold on to things more carefully. From this sobriety in material concerns will flow a similar moderation of spirit, so that feelings will not run riot as if intoxicated and disturb the tranquillity of virtue, but that she may both act well and use good sense. Let her be dedicated to piety and content with little, satisfied with her present situation. "Piety with acceptance of what one has is a great gain,"[234] according to the apostle. She will not seek what is absent or what belongs to another, whence arise envy and rivalry and curiosity about things that belong to others.

230. Terence *The Brothers* 643.

231. Jer. 3:3.

232. Erasmus *Adages* I viii 47 (*CWE* 32:149).

233. Aristotle *Economics* 1.3, 1343b (Barnes 2:2131).

234. 1 Tim. 6:6.

Especially proper to the female sex is devotion to sacred things. There is nothing more repugnant than a woman averse to religion; she should be avoided and detested like an ill-omened apparition.

85. She must frequently do battle with envy, which, shameful as it is for women to the point of absurdity, in some strange way afflicts that sex relentlessly. But one who is possessed of moderation and who is amply satisfied with simple necessities will have no desire to be envious of another or curious about some one else's home. A woman who is chaste and moderate and sober-minded will never be carried away by anger or give vent to abusiveness or be swept away by violence and inhumanity. Since it behooves the female sex to be meek and benevolent by nature in that it is weak and much in need of the help of others, who would tolerate uncontrolled anger and cruelty in a woman, which would make her wish to lose what she cannot preserve if she had need to? And who would suffer a mind that does not forget an injury, waiting for the occasion to avenge it? A woman of this kind is worthy of being visited with so many evils that, overwhelmed and shaken by their number and magnitude, she would admit defeat and cease to think of anger and revenge and other insanities, and be anxious only for her salvation.

We see this occur often to many by the just judgment of God, and not without the approval of those to whom her violence and cruelty were well known. Incautious women have to face a struggle with savage beasts—pride, anger, and envy—because to their inconstant and weak minds, every offense seems grave and intolerable and deserving of fierce revenge. It is no wonder that slight and minute matters present themselves to their inexperienced and defective eyes as huge and insuperable, all the more so because they are obscured by a cloud or by smoke. And so if these women do not avoid these terrible enemies by their ingenuity or conquer them by sheer endurance, there is danger that they will be undone by them and will suffer unending torment both in this life and in the next.

86. I think it is abundantly clear that chastity is, so to speak, the queen of female virtues. Two inseparable companions follow: modesty and sobriety, which it engenders, and from these two the whole chorus and firmament of female virtues is composed and fashioned: modesty, moderation, frugality, parsimony, diligence in household duties, the observance of religious obligations, meekness. Although I will expound on all these virtues in greater detail in other parts of the work, the young woman will find more copious treatments of the subject in the writings of wise and holy men. Contemplate the image of moral rectitude as it is delineated, a thing of such beauty and preeminence of form that if it could be seen by bodily eyes, as Plato writes in

the *Phaedrus*,[235] it would arouse extraordinary love in us. No other beauty so captures and entrances us as moral integrity, which, if it were revealed and shown to us, would sweep us away and carry us off with it.

87. Then the young woman will collect examples of virgins from what she hears and reads, which she will hold up to herself for imitation. She will desire to be like them and will make every effort to bring this about. The first model to place before herself, as I have said, is the queen and glory of virginity, Mary, the mother of Christ, God and man, whose life should be the exemplar not only for virgins to follow but for married women and widows as well. She became all things to all so that she might inspire and lead all women to the example of her chastity and of all lofty virtues. To virgins she was a most humble virgin, to married women a most chaste spouse, to widows a most pious widow. She was the first to enter upon this road of virginity, unknown to previous centuries, with great courage and pious determination. She was the first who lived in marriage a life above that of ordinary mortals, without carnal relations, an angelic life, taking not a husband, but a guardian of her chastity. Since these were miraculous things, so by a greater miracle, to the astonishment of nature, she brought forth a Son to the world. When she had become a widow, since her whole life was based on the spirit and though living in the body she had raised herself above the condition of the body, she found in God alone a most obedient Son, a most chaste spouse, and a most indulgent father, so that she who had despised all things for the sake of God found all things in God.

88. But, what am I about, Virgin Divine? What am I undertaking? To tell of your infinite praise? But this is a task beyond my dull wit, lack of eloquence, and narrow limits of this work. It would require a great amount of leisure time, a very practiced eloquence, a superior and very learned intelligence. Imitate her, virgins, all you who wish to preserve your chastity. Imitate her, you married women, whose concern it is to please your husbands and to fulfil the oath you made. Look to her at all times, you widows, and you will receive from her solace for your departed spouse, counsel for watching over your offspring, and a most useful example for passing the rest of your lives. Thousands from among our ranks have followed her mode of life, as the psalmist had foretold: "Virgins shall be led to the king in her train."[236] Their works are not only beneficial for the present moment but will be a model for all generations to come.

History is not silent about virgins in pagan times, ennobled by chastity

---

235. Plato *Phaedrus* 250D.

236. Ps. 45:15.

alone. Jerome does not hesitate to include a catalogue of them taken from Greek history in his polemic against Jovinian,[237] because he saw that in matters of this sort people are forcefully moved by example, since it does not seem difficult to do things that were once done. He introduced the examples of many women who preferred to sacrifice their lives rather than their chastity. I will not insult this revered and holy man by passing over what he compiled as if it were superfluous, or putting it into other words as if I could say it better. Rather, I shall transcribe just what he put down, which is as follows:

89.

When the thirty tyrants[238] of Athens had slain Pheidon at a banquet, they ordered his daughters to be brought to them and to be stripped like harlots and to cavort with unseemly gestures on the floor stained with their father's blood. They concealed their feelings of sorrow for a while, and then when they saw that the guests were drunk, they left the banquet hall as if to answer the needs of nature, embraced one another and plunged into a well to preserve their virginity by their death. The virgin daughter of Demotion, leader of the Areopagites, hearing of the death of her promised spouse Leosthenes,[239] who had stirred up the Lamian war, killed herself. She declared that although still unsullied, if she were forced to take another man, it would be the equivalent of having a second husband since in her heart she was still married to the first. The Spartans and the Messenians had a long friendship with each other, to such an extent that they even exchanged virgins for certain sacred rites. On one occasion when the Messenians tried to violate fifty virgins sent by the Lacedaemonians, of that great number none consented to their debauchery, but all willingly died for their chastity. Whence there arose a grave and prolonged war and after a long time the Mamertines[240] were defeated.

237. Jovinian was a monk who came to Rome probably from the northern Italy. He denied the superiority of virginity over matrimony, affirming that baptismal grace was given to all equally. His doctrines were condemned by Ambrose in a synod in Milan about A.D.390, and Jerome wrote his treatise, *Against Jovinianus*, in 393. It drew much criticism for its exaggerated and polemical tone, which Jerome answered in three letters to his friends in Rome, letters 48–50.

238. After the defeat of Athens in the Peloponnesian War, Lysander appointed thirty men to run the government. They lasted for only one year, from the spring of 404 BC to May 403 BC. This story concerning Pheidon, one of the thirty, is related only in Jerome *Against Jovinianus* 1.44 (*NPNF*, 2d ser., 6:381).

239. Leosthenes was an Athenian commander who defeated Antipater, Alexander's general, but was then killed by a stone while besieging the town of Lamia in 322 B.C.E.

240. The Mamertines were mercenary troops who had made themselves masters of the town of Messene in Sicily.

Aristoclides,[241] tyrant of Orchomenus, fell in love with a young girl of Stymphalus, who after her father was killed, took refuge at the shrine of Diana and, embracing her statue, could not be dragged away by force. She was run through on that very spot. All of Arcadia was so moved with sorrow at her death that war was declared officially and the virgin's murder was avenged. Aristomenes of Messenia,[242] a man of highest integrity, after the defeat of the Lacedaemonians, while they were celebrating nocturnal rites called the Hyacinthia,[243] carried off fifteen virgins from the chorus of dancers and fleeing through the night at a swift pace, left the borders of the Spartans behind him. When his companions wished to violate them, he warned them as sternly as he could not to do so and finally had to kill some who did not obey, which deterred the others. Afterwards the young girls were ransomed by their relatives, and seeing that Aristomenes was accused of murder, they would not return to their native country until, prostrate at the feet of the judges, they saw the defender of their chastity acquitted.

90.

What words of praise should be reserved for the daughters of Scedasus in Leuctra in Boeotia?[244] It is related that in the absence of their father they showed hospitality to two young men passing through the city, who, having indulged too much in wine, ravished the virgins in the course of the night. Not wishing to go on living after the loss of their virginity, they killed each other. Nor would it be right to omit mention the virgins of Locris, who were sent to Ilium according to a custom which had lasted for nearly a thousand years, and yet not one of them gave rise to slanderous talk concerning her reputation or the defilement of her virginity. Who could pass over in silence the seven virgins of Miletus, who, when the Gauls were sacking the city,

---

241. Either Jerome or the textual tradition is in error here; the tyrant's name was Aristocrates. The story is told in Pausanias *Guide to Greece* 8.5.11.

242. Aristomenes was a legendary hero of the Peloponnesian state of Messenia who resisted the incursions of neighboring Sparta.

243. The Hyacinthia was a mid-July festival held in Amyclae in Lacedaemonia honoring Hyacinth, beloved of Apollo.

244. The battle of Leuctra in 371 BCE took place near the tomb of the young girls who had been ravished by the Spartans some years previously and had then taken their lives. The spirit of Scedasus appeared to a general of the Theban army and requested the sacrifice of a white colt at the tomb. Plutarch, "Love Stories," *Moralia*, 773C–774D.

escaped disgrace by taking their lives rather than suffer any indignity from the enemy, leaving an example to all virgins that for noble souls chastity is a matter of greater concern than life? After the conquest and subjection of Thebes Nicanor[245] was overwhelmed with love for a young maiden he had taken captive. He sought to marry her and wished to receive her willing embraces, which one might expect a captive maiden would desire. But he realized that virginity was dearer to chaste minds than kingly power when with tears of mourning he held her in his arms, slain by her own hand. Greek writers tell of another virgin, also of Thebes, whom a Macedonian soldier had defiled. For a little while she concealed her sorrow but later while her ravisher was asleep, she cut his throat and then killed herself with the same sword, for she neither wished to continue to live after the loss of her chastity nor die without having avenged herself.[246]

91. Jerome relates all these stories so that, if there is any shame at all, Christian women may be ashamed, who, too little chaste, preserve their virtue under the most chaste Christ, son of the most chaste Mary, within the most chaste Church; while pagan women, worshipers of foul Jupiter and immoral Venus, have preferred chastity to the most priceless things of this world. Why should I bring forward examples of holy virgins to move those who are not ashamed to hear tell of the chastity of pagan women? Whom shall I propose for their imitation of the thousands that present themselves to us? Shall I mention Thecla[247] or Agnes[248] or Catherine[249] or Lucia[250] or Caecilia[251] or Agatha[252] or Barbara[253] or Margaret[254] or Dorothea?[255] Or,

245. Nicanor was a general of Alexander the Great involved in the destruction of Thebes in 335 B.C.E.

246. Jerome *Against Jovinianus* 1.41 (*NPNF* 2d ser., 6:380).

247. Cf. par. 25 n. above.

248. Saint Agnes was a Roman maiden martyred under Diocletian at the age of 12 or 13. She became the patroness of chastity.

249. Cf. par. 25 n. above.

250. Little is known of the life of Saint Lucia. She is said to have been martyred in Syracuse, where her tomb still exists in the catacomb named after her.

251. Saint Caecilia, one of the most famous of Roman martyrs, is patroness of music.

252. Saint Agatha was born in Catania and is mentioned in all the martyrologies.

253. Cf. par. 25 n. above.

254. Margaret is an Eastern saint born in Antioch, denounced by her father as a Christian, and decapitated, perhaps during the reign of Diocletian.

255. Saint Dorothea was a legendary martyr of Caesarea in Cappodocia.

rather, the army of eleven thousand virgins,[256] all of whom, marvelous to relate, preferred to face death rather than to offer their bodies to the lust of the enemy? You could hardly find among two men this unanimity in a holy cause that remained so firm and fixed in eleven thousand tender virgins. What number can be devised for those women who readily and willingly allowed themselves to have their throats cut, be slain, dismembered, suffocated, drowned, cut to pieces, burned alive, as long as they could preserve their chastity?

Not wishing to take their own lives, they sought death by clever stratagems when their chastity was at stake, like Brasilla,[257] a virgin of noble birth from Dyracchium, who, seeing that the cruel conqueror had designs on her chastity, made a pact with him that if he respected her virginity, she would give him an herb whose juice smeared over his body would make him invulnerable to all weapons. The soldier accepted the condition. She pulled up the first herb that came to hand in a nearby garden and invited him to test its efficacy on her. Smearing it on her throat she said: "Strike here to make proof of it, for there can be no doubt of its power." He struck and killed the virgin.

And what am I to say if even Jerome does not seem to condemn a woman who kills herself to preserve her chastity? And Ambrose on this question adduces the example of the martyr Pelagia in the third book of his *On Virgins*, saying: "There is no need to justify it when it is the deed of a fifteen-year old martyr, who threw herself into a river together with her mother and sisters."[258] Eusebius in his *Ecclesiastical History* relates that when the noblewoman Sophronia saw her husband, prefect of the city, hesitating and indecisive in defending her chastity from the lust of Maximinus, she secluded herself in her bedroom and plunged a sword into her breast. By the consensus of the church she was admitted into the list of martyrs.[259]

92. All these examples of chastity are read in church, and will an unchaste woman dare enter therein? Does she not shudder to introduce a

256. Saint Ursula and her companions are said to have suffered martyrdom at the hands of the Huns in Cologne in defense of their chastity.

257. Vives got this story from Francesco Barbaro, *On Marriage*, who in turn took it from the *Memorandarum rerum liber* of Giovanni Conversini of Ravenna. The Slavic pirate chieftain was named Ceric. The Venetians were familiar with these stories, since they had long waged wars with the Dalmatian pirates.

258. Ambrose *On Virgins* 3.7.33 (*NPNF*, 2d ser., 10:386).

259. This account is not contained in Eusebius's history as we have it, but in the Latin version of his translator, Rufinus, 8.14.17.

brothel into the company of virgins, to defile their pure eyes with her face, to pollute their delicate hearing with her words? Wicked woman, do you dare pronounce the names of Catherine or Agnes or Barbara, and contaminate their sacred names with your impure mouth? Do you adorn yourself with any of these names and wish to be known by a name to which your morals are inimical? Does it not occur to you when you are called by this name what kind of person she was whose name you bear? When you reflect how pure, chaste, and virtuous she was—whereas you are impure, unchaste, and wicked—do not the Furies hound you night and day? Do they not terrify you and pursue you with flaming torches? O most presumptuous of women, do you dare to celebrate the birthday of the Blessed Virgin, when you did not deserve to be born, and to show your shameless face to her most pure eyes? And do you wish her to look upon you or listen to you, buried in vice, when she, while she dwelt on earth, neither saw nor heard men, not even good men! It would have been better that you never came into their sight so that they would not take vengeance on you for the harm done to their sex, nor be called by one of their names, so that they would not exact punishment of you for the outrage done to that name!

I say in all seriousness, for this is no time for pleasantries, that it should be forbidden by public decree that any overtly unchaste woman should be called Mary. Why should we not render the same homage to that name, at which we rise to our feet and bend the knee, that pagans give to certain names of theirs? In Athens, from the time that Harmodius and Aristogiton had driven the tyrants from the city,[260] it was ordained by public decree that those names would not be given to slaves or anyone who did not exercise a liberal occupation.[261]

---

260. Actually, the attempt of the tyrannicides to kill the tyrant Hippias at the Panathenaic festival of 514 was unsuccessful, but they remained the patriotic symbol for the defeat of tyranny. Cf. Thucydides *History of the Peloponnesian War* 1.20.53.

261. Aulus Gellius *Attic Nights* 9.2.10.

CHAPTER XI

HOW SHE WILL
BEHAVE IN PUBLIC

93. She will appear in public on occasion, but as rarely as possible, for many reasons. First, because every time she issues forth in public she undergoes what we might almost call a fatal judgment of her beauty, modesty, prudence, propriety, and integrity, since there is nothing more fragile or more vulnerable than the reputation and good name of women; it may well seem to hang by a cobweb. That is because those qualities I mentioned are expected in a woman and our judgments are exacting and suspicious, and, as Ovid said: "The masses are prone to detect vice."[262] Moreover, to quote Cicero, "There is nothing more volatile than slander, nothing is uttered more easily, nothing is accepted so quickly, nothing is spread abroad so widely."[263]

If some slur has attached to a girl's reputation from men's opinion of her, it usually remains forever and is not erased except by clear proofs of her chastity and wisdom. If you speak little in public, you are thought to be uneducated; if you speak a lot, you are light-headed; unlearnedly, you are accounted ignorant; learnedly, you are malicious; if you are slow in responding, you are haughty and ill-mannered; ready with an answer, a little push will make you stumble; if you sit with composed mien, then you are a dissembler; if you gesticulate, you are stupid by nature; if you look at something, that means your mind is drawn there; if you laugh when someone else laughs, even if your attention was directed elsewhere, your smile has betrayed you; if you listen to a man, it means you approve of what he says and you will be an easy conquest.

What more can I say? How many occasions there are for corruption and misconduct when one is in public? Dinah, the daughter of Jacob, went

262. Ovid *Fasti* 4.312.

263. Cicero *In Defense of Plancius* 57.

out to see the women of the city. Immediately she found there one by whom she was reduced to shame and dishonor and was violated, which was the reason why all the male population of Shechem, together with their king and his son, were slaughtered by Simeon and Levi.[264] The tragedian was right in saying: "It is an impious act for young women to be seen in public."[265] How much more profitable would it be for them to remain at home than to incur such manifold and unjust criticisms and such imminent dangers! Never so apt was that Greek proverb: "Live a hidden life."[266] For that reason, Thucydides expressed the opinion that in the end, the best woman was the one of whom there was least talk, whether in praise or blame.[267]

94. A woman should live in seclusion and not be known to many. It is a sign of imperfect chastity and of uncertain reputation to be known by a great number of people. What good is it to be talked about all through the city or to be referred to by some mark or characteristic, as light-skinned, lame, cross-eyed, flat-nosed, bowlegged, night-blind, two-faced, small, big, fat, crippled, stuttering? These things should not be commonly known in a good woman. Should she never set foot outside her own house? Evidently that would be a great crime. Must she always hide herself at home, which certain vain women, anxious to see or be seen,[268] interpret to mean in prison for a life sentence?

She should go out at times, if circumstances demand it or a parent orders it. But before she steps over the threshold, let her prepare her mind as if she were entering a combat. Let her think about what she will see, what she will hear, what she will say. Let her reflect within herself that she will be confronted on all sides by things that will perturb and upset her chastity and her good conscience. Against these shafts of the devil hurled from every side, let her take up the shield[269] of a mind fortified with good precepts and examples, a firm commitment to chastity, a mind intent and fixed on Christ. She must not forget that she is pitted against vanity and the tricks and illusions of the devil and she must take care she is not ensnared. She must be persuaded that all she sees around her is nothing but a spectacle of human life, and not only must she not be corrupted by the contagion of the vices laid before her eyes, but she must emend her own. And the moment she

---

264. Gen. 34:1–27.

265. Euripides *Electra* 343.

266. This saying is attributed to Epicurus.

267. Thucydides *History of the Peloponnesian War* 2.45.

268. Ovid *The Art of Love* 1.99.

269. Eph. 6:16.

turns away from God toward men, whether to approve them or be approved by them, she departs from Christ into adultery.

If she sees good things, let her follow them for the sake of Christ; if she sees bad things, let her avoid them for the sake of Christ. Let her be on her guard that she does not comport herself, walk, act, or speak in such a way that she becomes a snare of the devil for men. Not only must she not sin herself, but she must, as far as possible, be responsible for seeing that she is not a cause or incitement to sin for others. Otherwise, she will be a member of the devil, whose instrument she already is, not of Christ. They say that the Blessed Virgin was of such modesty and composure in her actions and in her whole body that if any lascivious look were directed at her, that loathsome fire would immediately be extinguished like a live coal that has fallen into the water, or as if some radiating force of continence and temperance held in check the perverse desires of those who looked at her and converted their feelings to her own nature.

95. Armed with these and similar reflections, let her leave her house with her mother, if that is possible; if not, with a woman of austere morals: a widow, a married woman, or even a young woman of proven virtue, chaste and sober speech, and seemly behavior. Homer sings that the chaste Penelope went down to the assembly of the suitors not alone but accompanied by two virtuous handmaids,[270] but when he was at home her son Telemachus, already a young man, also took his place among the suitors. Saint Paul insists that a woman should not have her head uncovered.[271] As for the rest of her body, Jerome recommends that when she appears in public she should not expose her breast or neck, or throw back her pallium to reveal the back of her neck, but that she should conceal her face, leaving only one eye uncovered as she walks, to see her way.[272] She should not desire to see or be seen, or cast her glance this way and that, or be anxious to know who lives here or there when she should barely know who her neighbors are. He wishes that a young woman be completely covered except for her eyes, which guide her way.

I do not see how there can be any modesty or virtue in showing off one's neck (although this can be tolerated) but also the breast and the nipples, and the back; indeed, some even expose the shoulders. As the saying goes, even the blind can see how shameful that is.[273] Some loathe this

---

270. Homer *Odyssey* 1.331.

271. 1 Cor. 11:5–6.

272. Jerome *Letters* 130.18 (*NPNF,* 2d ser.,. 6:270).

273. Erasmus *Adages* I viii 93 (*CWE* 32:174.

kind of exposure as abominable, but the more wanton, seeing a part of the body not usually exposed to view, are enflamed as if they had caught fire. For what purpose were long sleeves and gloves invented? Was it to keep the hands snug in soft and fragrant wrappings? Antiquity was not so ingenious in luxury and self-indulgence. Certainly they were invented out of necessity and so that except when engaged in doing something, the hands would be hidden and that no part of the body, vile and useless servant, would be seen. The countenance, too, should reveal nothing but uprightness and modesty.

96. We read that the young women of Miletus were seized with such frenzy that they hanged themselves in various parts of the city. No remedy could be found for this plague. Edicts were passed forbidding this practice and threatening dire punishment, but these measures were ignored. What more horrible death could be devised than the one they meted out to themselves? They were kept under guard, but even in their confinement, their spirit found a way out. Finally, it was decreed that whoever killed herself would be dragged naked through the middle of the forum in broad daylight. This penalty alone deterred them, for they did not wish to be seen naked, even in death.[274] What incredible and laudable modesty! Those who despised death, the last of all evils, had concern for modesty, even in their dead body. Thus, that madness was restrained and laid to rest. What could I add, save that the providence of mother nature herself took thought for the modesty of women? Astonishing to relate, men's bodies float faceup when they are thrown into the sea, Pliny tells us in his *Natural History*,[275] while women's bodies lie facedown.[276] Therefore, when nature looks after their modesty, will they themselves neglect it?

97. In her walk, a woman should neither be too hurried nor deliberately slow. When she is present at a meeting in the company of men, her countenance and her whole body should exhibit great modesty of attire and adornment, born not of ostentation but of true Christian gentleness and humility of spirit. This, after all, is real and lasting modesty, which by its sincerity wins the favor of those who look at her. A sense of propriety, the adornment and embellishment of all the other virtues, must be joined to her modesty. She will keep her eyes cast down, and will raise them but rarely and with modesty and decorum. She will not stare at anyone intently or in an unbecoming manner.

---

274. Plutarch, "Bravery of Women," *Moralia*, 249B–D.

275. Pliny *Natural History* 7.17.

276. This bit of folklore was discredited by the anatomist Luigi Bonacciuoli in his *Enneas muliebris* (c. 1480). Cf. Ian Maclean, *The Renaissance Notion of Women* (Cambridge, 1980), 43.

If the men are seated apart and look at the young women and talk among themselves, she should not think that she is being looked at or that they are talking about her. For it happens that some young women, who have conceived a false opinion of their beauty and comeliness, think that the eyes of all are fixed upon them and that they are the subject of every conversation. So if a man turns his glance toward them, even if he is occupied with something else and his thoughts are directed elsewhere, they think their beauty is being admired, and they smile complacently. Then, to avoid giving the impression that this is the reason for their smile, they inject some vapid comment into the conversation that they think will provoke laughter. Sometimes one can see twenty damsels sitting together, and if anyone looks at them, they all break out into laughter, pretending that they are laughing at some witticism or action that is not at all funny, since each of them is convinced that she is the object of looks of admiration for her extraordinary and marvelous beauty, and in so doing gives clear proof of her shallowness and folly.

98. The young woman, as I envisage her, will have no regard for beauty and will not think herself beautiful; she will not laugh at insipid and frivolous remarks, nor will she find pleasure in being stared at as if she were the subject of young men's conversations. Rather, she should weep the more that this most prized of her possessions is assailed and attacked by so many enemies and engines of war that she is not certain she can resist, and that her face like a firebrand ignites the minds of young men to illicit and foul lusts. And since we were speaking of laughter, which is the surest index of a light and frivolous mind, let her take care that she does not laugh too freely so that her whole body seems so convulsed with boisterous laughter that she cannot regain her breath. Neither should she laugh for silly or stupid reasons, such as if someone is bald, or bowlegged, or knock-kneed, or lisps or stammers, or inverts a word; nor for trivial reasons, e.g., because someone wears his hat backwards or in an unusual way or if his shoes are untied or his belt broken or because a fly lands on someone's nose or a cat walks across the bench.

99. But especially to be avoided is that laughter or, I should say, derision, caused by someone's misfortune, since human calamities are common to us all, and their causes are unknown. It is the sign of a cruel and inhuman spirit to make light of human tragedies or make them the butt of insolence without any regard or consideration for these unexplained happenings. The designs of the divine mind should be admired and worshipped, which makes some unhappy in this brief life and others happy in accordance with the will of that most equitable wisdom of the eternal God, who is the moderator of all things. I need not even admonish the young woman not to return the

smile of a young man, which only a woman with no modesty or sense would do. She must not allow herself to be pinched or touched in a lewd manner. Let her change her place and leave if she cannot avoid it in any other way. She should not give anything to a man or receive anything from him. "To accept a kindness," a wise man said, "is to sell one's liberty."[277] And with good reason the French and the Spaniards repeat the saying "A woman who accepts sells herself; a woman who gives has given herself."[278] Therefore, the virtuous woman will neither give nor receive.

100. I do not wish that a young woman be talkative, not even among her girl companions. I am amazed that there are some men impudent enough to approve of this. The custom to give praise to a woman for her ability to converse wittily and eloquently with men for hours on end is something that is welcomed and prescribed by ordinances of hell, in my opinion. I ask you, what will an inexperienced girl talk about with a young man who is ignorant of good things, but expert in evil? What is fire doing with flax?[279] I suppose they will be talking about Christ or the Blessed Virgin or the subordination of the spirit? What could be the subject of such a long conversation? Will not both of them, burning with the same ardor, be forced to speak about the fire that consumes them, whether they will it or not? Are these the women they call ladies of the court or of the palace? Tell me, what is the derivation of that word? Is it from *palor,* "to stray abroad," or perhaps *balo,* "to bleat"?[280] Courtly dames they are, indeed, judging from the courts of our day, begetters of every vice, the abode of Satan, which not only the Christian will avoid but even the pagan who has a modicum of good sense. But not all of them are immodest, some will say. I really do not know, but even if they are pure in body, they are certainly most impure in mind and have prostituted themselves to men in mind if not in body. The only thing lacking in their impurity has been the opportunity, since they are constantly in view and engaged with many people. Ovid said, "The woman who did not yield because she did not have the opportunity, has already yielded."[281] Saint Augustine wisely said, "We are privy to the secrets of conscience through what we hear; we do not usurp judgment on things hidden from us."[282] If you

---

277. Publilius Syrus 89.

278. The French saying is "Femme qui prend, elle se vend. / Femme qui donne, s'abandonne." In Spanish:"La mujer que prende, su cuerpo vende."

279. Cf. the Spanish proverb: "La estopa de junto al fuego, quitala luego." and the English proverb: "Put not fire to flax."

280. The true derivation of the word *palatium* is *Mons Palatinus,* where the imperial palaces were built, beginning with that of Augustus.

281. Ovid *Amores* 2.4.4.

282. Augustine *The City of God* 1.26.

speak no differently than a prostitute, how can you dare to presume that I believe you are chaste?

101. You say, "You did not see me lying with a man." I did not see you plying the trade of a prostitute either. But do you wish to exempt yourself from the criterion we use in all of nature, that we judge the interior from the exterior? Do you want me to believe that a cask contains water when I see wine flowing out of it? But why dispute with such people? What man of worth approves such things? Who praises them, save those who do not even know the semblance of chastity, who would wish, if it were possible, that all women were unchaste so that they could more readily find an outlet for their boundless lust. Immersed up to their ears in shameless acts, crimes, and wrongdoing, they are unable to see their own vices or those of others. Let them first throw off this veil of depravity that envelops them, and then we will believe them when they give their opinions on virtue. Among Roman women of old, trained in that strict school of chastity, Tacitus tells us that affability was not looked upon with approval.[283] Plutarch reports that Postumia, the priestess of Vesta, was accused of incest solely because of her unrestrained laughter and her too-free discussions with men.[284] She was acquitted by the pontifex maximus, Spurius Minucius, with the warning that she should not engage in conversations that were unbecoming to a blameless life.

102. It is not to be permitted that a young woman and a man should converse alone anywhere for any length of time, not even if they are brother and sister. Many examples, both old and new, can be adduced of horrible crimes that even brothers and sisters dared to commit when the opportunity of seclusion offered itself. So it was that Amon, son of King David, violated his sister Thamar,[285] and Caunus his sister Byblis.[286] Augustine never consented to live with his sister. "It is evil," he said, "to see a woman, worse to talk to her, and worst of all to touch her."[287] When the sister of the Abbot Pion was sick, he was asked to visit her before she died, but he came to her room reluctantly, led by another with his eyes closed. After addressing a few words to her, he departed in the same way in which he came. I would not allow brothers and sisters or close relatives, no matter how chaste they are and of proven virtue, to play together, kiss each other, touch or tickle each other. What else is this but to enflame the young girl and weaken her

283. Tacitus *Dialogue on Orators* 28.4–6.

284. Plutarch, "How to Profit from One's Enemies," *Moralia*, 89F.

285. 2 Sam. 13:10–14.

286. Ovid *Metamorphoses* 9.450–665.

287. Augustine *Sermons* 349.4 (PL 39:1531).

defenses for more shameless acts so that if more aggressive advances are made upon her, in her aroused state, she may conceive of things not conducive to her chastity?

103. Nor would I have them retreat into a corner of a crowded hall or room. What will they say to each other in solitude that others cannot hear if their conversation is to be pure and chaste? Conversations about good things do not require secrecy. That is necessary only when there is fear of a witness and when embarrassment will result from the divulging of their words to others. It is not becoming that many words be exchanged between young people of opposite sex even if there are others present, unless the whole tenor of the conversation is so clearly pure and virtuous that no suspicion of indecency could arise. There are some who are so clever in their wickedness, who disguise their feelings in such ambiguous and indirect language, that their intentions are not difficult to divine by the woman to whom they address their words. Yet their ambiguity may enable them to deny that these were their sentiments and to reproach their hearers as malicious for turning to evil purpose what they said in a pure and simple spirit. And they think themselves quite clever if they are good at these wiles, devoid of all good qualities, but expert and cunning in the devising of evil. This is no proof of cleverness but rather of a perverse zeal for evil, which, as Seneca said, is worse than sleep and idleness.[288] Talent is not to be measured by fraud and deceit, unless we give precedence to devils over angels in intelligence, whereas one of the holy angels is more keen-witted and wise than all the devils put together.

104. To sum up, it is best to have as little contact with men as possible; few words are to be exchanged with them, and those should be instinct with modesty, propriety, and discretion. You will not be accounted a more inarticulate young woman but rather a wiser one. If judgment is to be pronounced on your character, I prefer that you appear deficient in learning to the wicked rather than lacking in virtue to the good. Tell me, how many words of Mary do you find in the whole story of the four Gospels? The angel comes to her and in a few words she accepts the message of so great a mystery, words of great wisdom and holiness.[289] She goes to visit Elizabeth, and she opens her mouth only to praise God.[290] She brings forth her divine Son, she is extolled by the angels, adored by the shepherds, and she remains silent, treasuring all that was said to her and pondering it in her heart.[291] She

288. Seneca the Elder *Controversies* 1.8.2.
289. Luke 2:19.
290. Luke 1:46–55.
291. Luke 2:8–19.

receives the homage of the Magi, who had come there from afar. What do you read that she said? Another woman might have asked them perhaps about their country, about its riches, about their wisdom, about the star, but as befitted a young maiden, she uttered not a word.

She offers her Son in the temple. When Simeon made prophesies about him, another woman would have put various questions to him or asked the meaning and substance of what he said. The old man addressed her with these words: "Behold this child is set for the fall and the rise of many in Israel and he will be a sign that will be contradicted. And your own soul a sword shall pierce so that the thoughts of many hearts may be revealed."[292] Another woman would have inquired when, how, and where this would take place. She is reported as having said nothing.

She loses her beloved Son in Jerusalem. After seeking him for three days and finally finding him, how many words does she speak to him? "My Son, why have you treated us in this way? Behold, your father and I have been looking for you anxiously."[293]

When he was a grown man, she makes this simple observation: "My Son, they have no wine."[294] At the cross she was entirely speechless; she asked nothing of her Son—to whom he would leave her, or what his dying wishes were—because she had learned not to speak in public. Imitate her, virgins and all women, imitate this woman of few words, but of remarkable wisdom.

105. Theano of Metapontum, a most learned young woman and a prophetess, was of the opinion that silence was the greatest adornment of a woman.[295] Sophocles was of the same opinion,[296] and indeed silence is a sweet seasoning for chastity and prudence. In conclusion, the most eloquent woman for me is the one who, when required to speak to men, will become flushed in her whole countenance, perturbed in spirit, and at a loss for words. O extraordinary and effective eloquence! You are not an advocate, my child, nor are you pleading a case in the forum, where your silence would do harm to your cause or that of your client. Show as much courage by your silence as others do in speaking in the forum. In that way you will better defend your cause of chastity, which in the eyes of fair judges will be made stronger by your silence than by your speaking. Writers of history relate that a boy was brought forward to the rostrum of Rome on a charge

292. Luke 2:34–35.
293. Luke 2:48.
294. John 2:3.
295. Porphyry *Life of Pythagoras* 19.
296. Sophocles *Ajax* 293.

involving chastity, and with his eyes fixed on the ground and with unwavering silence, he commended his chastity more strongly to the people than the most eloquent orators could have done in long, elaborate speeches.[297]

106. But to return to women, Saint Susannah acquitted herself of the accusation of adultery by her resolute silence, not by a prepared speech. Let us listen to the words of Saint Ambrose: "Susannah kept silence and defeated her enemies. Before the judge Daniel she did not defend herself by verbal argumentation nor did she protect herself with the language of the law court, but in this holy woman, though her tongue was silent, chastity spoke in its place."[298] The same author in the third book of his *On Virgins* said, "I prefer that speech be lacking to a virgin rather than it be copious. For if women are bidden to be silent even concerning divine things in church, and to ask questions of their husbands at home, what precautions should be taken in the case of virgins, in whom modesty is their greatest adornment and silence the greatest commendation of their modesty?"[299] These are the words of Saint Ambrose.

She will not only comport herself in this manner before men, but among women too; modest and restrained speech will become her, not loud or arrogant or typical of a man's spirit, or interspersed with oaths, which, while unseemly in men, cannot but be a very grave defect in women. For a woman to swear seems as unnatural to me as for her to bear arms. Her voice should not be affected or delicate, and her countenance should not have a cruel or fierce expression or one that denotes severity or sadness or disgust; nor should it be changeable or display an air of superiority or disdain, not grinning, shifting, wayward, and uninhibited, since this is a sure indicator of a similar mind.

107. There are some women of such inconstant and unsound mind that among their peers they blurt out everything loquaciously, their own and other people's affairs, giving no thought to what they say. Whatever comes to their mind[300] they make public knowledge of it. From this comes their inclination to tell lies, when they don't know the truth. They invent fantastic tales—of a single crow, they invent a hundred; one slain man becomes a thousand; and a dog of average size they magnify into one bigger than an

---

297. Valerius Maximus 6.1.7.

298. The homily from which this excerpt is taken is sometimes ascribed to Ambrose, but it is by St. Maximus of Turin, a younger contemporary who imitated Ambrose's style in his sermons. Maximus of Turin *Homilies* 46 (*PL* 57 : 333).

299. Ambrose *On Virgins* 3.3.9 (*NPNF*, 2d ser., 10 : 382).

300. Cicero *Letters to Atticus* 12.1.2. This Ciceronian phrase was a favorite with humanist writers.

Indian elephant—to such an extent that it is impossible to find words to reprehend something so preposterous and ridiculous. Everyone takes these stories with a grain of salt and mockery. Their very recounting of such tales is reproof enough. Some do this for fear that they may appear impolite if they keep silence or unfriendly if they do not pour out into someone else's bosom things that should be kept secret even when this involves some risk. There are some who think they do nothing wrong in this. Others who speak before they think blurt out things that should have remained unspoken before they think of what they are going to say or consider whether it is suitable to be said. They give utterance to their thoughts without even being aware that they are speaking. Many are under the vain illusion that by revealing secrets, they will be thought to be worthy of having important things confided to them. Poor fool! Who is going to confide her own affairs to you after seeing how you treat the secrets of others? This is what gave rise to the precept "A secret should never be confided to a woman, not to your sister, nor your mother, nor your wife."

108. But that this is the vice only of certain women, and not of their entire sex, is proven by some examples of women of great constancy, who even under torture did not reveal what they knew, like that disciple of Pythagoras who bit off her own tongue and spat it in the face of the tyrant who was torturing her, so that she could not be forced to speak.[301] I shall not mention the women of Miletus who for many days, as long as was necessary, guarded with fidelity and prudence the plans of their husbands in Marseilles. Tacitus tells us how Epicharis, who knew of the Piso conspiracy, was condemned to be torn to pieces with the most cruel torment to make her reveal her secret. On the first day, neither beatings nor fire nor the wrath of her tormentors, who did not wish to be scorned by a woman, could move her to confess to what she knew. On the next day, when she was being delivered to the same torture seated on a saddle (since she could no longer stand up on her weakened limbs), she took a band that was tied around her breasts, fastened it in the form of a loop to the pommel of the saddle, then tied it around her neck and let her body fall under its own weight and breathed forth the little life she had left in her.[302] The Athenians commemorated the memory of Leaena,[303] the friend of Aristogiton, who drove out the

301. Plutarch, "Concerning Talkativeness," *Moralia*, 506A. The woman in question was Leaena, mistress of Aristogiton, the tyrannicide. The plot failed and both Aristogiton and Harmodius were put to death, but Leaena refused to reveal the names of others involved in the conspiracy.

302. Tacitus *Annals* 15.57.

303. The Athenians erected a monument of a tongueless lioness to Leaena (Greek for *lioness*) to commemorate her heroism.

sons of Pisistratus, because she suffered every torment in silence rather than betray her friend. If unchaste women could do this, what of chaste women?

109. Curiosity about another household should be avoided. Do not be eager to pry into and investigate everything or desire to understand and know more than is allowed. You must not dispute or quarrel in public, neither concerning trivial matters, nor even if some great possessions were at stake. It is better to suffer loss of fortune rather than of name, reputation, and things rightly most dear to us. Concerning feast days, celebrations, and banquets, I do not know what instruction to give to Christians with respect to these worse-than-pagan customs. They have become so firmly established that anyone who would not let himself be carried away by them with everyone else would be regarded as mad to resist the popular frenzy, and stand alone or with few others.

110. Those who do not wish to listen to a Christian may heed what the pagans have to say. In his scandalous manual on the art of love, Ovid says this about public spectacles:

> They come to see and also to be seen.
> That place bodes ill for purity of life.[304]

Juvenal in his famous satire says that in theatres, dances, and crowded places, women who would make obedient and complacent wives for a dignified and honorable man are not to be found.[305] The same Ovid testifies that banquets are the weapons of Venus and Cupid.[306] And, in fact, what safeguard is there for chastity when a girl is the center of so much attraction, when so many glances are fixed on her, and she herself gazes at so many men? She cannot but be enflamed with desire in turn and, unless she is made of stone, grow hot with her own fire. Much fuel is added to the fire at a banquet: food, drink, conversations, cajoling smiles, enticing looks, touches, pinching, and other such things, to which Bacchus gives free rein. What mind can remain pure and unblemished, undefiled by any lustful thought amid all this? The foolish crowd thinks that girls cannot sin except by lying with a man. You who were baptized in the gospel of Christ, how do you read or hear those words of Christ in the gospel: "For every idle word an account must be rendered on the day of judgment."[307] But in gatherings and drinking parties among young men and women, how many words fly about that are not

---

304. Ovid *The Art of Love* 1.99–100.
305. Juvenal *Satires* 6.60–62.
306. Ovid *The Art of Love* 1.229.
307. Matt. 12:36.

only idle but are deadly shafts, which our corrupted morals even consider praiseworthy?

111. Then there is this precept of the Lord: "Whoever will look upon another woman with desire for her has already committed adultery with her in his heart."[308] Do you not think that this saying also applies to a woman looking at a man? A secular writer has said, "A woman who desires illicit intercourse is unchaste even without engaging in intercourse."[309] And Menander writes, "Bad company corrupts good morals."[310] Paul consecrated this verse by including it in one of his Epistles.[311] Finally, you are not a Christian and a spiritual person, but a sensual pagan, I should say a brute beast, if you do not understand that the source of virtues and vices is inside us, in the mind, and it is not the body that matters, but the mind. I would venture to say that after the age of puberty, few girls return from these banquets and celebrations among men with the same virginal spirit they had when they went. Some are captivated by beauty and are caught in the net, so to speak; others are swayed by talent, others by riches, others by eloquence, others by quickness of intellect. In the assembly of men, a girl finds all these things laid out as in a trap. It seems difficult that she should not be captured by things to which she is naturally drawn.

112. How much better not to love danger, lest, according to the advice of the wise man, you perish in it![312] My opinion, or, I should say, Christ's opinion, is that young women should be kept at home, should stay out of public, except for attendance at sacred offices, and be well covered, separated from the view of men, which Saint John Chrysostom[313] writes was the custom of his time, so that they will neither provide a snare nor discover one. A Christian young woman should have nothing or as little as possible to do with weddings, male gatherings, or banquets. A woman may be present at a hundred meetings and banquets. In none of these will she hear or see anything by which she will return home better, but in all of them she will see things that will make her return home worse.

---

308. Matt. 5:28.

309. Seneca the Elder *Controversies* 6.8.

310. Menander, *Sententiae*, 803, ed. Siegfried Jaekel (Leipzig, 1964), 79. Menander, the greatest writer of Greek New Comedy, wrote plays based on domestic plots that often featured a love interest. Portions of his plays remain; and one complete play, *The Ill-Tempered Man*, was discovered only recently. A collection of maxims attributed to him also survives, but they are not all genuine.

311. 1 Cor. 15:33.

312. Sirach 3:27.

313. John Chrysostom, *Homily 78 on the Gospel of Matthew* (*NPNF*, 1st ser., 10:471).

There is no small number of persons whose sole occupation it is to seek out these festivities and say or do things there that will detract from their good name. My feelings concerning young women can be deduced from the fact that I am also contrary to young men participating in banquets, both because it is harmful to their strength and health in their adolescent years and because all banquets in the present moral atmosphere are the seedbed of numerous vices, no matter how moderate and temperate they may be. The young man sees many shameful things there; he learns many disgraceful habits even among old men of good morals. What shall I say of meetings where both men and women are present, where souls are so enkindled to lust by internal and external factors, despite the constraints of modesty, that they burst forth and are transported in a wild and base manner, and oblivious of the reins, drag the rider along with them. What if, in addition, they are goaded on with spurs? Then there will be measure, no moderation, no respect for decency.

XII

ON DANCING

113. Let us say a few words also about an activity in which many women find great delight and which they are taught with great diligence even by their parents, namely the art of dancing skillfully. I do not wish here to discuss the rules of gesticulation and the ancient palestra, which Plato[314] and most of the Stoics said were useful for freeborn children and which Cicero[315] and Quintilian[316] considered essential for the orator. This consisted of a specific training in every gesture and movement, which ensured a graceful bearing, an art that, like many others, has fallen into complete disuse. I refer to the type of dancing—to call it that—not only the *tripudium*[317] but also the palestra of these times, that is performed with a languid step. For in both the offense to decency is similar, or, I should say, the same.

Both the palestra and the art of gesticulation cannot be executed without some little dance steps, even if it merely consists of short, jerky movements that do not rise too far off the ground. We see that dancing was repudiated not only by the severe Romans, but also by those Greeks who were a little more sensible and sober-minded. When the orator Demosthenes was denouncing the followers of Philip, king of Macedon, before the Athenian people, he could make no more grave accusation than to say that they indulged in drunken dancing and that men of good sense and integrity who did not abide dancing shunned their company. We do not read that any of those Roman matrons of old, famed for their chastity, ever danced. Sallust

---

314. Plato *Laws* 795D (on gesticulation); *Republic* 403C (on the palestra).

315. Cicero *Tusculan Disputations* 2.36.

316. Quintilian 1.11.17, 1.2.16.

317. The *tripudium* was a ritual dance in triple time performed by priests in honor of Mars. Dancers of the *tripudium* leaped into the air, hence their name, *Salii.*

writes that Sempronia sang and danced with more skill than befitted a woman of good morals.[318] In his defense of Murena, Cicero mentions that the defendant was accused by Cato of having danced in public while in Asia Minor. This was such a serious charge that Cicero did not attempt to defend this action but consistently denied it. He said, "Hardly anyone dances when he is sober unless he is out of his mind, whether he be alone or at a respectable banquet. Dancing is the final escort of dinner parties starting at an early hour, in attractive surroundings and amidst all sorts of sensuous delights."[319] Thus, it must be considered, as it were, the culmination of all vices.

114. But we have dance schools in Christian cities, side by side with public brothels; to such a degree do pagans surpass us in the austerity of their morals. And they were not familiar with this new type of dancing that we have—uncontrolled, audacious, arousing the passions, full of unchaste touches and kisses. What is the meaning of all these kisses? I suppose, to imitate doves, the birds of Venus,[320] as the ancients thought. At one time kissing was allowed only among relatives; now kisses are bestowed indiscriminately on anyone in France and in England.[321] I suppose this is because baptism makes us all brothers, if you please! I for one would like to know what is the point of all this kissing, as if there were no other way of demonstrating friendship and affection to women. It is the beginning of shameful actions that I prefer not to mention. As far as I am concerned, it is an utterly vile and barbaric custom.

115. I return to the subject of dancing. What is the purpose of these dances in which the girls' elbows are supported by their male partners so that they can go higher into the air? How can they move in this frenzied way until the middle of the night without having enough or becoming tired? But if they are asked to pay a visit to a nearby church, they say that they cannot go except on horseback or in a carriage. Do they not make it clear that they are carried away by their excesses? I remember being told once that certain men had been brought to our part of the world from far-off Asia, and when they saw women dancing, they fled in terror because they thought they were victims of some strange and unfamiliar type of madness.

In fact, who would not believe women are mad when they are dancing

---

318. Sallust *Catiline* 25.2.

319. Cicero *Pro Murena* 13.

320. Virgil *Aeneid* 6.190.

321. Erasmus writes exaggeratedly about this English custom to his friend Fausto Andrelini in 1499: "When you arrive anywhere, you are received with kisses on all sides, and when you take your leave they speed you on your way with kisses." Ep. 103 (*CWE* 1 : 193).

if he had never seen women dancing before? Who would not believe they were not mentally deranged when to the sound of a skin or a string they move their hands, their heads, and their whole body in wild gesticulations? It is interesting to see how they behave in these crowded gatherings, how some of the female spectators sit there composed while others dance or strut about with such movements, such a bearing, such mastery, and such haughtiness. You can recognize their madness from the fact that they try to make such a stupid thing appear sensible. All their mental concentration has leaped down from their head to their feet, where, evidently, it is more necessary when one dances than it is in the brain or the heart.

Do we read that holy women ever danced? How few of those respected matrons who have learned wisdom through experience would admit to knowing this art, or, if asked to participate, would not refuse and consider it an insult to be asked! Obviously they regard it as something absurd, otherwise they would willingly learn it themselves. Such women do not frequent places where there is dancing unless obliged to do so through some duty, and they conduct themselves in such a way as to give the impression that they do not wish to be there; their facial expression and attitude indicate their aversion and disapproval. In these places, what safeguard can there be for chastity, when so many men's bodies are visible and the soul is attacked through the portals of the eyes by the wiles of our most subtle and astute enemy?

116. Concerning the art of dancing, a holy man declared that he preferred to plough and dig on feast days rather than dance. Writing to his sister, Saint Ambrose said:

> Happiness of mind must be found in a good conscience, not in wild banqueting or nuptial music. For where dancing is the last escort of self-indulgence, modesty is threatened and sensual enticements are everywhere present. From this I wish the virgins of God to be far removed. No one, as a certain learned man of the world wrote, dances when he is sober, unless he is out of his mind.[322] If according to the wisdom of the world drunkenness or madness instigate us to dance, what precautions do the holy Scriptures set before us by example, as in the slaying of John, the precursor of Christ, at the wish of a dancing girl?[323] It proves that the incitement of the dance was more harmful than the madness of sacrilegious frenzy. The funeral banquet is

322. See note 319 above.
323. Matt. 14:6–11.

prepared with regal luxury and at the moment when a great crowd of people had gathered, the daughter of the tyrant under secret instructions is brought forth to dance before the male onlookers. What could the daughter of an adulterous mother learn but the loss of all decency? Is there anything more conducive to carnal lust than to reveal with crude movements those hidden regions of the body which either nature or moral discipline has concealed, to cavort with the eyes, to roll the head around, to toss back the hair? As a natural consequence this will lead to an offense against the divinity. What sense of shame can exist where there is dancing, loud confusion and noise? Then the king, delighted with the spectacle, told the girl she could ask of him what she wished.[324]

117. There is a custom of recent institution for men and women to run about the city wearing masks, dancing in famous houses, as those of leading citizens, the rich, or where there is banqueting, or, I should say, a drinking party going on. There are some so dedicated to this pastime that they claim there is nothing equally enjoyable as to go the round of people's houses with their heads covered in this manner. They see and know everyone but are not recognized by anyone, like little children who take great pleasure in covering their face with their hands and thinking that they are not seen by anyone and hearing people calling them by name.

But under that mask many shameful things are concealed. The first of them is the uncontrolled curiosity of women, who are dying to know what is happening everywhere: who is out banqueting, at whose invitation, how they are dressed, with what splendid apparel. From this arise envy, talkativeness, detraction, and defamation. You may think you are receiving a friend into your house with his face covered, but it is an enemy, a deadly enemy who enters, in order to find out how he may harm you. You can exclude an enemy who is visible but not one whose identity is hidden.

Then female shamelessness is given free rein. A woman who would be ashamed to go out and dance if she were known is not afraid to do so when she is masked, and consequently there is no respect for age, social status, fortune, or reputation in those circumstances. Not only do they hear obscenities and things unworthy of them, but they say fearlessly what they would not dare to think if they were recognized. But a mask levels everything in the eyes of the beholder as if darkness were cast around them. Thus little by little they become used to shamelessness so that the harm

324. Ambrose *On Virgins* 3.6.27 (*NPNF*, 2d ser., 6:385).

that modesty suffered under the mask is now flaunted and displayed without the mask. Even in France, Germany, and England, where people live more simply and social relations are less sophisticated, they imitate these shameful actions, which are not to be regarded as of no consequence. In Spain, Italy, and other regions, where through greater acuteness of intellect there is more cleverness and ingenuity, it is to be feared that these amusements may be the occasion of great misconduct. Up to now there have been few instances of this, but there have been some, even though the custom has been introduced quite recently. But it is preferable to leave these evils to everyone's imagination than to explain them in words, lest I seem more to rebuke than to correct.

XIII

ON LOVE AFFAIRS

118. From meetings and conversations with men, love affairs arise. In the midst of pleasures, banquets, dances, laughter, and self-indulgence, Venus and her son Cupid reign supreme. Such things attract and ensnare human minds, but especially those of women, over which pleasure exercises an uncontrolled tyranny. Poor young girl, if you emerge from these encounters a captive prey! How much better it would have been to remain at home or to have broken a leg of the body rather than of the mind! I shall try to be of help, if you have not yet been captured, so that you will not be captured, and if you are already caught, so that you may escape. First of all, I shall omit all that has been said by philosophers, holy men, and all men of wisdom against passionate love. I shall also refrain from mentioning things that have been written by those who seem overtly to have sung the praises of love. What censures those first mentioned heap upon it! They call it tyrannical, stern, harsh, vile, cruel, ugly, wicked, accursed, impious, the author and instigator of the worst crimes. Taking his cue from Aristotle, Seneca, and Plutarch, Saint Jerome writes, "Love of beauty is the oblivion of reason and close to madness, an ugly vice that ill befits a sound mind. It bewilders judgment, breaks lofty and noble spirits and drags them down from great thoughts to lowly ones. It makes them querulous, irascible, temerarious, harshly imperious, servilely flattering, useless for everything, in the end even for love. For although it burns with insatiable desire for pleasure, it wastes much time in suspicions, tears and complaints, it makes itself hateful, and in the end becomes hateful even to itself."[325] So writes Saint Jerome.

119. Who can rehearse in words how many perjuries, deceptions, murders, catastrophes, and destruction of cities, people, and regions this love

325. Jerome *Against Jovinianus* 1.49 (*NPNF,* 2d ser., 6:385).

has brought about? Shall I recount here how Troy fell for the sake of Helen and how so many armies were slaughtered? Shall I tell of the great war between the Spartans and the Messenians because of the abduction of young girls? Or of the breaking of the power of the Spartans by the Theban Epaminondas at Leuctra in Boeotia when, as Plutarch tells us, the spirit of Scedasus revenged the rape of his daughters by Spartan youths and a father's plaint ignored by the magistrates?[326] King Rodrigo by lying with Cava, daughter of Don Julián, caused the ruin of the flourishing country of Spain and left it to be ravished and crushed by the Moors.[327] Adam caused the downfall and affliction of the human race through his love for Eve.

120. The poet cries out, "To what excesses does gold not drive us?"[328] With more truth he could have said the same of savage love. It drove mild-mannered David to expose the innocent Uriah to imminent danger so that he could freely possess Bathsheba.[329] It drove Solomon, wisest of kings, to madness, to the point of idolatry.[330] It weakened Samson, it forced Medea to rend her brother limb from limb and kill her children. It led Catiline to slay his own son so that he could bring Orestilla into an empty house.[331]

Girls hate their parents and relatives because they stand in the way of their love. There are those who have poisoned their own mothers, who gave them birth and by whom they were brought up, so that they could fly away with their lovers. Messalina, wife of the emperor Claudius, while he was still alive and had left for Ostia, sixteen miles from Rome, with no mention of divorce, publicly and in broad daylight, dared to marry Gaius Silius in Rome.[332] I won't mention the fact that from an empress she became an ordinary citizen. Of course, that augmented the danger as a result of which she and Silius and all those who were accomplices of the wicked marriage were doomed to die, as indeed came to pass. Would an Orestes or an Ajax or any of those who we learn were hounded by the Furies do such things? Such frenzy is not observed in tigers, lions, wolves or bears. The consciousness of

326. See note 244 above.

327. The daughter of the Spanish nobleman Don Julián, who governed Ceuta in North Africa, was raped by King Rodrigo. In retaliation, Don Julián assisted the Arabs in crossing the strait and invading Spain about 711. The story is told by Alfonso el Sábio, *Primera crónica general*, and in the Spanish version of the Latin *Historia góthica* by Rodrigo Jiménez de Rada, archbishop of Toledo.

328. Virgil *Aeneid* 3.56.

329. 2 Sam. 11:14–15.

330. 1 Kings 11:4–5.

331. Sallust *Catiline* 15.2.

332. Tacitus *Annals* 11.26.

the crime, roused by passion, pushed them to extremes which not even the most deranged mind could conceive of without anxiety. If one could see this monstrous and dreadful passion with bodily eyes, he would be as terrified and horrified as if a ferocious beast were to cross his path, and would flee in terror as far as he could.

121. If you have not yet been stricken by the poison of this scorpion, you should meditate on this verse of the Mime: "Love is taken up at the mind's discretion, but not put aside." [333] It is in your power to let love in, but once you have let it in, you no longer belong to yourself, but to it. You cannot drive it out at your pleasure, but it will be able and will take pleasure in ousting you from your own house. So if you do not drive this guest away upon arrival, you will be driven away by him. You must do what would later be done to you if you do not do it. You must understand that in order to gain more unlimited and extensive dominion over our mind and willfully throw everything into confusion, engulf and muddle everything from top to bottom, love first of all blinds the mind or banishes it so that when it sees nothing or is far removed, it cannot know what is happening in its own dwelling. It lets itself be managed and directed entirely according to the whims of love. Love is a deadly poison that deprives us of our sight and drags us in our blindness over a thousand ravines and precipices and often plunges us to our death in an abyss! There is no deed so inhuman, so monstrous, strange, and unheard of that we would not undertake if we have to give heed to love or gratify its wishes: to defraud friends, kill relatives, cut the throats of parents, slaughter those to whom you gave birth, are trifling matters in order to satisfy love. It is of no great consequence to destroy utterly one's native land or the human race from the very base.

122. In all this turmoil, can there be any remembrance of what is holy, pious, and just? God and religion and a good conscience are mere trifles to one who has forgotten himself. Anyone of sane mind who would reflect on these things and not take every care that he never become a victim of this madness and total blindness deserves to be its prisoner forever and find no end or limit to his woes, but be tormented night and day by Cupid's torch. May he not take food, nor sleep, nor see, nor rest, and though he be a human being, let him not perform any human function. While this passion violently sweeps away all human hearts, it does so all the more with women's feelings, which are more tender than men's. Wherefore it behooves them to be all the more cautious that they do not slowly imbibe it without knowing it. For it will steal upon them without warning when they are in critical situations or

333 Publilius Syrus 47.

in the right circumstances, thinking themselves free of any assault upon their emotions. When once love has crept into their hearts, they embrace and cherish it as something sweet and pleasant, unaware that a deadly and terrible pestilence is hidden beneath those external blandishments.

123. Therefore, a strong resistance must be made to the first stirrings, which even Ovid, the preceptor of love, counsels.[334] Do not allow the children of Babylon to grow up, but, according to the advice of the psalmist, "Dash them against the rock"[335] and crush them on the groundwork of the religion of Christ Jesus, who admonishes the virgins in the Canticle, "Capture for us the little foxes that destroy the vineyards."[336] And he admonishes this all the more carefully if the vineyard already shows the blossoms of good fruit. Love gathers strength with time, as do many other things. As Ovid says:

> I saw a wound at first susceptible of cure,
> But neglected, suffered the bane of long delay.[337]

A lover should be listened to no more than one who casts spells or a poisoner. He approaches smoothly and persuasively; first he praises the girl, says that he has been captured by her beauty, and last of all he says that he is perishing of his uncontrollable love. He is well aware of the vain minds of many women, who take singular pleasure in being praised. In this way the fowler deceives the bird with birdlime and the decoy's cry. He calls you beautiful, charming, clever, eloquent, noble—and perhaps you are none of these things, but you like to hear those lies. Stupid girl, do you think you appear such, when you are not? But suppose you are. He did not mention that you were prudent or that you were chaste, did he? If he omitted these, he said nothing; but if he did add them, what does he hope for from you? If he does hope, it is evident that he lied. How did he plead his case? Did he say that he was captivated by your good qualities? Then what? That he would die unless he had you? Now we know the reason for those tears.[338]

124. Make sure you are not captured by his words, for then the two of you will perish together. He swears he will die and even (may the gods forgive me!) that he is dying. Do you believe this? You fool, let him produce evidence of how many have died of love out of so many thousands of lovers.

334. Ovid *The Remedy of Love* 91.
335. Ps. 137:9.
336. Song of Sol. 2:15.
337. Ovid *The Remedy of Love* 101–2.
338. Terence *Andria* 99; Erasmus *Adages* I iii 68 (*CWE* 31:292).

Love torments us at times, but it does not kill us. But if he dies, how much better it is for you that he die and not you, or that one die instead of two? What is the use of explaining that this is the ready and common refrain of all lovers, who know it by heart, although often they have not been touched by a drop of love. They sing this song only to deceive.

There was a certain French girl among the retinue of those who accompanied Marguerite of Valois to Spain to see her brother Francis I, king of France, who was held captive by the emperor Charles.[339] When she heard young Spaniards constantly crying out, "I am dying of love," she said, "Well, die and be done with it so that I can see some lover die of all those who say they are going to die." But if a lover enjoys you until he is tired of you, then he will show how much he loved you. If he had loved you, that is to say, your soul, he would have never become bored or sated with you. But since he was dying only for your body and the brief pleasure he could get from you, when the body became droopy his ardor waned, and after satisfying his pleasure he grew tired of the easy availability.

125. Examples are not rare, and it is not necessary to invoke the past. No one is so inexperienced that he has not heard of or seen thousands of men who take advantage of girls and then consign them to a brothel, since they had never loved them. There are others who fell in love, and their burning love turned to deadly hatred, so they killed or strangled their mistresses. There is no city in which these things are not heard daily, which makes me wonder all the more at the madness of young girls, who willingly immerse themselves in such a sea of evils. Whence come so many whorehouses, I ask you? I must beg your indulgence, but these things should not be kept silent, for Saint Jerome did not hesitate to use similar language.[340] Why are there so many prostitutes, and some of them of good family? Why are there so many beautiful young women with festering ulcers in poorhouses and hospitals? Why are there so many begging for alms, pale and sick, consumed with ugly sores, except that they were of this number? If you cannot be moved by virtue, honor, chastity, or respect for religion, if the deeds and examples of holy virgins do not dissuade you, then let the fate of these miserable young women, at least, influence you—a fate that undoubtedly awaits you if you enter upon that same path.

126. Your lover will deceive, either because he is used to deceiving or

---

339. In 1525, after the battle of Pavia, Francis I was taken prisoner by the troops of Charles V and imprisoned in Madrid, but was quickly freed. In a letter of 12 March 1525 addressed to Henry VIII, Vives pleads for leniency for France and its king. This probably was not a politically wise move.

340. Jerome *Against Jovinianus* 1.13 (*NPNF*, 2d ser., 6:356)

because this is the reward of an illicit love or because satiety of pleasure will persuade him to do so. Many of the things I said about the safeguarding of chastity will be profitable to you, so that love will not be engendered or nurtured by your diet or through leisure time or dealings with men. In the dialogues of the sophist Lucian, Venus asks of her child Cupid why he transfixes with his arrows Jupiter, Neptune, Apollo, Juno, and even herself, his mother, and in general all the gods, but does not lay a hand on Minerva, the Muses, and Diana. He answered, "Minerva threatens me when I approach her, she takes countermeasures and puts up a resistance. The Muses are to be respected and are always occupied in honorable activities; they defend themselves from love by their majestic presence and their attention to their task. Diana wanders in the woods and solitudes; her way of life makes her immune to love." [341] A great part of love is instilled through the senses, and it is then nourished and increased by tender thoughts.

But the girl has been captured. We must find a remedy for this plague before it forces her to perpetuate that which will bring eternal punishment. The first thing to regret is that you threw yourself into this abyss knowingly and wittingly. We cannot give ear to those who say that it was not in their power to turn love away. Those are the words of persons who cloak their misdeed with the excuse of necessity as if they acted unwillingly and were ignorant of the nature and the force of love. You should meditate on the verse of the Mime: "Love cannot be obtained by force, but it can slip away." [342] This clearly indicates that love does not break in by force, nor can it be expelled by force; but, as it slipped in little by little, so can it be gradually squeezed out. Do not allow your mind to wander, because it will always return to thoughts of love of its own accord.

127.   There are some judicious women who expel amatory thoughts by other thoughts of a different nature, like driving out a nail with a nail. [343] For example, they give themselves over entirely with great zeal to some activity that absorbs all their attention and that excludes all other cares and concerns. So they prepare a job of weaving with hope of remuneration, or they eagerly learn how to embroider or read or write, or study Latin, which either by the prospect of present advantage or hope of it in the future diverts the mind and recalls it to itself. Then when the stimulants of love are quieted and the soul is relieved of its violent constraints, you will have leisure to see things with your mind and reflect within yourself on how many stupid, blind

341. Lucian *Dialogues of the Gods* 8.19.1.
342. Publilius Syrus 39.
343. Erasmus *Adages* I ii 4 (*CWE* 31 : 148).

things you did thoughtlessly and senselessly. You will see how much valuable time you spent on useless and inane cares and lost so many excellent opportunities; with what passion you were consumed, how many silly, insane, and even impious things you thought, said, and did; into what a hotbed of wickedness you blindly hurled yourself. What a blessing that your vision has been restored to you and that you are willing to return to a better state of mind. This is no small favor of God and no small gratitude is owed to him for it. Then return to your task. Be sure not to see the beloved object or hear anything about it. If it comes to mind, divert your attention elsewhere, either by reading or prayer or conversation or even an uplifting song or the thought of something pleasant, provided it be pure and chaste.

128. Next, if the one you love has some defect or some deformity, concentrate on that rather than on something good and beautiful. There is no mortal in whom there is not something to criticize. Let that occur to you first when you are thinking of him. Consider that beneath the appearance of virtue there lurk great evils and many pernicious things under the guise of integrity. Beauty renders men proud and haughty, nobility makes them insolent, riches make them presumptuous, strength of body makes them fierce and cruel. Recall to mind not the things he said that pleased you, but those that displeased you. You cannot help but remember that he did or said something fatuous, silly, stupid, base, offensive, abominable, wicked, criminal, mad, nefarious. From what has emerged you can conjecture what other defects are kept carefully hidden. There is no one who does not conceal his vices, as far as possible, no one who does not show off his virtues. It thus happens that the latter are always less than they seem and the former greater. Add to this that we are deceived by the similarities between vice and virtue, since everyone strives to appear better than he is and we in our ignorance measure virtues according to a popular scale of values. Therefore, we call liberal one who is extravagant, courageous one who is foolhardy, eloquent one who is loquacious, clever one who is light-headed. Girls are often captivated by these qualities, since they are not capable of making judgment and they judge a man from externals that all can see, especially since no one approaches a girl without putting on the airs of an excellent and fortunate gentleman, lest he be thought lacking in anything that could be desired in any mortal for the winning over of love.

129. In this way they deceive unwary girls, covering over the yawning chasms of evil with their veneer of goodness, as the fowler hides the birdlime under food and the fisherman places bait on the hook. A girl should reflect on these things before she is seized by repentance when it is too late and begins to have some sense when all is of no avail. But if you expel love

altogether, then, as if restored to health and regaining your eyesight, you will understand that, as with innumerable other blessings, you will be forever indebted to God for having delivered you from the ranks of the foolish and placed you among the wise. What holy Christian or pagan woman who had any reputation for wisdom and decency ever fell in love with anyone except her husband? You would not wish to be loved with this kind of love, nor would you kindle passion in a man by devious arts, knowing that the fire will easily spread to you because of its proximity. Some women boast that they have lovers whom they enflame of set purpose. These women are led by the devil on this hunt, and, through the lavishing of their beauty, adornment, and conversation, they spread the net no less for themselves than for their quarry. They make the safeguarding of their chastity all the more difficult, as it is the target and object of so many men's assaults.

130. It is difficult to hold on to what so many are intent to wrest away from you. They justly merit the fate predicted by Jesus, son of Sirach: "If one throws a stone into the air, it will fall on his own head and a treacherous blow cuts both ways. He who digs a ditch will fall into it and he who places a stone in his neighbor's path will stumble upon it himself. He who lays a snare for another will perish in it."[344] Impious girl, don't you see that by driving him into the devil's snares by your deception you will fall into them together with him and so receive the reward for your service? He will burn because he was defeated by the devil and you because you were victorious thanks to the devil. Each of you will merit ample reward for your sin. "The wages of sin is death,"[345] as the apostle testifies. The law of Christ, which is the standard of mutual love, places the soul of one's neighbor not only above external raiment and all incidental things, but above the body itself and the blood and life of each of us. All of us set out on our journey intent and unencumbered, pressing on to our destined goal of eternal happiness. As it befits us to rejoice when by example, precept, or encouragement we have been of profit to our brother in his striving after virtue, so we should be sad when he becomes worse because of us. If the Lord detests those through whom scandal comes,[346] what will become of him who knowingly and wittingly casts obstacles in the path of his neighbor so that he will run into them and suffer a grave fall?

---

344. Sirach 27:28–29. Jesus, son of Sirach, was a scribe and teacher in Jerusalem who wrote the book known either as the Book of Sirach or Ecclesiasticus, accepted as a canonical book in the Catholic Bible.

345. Rom. 6:23.

346. Matt. 18:7.

131. An upright woman will feel the same grief for having been the occasion of sin to a person as she would if she had killed him. How much less serious, obviously, it is to cut a man's throat than to annihilate his soul or to sever his head from his body rather than his soul from God. The body will die without the soul, but the soul will live on. But without God, neither the body nor the soul will live. Therefore, a woman will strive with strenuous effort to bring back to his right senses a man whom she has driven mad. She will do this first by words and admonitions as much as she can, and if these are of no profit, by keeping away from him herself and by rejecting him. She will speak to him more rarely and see him more rarely. She will minimize the things that ensnared him: beauty, charm, adornment, conversation. She will resolve not to adorn herself with those things that bring about the destruction of her brother and make of her a minister of the devil and cause offense to God.

One cannot be called a Christian who does not even at the risk of his own body procure the salvation of his brother's soul. In pagan chronicles, we read that a young man of exceptional beauty, seeing that some young girls were passionately in love with him, disfigured his face with a knife. What an example for all women! O noble young man worthy of illustrious memory! This was done by a man, and a pagan. Will a Christian girl or woman not sacrifice one tiny bit of her adornment, her words and conversations, by which she both destroys her brother and violates the majesty of Christ? There is no lack of examples for women from their own sex if they have a mind to imitate what is better. There was a woman of Barcelona who, to bring her desperate lover back to his senses, kept rotten cabbages under her armpits for a period of time. She also ate raw cabbage and, drawing close to her lover as if to initiate a conversation, frightened him off with the foul odor and chased him away forever.

XIV

ON THE LOVE
BEFITTING A VIRGIN

132. And since human minds have a tendency and aptitude for loving, I shall point out to you pure and holy loves that will drive away this depraved and adulterated love. You have, first of all, one whom you can love: God the Father, and your spouse, Christ. You have his mother and your sister, the Blessed Virgin. You have one like yourself, the church of God. You have so many holy virgins, whose souls lead a blessed existence in heaven, and whose names are sanctified on earth. You have your parents, who gave birth to you, who take the place of God, who nourished you with such care, brought you up with such love and solicitude, whom you can love and help according to your means. You must hold their commands as sacrosanct and obey them with all humility. Do not show in mind, countenance, or gesture any defiance toward them, and think of them as a true and solid image of God, creator of all things. You have your own soul to love, commended to you by the voice of nature. You have in others virtues and minds dedicated to Christ. You have those who wish you to be safe and uncorrupted; finally, you have eternal joy and that highest and never-ending happiness.

These are, in the end, true and right loves. For physical love is feigned and a perverse imitator of true love. It should more justly be called lust rather than love. If you love all those things in good faith, you will neither prefer man to God nor a young libertine to your spouse, Christ, nor a procuress to the Blessed Virgin, nor a brothel to the church of God, nor immoral companions to the company of holy virgins, nor outsiders or even enemies to your parents, nor your body to your soul, nor vices to other people's virtues, nor souls subservient to the devil to souls dedicated to Christ, nor those who wish to ruin and corrupt you to those who desire your salvation and integrity, nor a brief and ephemeral pleasure to eternal happiness, nor the misery of the damned to perfect beatitude.

133. Therefore, the ordinances of God will have more efficacy for you than the deceitful persuasions of men, and you will prefer to place your trust in Christ rather than in the words of a vile scoundrel, and you will follow where the Blessed Virgin leads you and not the promptings of lust, and you will hold dear him whom she commends to you rather than the man procured for you by a brothel-keeper. You will not violate the laws of the church in order to keep those of the brothel, and you will prefer to be numbered among the flock of Catherine, Agnes, Clara, Margaret, Barbara, Thecla, and Agatha rather than among unchaste women, whose names are as unknown to men as their lives are to God, while both their names and their lives are known and recorded by the devil. Do not desert your parents to follow after lovers nor cause them unending anguish of heart in order to give your fraudulent lover some short-lived pleasure; do not prefer the well-being of your body to that of your soul and physical pleasure to sadness of soul. You will not listen to what someone says out of wickedness in preference to what someone says with virtuous intent, nor will you put more credence in a henchman of the devil than in a servant of Christ. Confide not in one who wishes to destroy you but in one who wishes to save you, and choose to enjoy perfect and eternal happiness in heaven rather than to be touched by the false image of joy here on earth, which is not only fleeting, but so mixed with sadness that it might more rightly be called and thought of as sadness.

Then you will shun that endless misery rather than aspire after the pleasure of this world, if indeed it deserves this name; and you will meditate on that saying of a holy man: "Present delights are momentary, torment is eternal." When you are surrounded and protected by so many great loves, love of God, of Christ, of Mary, of the church, of virgins, of parents, of yourself, of divine beatitude, what door will lie open to obscene behavior? Cupid will not be so rash and impudent as not to dread attacking a place fortified and hedged in by such respected sentinels, since he is one who reveres the Muses for their studious pursuits. But if he should hazard an attack, his shaft will be turned back upon himself, for in a girl of this sort the arrow will not find a vulnerable spot.

XV

ON SEEKING A SPOUSE

134. The human race, mortal in each of its members when taken singly, becomes eternal through the continuity of offspring. So that this offspring would be holy and pure, God instituted marriage, by whose sanction we may serve nature without sin. Therefore, Paul said, "He who gives his daughter to a man in marriage does not act wrongly, as long as it is done in the Lord."[347] And since a man is sought for a woman to share all her fortunes publicly and privately as her indivisible and inseparable companion—so that only the death of either party can separate them—this decision is greater and more serious than people think, being one of those in which, as it is said, you cannot err twice. If an error has been made once, whatever happens afterwards must be suffered, whether you like it or not. Therefore, the greatest care must be taken not to make a mistake.

True virginity knows nothing of sexual union nor seeks after it and indeed does not even think of it, being protected and free of all such feelings through a heavenly gift. Therefore, when her parents are deliberating about her marriage, the young woman will leave all of that concern to those who wish as much good for her as she does for herself through the love enkindled in their hearts by nature, and who by their years and experience see further ahead. For how can a girl who has been confined within the walls of her house know the character and morals of men so that she can choose among them, or in her complete inexperience know what is best for her?

135. In Homer, when Nausicaa was instructed in her sleep by Minerva to wash her clothes, since she was soon to be married, she asked her father, Alcinous, for the chariot so that she might wash her clothes in the river. She gave another excuse, however, for she was ashamed even to mention

347. 1 Cor. 7:38–39.

marriage.[348] Imitating this passage in the twelfth book of the *Aeneid*, in which Latinus and his wife, Amata, are talking to Turnus, the future spouse of their daughter, Lavinia, Virgil merely makes reference to her tears and maidenly modesty, but does not have her speak a word.[349] By this he wished to signify that it does not befit a young woman to speak when her mother and father are discussing her marriage.

It was an ancient Roman custom[350] among those famous matrons, examples of modesty, that on the day when the bride was escorted to her husband's house, she did not cross the threshold herself but was carried in as if she unwillingly and forcibly entered that place where she would lose the honor of her virginity. How can a young woman pretend to do this when she has sought and asked for the marriage of her own will?

136. Saint Ambrose says this of Rebecca:

> It is not becoming to virginal modesty to choose a husband, but once a girl is betrothed to a man a decision is made about the day of the procession. And with good reason she did not interpose any delay. It was fitting that she hasten to her husband. Hence the clarity of that saying of Euripides, which made many people wonder where it came from. He said in the person of a woman who wished to leave her husband and was sought after for another marriage: 'My father will attend to my marriage, for that is not mine to decide.'[351] Therefore, young women, observe this modesty, which even the philosophers marveled at.[352]

So says Ambrose, who does not even permit widows to look after their marital situation. In the prayer of Sarah, daughter of Raguel, we find these words: "You know, Lord God, that I never desired a man, and I kept my soul free of all concupiscence. I never joined in with those who play nor did I share the company of those who walk in fickleness."[353] Let us hear how she says she received the men who were given to her by her parents: "I have consented to take a man out of respect for you, not because of my desire."[354]

137. Therefore, when her parents are engaged in these considerations,

---

348. Homer *Odyssey* 6.66.
349. Virgil *Aeneid* 12.64–66.
350. Plutarch, "Roman Questions," *Moralia*, 271D.
351. Euripides *Andromache* 987–88.
352. Ambrose *On Abraham* 1.91 (*PL* 14:153).
353. Tob. 3:16–17.
354. Tob. 3:18.

the young girl should help them by her prayers and supplications. Let her ask of Christ with purest intention that she be given a spouse who will not discourage, distract, or impede her from the practice of piety, but will invite, exhort, and assist her; and, according to the prediction of the apostle, "Let the unbelieving wife be sanctified by the believing husband."[355] In making this decision, parents should not only have and exhibit the affection of parents toward their children, but they should also assume the feelings of their daughter. Then they will make a choice that they would make if they themselves were to marry. It often happens that many parents, whether unknowingly or through deliberate malice, act wrongly in this decision because they think that the son-in-law whom they deem desirable for themselves would also be a good husband for their daughter. Often they look only to riches, noble lineage, wealth, and power in their son-in-law, things that will be to their own advantage, not what is best for their daughter, who must live with him within the same walls. These are enemies, not parents, or, to put it more aptly, vendors of their own daughters, whom they sell for their own advantage.

138. Marriage is a knot that cannot be untied. If you are going to let your son go out to dinner, you will first carefully inquire who the invited guests are. If he is to undertake a journey, you will find out who will accompany him. If you admit a dependent or servant into your house, you will inquire who he is, from what country he hales, who his relatives are, what his morals are, and how trustworthy he is. With what scrupulosity you will investigate all these matters, although they are associations of brief duration. For your tender young daughter, innocent and inexperienced in worldly affairs; who puts all her trust in you and places all her hopes and aspirations in your hands; who will have no other partner in life but the one you give her and no other future or destiny, will you have no qualms about coupling her with a person whom you would not wish for a servant, who is as ill-adapted to human fellowship as a bear, a wolf, or a pig? The French proverb is to the point: "He who is not happily married was not happily born."[356] So much does unhappy marriage outweigh nobility, beauty, health, wealth, and power and lead to complete misery. If this can be said of a man, how much more truly can it be said of a woman, for whom greater diligence must be exercised in procuring a good husband than a good woman for a man, since it is easier to rule over an evil person than to obey one?

355. 1 Cor. 7:14.
356. A proverb from Auvergne illustrates this: "Un homme mal marié, il vaudrait mieux qu'il fût noyé."

139. Two things should be considered in marriage: living together and offspring. The first includes the necessities of life, family existence, and daily habit. First, care must be given to material sustenance, although that is of little consequence; second, the physical well-being of the husband; third, the offspring; and fourth and most important, character and morals, all of which I shall discuss one by one. In all of this, one thing must be heeded: that there be a certain equality, or better, similarity, between husband and wife, that unites their souls and holds them together more tenaciously than anything else. Likeness is the tightest bond of love, which was what Pittacus of Mytilene, the most famous of the Seven Sages of ancient Greece, taught. When asked by a young man whom he should marry of two women who sought him in marriage—one superior to him in family and wealth, the other equal to him—the wise man directed him to a group of boys who were playing and shouting out, "Keep to your own place![357] By this he intimated what the young man should do.

Of very little concern, and, if its true value be esteemed, of least importance, is thought for the sustenance of the body. But unavoidable necessity has dictated that if not the greatest concern, it is at any rate the first. If you have to collect enough money for your daughter as a dowry to provide for the maintenance of the family, concentrate all your attention on the son-in-law, on his physical and moral qualities. If he must contribute something, you must consider not what riches he possesses but how he will acquire what he does not have and how he will hold on to what he has acquired. There are no resources so great that if you do not know how to protect and maintain them they are exhausted in a short time. The advice of the Greek leader Themistocles concerning the choosing of a marriage partner was that he preferred a man without money to money without a man.[358] One who is not adept at being thrifty and does not possess any money I esteem more worthy of slavery than of marriage.

140. A marriage should not be without patrimony. The woman brings one thing, namely, womanly virtues and the ability to bring forth children, and the man's contribution is to provide sustenance. Of life's occupations, some should be avoided altogether as dishonorable, such as that which accumulates wealth by lending out money at interest. Others are cruel and inhuman, such as the occupations of executioners, pirates, and mercenary soldiers, who, for the sake of small gain, use their hands to slaughter human

---

357. Diogenes Laertius 1.80. Plutarch also refers to this saying in "Education of Children," *Moralia*, 13F, where he states that those who take wives far above their station unwittingly become not their husbands but their slaves.

358. Valerius Maximus 7.2.9.

beings, to devastate property, and to burn buildings, acts of the most savage brutality. There are other disreputable livelihoods, such as those of shop-keepers and go-betweens, to which we will not descend unless we have despaired of finding any other livelihood or we are of that same class. Immoderate wealth, far superior to our own, makes husbands insolent and disdainful of their wives, whom they regard not so much as legitimate spouses as servants, all the more so if joined to wealth are power or illustrious ancestry.

141. In the body we consider beauty, age, and health. Beauty is a slight and short-lived blessing, and ugliness should not be an impediment to marriage if the other qualities are not missing, unless it is truly horrendous and abominable. Age is a more important factor. It should not be less than what is required to exercise paternal authority and to govern wife, children, and servants, nor too advanced to possess the strength necessary for domestic obligations, nor such that at the very beginning of the marriage, while the children are still infants, he should pay his debt to nature and leave wife and children bereft of his support. Much attention should be given to good health, both for the sake of household duties, which often demand a healthy person at the helm, and for wife and children, whom he will afflict with his illness if it is contagious. This is to be guarded against all the more carefully if it is a foul and horrible disease, one of those that doctors call hereditary. And what should be said of insanity or some form of mental illness which is proven by many examples to be transmitted to one's offspring? The greatest care and consideration, as I said previously, must be given to the future husband's character and morals. This is the one criterion we should use. On this we must base our judgment of a man. There is nothing in physical attributes or material well-being that can provide us with a sure estimation of a man: not riches, possessions, race, power, influence, dignity, entourage, beauty, health, age, soundness of body, stature, nor their opposites—nothing, in a word, but his character, in which are to be found intelligence, learning, and virtues, or their opposites: dullness, ignorance, and vice.

142. Many unpleasant things occur during the course of a marriage; many distasteful and painful things must be swallowed. Paul made this prediction of spouses: "They will have infirmities of the flesh."[359] Many things can exacerbate this way of life. Only one thing can make it palatable and alleviate it: the good fortune of having a good and wise husband. An upright woman is a singular gift of God to a man,[360] as the wise man said, which is conferred upon him for his good deeds. What is a good man to a woman?

359. Rom. 6:9.
360. Prov. 12:4; 18:22.

Surely we do not think it more pleasant and profitable to have a good servant rather than a good master. O stupid parents! O senseless and foolish girls who prefer handsome, rich, or noble spouses to good ones. You increase your cares, anxieties, and troubles, which a marriage brings with it of itself. Marriages based on money or sensual pleasure are disastrous, like that of Helen and Paris; she desirous of the riches of Asia and he lusting after exceptional physical beauty. In contrast, the union between Ulysses and Penelope was happy and peaceful, since he was a sober-minded and wise husband, she a temperate and chaste wife.

143. If one were to choose a companion for a journey out of a given number of men, would she not be accounted mad by everyone if she should prefer a rich or well-dressed or handsome man over one who was cheerful and eloquent, who is like a vehicle upon the journey, as the ancient proverb has it,[361] or wise and provident, who can mitigate the tedium of the journey and be a helper in danger? If life is nothing but a journey, what madness it is to increase the host of difficulties with which it is encumbered by adding marital discord. If you marry a handsome man, his beauty will make him conceited; a rich man, his riches will make him contemptuous. Marry a nobleman, and his noble birth will make him insolent. Finally, pride, which is born of fortuitous gifts, will not allow concord founded on good faith to exist between you. If you marry a handsome man for the sake of his beauty, in whom there is no sense, or honesty, or a grain of salt, as the saying goes[362] (just as it is usually the case that in the most elegant dwelling places there dwells the most repulsive of hosts), you might just as well seek to marry a painting or a marble statue that is beautifully carved or painted. Do you wish an insipid rich man for the sake of his riches? Why not marry a golden statue? Do you want someone of illustrious family, but who is filthy and licentious, merely because of his blood? Why not settle for a statue of Scipio or Caesar? How much better it would be to lead your life with images, paintings, and statues than with an unprincipled and intolerable man! And yet my comparison of wicked men with mute objects was not altogether apposite. It would have been more accurate to compare them to asses, swine, bears, and wolves.

144. I used to think that the mating of Pasiphae with a bull[363] was a fairy tale. In reality, it is a plausible fact,[364] since I have seen women who

---

361. Publilius Syrus 17.

362. Erasmus *Adages* II iii 51 (*CWE* 33 : 163.

363. Pasiphae, the wife of King Minos of Crete, mated with a bull. The offspring of this union was the Minotaur.

364. Cf. Plutarch, "Advice to Bride and Groom," *Moralia,* 139A.

do not recoil from men whose nature is worse than that of brute beasts—dirty, drunk, wrathful, stupid, imprudent, idiotic, cruel, and bloodthirsty, who have less in common with men than with wild beasts, who flee and avoid the company of wise and temperate men. This conduct inspired one of our own writers, using the vernacular tongue,[365] to attack them, saying that they have the instinct of she-wolves in choosing a mate, since they are said to choose the vilest and most foul-smelling of the males that follow after them. From this characteristic the name of she-wolf has been assigned to women. Men are not easily captured by women in whom no quality of fortune or physical beauty or talent stands out. Some women love certain men simply because they think nothing is truly worthy of love, which shows clearly that they have no concern for discretion, reason, judgment, or good sense. These have no influence on them, so that whatever they do is done under the impulse of their sick minds, devoid of reason or, rather, totally averse to reason.

145. It cannot be estimated how great a part of our youth is corrupted by this type of—shall I call her a woman or a stinking corpse? I cannot even mention such squandering of life without a feeling of disgust. Inexperienced young men, devoid of better judgment, aspire to receive the approval of the girls they love and desire. They see that this cannot be attained except by dissociating themselves from every honorable practice and from the cultivation of talent and good morals. They make everything subservient to the tyranny of love. Thus, love for that type of woman is very much like the potions of that famed witch Circe, by which they say she turned men into wild beasts.[366] Just as boys absorbed in their games (who at that age know nothing better or more elevated) have admiration only for those who excel in those games, with no appreciation of the pursuits of wise men that they cannot even imagine, so women addicted to pleasures, sexual license, and madness attribute great wisdom to those who are immersed in such pursuits and esteem them of great importance. Whatever is redolent of a sounder mind they reject as worthless trash and madness with expressions of great disdain. They love, admire, and look up to those that are stupid and insane, consider them wise, and openly confess it. On the contrary, they despise the wise, avoid them, say they are stupid and insipid—like people burning

---

365. The verses are "De natura de lobas son / ciertamente 'n escoger" ("They are of the nature of she-wolves, certainly in choosing"), Pere Torroella, *Maldezir de mugeres*, 3.1–2. Torroella was a bilingual poet (Spanish and Catalan) of the second half of the fifteenth century. His poems appeared in the *Cancionero general*, published in Valencia in 1511 and 1514.

366. Homer *Odyssey* 10.234.

with fever who spit out things tasting of honey as if it were gall and as swine find the smell of mud better than that of marjoram.[367]

146. But if they knew how much good they could do for others if they changed their perverse opinions, I have no such low opinion of them as not to believe that they would be wiser in their choices and in their whole way of life. I daresay that the good advice and exhortations to virtue of all preachers, parents, and magistrates would not have the same efficacy as the sound minds and words worthy of sound minds of these women. Whatever the one you love or wish to please says or does has very great authority. Plutarch tells us in his life of Lycurgus that the lawgiver of the Spartans understood this.[368]

147. I remember that when I was very young, I was told that there was a city in Spain where the youth of the nobility, in their idleness and opulence, began to abandon themselves to the pursuit of pleasure, to the point that they cared for nothing but banquets, dancing, love affairs, gambling, and other pastimes that contributed nothing to good sense or wisdom. This caused great grief in the older citizens, who, in those beginnings, prophesied great ruin for their republic. Many of them deliberated day and night how they could take countermeasures against the vices of these young men, for they saw that once they were dead and gone, the city would fall into the hands of morally depraved men.

One of them had a very salutary plan. He saw that these young men were aspiring Don Juans who put much faith in the caprices and judgment of women. Thus, he suggested to his fellow conspirators that each of them should explain the perilous state of the republic to his daughters and daughters-in-law and those women charged to his care, how from a flourishing and prosperous city, it would fall into utter wrack and ruin once these crazed men took control of it. The result would be that the women, who were now enjoying a luxurious existence in its great wealth, would have to endure a very hard life when present prosperity would be turned into indigence and squalor. The only remedy left to them was if they, to whose judgment the young men ascribed such importance, were to urge them on to the pursuit of wisdom and interest in the public good. This could easily be achieved if they were to shun the company of the would-be dancers, chatterers, misfits, clowns, banqueters, and gamblers, giving open display of their contempt. As for honest, moderate, sober-minded young men, who gave some sign of good sense, they would welcome them with courtesy and

367. Lucretius *On the Nature of Things* 6.973.
368. Plutarch, "Sayings of Spartans," *Moralia,* 228A, *Life of Lycurgus* 14.5.

kindness. They would praise them as future pillars of the state and would revile the others as worthless and depraved, of no merit, and destined to bring dishonor and ruin upon their country.

The plan met with the old men's approval, and it was explained to the women with great urgency and approved in view of the evident danger, and they put it into execution with all discretion. Within a short time, the young men changed from profligate and debauched youth into men of great sagacity, skilled in public and private administration, and that city emerged more thriving under those young men than it had been under the old men, and in intelligence and experience they far surpassed their ancestors.

148. You poor creatures! What will you do with men laden down with gold and deprived of any good sense? Would you rather be in perpetual mourning wrapped in gold and silk than to lead a happy life clothed in wool and hemp? Do you prefer to be hated and beaten dressed in purple garments or to be loved and offer yourself to your husband's embraces dressed in drab colors? If it is the former that you prefer, take what you asked for and do not complain that you received as your lot what you choose consciously and deliberately, though blindly and imprudently. What shall we say of those husbands who, we are told, driven on solely by madness, ended up killing their innocent wives? Justina, a noble Roman virgin, the most beautiful young woman of her time, was given in marriage to a rich but senseless and raging madman. He became suspicious of his bride's exceptional beauty. When on his wedding night he caught sight of her immaculate white neck as she was bending down to take off her shoes, seized by a frenzy of jealousy, he butchered the young maiden and new bride. This epigram tells about this terrible crime:

> My cruel husband cut off my head
> As I stooped down to loose the fastenings
> Around my snow-white foot,
> Pitilessly, and beside that very bed
> Where I had lain with him not long before,
> And where I lost the honor of my maidenhood.
> And yet I did not merit this cruel death,
> I call upon the gods to be my witnesses.
> But here I lie, the victim of harsh fate.
> Learn, fathers, from the example of Justina
> Not to marry your daughter to a senseless man.[369]

369. This epigram is found in a Vatican manuscript, *Vat. lat.* 1610, 58b.

149. If Plato rightly prescribes that men, like diligent and industrious farmers, should be careful into what field they scatter their noble seed, lest it degenerate because of a defect of the soil,[370] how much more care should a woman take, since she is the ploughed field itself? For if feeling were given to the seed and the soil, there is no doubt that each would require the other to be good. Crops are produced from the combined powers of both, but the earth would be more careful and meticulous, since crops receive most of their vigor from the seed rather than from the earth.

A mare of good breeding mates only with a stallion of good breeding. It is commonly desired that offspring resemble their parents. Would you, the wife, wish your children to resemble such a father? Or would you, the father-in-law, wish grandchildren who resembled him? What madness it is to adopt into one's family the kind of son-in-law that if someone were to express the wish that you would have grandchildren like him you would regard it as a curse. How much more nobly Aristides of Locri, an intimate friend of Plato, conducted himself. When Dionysius II asked for the hand of one of his daughters, he responded that he would be much more content to see her dead than married to a tyrant.[371]

Living together consists of talking together and sharing all fortunes. What would such a dolt, totally ignorant of everything, talk about? What a torture it will be to hear the ass constantly braying. And how much more irksome if you are not lacking in intelligence, as it is commonly said that there is no greater torment for a person of intelligence than to be stuck with one who is ignorant.

150. The apostle Paul does not allow women to speak in church, whether it be to teach or to learn; instead, if they wish to know something, they should ask their husbands at home.[372] Whom will you ask, you poor thing, if you have any doubts about piety or about religion? Will you ask this of the beauty, nobility, or riches that you sought after in a demented person? Who will look after the family? Who will educate your children? In prosperity there is need of moderation; in adversity, of consolation; in both cases there is need of sound and effective judgment. Who will provide this when you have a husband totally devoid of judgment and reason? If you go over to the morals of your evil husband, you become evil. If you contradict him, you will be hated. What quarrels! What unending hatred! In order to avoid this, at times you will acquiesce to what seem like wicked actions or

---

370. Plato *Phaedrus* 276B.

371. Plutarch *Timoleon* 6.3–4.

372. 1 Cor 14·34

will even indicate approval. The reason why the church does not allow a Christian woman to marry a pagan or a heretic, or vice versa, a man of the Christian faith to marry an unbelieving woman, is so that neither will be tainted by the contagion of the other.

151. Consider, on the other hand, what conversations you will enjoy with a gifted and prudent man, such that no sweeter harmony could be found than the speech of this man, and all the more if added to that is the gift of eloquence. What training for the children! What a model of the family of a prudent man! How suited to practical realities, how unshaken in its stability, how irreproachable in its honor! If you wish to learn something, you have a teacher at your disposal; if you are in need of advice, whether it be to conduct yourself wisely in prosperity or courageously in adversity, you have at hand a fountain from which you can draw copiously. Not only this, but precepts, recommendations, exhortations, consolations—in a word, all that is necessary at any moment in the tempests of life. With a good man, what mildness of manner! What peace and tranquillity! What growth in piety with the help of your husband, not only by precept and idle philosophizing but by the example of his actions, so that you will find that it is not a husband that you have acquired but an angel sent from heaven, a guide for your whole life.

152. This is true and genuine tranquillity, a foretaste of eternal bliss. Because of such a husband, the Lord will rain down blessings upon wife, children, and the whole family, relatives too and close friends. Because of Abraham, God gave a son to Sarah; because of Isaac, he gave twins to Rebecca. God looks after the generation of the just, as he himself testifies in his prophecies in more than one place. So many times did he pardon the grave crimes of the race of Israel because of Abraham, Isaac, and Jacob. "The generation of the righteous will be blessed,"[373] said the psalmist, and elsewhere he says, "I was young, and I grew old and I did not see the just man abandoned nor his seed in search of bread. All the day he has mercy and takes pity, and his seed will be blessed."[374] Then Solomon in the Book of Proverbs says, "He who dwells in justice without blame will leave his children blessed."[375] In human society, what commendation can be compared with this: "Wife of an excellent husband," "Son of an excellent father"? As soon as Evander, king of the Arcadians, saw Aeneas, he embraced him, remembering his father, Anchises:

373. Ps. 112:2.
374. Ps. 37:25–26.
375. Prov. 20:7.

Bravest of the Trojan line,
How gladly I receive and remember you,
How you remind me of your father's speech,
The voice and features of great Anchises![376]

153. What of the father-in-law? What security they provide for themselves if their sons-in-law are men of good character, mindful of their duties and of filial piety! But if they are corrupt, morally depraved, stupid, deceitful, arrogant, and wicked, then one acquires an enemy. A bad son-in-law is an enemy, not a relative. A good one is not so much a son-in-law as a son. Peter's mother-in-law was delivered from a strong fever because her son-in-law had interceded for her.[377] It was of such profit for her to have such a son-in-law, whom Christ did not disdain to join to himself as his companion and disciple.

Of the daughter-in-law, we read in the Book of Ruth that when Naomi returned from the land of Moab to her native land of Judah, bereft of husband and children, two Moabite daughters-in-law accompanied the old woman. One of them, Orpah by name, returned home to her people, but Ruth continued to accompany her mother-in-law,[378] whom she consoled with her words, nourished, and cared for. So Naomi found in Ruth both the loyalty of a daughter and the care of a son. She would have truly been a widow and an abandoned old woman if she had not had the good fortune to have a better daughter-in-law than Orpah. But since she had Ruth, she did not appear to be entirely bereft of children, nor did she have reason to be called Mara, which means embittered, as she wished to be called.[379] Moreover, when Ruth bore Obed of Boaz, Naomi's neighbors congratulated her so warmly that it did not seem that she had a grandchild born of her daughter or her son, but that she had seven sons of her own. These were the words of those who congratulated her: "Blessed is the Lord who has not left you this day without next of kin and may his name be renowned in Israel. You have one who will console your spirit and provide for your old age. He is born of your daughter-in-law, who loves you and who is more to you than seven sons."[380] So much for the spouse himself.

154. Now I shall briefly discuss how he is to be sought and acquired. I

---

376. Virgil *Aeneid* 8.154–55.
377. Luke 4:38.
378. Ruth 1:6–18.
379. Ruth 1:20.
380. Ruth 4:14, 16

shall begin by saying that men are often changed by marriage, so that one whom everyone despised when he was single suddenly becomes one whom everyone would like for their daughters. Others, however, take a turn for the worse. When a young woman's marriage is being contemplated, some think that it is expedient that marriageable girls should be seen frequently in public; should be dressed and adorned with elegance and splendor, should associate and converse with men; be eloquent, skilled in dancing and in playing the cithara; and sometimes even should fall in love with the man destined to be their husband, for in this way they may find a match more easily.

In answer to this dangerous opinion, I could cite some of the general precepts I have given, but I shall examine these points one by one to give satisfaction not only to the wise but also to the ignorant and inexperienced. Would any sensible person ever give this advice, knowing that we should not do evil so that good may come thereof, especially when the present evil is certain and the good not certain or not at all commonly to be expected? My dear young woman, if the only way you can get married is through these corruptions of the soul and these risks to chastity, it is better never to get married or to have only Christ as your spouse. Otherwise, you would be first marrying the devil so that you can then marry a man—or rather, that you can have two husbands at the same time, the second being an adulterer, namely, the one to whom you were joined second, your mortal husband. I have previously explained what perils and what evils there are in all these things. I am confident that my views will receive the approbation of those whose first and principal care is for Christ and for piety.

155. Let us talk now with those who wrongly and impiously consider the things of the world to be more important than those of Christ. I observe that there are two things that are of most importance for a woman to bring to her husband—unblemished chastity and unblemished reputation. No one is so insane, no one so much a slave of beauty or wealth or nobility, no one so vile and devoid of all principles, that he would not take any woman who had these two qualities, just as no one would wish to have a woman who did not possess them.

Which girl guards her chastity and her good name more irreproachably: the one who stays at home or the one who appears frequently in public? At home there is no occasion to commit wrong; outside there are innumerable occasions that crop up on all sides and multiply like the heads of the hydra. On the girl hidden away in her house, no one passes judgment. On one who is often seen in public, everyone has something to say, whence arises dishonor, and her reputation is easily besmirched according to the diverse opinions of her critics. There is no one more susceptible to these stains to their reputation than a young girl, and no one has more difficulty in removing them.

Which girl do men admire more; which do they respect and regard as more chaste: one whom they see but rarely or never, or one they run into everywhere, even to the point of boredom? They do not easily believe that chastity can be rightly preserved by a girl who spends so much time in public. Certainly, to ensure a girl's successful marriage, it is of more advantage that she be heard about rather than seen, since men's characters and opinions are so varying. A girl in the public eye will either say or do something that may displease her future spouse, one of those who counsel him, or one in whom he places much trust. This one thing is sufficient to destroy many marriages that had almost been joined. There is much truth in the popular saying that marriages that are long in the making rarely come together.

156. Let us speak of dress and cosmetics. If that is why someone marries you, don't you see that you will excite his aversion when you will be without them? And yet eventually you will have to put off this mask and deal simply and openly with your husband. Are we not aware that we derive most pleasure from things in which we encounter some unexpected good and most displeasure from things that delude our good hopes? If you seem beautiful to your spouse when you are adorned and made up, but you are really not beautiful, after forming such a high opinion of your beauty, he cannot help but dislike you when he finds out that he has been deceived. I can name any number of women, no longer young, in this region and in my native Valencia, who are still unwed because of their excesses in personal adornment. They say, "The whole dowry and all the wedding gifts will be lavished on one dress or a necklace." This finery in the case of the bride is a heavy burden for the husband and in the unmarried girl for the father. For that reason there is sadness in a household when a daughter is born, because they immediately calculate how much it is going to cost them. Add to this the fact that too much adornment makes women suspect of frivolity and vanity, whereas one who uses discretion in adorning herself is considered to be frugal, wise, and dignified—the kind everyone would want as his wife.

157. As for those who freely associate with men, who does not direct some adverse criticism against them? Atalanta, daughter of Iasius, king of Argon, who spurned the pleasures of the city and lived a life dedicated to hunting in the woods and who first pierced the famous Calydonian boar with an arrow, was a virgin huntress, according to legend. Certain rhetoricians, however, called her chastity into question because she often wandered

through the woods with young men.[381] With regard to a girl's chastity, there is no adverse rumor so insignificant that it does not spread like a spot of oil. It will be magnified in the talk of the crowd, always ready to find imperfections. Then what husband has the patience to put up with a wife who is accustomed to associate with men and join in conversations with them? Who would not prefer a woman who is content to sit and talk with her husband rather than with a crowd of men, among whom one is attractive for his beauty, another for his wealth, another for his liberality, another for his intelligence, another for his eloquence, noble birth, or physical strength? When young women are eloquent, that is, garrulous (for what is eloquence in a woman but garrulity?), it is proof of levity and perverse character, so that the man who intends to marry her will think he is marrying a viper, not a woman.

Young men praise to her face a woman who is loquacious, skilled in dancing, witty and carefree; they call her unaffected, congenial, well-bred— but only to deceive and corrupt her, not to marry her. They all think that such a girl will be an easy conquest. No one will be willing to take a woman to wife when he sees that she makes herself so available to others. They praise what they do in their presence because they enjoy it.

158. Poor wretches! If they could only hear what these young men say to one another afterwards when they are among themselves and have thrown off their masks! Then they would know what their real sentiments were in praising them, smiling at them, and exciting them by word and gesture. They would understand that when they call someone congenial, they mean of loose morals; when they call her eloquent, they mean talkative and garrulous; when they call her agile, they refer more to lightness of mind than of body; when they call her sophisticated, they mean shameless; when they call her polite, they mean forward and assertive. Did they say she was unaffected and guileless? What they really meant was silly and ignorant of feminine propriety. But will such girls find a marriage partner? I admit that some will, either through the efforts and foresight of their parents and relatives or because of the imprudence and stupidity of their husbands. But how many do not find a match! How many marry better husbands and more happily who do not lure them with false blandishments, who, when they realize they have been trapped, kill them with ill-treatment. You will never

---

381. In the Calydonian boar hunt, Atalanta was the first to wound the animal, but Meleager killed it. According to some versions of the myth, she bore a son to Meleager but hid it in order to preserve her reputation as a virgin.

get a good, exemplary husband if you win him over by wiles and cunning. In short, if there is anyone so insane, so base and depraved as to prefer such a woman over one who is shy, austere, of simple dress, silent, let my neighbor give him his daughter; I would not give mine. For if one puts frivolity and vice before dignity, holiness, and other virtues, it must be those things that he loves.

159. A few things must be said about love, which miserably deceives the majority of young women and precipitates them into a thousand perils. It will be evident that a girl must not give even a sign of her desire for marriage or that she loves a young man in order to marry him. If you love him before he is your husband, what will he suspect but that you will easily fall in love with someone else other than him, to whom you should not yet have shown your love. Naturally, he will think that he is not the only one loved, since there is no reason to think that you will not love others; and after you have been legitimately joined to him, you will fall in love with others, since you have such a strong inclination toward love.

Others may gloss over this fact with whatever pretexts they wish: A woman who loves a man who is not her husband is a prostitute in her body if she has carnal relations with him, and in her mind if she does not. It does not matter who the man is, if she does not yet love her husband. Foolish girl! Have you never heard it said that many women have been drawn into these premature love affairs intending to surrender themselves to the ones they thought would be their husbands? But when these men had given satisfaction to their lust, they left them deluded and scorned. And they acted rightly and wisely, for these women were not worthy of marriage, since they openly showed that they could lie together with a man who was not their legitimate husband. They would do the same thing with other suitors before marriage and with adulterers when they are married.

160. No day goes by without these things happening in every city. There is no woman so remote from reports of events that take place among the people as not to have heard about them. I hear that in this region where I live, many suitors have been rejected by young women for the sole reason that there was no intimacy between them beforehand. They said that they could not live a happy and pleasant life with husbands whom they had not loved or knew before marriage. They say this is very common in Crete. As if love could not coalesce in marriage! What need is there to berate such individuals with words? A woman who does not see their shamelessness is all the more shameless herself. Will you not love a man because he was joined to you by the laws of God, by God's command and with God as the godfather, as it were—but because you became used to his love before a

holy and legitimate marriage? Do you approach the marriage-bed through lust awakened by being in his company? Whores do this too, and that is why they love their lovers; and you, to be sure, are not very different from them. And so it happens to girls of this type that almost by divine vengeance all the flame of love that should burn in wedlock burns before their marriage. In the first wedding embraces, it dies down and is extinguished. Whence the popular saying: "Those who marry for love live in sorrow."

161. In many cases, hatred takes the place of the extinguished love, and this subject has given rise to many a story in all cities, when they hear tell that the most ardent lovers three or four days after the wedding have had quarrels and even come to blows and are divorced before all the wedding bread has been consumed. No wonder. Fire that lacks fuel and kindling wood cannot last, nor can love that is not nourished by good morals. As Cicero says, "There is no firm friendship between evil-minded persons."[382] But if it is not expedient that marriages be brought about by love affairs and if that holy love cannot be held together by such disreputable and fragile bonds, how much less so through discord, quarrels, lawsuits, and mutual hatred, as when in a legal dispute a woman claims some man as her husband or a man claims some woman as his wife. I have never read, seen, or heard anything more foolish and absurd than that you drag to yourself by force a person who is unwilling and reluctant, with whom you must live inseparably, and who will ruin your existence if he does not love you. As if someone could be forced to love! Love is not obtained by force, but elicited, and one who has been dragged somewhere by force against his will and is there held prisoner will never be a friend.

162. What madness it is to enter upon the mystery of consecrated love out of hatred! I would not wish to keep a servant against his will, so help me God, never mind a wife! I do not merely say that a man should not be seized against his will in spite of his refusal, but that you should not marry a man unless he gladly and eagerly desires the marriage. It is not fitting that the girl's father or guardians ask or solicit the marriage or that the girl offer herself spontaneously. On the contrary, it is the man who should demand the marriage. That is the way it would be done if money did not set the standard and govern everything. Now the woman marries because of money and so does the man, and as Seneca said with no less truth than humor, "We take a wife counting on our fingers."

That is why we see so many unhappy marriages, when each of the spouses thinks he or she is married to money, not to a person. Each party

---

382. Sallust *Catiline* 20.4.

tightly embraces it as if it were his legitimate mate; the husband regards his wife as a mistress, and the wife regards her husband as an adulterer for the purpose of lust, while everything else is hateful to them. Those who marry for the sake of riches inhabit the same house together, but do not live together. In the case of those who marry for sensual pleasure and beauty, as these fade so does conjugal affection. Those who marry out of true and genuine love form one soul out of two persons, which is the natural effect of true love. Therefore, those who wish to preserve the natural order of things pure and intact and not corrupt it with perverse opinions look upon marriage as a union of love, benevolence, friendship, charity, piety, and all that is sweet, pleasant, and endearing, which bolster and support it. Therefore, they do not deceive with artful stratagems the person who is to be their inseparable companion, and they do not carry him off by brute force; but, as is expressed in the term used for this contract, they lead and are led into matrimony [383] openly, sincerely, purely, honorably. Neither of them will have cause to complain that they were captured, defrauded, or dragged by force with irreparable damage to both parties. Let a holy and happy concord exist between them, the sweet condiment of marriage.

383. The Latin expression for "marry" is *ducere in matrimonium*.

BOOK II

WHICH TREATS OF
MARRIED WOMEN

I

WHAT THOUGHTS
SHOULD OCCUPY THE MIND
OF A WOMAN WHEN
SHE MARRIES

1. When a woman marries, she must call to mind the origins of marriage and frequently review its laws in thought and meditation. She must so prepare herself that, having first understood this great mystery, she may later fulfill its obligations. God, the originator and founder of this great institution, after bringing man into the world, thought it was not fitting to leave him alone.[1] So he joined to him a living partner, like to him in mind and body, with whom he could associate, converse, and spend his life suitably and agreeably; and, finally, provide for the procreation of offspring, if he so desired. For marriage was instituted not so much for the production of offspring as for community of life and indissoluble companionship. The name of "husband" does not signify the gratification of lust, but a mutual association in all the activities of life. God brought woman to man, which means that God himself was the chief author and mediator of marriage. Therefore, Christ in the gospel refers to them as joined by God.[2]

As soon as man looked upon the female of the species, he began to love her above all else and said, "This is now bone of my bone and flesh of my flesh. She shall be called woman[3] because out of man was she taken. Because of her, man will leave father and mother and will cleave to his wife and they shall be two in one flesh."[4] When he says "one flesh," it means literally one flesh. Moreover, flesh means mankind, both male and female, according to

1. Gen. 2:18.

2. Matt. 19:6.

3. The Latin word used for "woman" in the Vulgate in this context is *virago*, which is from the same root as *vir*, "man." This similarity is also present in the original Hebrew words: *ish* and *isha*.

4. Gen. 2:23–24.

the true sense of the Hebrew word.[5] Therefore, those who were previously two human beings become one, joined together in matrimony. This is the marvelous mystery of marriage, that it so joins and unites the two spouses that the two become one, which was true also of Christ and the church, as the apostle Paul teaches.[6] No power could bring this about except it were divine. Of necessity, this must be a very holy thing, since God is present in it in such a special manner.

2. Therefore, a woman should not think that she is on her way to dances, amusements, and banqueting when she approaches the marriage ceremony, but must think of higher things. God is the sponsor,[7] and the church is the matron of honor. Therefore, Christ does not allow that what has been joined and ratified before such witnesses should be undone and dissolved by any mortal, and that those who from two have become one should become two from one. For he says in the gospel, "What God has joined together, let no man put asunder."[8] Now if it is a crime to separate them, and if the knot that God has tied cannot be loosed by human hands, then no other should try to open what has been closed with the key of David,[9] which only the immaculate Lamb[10] holds in his possession.

3. Right now, from the beginning, good woman, prepare to join to yourself in love the one whom God has joined to you in the sacrament in such a way that the joining may become easy and light for you. Do not wish that the bond be dissolved or loosened, lest you involve yourself and your companion in inextricable trouble and unending misery; for a great part of this lies in your hands. By your chastity, modesty, and obedience, you can enjoy the pleasant companionship of your husband, and you will live happily together. On the other hand, by your vices of mind and body, you will render him harsh and bitter and create torture and exasperation for yourself and for him that will not end, even with death. You will be a maidservant in eternal drudgery; you will work, pull the millstone, cry, be afflicted; you will curse the day you were joined to him in the marriage bed, the day on which you were born, and your parents and relatives and whoever else had a hand

---

5. The Hebrew word *basar*, meaning "flesh," can also be used generically to denote the whole human race, male and female.

6. Eph. 5:31–32.

7. Vives uses words from the Roman marriage ceremony: *auspex*, a functionary who originally took the auspices; and *pronuba*, a married woman who conducted the bride to the bridal chamber.

8. Matt. 19:6; Mark 10:9.

9. Apoc. 3:7.

10. Apoc. 5:9; 1 Peter 1:19.

in arranging such a marriage, if by your vices you offend your husband and inspire his hatred. But you will be mistress of a happy household, you will be happy, exultant, and will bless the day you were married and those who joined you to him if by your virtues, modesty, and compliance you render yourself lovable to him. The wise writer of mimes said, "The good woman by obeying rules her husband."[11] Pliny the Younger, who had the wife whom he desired and showed himself in turn to be a pliable and agreeable husband, thanked Hispulla, his wife's aunt, in his own name and in that of his wife: "I, because you gave her to me, and she, because you gave me to her, as if you chose us for each other."[12]

4. Above all these considerations, this is the first and perhaps only law of marriage: "They shall be two in one flesh."[13] This is the hinge of marriage, the bond of a most sacred fellowship. If a woman will direct her thoughts, words, and deeds to this goal, then it follows of necessity that she will guard and protect the holiness of marriage with honor and integrity and will live an excellent and happy life. This a chaste and honorable woman must always keep before her mind. To fulfill this law and express and manifest it in her deeds will be her one thought night and day, conscious that no virtue will be lacking in the one who considers herself to be one with her husband. May she so live that she both plainly appear to be and truly be one with him. On the contrary, she who does not do this will be entirely without virtue.

5. This precept is very similar to that which Christ often declared was the only one he left to his disciples: that they should love one another.[14] That most wise fashioner of human emotions was aware that whatever alliance was joined together with this glue would not need any other laws, edicts, statutes, pacts, or agreements. All would proceed in the greatest tranquillity and harmony; there would be no quarrels or litigations or complaints. For no woman is envious or becomes angry or does harm or causes trouble or brings a lawsuit or wishes to be preferred to the one she loves. She will think of that person as she would of herself and will wish no less good for him than she wishes for herself, since she will consider everything that is his as being hers as well, and that he is her alter ego as she is his. O what force in the divine word, worthy of our total adoration! Obviously, the Lord used very concise language, which was instilled with divine wisdom far

11. Publilius Syrus 108.
12. Pliny *Letters* 4.19.
13. Matt. 19:5.
14. John 13:34, 15:17.

surpassing all human wisdom. He spoke only three words and gave expression to what mortals cannot explain in the longest speeches but merely labor and try to explain in their infantile stammerings.

I propose no other law of marriage; this alone suffices, this alone contains all that human ingenuity can devise or mortal eloquence express. Let women not rely on my word, but believe the first parent of our race, Adam; or, rather, let them harken to the words of Christ in the gospel, who commands that they be two in one person and says, "What God has joined together. . . ." [15] For she who lives in such a way as to be convinced that she and her husband are one in every respect fulfills to perfection all the duties of a holy wife. We would have been spared the labor and care of writing by this one precept of God if it had penetrated so deeply into the minds of women that they would be able and willing to readily understand it, uphold it, and put it into practice. But in order that it adhere more strongly and have deeper roots, I must place it before your eyes—developed and elaborated in many ways, given various forms, and taught in such a way that it will be more easily grasped and retained. Let the prudent woman remember, however, that whatever we say does not deviate from that one teaching, just as a person remains the same no matter how often he changes his clothes.

6. On the day of the wedding (since this is the beginning of a new life, whose outcome remains uncertain), there is no need of dancing, round dances, and all that hubbub of drinking and uncontrolled and prolonged gaiety, lest the wise man's words be verified: "Laughter will be mixed with sadness and grief occupies the last moments of mirth." [16] Rather, the man and woman should begin with prayers and supplications that he in whose hands they are may grant them a happy outcome. When it is necessary to set out on a long, varied, and uncertain journey, one does not send for a flute player and invite his friends to a dance. Instead, he implores the help of God so that what he is undertaking may turn out well and prosperously. With how much more solicitude and more pious spirit must this be done on the wedding day, which is the birthday of both spouses either for happiness or misfortune! Strange to say how the devil, counselor and instigator of the worst possible examples, perverts men's senses so that to those antidotes given us by God against poison, we mix in so much poison that they become lethal; and from that source whence salvation was hoped for, destruction arises. We profess in baptism to renounce the pomps of Satan, yet we have added immense pomp to baptism. Marriage was permitted as a remedy for

15. Matt. 19:6.
16. Prov. 14.13.

lust, and we have made of the wedding day an occasion for unbridled lust. Saint John Chrysostom bitterly complains that immediately on the wedding day itself, the mind of the young girl is assailed on all sides by the machinations of vice.[17] We would behave well enough if in this storm of perturbations we could keep the rudder of our mind on a straight course, not to say arrive safely in port after being buffeted by these winds.

17. John Chrysostom, *Homily 56, on Genesis, ch. 29* (PG 54:486–87).

TWO POINTS OF GREATEST IMPORTANCE FOR THE MARRIED WOMAN

7. Among the virtues proper to a married woman, two must be regarded as the most important, surpassing all others. If these two are present, they can render marriages strong, stable, lasting, easy, light, pleasant, happy. If either of them is absent, they become weak, burdensome, unloving, intolerable, and full of misery. These two virtues are chastity and great love for one's husband. The first she brings with her from her father's house, the second she assumes when she crosses the threshold of her husband's house, so that after leaving behind parents, relatives, and friends, she has no doubt that she will find them all again in her husband. In each of these virtues she reflects the image of the church, which is most chaste and tenaciously preserves unshaken faith in its spouse, Christ. Though harassed internally by suitors, which is to say, baptized heretics, and attacked externally by pagans, Moors, and Jews, it has never been contaminated by the least stain, and it believes and senses that all its good is found in its spouse, Christ. Chastity must be greater in a married woman than in an unmarried one, for if you pollute and violate it now (God forbid!), see the harm you do to many and how many avengers you incite against you by one wicked deed. In the first place, you harm two persons, than whom none should be greater, better, or dearer to you: God, by whose authority you were joined and by whose divinity you swore to the purity of the marriage bed; and after him your husband, next to God, to whom you dedicated yourself and to him alone, in whom you violate all loves and loyalties; for you are to him what Eve was to Adam— daughter, sister, companion, and wife.

8. Add to this the fact that he is a second self; and so it is as if you laid hands on yourself. You will have dissolved the greatest of bonds, broken the holiest association that exists in human affairs: trust, which many have given even to an armed enemy and kept it, although it meant their own certain destruction. You will have broken faith with your husband and that breast

which should have been dearer to you than your very self. You contaminate the immaculate church, which sanctified your union. You destroy civil society; you violate the laws of your country; you lash your father with a bitter scourge; you beat your mother, sisters, brothers, near ones, your kinsmen by marriage, your close friends. You are an example of wicked behavior to your peers; you sear an indelible brand into your family; and like a crazed and cruel mother you reduce your children to the point of being unable to hear about their mother without shame or about their father without doubt. You subject yourself to perjury and sacrilege, since your bodies are dedicated to God by vow and sacrament. Then, besides the defilement brought upon your family, you transfer the heredity from its rightful owner to strangers. You drag your brothers into the danger of having incestuous relations with their sisters. What greater sin do they commit or what fouler contamination do they contract who overthrow their country, do away with laws and justice, slit their parents' throats, defile and adulterate both the sacred and the profane?

9. What gods or what men do you think can be well disposed toward you? You are condemned and punished by your fellow citizens, the laws, human rights, your country, your parents, your relatives, your children, your husband. God will exact terrible vengeance for the wrong done to his majesty, which you have crushed underfoot. And do not mistake the fact, woman, that modesty and chastity have been entrusted to you, given into your custody, and commended to you by your husband. For which reason it is more unjust that you give away what belongs to another without the consent of the owner, so that you add to your other crimes also the crime of theft. A Lacedemonian married woman gave this answer to a young man who asked a base thing of her: "I would give it if what you asked were mine to give, but what you ask belonged to my father, while I was a young girl, and now belongs to my husband after I was married."[18] That was a shrewd and clever answer, but it was also wise advice for good women. No less apt was the answer of the Insubrian woman who loved her husband, Marfidius, tenderly; and when a would-be lover asked a disgraceful thing of her by the life and health of Marfidius, she said, "But Marfidius would prefer to die a hundred times rather than that I submit once to what you ask of me by his health. Go ask it of him."

10. The apostle Paul was teaching the Church of God when he said, "A woman does not have power over her own body but the husband does."[19] According to this statement, it is right to keep every shameful and lowly

---

18. Plutarch, "Sayings of the Spartan Women," *Moralia*, 242B.
19. 1 Cor. 7:4.

thing away from a woman, unless she is completely depraved, to the extent that Augustine even forbids the vow or practice of continence in a married woman unless her husband approves it.[20] In his letter to Celantia, Jerome—or whoever wrote it,[21] undoubtedly a learned and holy man—reprehends her, an exemplary matron, because she had taken a vow of perpetual continence without consulting her husband. A woman does not have the right over her own body, even when it comes to the virtue of continence. How much right do you think she has when it is a question of the vice of unchastity?

Continence is censured when it is practiced without the knowledge of the husband. What shall we say of adultery entered into against the will of the husband? Listen to the words he employs: "I have learned also to my great consternation and distress that you have begun to practice this good proposal of continence without the consent and agreement of your husband, although the authority of the apostle prohibits this categorically, which in this case not only subjects the wife to the husband but also the husband to the wife. 'The wife,' he said, 'has no power over her body, but the husband does,' and similarly, 'The husband has no power over his body, but the wife does.'[22] But you, oblivious, as it were, of the marriage contract and unmindful of the compact and of the marriage rights, inadvisedly vowed your chastity to God. But it is dangerous to promise what is in the power of another, and I do not know how it can be a pleasing gift to God if one offers that which belongs to two."[23] Such are his words, and this is the unanimous opinion of all the sacred writers. But if he upbraids a respectable matron so harshly for a holy resolution, since it was not in her power, what words would he use to rebuke a wicked woman involved in a disgraceful act?

11. And that you may understand how great an offense adultery is considered to be by God and men, when Christ proclaimed in the gospel that wives should be kept at all costs and allowed no possibility for divorce, he made the sole exception of adultery.[24] Therefore, one must tolerate a wife who is drunk, hot-tempered, extravagant, lazy, gluttonous, lying, fickle, of fragile health, quarrelsome, slanderous, foolish, insane;[25] only the adulteress

---

20. Augustine *On the Good of Marriage* 6 (*NPNF,* 1st ser., 3 : 401).

21. The letter is also attributed to Paulinus of Nola. The style does not seem to be that of Jerome.

22. 1 Cor. 7 : 4.

23. Jerome *Letters* 148.28 (*PL* 22 : 1217).

24. Matt. 19 : 9.

25. Cf. Isidore of Seville *On Ecclesiastical Duties* 2.19.1 (*PL* 83 : 737).

can be cast out. The other vices are serious, but they can be tolerated; not keeping faith to the marriage bed, however, cannot be tolerated. Homer, enumerating the curses and bad omens that may befall a man, says, "To have a wife who has carnal relations with other men is the worst of all."[26] Job also says that if he were to lie in wait for a woman at his friend's door, he would call down this imprecation upon his head: "May my wife be the harlot of another man, and may others kneel on top of her."[27] All of which shows that this vice is totally opposed to the nature of marriage, which is based on mutual love. From the moment a woman admits another man other than her legitimate husband into her heart, she is immediately stricken by those intemperate desires and by fear of her husband so that she hates no one more implacably than him; he can never be present to her without her becoming terrified and shuddering with fear as if she were being hounded by the Furies[28] with their burning torches, as it is recounted in fables.

12. There are two other blessings that nature bestowed upon marriage: offspring and family possessions. These, too, are defiled and contaminated by adultery, since it creates doubt about the offspring, as I said a little earlier,[29] and it ruins the domestic economy. For a woman who has been estranged by adultery neglects the home, and, unmindful of herself, she cannot have any love for the fortunes of the one whose life she hates and not even for her children. What will a woman not grant to the man to whom she has prostituted herself and her chastity, that is, her most precious possessions? Are we to think that she will deny money or power or the death of her children to the man to whom she did not deny herself and to whom she betrayed her conscience?

When Livia,[30] the sister of Germanicus, had surrendered her chastity to

26. Homer *Odyssey* 11.427–28.

27. Job 31:10.

28. The Furies are goddesses of retribution who drive men mad as punishment for crimes. They are usually represented in art and literature as being dressed in black and carrying torches and scourges, with snakes for hair.

29. Ch. 2 above.

30. This is Livia Julia, also called Livilla. She was the daughter of Nero Claudius Drusus, the younger brother of the later emperor Tiberius who was entrusted with the conquest of Germany by Augustus. Nero reached the Elbe in 9 B.C.E. but died in camp after falling from his horse. The Senate voted to him and his descendants the title of Germanicus. His son, Julius Caesar Germanicus, continued his father's campaigns in Germany but fell victim to a plot in the east. Both men were buried in the mausoleum of Augustus. Not only did Livilla defile their memories, but she was suspected of poisoning her second husband, Drusus Julius Caesar, in complicity with her paramour, Aelius Sejanus, who had risen to great powers under Tiberius. This passage of Vives is inspired by Tacitus *Annals* 4.3.

Sejanus, a man well past his prime, of low birth and vile character, she could not deny to him the death of her husband, Drusus, son of Tiberius Caesar, heir to a vast empire, a youth of exceptional beauty, nobility, and courage. She sacrificed, too, the children she had from him, spurning the most certain prospects of rule, casting away her children's devotion to her; showing no respect for her mother, Antonia, or her grandmother, Augusta, both of them revered matrons of their time; unmindful of her noble blood, her father and brother, whom the human race venerated as gods for their moral rectitude. In the end, torments were made ready under the direction of her shrewd and cruel father-in-law, by which the lives of Livia herself and Sejanus and all their friends would be exacted of them, as indeed it happened, in all manner of violent deaths.

13. Evidently, a woman who has thrown away her chastity makes no provision for her future. Not only holy Christian women were aware of this, but pagan women as well, among whom some who, when they suffered defilement, deemed themselves unworthy of living—women like Lucretia,[31] the wife of Collatinus, whose deed, done out of an admirable love of chastity, is justly famous. Others likewise took their lives to preserve their chastity. When Athens was captured by Lysander,[32] king of Sparta, and thirty men were set over the city as rulers, who conducted themselves so haughtily and insolently that they earned the name of tyrants, and made sport of the chastity of many women, the wife of Niceratus committed suicide so that she would not be forced to satisfy their lust.

Need I recount single instances? The wives of the Teutones,[33] who, after the defeat at Aquae Sextiae at the hands of Caius Marius, were slaughtered in great numbers, begged Marius that they be given as a gift to the sacred Vestal Virgins, since, like them, they would live without any carnal relations with men. When the hard-hearted Marius denied their prayers, they all hanged themselves on the following night.

14. In the war between the Phocians and the Thessalians,[34] when the

---

31. See Book 1, par. 15 above.

32. See Book 1, n. 238.

33. The Teutones, a Germanic tribe that had migrated to southern France, were annihilated by the army of Caius Marius at Aquae Sextiae (the modern Aix-en-Provence) in 102 B.C. Cf. Valerius Maximus 6.1.3. Valerius Maximus wrote a handbook of illustrative examples of memorable deeds and sayings, *Factorum ac dictorum memorabilium libri IX*, during the reign of the Emperor Tiberius. It was very popular during the Middle Ages and the Renaissance, and is frequently cited by Vives in this treatise. The reference will be given simply as Valerius Maximus.

34. Plutarch, "Bravery of Women," *Moralia*, 244B–D. The Thessalians, a people from the north of Greece, made several attempts to gain control of Delphi in the enemy territory of Phocis. The incident referred to here took place sometime before the Persian Wars.

Thessalians invaded the land of the Phocians with a huge army, Daiphantus, the chief magistrate among the Phocians, proposed to the people that they form a strong contingent and go out to meet the enemy; but that children, old men, women, and all others who could not bear arms should be confined in a hidden place. There they piled up a great supply of wood and straw so that if they were defeated, those stationed there would set it afire and burn themselves to death.

When the assembled multitude gave their approval to this plan, an elderly man stood up and expressed the opinion that the women should be consulted in this matter. If they agreed, then it would be done, but if they thought otherwise, it would be unjust to make this decision against their will. The question was put to the women, who, after deliberating among themselves, answered that they approved the measure of Daiphantus and indeed were most grateful to him for having provided both for the best interests of the city and for their safety.

Therefore, they were led off to a more secret place for that purpose. But the Phocians, as this heroic chastity of their wives deserved, returned home from the war victorious. When Damo, the daughter of Pythagoras, was asked when a woman remained undefiled by sexual contact with a man, she answered, "With her husband instantly, with another never."[35] Such examples were given by pagan women in the darkness of their ignorance, to whom everything was obscure and uncertain and who knew nothing of the great mystery of marriage. Wherefore Christian women should be all the more ashamed, since they have been redeemed by the blood of the Lord, cleansed by baptism, instructed by the gospel, and illumined by the light divine.

35. Diogenes Laertius 8.43.

III

HOW SHE SHOULD BEHAVE
TOWARD HER HUSBAND

15. The duties of a wife to her husband, difficult to set out in words, were summarized, as I mentioned previously,[36] in one word by our Lord. Let a woman remember what I said: that she is one person with her husband and for that reason should love him no less than herself. I have said this before, but it must be repeated often, for it is the epitome of all the virtues of a married woman. This is the meaning and lesson of matrimony: that a woman should think that her husband is everything to her and that this one name substitutes for all the other names dear to her—father, mother, brothers, sisters. This is what Adam was to Eve, what the virtuous Andromache said Hector was to her in the passage in Homer:

> Father and mother are you to me,
> Brother and well-beloved spouse.[37]

If friendship between two souls renders them one, how much more truly and effectively must this result from marriage, which far surpasses all other friendships? Therefore, it is said that wedlock does not make just one mind or one body of two, but one person in every respect. Wherefore, what the man said of the woman, "For her sake a man shall leave father and mother and cleave to his wife,"[38] should be said with all the more reason by the woman, since, even if one is created out of two, the woman is still the daughter of the man and weaker, and for that reason needs his protection. And when she is bereft of her husband, she is alone, naked, exposed to harm. As

36. Cf. par. 4 above.
37. Homer *Iliad* 6.429–30.
38. Gen. 2:4.

the companion of her husband, wherever he is, there she has a country, home, hearth, parents, close friends, and wealth. Examples of this abound.

16. Hypsicratea, wife of Mithradates,[39] king of Pontus, followed her husband in male disguise when he was defeated and put to flight, wherever he sought refuge, even in the most remote solitude. She considered that wherever her husband was, there she would find her kingdom, her riches, and her country, which was of the greatest comfort and solace to Mithradates in his many misfortunes. Flaccilla followed her husband, Nonius Priscus, into exile, and Egnatia Maximilla followed Glitio Gallus with a loss of great wealth because they had to leave Rome and Italy.[40] But they were convinced that their husbands surpassed and more than compensated for everything they had left behind in their native country. For this reason, they acquired great glory in the eyes of all. No less glory accrued to Turia,[41] who hid her husband, recently proscribed by the triumvirs, between the ceiling and the roof of her bedroom with the complicity of a handmaid, thus saving him from imminent death, at great peril to her own life. And Sulpicia, wife of Lentulus,[42] who was diligently guarded by her mother, Tullia, so that she would not follow her husband, who had been proscribed by the triumvirs, put on the guise of a servant and with two female and male servants reached him after a clandestine flight, not hesitating to exile herself in order to demonstrate her fidelity to an exiled spouse.

17. There were many women who preferred to endure danger themselves rather than that their husbands should do so. When Fernán González,[43] Count of Castille, was being held in custody by the king of León, a city in the Asturias, his wife came to the prison pretending to pay him a visit. She persuaded her husband to change clothes with her and make his escape, and to leave her to face the danger, which he did. The king, in

39. Mithradates VI Eupator Dionysus (120–63 B.C.E.) was the greatest Hellenistic king of that name. He ruled Pontus in Asia Minor, a formidable enemy of Rome in the the first century B.C.E. The story of Hypsicratea is a favorite one in accounts of the lives of famous women, including those by Boccaccio and Christine de Pizan. Cf. Valerius Maximus 4.6., ext. 2.

40. Tacitus *Annals* 15.71. Novius Priscus was a friend of Seneca and was probably exiled for that reason. Egnatia Maximilla was mistress of a great fortune that was confiscated when her husband was exiled. The pair returned to Rome after the death of Nero.

41. Valerius Maximus 6.7.2.

42. Valerius Maximus 6.7.3. Lentulus Cruscellio had been exiled to Sicily by the triumvirs.

43. Fernán González (c. 915–70) was a legendary figure who secured the independence of Castille from León and fought against the Moors. *El poema de Fernán González*, composed about 1260, recounts his exploits. The story of his rescue by Doña Sancha is told in *La leyenda de Fernán González*, ed. Evaristo Correa Calderón (Madrid, 1964), p. 267.

admiration of the woman's loyalty and praying for wives like her for himself and his children, sent her back to her husband. Of that same caliber was the wife of Robert,[44] king of England. In an expedition against the Syrians, her husband had sustained a grievous wound in his arm from a poisoned sword. After returning to his native land, he was not able to have it cured, unless someone would suck out the poisonous pus. The king, knowing that anyone who would undertake this task would meet certain death, would not allow anyone to expose himself to such danger. At night, his wife undid the bandaging of the wound and at first without her husband's knowledge and then with his permission, sucked out the poison. She spat it out little by little until she had drawn it all out and rendered the wound easily curable for the physicians. How sorry I am (if this story is to be believed) not to know the name of such a noble matron, worthy to be celebrated with the most eloquent of encomiums! Yet her name has not remained in silence, for it is contained, if I am not mistaken, in the chronicles of Spain written by Rodrigo,[45] archbishop of Toledo; and I shall introduce it into my own writings one day with honorable recognition.

18. When the Etruscans migrated in great numbers to Sparta from their island and aroused suspicion in the Spartans that they were plotting a political uprising, they were all delivered into public custody and condemned to capital punishment. Their wives, obtaining permission from the guards to visit their husbands to greet and console them, changed clothes with them. The men with their heads veiled, as was the custom among Etruscan women, escaped from the prison and left their wives in their place. They later recovered them together with their children and possessions, striking fear into the Spartans, since they occupied Mount Taygetus, making it their citadel. This outstanding deed is recounted by Valerius Maximus and Plutarch.[46] When Acastus, the son of Pelias, wished to put his sisters to death—they had killed their father, albeit unintentionally, for they wanted to restore him to the vigor of youth—one of them, Alcestis, was with her husband,

---

44. This may be Robert Curthouse (1054–1134), eldest son of William the Conqueror, who became Duke of Normandy but failed in his attempt to gain the English crown. He was a heroic warrior during the First Crusade and participated in the siege of Antioch. Many legends survive concerning him, of which this may be one.

45. Rodrigo Jiménez de Rada was made archbishop of Toledo in 1208 and died in 1247. He wrote a *Historia de rebus Hispaniae*, ed. Juan Fernández Valverde (Turnhout, 1987), translated into Spanish at an early date as *Historia gótica*. The story related here is not found in his extant works.

46. Valerius Maximus 4.6,.ext.3; Plutarch, "Bravery of Women," *Moralia*, 247B–C. In Herodotus's account of this incident (4.145), the women are Spartans married to descendants of the heroes of the *Argo*.

Admetus. Acastus took him captive and threatened to kill him unless he delivered over his wife. He persisted in refusing, almost to the point of being killed, when Alcestis freely offered herself to die in order to save her husband's life.[47]

19. There were those who chose not to survive their husband's death. When Laodamia[48] heard the news that her husband, Protesilaus, had been killed before the walls of Troy by Hector, she killed herself. Paulina, the wife of Seneca, wished to die with her husband. She opened her veins, but she was restrained by Nero and kept alive; her arms were bound up and the blood was stanched either against her will or without her knowing it. She lived a few years longer, her countenance and limbs so pale that the condition of her body gave clear evidence of her conjugal fidelity.[49] When the unmarried daughter of Demotion, prince of the Areopagus, heard of the death of her promised spouse, Leosthenes, she killed herself, declaring that even if she were still a virgin, she was spiritually married to him, and would be committing adultery with whomever else she married.[50] Ancient writers tell the story of Halcyon, who did not allow herself to survive her husband, Ceyx, but plunged headlong into the sea.[51] The fables, which often provide teachings on how to live, add that they were turned into birds called halcyons, who are so endeared to Thetis that whenever they build their nests, there is the greatest calm at sea and in the heavens. This occurs on fixed days every year, which for that reason are called the halcyon days. This was the gods' tribute to a wife's fidelity to her husband. The same writers tell us that Andromeda, daughter of Cepheus, was transported by Pallas Athena to the stars, because she had preferred her husband, Perseus, to her country and her parents.[52] Evadne, assisting at the funeral rites of her husband,

---

47. Jerome *Against Jovinianus* 1.45 (*NPNF,* ser. 2, 6:382); Valerius Maximus 4.6.1.

48. Jerome *Against Jovinianus,* 1.45 (*NPNF,* ser. 2, 6:382) According to one version of the myth, the gods granted to Laodamia that her husband return to the upper world for three hours. After this she died with him and accompanied him to the underworld.

49. Tacitus *Annals* 15.63–64.

50. Jerome *Against Jovinianus* 1.41 (*NPNF,* ser. 2, 6:380). Leosthenes, commander of the combined Greek army in the Lamian War, died at the siege of Lamia in 322 B.C.E.

51. Ovid *Metamorphoses* 11.674–748.

52. This sequel to the myth of Perseus and Andromeda is contained only in the *Astronomica,* a work attributed to the grammarian Gaius Julius Hyginus, who was appointed librarian of the Palatine Library by Emperor Augustus. He was thought to be a Spaniard by birth, and perhaps for this reason Vives lectured on him in Louvain as a young man. It is now generally agreed, however, that the writer of this treatise is not to be identified with Gaius Julius Hyginus. Hyginus *Astronomica* 2.11.

Capaneus,[53] threw herself upon the pyre so that she would not be separated even in death from her dear spouse.

20. Caecina Paetus had a wife named Arria. When he joined a mutinous rebellion led by Scribonianus in Illyria against Emperor Claudius, he was brought back a prisoner to Rome. Arria begged the soldiers that they let her minister to her husband's needs instead of the servants that were assigned to him, because of his consular rank. When she failed to obtain this request, she hired a small fishing smack, followed the sailing vessel, and, arriving in Rome a few days after her husband's execution, took her own life, although her daughter was still living and married to Thrasea, a respected and learned man of those times.[54] Porcia, the daughter of Cato, wife of Marcus Brutus, was determined to die after her husband had been defeated and killed. They took every weapon away from her, but she put burning coals in her mouth and died of suffocation.[55] Panthea, wife of the king of Susa, remained faithful to her husband while he was imprisoned. Expending all her resources for his safety, she took her own life when he was killed in war.[56] Julia, the daughter of Caesar the dictator, on seeing the bloody garments of her husband, Pompey the Great, brought home from the battlefield, suspected that her husband was wounded and fell half-dead to the ground. In her state of shock, she gave birth prematurely and died.[57] Cornelia, the last wife of that same Pompey, said it was a disgrace not to be able to die of grief alone when one's husband was killed.[58] Artemisia, Queen of the Lydians, as

53. Capaneus was one of the seven Argive chieftains in the expedition against Thebes. Zeus struck him down with a thunderbolt for his blasphemy and impiety. Ovid *The Art of Love* 3.21.

54. Pliny *Letters* 3.16. The more famous story of Arria's death, referred to obliquely in this letter, recounts how she thrust a sword into her breast, pulled it out, and then handed it to her husband, saying, "It does not hurt, Paetus." This story is also the subject of an epigram of Martial, 1.13. Arria's daughter, Arria Minor, did not follow her mother's example, but chose to live for the sake of her daughter: Tacitus *Annals* 16.34.

55. Valerius Maximus 4.6, ext. 1; Plutarch *Brutus* 53.4.

56. Xenophon in his prose romance, the *Cyropaedia*, 6.4.3, relates that when Panthea's husband, Abradatas, king of Susa, was killed in battle, she sought out his corpse and committed suicide on it.

57. Valerius Maximus 4.6.4; Plutarch *Pompey* 53. Vives is somewhat inexact in his re-telling of the events. According to the ancient sources, a tumult at the election of aediles resulted in the loss of many lives. During the mêlée, Pompey got spattered with blood, so he changed his garments. Servants carried his bloodstained toga home, and the shock of this sight caused Julia to have a miscarriage.

58. Plutarch *Pompey* 74.3; Lucan *Pharsalia* 8.72–85. In his flight from Caesar after the battle of Pharsalus, Pompey stopped at Mytilene to take aboard his last wife, Cornelia, and his sons. Cornelia blamed herself for his misfortune, but Pompey consoled her by saying that it was necessary to accept ill fortune along with the good.

it has been recorded, out of her boundless love, drank the ashes of her dead husband, Mausolus, diluted in a potion, wishing to be his living sepulcher.[59]

21. The extraordinary deed of Camma[60] must not be passed over in silence. I shall reproduce the story in Latin literally from Plutarch's Greek, for I could not improve on his version:

> In Galatia there were two men named Sinatus and Sinorix, the most powerful of the tetrarchs in that region, related by ties of blood. Sinatus had a wife named Camma of exceptional beauty and charm but especially renowned for her exemplary virtue. She was not only modest and devoted to her husband but judicious and generous, and because of her pleasant manner and benevolence was beloved by her subjects. In addition to all these qualities was her fame as a priestess of Diana, a goddess whom the Galatians hold in special reverence and veneration. In her festivities and solemnities Camma stood out for the magnificence of her attire. Sinorix was smitten with love for her, but unable to win her over by persuasion or by force, he slew Sinatus in a foul and treacherous manner. Not long afterwards he spoke to Camma of marriage as she performed her sacred duties in the temple, bearing up with the killing of her husband not in a mournful or abject way, but repressing the anger in her heart and awaiting the opportunity to avenge the crime of Sinorix. He humbly entreated her and resorted to supplications that seemed not altogether inappropriate, protesting that he was superior to Sinatus in material possessions and would never have committed this atrocious murder if he had not been driven to it by his uncontrollable love for Camma. The woman at first refused his advances, without showing anger, then little by little seemed to weaken and give way, for her friends and relatives gave support to his desires, persuading her, dinning it into her ears and almost coercing her since they were eager to gain favor with Sinorix. Finally she yielded and summoned him to the temple so that their mutual consent and approval of the marriage agreement could be formalized before the goddess as witness and judge. When he entered the temple she received him cordially, led him to the altar and offered him to drink from a cup from which she had already drunk, presenting the rest for

---

59. At the death of her husband, Mausolus, king of Caria, in 335 B.C.E., Artemisia had a huge tomb built. Known as the Mausoleum, it is numbered among the Seven Wonders of the Ancient World. The account of Artemisia's death given here is contained in Valerius Maximus 4.6., ext. 1.

60. Plutarch, "Bravery of Women," *Moralia*, 257F–258C.

him to drink. It contained a drink made from honey and wine mixed with poison. When she saw him quaff the drink, she uttered a loud cry and throwing herself on her knees before the goddess, said 'I invoke you as my witness, holy and venerable deity, that for the sake of this day and this moment I have lived on to survive my husband, making use of this interim period of life for no other reason than the hope of revenge, and now that I have attained it, I descend to my husband. As for you, most wicked and impious of men, let your servants prepare your tomb rather than the nuptial bed.' When Sinorix heard this, feeling the poison creep through his vital parts and his whole body shaking, climbed into a chariot so that he could find strength to move his limbs, but already powerless he was placed on a litter and expired as evening drew nigh. Camma prolonged her life through the night and after she learned that he was dead gladly and happily gave up her spirit.

22. Because of women like these, the whole female sex has a good reputation, and it is a pleasure to marry wives, have daughters, and educate them with good hopes, just as we are affected in an entirely opposite way when we observe only those women who either spurn or neglect the duties of female virtue. I have proposed these heroic examples in order to shame those women who do not exhibit at least ordinary acts of virtue. How much more intolerable is the inhuman lack of loyalty of those women who can allow ignominy, harm, or any adversity to befall their husbands for the sake of money, although they have enough coin in their coffers to free their husbands from such calamities. Even if they did not have the money, they should not endure it. O soul more ruthless than a wild beast! You can suffer your own blood, your own body, you yourself to be afflicted in this way in the person of your husband! Obviously, public customs and the laws that tolerate them gave greater importance to money than to trust and loyalty. But these things and many others that are still among us, the legacy of paganism, have clung more tenaciously to Christians than the law of Christ permitted. According to this law, not only a wife for her husband, but a Christian for any other Christian, even one unknown to him, should give freely whatever clothes, metals, and other possessions are hoarded away in family chests.

In this regard, a woman who would not spend her entire substance to free her husband from the least discomfort should account herself unworthy of the name of Christian, upright woman, or wife. The most sure sign of chastity is to love one's husband with one's whole heart, as the saying goes.

So renowned was the chastity of Agrippina, wife of Germanicus, because of her love for her husband, that when Tiberius Caesar out of hatred tried to incriminate her and her sons to cause their ruin by whatever pretext, he trumped up the charge of unchastity against her son Nero. He did not dare to make this accusation against her, although he had accused her of other gross offenses.[61]

23. Husbands show gratitude to their wives by whom they know they are loved by loving them in return. Thus it is told that Ulysses spurned the goddesses Circe and Calypso for the love of Penelope, a mere mortal, and, while wandering the seas for ten years, he kept course for home and arrived there after many perils and hardships. Hector so loved Andromache that in return for her steadfast and undivided love for him, he said that his grief for the fall of Troy was not for the sake of parents or brothers, but for his wife.[62] I am not going to debate whether these are fables or not. What is certain is that they were fashioned by a poet of great genius after the model of human life. But to turn to actual historical events, Cicero, Valerius Maximus, Pliny,[63] and others relate that Tiberius Gracchus was asked whose life he would prefer to save, his own or that of his wife Cornelia, whom he fondly loved. Aware that one or the other would have to be victims of fate, he preferred to die himself rather than that his wife die. O happy wife, who had such a husband! Unhappy that she survived him!

24. A husband is not to be loved as we love a friend or a twin brother, where only love is required. A great amount of respect and veneration, obedience, and compliance must be included. Not only the traditions and institutions of our ancestors, but all laws, human and divine, and nature itself, proclaim that a woman must be subject to a man and obey him. In all races of animals, the female obeys and follows the male; she fawns upon him and allows herself to be beaten and punished by him, and nature has taught that this is the way things should be. This same nature, as Aristotle demonstrates in his books on *The History of Animals*,[64] has given less muscles and

61. Tacitus *Annals* 5.3. Agrippina the Elder was the daughter of Marcus Vipsanius Agrippa, lifelong friend and supporter of Augustus; and Julia, daughter of Augustus. After the death of Livia, wife of the emperor, Tiberius became more openly hostile to all descendants of Augustus. In a letter to the Senate, he accused Nero, firstborn son of Germanicus and Agrippina, of love affairs with young men and moral depravity. He could not fabricate such a charge against Agrippina, but instead denounced her arrogant and refractory spirit. Mother and son were exiled to the island of Pandateria, where Nero killed himself and Agrippina died of starvation.

62. Homer *Iliad* 6.450–54.

63. Cicero *On Divination* 1.18.36; Valerius Maximus 4.6.1; Pliny *Natural History*, 7.172.

64. Aristotle *The History of Animals* 5.11, 538b (Barnes 1:851).

strength to females than to males and a softer flesh and more delicate hair. Likewise, it denied many female animals those parts that are more suitable for defense, such as teeth, horns, spurs, and the like, as with deer and boar. If it did concede such weapons to the female, it gave stronger ones to the male, as the horns of a bull are stronger than those of a cow. In all of this, nature in her great wisdom has instructed us that the male has the role of defender, and the female follows the male. She takes refuge under his protection and shows herself obedient to him in order to live more safely and comfortably.

25. But from the actions of beasts, which put us to shame if we do not excel them, let us pass to human reason. What woman has reached that point of arrogance and presumption that she is unwilling to harken to her husband's word—if she reflects that he takes the place of father, mother, and all her kin, that she owes all her love to him alone and all the loyalty due to all others? The madwoman who does not obey her husband does not think of this, unless perhaps she began by not obeying her father, mother, and nearest of kin. For if she obeys them, then she must obey her husband, in whose authority everything has been placed by every law, custom, statute, and natural precept, human and divine. A woman does not achieve more honor in the eyes of men by arrogating more honor to herself than is given to her husband, but becomes more foolish and ridiculous. By the same token, she becomes hated and abominable to all as if she were attempting to invert the laws sanctioned by nature, like a soldier demanding the right to give orders to a general, as if the moon were superior to the sun or the arm to the head. In marriage as in human nature, the man stands for the mind, the woman for the body. He must command, and she must serve, if man is to live.

26. Nature herself has declared this by making the man more fit for governing than the woman. In great affairs and in moments of crisis, the woman is so shaken and confused by fear that she cannot use her reason or judgment, since that emotion is uncontrollable and deprives us of all use of discretion. A man is courageous and is not so shaken by fear as not to perceive clearly what is fitting to be done in the immediate circumstances. Moreover, since more frequent perturbations arise in women, their judgment is always influenced by some emotion and it is less consistent, tossed about by the storms of passion that pull it in various directions, so that often it is impotent and ineffectual. With great wisdom, as in other matters, Paul said, "The head of man is Christ, the head of woman is man."[65]

65 1 Cor 11:3

The man who does not have Christ as his head is truncated and completely dead. The woman not subject to a man is reckless and raging. Here I am entering into the divine commandments, which among men of good sense are duly and rightfully more efficacious than all laws, all human reasoning, and the voice of nature itself, since nature is often twisted and perverted. God is always unchanged, always identical and like unto himself, and God is the creator of nature, wherefore in our minds also he should be more powerful, more worthy of respect and firmer trust.

27. The author of this whole fabric of the universe, when the world was still new and inexperienced and he was establishing laws for the human race, said to the woman, "You shall be under the power of the man, and he shall have dominion over you."[66] In these words it is worthy of note that not only is man given right and dominion over the woman, but also use and possession. The apostle Paul, teacher of Christian, that is, divine, wisdom, does not permit the woman to have mastery over the man but to be subject to him, and he says this in more than one place.[67] This is the pronouncement of Peter, prince of the apostles: "Let women be subject to their husbands, as were the holy women, hoping in the Lord. So Sarah obeyed Abraham, calling him lord."[68] Jerome gives these instructions to Celantia: "First and foremost his authority must be safeguarded, and let the whole household learn from you how much honor is due him. Show him to be master by your obedience, and show him to be great by your humility. You will be so much the more honored as you honor him more. For, as the Apostle said, the head of the woman is man and the rest of the body cannot receive more distinction than from the dignity of the head."[69]

28. Foolish women do not consider that since all honor derives from their husbands, they will be without honor if they have husbands whom women can command. Thus, while they seek honor, they lose it, since they immediately lose that which gives greatest honor to women, namely, to be wedded to husbands who are honored. Race, wealth, fortune will be of no avail; you will be without honor if your husband is without it. But who can have respect for a man who he sees is ruled by a woman? On the contrary, lowness of birth will be no obstacle, nor will poverty or unbecoming appearance. You will be honored if your husband is given honor. Neither beauty, lineage, or riches saved Orestilla from being an object of contempt

66. Gen. 3:16.
67. Eph. 5:22; Col. 3:18.
68. 1 Peter 3:5–6.
69. Jerome *Letters* 148.26 (*PL* 22:1216).

and hatred as the wife of the wicked Catiline.[70] The penury of Salonia did not prevent her from being loved and admired by the people of Rome as wife of Cato the Censor.[71]

But that you may better obey your husband and accomplish everything to his liking, you must first be thoroughly acquainted with his character and consider the circumstances of his nature and fortune. In these respects, there are many kinds of husbands. All husbands must be loved, respected, and revered; all must be obeyed, but not all are to be treated in the same way, like a white line on a white stone, as the saying goes. I think that what Terence said of human life, taking his cue from Plato,[72] can be well adapted to husbands: "The life of man is like a game of dice," he said, "if what comes out in the throw is not what you needed, correct it by skillful playing."[73] So with husbands, if you get the one you desired, you should be glad. He is to be honored, loved, and followed. If he is not very desirable, you must correct him skillfully, if you can, or at least make him less troublesome.

29. Your husband will either be fortunate or unfortunate. By fortunate, I mean those blessed with some good, either in their lives, in body, or in mind; unfortunate are those who lack any of these three blessings. Fortunate men easily satisfy their wives. We must turn our attention to the unfortunate. Yet at the beginning of all marriages, women should be warned not to put their love in the fortune of the husband, but rather in the husband himself. Otherwise, their love would be less solid and less enduring. If fortune, which is fleeting and inconstant, were to depart, it would take love away with it at the same time. They should not love handsome men for their beauty, or rich men for their money, or magistrates for their rank, for when they become sick, poor, and private citizens, they will hate them. If it is your fortune to find a learned man, you should absorb holy precepts from him; if you find a good man, you should take good examples from him to emulate. But if your husband is unfortunate, you should call to mind the speech of Gnaeus Pom-

---

70. According to the historian Sallust, Catiline had his son from a previous marriage killed at Orestilla's wish so that he could marry her. Sallust *Catiline* 15.2.

71. Plutarch *Cato* 24.2–3. After the death of his first wife, Cato slept with one of his slaves, an act that displeased his son and daughter-in-law, who lived in the same house. Cato then asked his former secretary, Salonius, if he had found a husband for his daughter. When Salonius replied that he had not, Cato said that he knew of a possible match for her, although the man was rather old. Salonius agreed to Cato's proposal and then discovered that the suitor was Cato himself.

72. Plato *Republic* 604C.

73. Terence *The Brothers* 739–41.

pey, a great and prudent man beyond all doubt, to his wife Cornelia, which Lucan expressed in verse.[74]

30. When Pompey was defeated by Julius Caesar, he set out for the island of Lesbos to meet his wife, whom he was to take with him in his flight. When his wife saw her defeated husband, she fell to the ground in a swoon, not sorrowful that she had fallen, but that he had fallen low. Pompey raised her from the ground and when she had recovered her senses, consoled her in this way: "My dear wife Cornelia, dearest to me of all things on earth, I marvel that a woman of your lineage should be so prostrated by the first blow of ill fortune. Now the path to immortal glory is open to you. For the subject of praise in the female sex is not eloquence, nor answering questions about law, nor waging war, but only this: to have a husband who has suffered adversity. If you love and cherish him, if you are not resentful at his ill fortune but treat him as a husband should be treated, all ages will celebrate your name with immense praise. It will be a greater glory for you to have loved the defeated Pompey than the leader of the Roman people, head of the Senate, and lord of kings. It is easy even for a stupid and dishonest wife to love such things, but to embrace one stricken by misfortune is the mark of an exceptional wife. Therefore, you should love my defeat as an occasion to display your virtue, for if you long and mourn for anything while I am alive, you show that you loved that which has perished, not me, who am still alive."[75]

31. These and similar words he used to comfort her sick spirit. A good woman will turn these words over in her mind as if they were an oracle so that she will not be afflicted when her husband suffers misfortune, will not hate or despise him on that account. Rather, if he is poor, she must console him with the thought that virtue is the only true wealth; you must help him by exemplary behavior, which you know will please him, which will have the approval of friends and acquaintances, and which befits the integrity of a good woman. See that you do not plunge into such a wretched state of mind that you would wish him to engage in some unseemly pursuits for the sake of money or commit some disgraceful action so that you may live more luxuriously and extravagantly, or dress more elegantly or live in a more comfortable house—in a word, to have him toil and sweat and even endure danger so that you may have a more pleasant life. It is preferable that you eat stale bread and drink turbid water rather than compel your husband to

---

74. Lucan *Pharsalia* 8.72–85.
75. Lucan *Pharsalia* 8.72–85. Vives' rendering is a free paraphrase of the passage.

submit himself—let us not say to occupations that are vile and sordid, or to excessive labor—but to any activity whatever that he undertakes against his will, simply to please you, avoid domestic quarrels, and have some peace at home.

32. The husband is his own master and lord over his wife, rather than the wife over her husband, and a wife should not ask more of her husband than she sees he will grant her gladly and willingly. Many wives do wrong in this regard. Through their insistent demands, constant nagging, and importunate behavior, they drive their husbands to unlawful pursuits and grave deeds, even crimes, to earn money, looking to their own gluttony and pride, not the interests of their husbands. What shall I say of those women who are annoyed and hostile toward the virtues of their spouses if they see that these are detrimental to the family economy? This is all the more disgraceful, since although it is the female sex that exhibits more piety and is by nature more devout in sacred worship than the male, she forgets herself and casts off all piety for the sake of money. The sacred Scriptures confute these women in the wives of Job and Tobias,[76] who foolishly blamed their husbands' ill fortune on their piety and great virtues. In so doing they were not only stupid but impious, because they did not recognize that the riches that are acquired by virtue are of greater value, and that it lies in the hands of the Lord to make anyone he wishes rich and prosperous in a single moment.

33. What need is there of other tyrants to obtain the crown of martyrdom? These irreligious women persecute their husbands for their faith in the same way the apostles were persecuted by Nero, and other Christians by Domitian, Maximinus, Decius, and Diocletian.[77] I think Job's wife was the only possession left to him so that she could add to his misery and with her malicious tongue make his burden even greater.[78] O detestable and impious woman! You reproach your husband for his holiness as if it were a crime! Not even devils would dare to do this. The devil destroyed all of Job's fortunes, slew all his servants, took away his children, covered him with ulcerous sores, but he never reproached him for persevering in his original purity of soul. His wife reproached him, showing that she was more shameless than

76. Sarah, the wife of Tobias, is not so depicted in the Book of Tobias.

77. Domitian, emperor from A.D. 81–96, favored the cult of Isis and proclaimed himself a god. He persecuted both the Jews and the Christians. Maximinus Daia was made caesar in 305. An ardent pagan, he enforced worship of the state deities. The persecution of Decius during his three-year reign was particularly severe. He believed the restoration of the state cults was essential to the preservation of the empire. Diocletian conducted the first systematic persecution of the Christians in four edicts passed during the last two years of his reign, A.D. 303–5.

78. Job 2:9.

the devil. Let his wife insult him as she will; her spouse will rejoice in this no less than the apostles in that they were considered worthy of suffering indignity for the name of the Lord Jesus.[79]

34. But you, good daughter, put it far from your mind ever to turn your spouse away from uprightness of life. Even at the certain cost of losing all your family possessions, in imitation of countless holy women, exhort him to innocence, piety, and mindfulness of divine goodness and power, so that the words of Paul may be verified in you: "An unfaithful husband is sanctified by a faithful woman."[80] In this way, great resources and immense wealth are obtained. Recall the word of the Lord that there is no one who neglects anything in this world for his sake who will not receive much more, both in the next world and in this one as well.[81] First of all, those riches are certain and lasting that are guarded without being exposed to the dangers of chance, whether from within, as rust in metals, moths in clothing, or from without, as thieves,[82] robbers, a violent and unjust ruler, or a rapacious judge. In addition, the psalmist declares that after a long life, he learned that he had never seen a just man abandoned or his seed in search of bread.[83] We have our Lord's solemn promise in the Gospels, by which we are bidden to hope abundantly in his kindness, that our heavenly Father knows what we need to live; he will provide all of these things for us, when we have sought his kingdom and his justice.[84]

35. If your husband is ugly, love his soul, which you have married. If he is sick, then you can show yourself a true wife. He must be consoled, tended, cared for, and held no less dear and cherished than if he were healthy and strong, and in that way you will divert a great part of the illness to yourself. He will suffer less when he sees that he has someone to share his suffering. She is not a good wife who is happy while her husband is sad or vaunts her health while her husband is ill. You should be constantly at his bedside, alleviating his pain with your words and soothing him with hot compresses. Treat his wounds and his sores yourself with your own hands and comfort his physical anguish. Dress him, undress him, dry him, give him to drink, bring him the bedpan. Do not shrink from these tasks any more than you would if it were for yourself. Do not pass these duties on to

79. Acts 5:41.
80. 1 Cor. 7:14.
81. Luke 18:29–30.
82. Matt. 6:19–20.
83. Ps. 37:25.
84. Matt. 6:33.

servants, who will execute them in a careless and slovenly manner because they do not love him; when the sick person senses that he is not loved, his physical illness is aggravated by sickness of soul.

Am I to call those women wives, matrons, and holy women, (heaven willing!) who are so indifferent when their husbands are ill that they are content to have servants look after him, ignoring their wifely duties? When I see that some women do not discontinue their customary attendance at sacred functions, banquets, visits and meetings with their friends, and their usual amusements while their husbands are confined to the house through illness, you would not say they are fulfilling the role of wives, rather, of concubines, or even, to speak more frankly, of prostitutes, bought with a price, who share their bed with men. Why should I be ashamed to call them by that name when they are not ashamed to act in such a way as to merit it? What am I to say if you think there is no difference whether it is your husband who is sick or a neighbor, except that your husband is at home and your neighbor outside the home? You are really brazen if you demand to be called a wife when you do not show yourself to be a wife. Do you wish to be called a weaver when you never learned how to lay the warp, or throw the shuttle, or strike the web with the comb? And although virtue without the help of any external light shines in the dark of its own light and is bright and lustrous, yet as far as it lies in me, I shall not allow those of the present and of future ages to be ignorant of what I saw with my own eyes and what many others know besides me.

36. When Clara Cervent,[85] the wife of Bernardo Valdaura, a young and beautiful girl from Bruges, was married to a husband more than forty years old, on the wedding night she saw that his legs were wrapped in bandages and discovered that she had married an infirm and sickly husband. Nevertheless, not put off by this, she did not show any dislike for him, in spite of the fact that it did not seem possible that she could feel any love for him. Not long afterwards, Valdaura fell victim to a very serious illness and the doctors despaired of his life. She and her mother stayed at his bedside for six weeks with such care and assiduity that they never took off their clothes, except to change their underwear; and never rested more than one or two hours, and then fully clothed; and passed many sleepless nights.

The cause of the illness was the Indian disease, which here we call the French pox, a violent and contagious illness. The doctors advised her not to touch him or go close to him. Her friends gave the same advice. Women of

---

85. Clara Cervent and Bernard Valdaura were the parents of Vives' wife, Margaret Valdaura.

her own age considered it to be against religious principles to struggle so indefatigably (these were their words) to save the life of a man destined to die, and more dead than alive; thought should be given to his soul, and no concern taken for the body except to provide for its burial. She was not deterred by these words but cared for both soul and body. She went in person to the kitchen to prepare the broth used for his cure; she changed the bedding frequently, for he suffered from severe diarrhea and from other parts of his body foul suppurations exuded. This she did, running about all the day long, sustaining her frail body with her spirit, since her body was not equal to the task save that the force of love gave her strength. Thus, Valdaura survived a very grave crisis. The doctors swore that his wife had snatched him from the jaws of death by force. One person said, more jokingly than with a true Christian spirit, that God had decreed the death of Valdaura, but his wife had made up her mind that she would not let him go.

37. Then the soft fleshy tissue inside his nostrils began to become cankerous, caused by a burning humor that flowed down from his head. The doctors prescribed a powder to be sprinkled on the ulcer by gently blowing through a reed, and since no one could be found who did not recoil at this task in abhorrence, only his wife volunteered to do it. Then, when pustules caused by the disease broke out on his cheeks and chin, since no barber could or would shave him, his wife cut them with scissors very skillfully every eight days.

Then he sank into another protracted illness, which lasted almost seven years. Once again she attended to him with indefatigable care. She prepared his food, although he had two maidservants and a grown daughter; she anointed his ugly sores; bandaged daily his foul-smelling legs dripping with purulent matter; applied powdered substances and poultices; and dressed his wounds as if she were handling musk instead of fetid sores. And his breath, which no one could tolerate even ten paces away, she swore was sweet-smelling. Once she became very angry with me when I said that it stank. She insisted that it reminded her of the fragrance of sweet, ripe apples.

38. And during all the time of this illness—when great expenses had to be assumed daily to nourish and cure a man afflicted with so many diseases, in that household where there had been no income for many years— she willingly despoiled herself of gold rings and necklaces, jewels and clothing, and emptied her cupboard of silver vessels so that her husband would lack nothing. She was content with any fare as long as there were sufficient provisions to care for the needs of her husband's body, afflicted by such grave ills. So through his wife's care, his life dragged on for ten years after

his first illness in his cadaverous body, or, more truly, a living tomb. During this time she bore him two children in addition to the six to whom she had already given birth since her marriage at the age of twenty, never becoming infected with her husband's contagious disease or any other scurvy, and her children also were endowed with healthy and clean bodies.

39. From this example, it becomes clear how great is the virtue and holiness of those women who love their husbands with their whole heart, as is fitting, and how God rewards them in this life. At length the sick old man passed away, or, rather, escaped from his unending torment. Clara was so stricken with grief that those who know her say that never has a young husband of sound body, handsome and rich, inspired such regret, mourning, and grief in a loving spouse. Many thought there was more occasion for congratulations than consolation. She all but cursed them, expressing the wish that her husband might return, just as he was, if it were possible, even if she had to suffer the loss of the five children that remained to her. Although she was still of youthful age, she decided never to marry again because she said that she would never find another Bernardo Valdaura.

I do not mention her chastity, of which she is an exemplar. I do not mention the sanctity of her life. I speak of her loyalty to her husband, which never comes alone, but always accompanied by all the other virtues. Who cannot perceive that she was married not to the body of Bernardo Valdaura, but to his soul, or that his body was her body? And what of the fact that she continues to observe the commands and wishes of her husband with such respect as if he were still alive and does many things according to his prescripts, saying that he had decided or ordered it? If you had had such a wife, Euripides, you would have praised women as much as you criticized them. If you, Agamemnon, had such a one, your country would have beheld you living for many years happy and triumphant after the defeat of Troy.

40. These things could not be passed over in silence when often lesser accomplishments are recorded to remind wives of their duties. "But these are the actions of lowborn women," some noble lady will say. First of all, Clara Valdaura was not at all of lowly origin. She was young, very beautiful, refined, and had many servants, to whom she could have assigned a great part of these duties if she wished. But there are many noblewomen who lend themselves to these same services, both of our own day and from the past, all of whom I cannot enumerate. For the most part, succeeding ages remember only the vices of those who lived before them.

Are you nobler than the wife of Themistocles—leader of Athens or, rather, all of Greece—who ministered to her husband unassisted when he was in poor health? Nobler than Stratonica,[86] the wife of King Deiotarus,[87] who, when her husband was old, disillusioned, and invalid, was cook, doctor, and surgeon to him, and nothing gave her more grief than the fact that sometimes the difficult and cantankerous old man intimated that she did not give him sufficient attention? Are you nobler than that queen of England who sucked her husband's wounds?[88] The high-ranking Roman matrons did not allow their sick husbands to be touched by any other hands than their own. Do you think you surpass even the Romans in nobility, when any family that can trace its origins to them is regarded as one of great nobility? But why must we confine nobility to lineage and riches? They are noble who are illustrious in virtue and noble deeds. You with your nobility will lie obscure and ignoble while every age and every sex will know and celebrate the truly noble. Go, then, and vaunt your nobility, which no one will recognize, whether you are dead or alive.

41. You say, "I have offered money to hire someone to do this." Therefore, your husband wedded your money, not you. Do you think you are a wife merely because a man sleeps with you? Do you think marriage consists in this alone? You are clearly violating the laws of God and of nature, for if you do not feel revulsion in touching your own body and looking at and putting your hands on pustules and ulcers, why do you turn away from your husband in disgust when he is afflicted in this same way? You are two in one flesh, or, to use more precise Latin, one human being. Or perhaps you think this does not apply to you. Where is that spouse, inseparable companion and mate of her husband if at the moment when you should be closest to him you take your leave? Would you not perform this service for a blood brother, a father, or a mother who brought you into the world? If you are ashamed to admit this, then you should likewise be ashamed even to think it with regard to your husband, whom you should prefer to all of these. Yet there are women like this who desert even their sick mothers and love no one but themselves, worthy in turn to be loved by no one else, just as they love no one else.

42. How often have we seen the female among dumb creatures licking

---

86. Plutarch, "Bravery of Women," *Moralia*, 258D. Since she had no children of her own, Stratonica prevailed upon her husband to have a child with a prisoner of war, and she treated the son of this union in kingly fashion.

87. Deiotarus was king of Galatia in Asia Minor and a friend of the Romans. A speech of Cicero in his defense is extant.

88. Cf. note 44 above. At this point the Spanish translator, Juan Justiniano, adds several examples from recent Spanish history.

the gore and sores of her mate? This is done by cattle, dogs, lions, bears, both tame and wild beasts. Will a woman refuse to touch or even to look at her husband's sores? Do you wish me to speak frankly? Not a few women who do not touch their husband's wounds touch those of an adulterer, for some have been caught doing this, making it clear that it was not nature that deterred them, but their own wickedness. Thus Juvenal does not seem unjust when he attacks them in this way:

> A wife away with her lover has a strong stomach.[89]

This same woman is very squeamish with her husband and cannot suffer the slightest annoyances. I could go on to enumerate other kinds of unfortunate husbands, although I cannot name them all, nor do I wish to. If he is a man of disagreeable character, he must be tolerated. You must not vie with him in disagreeableness, or there will be no end of ills and misery. Do not counter his insolence with insolence of your own or quell anger with anger. That would only stimulate and irritate his illness, not cure it. Do not hope that you can clean mud with mud or extinguish a fire by throwing oil on it. Turn your attention to those women who have husbands with more vices, or certainly greater ones, who are violent and intolerable, and from their misfortunes take consolation for your own. You cannot love him for his vices, but love him because he lacks many others that are no less troublesome. Do not look at those women who seem to be more happily married. This manner of thinking will render your whole life unpleasant, although you really do not know the secrets of their household. Look at those whose situation is more difficult.

43. When your husband shows himself more tractable, then admonish him politely and gently that he be willing to live a better life. If he listens to you, you will have been of great profit to both of you; but if he begins to flare up, do not struggle with him and make two madmen out of one: you and him. You have fulfilled your duty; persevere, and you will have great glory before men and immense merits in the eyes of God. But if through his proclivity to vice or lack of control he beats you, consider that you are being corrected by God, and that this is happening to you because of some of your sins, which are expiated in that way. Blessed are you if by a minor hardship in this life you can redeem great torment in the next. But good and prudent wives are rarely beaten by their husbands, no matter how wicked and insane they may be. Devour your grief at home, do not broadcast it in the neighborhood or complain to others about your husband so that it may not appear

---

89. Juvenal *Satires* 6.100.

that you appoint a judge between him and you. Keep domestic problems within the walls and threshold of the house so that they will not be spread abroad. In that way you will render your husband more amenable when you would only further exacerbate him with your complaints and your useless tongue.

44. There are some husbands who are mentally feeble and deranged. A good wife will treat such a mate tactfully and will not irritate him or be lacking in respect. Rather, she will convince him that she will do everything in accordance with his wishes and to his best advantage and will guide him gently like a tamed animal. A woman will comport herself with such men as mothers do toward children with similar defects, moved by their distress to great pity. Pity increases love, so that they more often love weak, crippled, stupid, deformed, and sickly children than those that are strong, unimpaired, intelligent, beautiful, and robust.

I do not wish to run through other types of bad husbands but to give one general rule of conduct. Whatever his qualities, you married him. God, the church, and your parents gave him to you as your man, husband, and master. Of the many thousands of men, he is your lot and your portion. That which cannot be changed must be borne with equanimity, and he must be loved, respected, and honored—if not for his own sake, then for the sake of those by whom he was allotted and commended to you because of the promise you gave, just as many persons do good to those totally unworthy of it for the sole reason that they have been commended to them by those whom they hold dear. Many do certain things merely because they promised it; otherwise they would not do them. And you must take care that what you do even against your will both appear and will be done willingly. Thus, you make lighter and more pleasant a task that would be burdensome and painful if you were to do it unwillingly. Necessity will teach you to bear up with fortitude; habit, which finds solace even in the harshest calamities, will facilitate it, "quickly making even the most painful things seem familiar," as Seneca said.[90] Think that you owe this to your husband and that in this way a great reward is stored up for you with God, and a great and honorable name among men.

45. At this point, I see that some women may have doubts about how far they should obey their husbands. Since the unscrupulousness and willful disobedience of some women has made this a vexed question, I shall give a rather lengthy explanation of the husband's authority over his wife. In matters having to do with virtue or that are neither good nor bad, there can be

90. Seneca *On Tranquillity* 10.2.

no doubt that a wife must obey her husband's commands as if they were the law of God. The husband takes God's place on earth, and, after the divine majesty, it is to him alone that a wife owes all her love, respect, and obedience.

Therefore, if a wife should wish to give to God what is not commanded by God, she should not do so without her husband's permission. What can a woman consider more her own than her body and soul? But Paul bears witness that a married woman does not have power over her own body [91] and cannot offer continence to God without her husband's knowledge, not to speak of acting without his consent. Therefore, if your husband has need of your service and you answer that you want to go, let us not say to a dance or to a public entertainment or a banquet or some other pastime (for that would obviously be more appropriate for harlots), but to pray and pay a visit to the church, know that your prayers will not be pleasing to God and you will not find him in church. God wishes you to pray, but only when you are free of marital obligations; he wishes you to visit his temple, but only when your husband does not need you at home. These are the duties of marriage that God placed upon a wife. He wishes you to approach his altar, but only when you have reconciled yourself to your friend. [92] How much more will he require that you be reconciled with your husband, your greatest friend? Why do you attend sacred functions and travel from church to church when your husband either expressly orders or tacitly demands something else of you? Do you seek God in church when you abandon your consort, to whom God joined you, sick and hungry at home? Around his bed are all sacred things: there are the altars, there is God, where peace and concord reign, especially between those who are bound to each other by these vows to remain inseparable. It will be easy for you to make God your friend if you make your husband your friend.

God has no need of our services; he reserved for himself piety and supreme worship. He demands obedience, not sacrifice. [93] Practically everything else he prescribes for mankind is for their mutual benefit, that they may live in harmony and friendship. That is why he so often inculcates mutual love and declares that he admits into his kingdom and promises the reward of beatitude to those who show kindness to their neighbor. He casts out and detests those who were neither beneficent nor benevolent toward their neighbor. God will easily be reconciled to you if you reconcile yourself

91. 1 Cor. 7:4.
92. Matt. 5:23–24.
93. Matt. 9:13.

with your neighbor. There is no more accessible path to the favor of God than through the favor of men.

46. So let a woman be convinced that she performs great acts of worship when she serves her husband and goes the round of the great churches [94] when she stays at her husband's bedside. And yet there are some women who would not give up their visits to church no matter how gravely ill their husbands might be, not so much for the sake of piety, in my opinion, as through habit and personal satisfaction. Why should we discuss such women? As for those who are motivated by religious devotion, Paul gives this warning: "The unmarried woman thinks of what pertains to the Lord, how she may please God; the married woman thinks of what pertains to her husband and how she may please her husband." [95] He does not take away the practice of religion from wives, but he shows that it is now of less importance, because an unmarried woman belongs totally to the Lord, and has the time to think only of him, whereas the married woman is divided between God and her husband. While previously she occupied herself exclusively with the contemplation of the heavenly life, now she must descend to the cares of this life for her husband's sake.

It is not that this way of life is alien to the Lord, since he instituted it, but the other is more lofty and closer to the Lord. The wife is pleasing to the Lord but through the intermediacy of her husband, because she is anxious to please her husband, whom God placed over her. The unmarried woman and the widow are pleasing to God without a man and without an intermediary, as it were. Their thoughts are different as the activities of Martha and Mary were different, [96] not through opposition but in degree, as the thoughts of an unmarried woman are more elevated than those of a married woman. Therefore, the greatest part of piety in a married woman is the care and ministry of her husband.

47. When the apostle said, "The wife thinks of things that concern her husband," [97] let no one think that he was implying that this was what a woman usually does rather than what she ought to do. Paul does not induce us into bad habits, nor does he leave an opening for them to rush in. What of the fact that not all unmarried women think of the Lord, and not all wives think of their husbands? He teaches us what is fitting to be done in both states of life, so that what befitted a woman in an unmarried state, namely,

---

94. Probably referring to the pilgrimage to the Roman basilicas.
95. 1 Cor. 7:34.
96. Luke 10:42.
97. 1 Cor. 7:34.

total absorption in the Lord, she should now convert to her marital duties. Otherwise, she would not satisfy her master, Saint Paul, or Christ the Lord, and in her very devotion she would lose the devotion that she is trying to attain.

The same apostle Paul, writing to Timothy, laid down this precept concerning the duties of a wife: "Let a woman learn in silence, with all submissiveness. I do not allow a woman to teach or have authority over men, but to remain silent."⁹⁸ And to the Corinthians he writes: "Let your wives not speak in church; if they have any questions, let them ask their husbands at home."⁹⁹ This law clearly seems to me to mean that a wife should learn from her husband and in matters of doubt should follow his opinion and believe the same things he does. If the husband should err, he is solely to blame; the wife is innocent, unless his errors are so manifest that they could not be ignored without blame, or are contrary to the teachings of those in whom her husband should have put his faith. Acts of impiety should never be committed, no matter how much her husband orders and demands it of you, if you know them to be such. One person must be acknowledged as superior and dearer than your husband, and that is Christ.

The head of the woman is man, but the head of the man is Christ.¹⁰⁰ Many holy women of our religion have even suffered torture at the hands of their husbands in order to remain faithful to Christ's commandments against the will of their husbands. Nevertheless, care must be taken that you do not judge rashly or in accordance with another's opinion concerning your husband's piety. This is too serious a matter for you to trust anyone else's opinion, one on which there are widespread differences of opinion among mankind. The apostle forbade a wife to leave an impious husband, unless he allowed it.¹⁰¹ So strong is the bond of marriage that, according to Paul, not even piety can dissolve it unless impiety permits it. What rules must be laid down when both are good and pious Christians? What attitude should a wife display toward a good husband?

48. I do not wish, nor should I pass over in silence, the grave recommendations concerning a wife's duties that are contained in the last book of the *Economics,* a work attributed to Aristotle:

> The virtuous woman should esteem that the customary mode of behavior of her husband is the law of her life, imposed by God through

---

98. 1 Tim. 2:11–12.
99. 1 Cor. 14:34–35.
100. 1 Cor. 11:3.
101. 1 Cor. 7:13.

the bond of marriage and community of life. If she supports it with resignation, she will govern the house with great ease; if not, it will be more difficult. Therefore it behooves her to show herself of one mind with her husband not only in prosperity and good fortune but also in adversity. If there be some lack of material things or sickness of body or alienation of mind, she should bear it patiently and obey, unless it is something base and unworthy. And if her husband should commit some fault through some mental aberration, she should not retain it in her mind, but ascribe it to his emotional state or to ignorance. The more scrupulously she obeys him in these circumstances the more grateful he will be to her when his troubled mental state is calmed; and if the base thing be demanded of her does not turn out well, he will appreciate it the more when he returns to his senses. Therefore a woman should be cautious at such times but in other things she should show herself more obedient than if she had come into that house as a bought slave. Indeed she was bought at a great price—partnership in life and the procreation of children, which are the greatest and most sacred things that exist. Besides, if she lived with a successful husband, her virtue would not have stood out so clearly. It is a matter of little account to enjoy the fruits of prosperity. But it is considered a much greater thing to suffer adversity with patience. Not to be cast down in the midst of great calamities is the mark of a noble spirit. One must pray that no such misfortune will befall your husband, but if he does suffer the blows of fortune she should think that she will receive great praise if she acts courageously, reflecting within herself that neither Alcestis would have won such renown nor Penelope merited such praise if they had lived with husbands who enjoyed good fortune. Whereas the troubles of Admetus and Ulysses procured these women everlasting fame. By maintaining loyalty and justice toward their spouses in their adversities they not undeservedly attained undying glory. It is easy to find companions in prosperity but women refuse to be companions of misery, except those of exceptional mettle. For all these reasons it is better to hold one's husband in honor and not despise him.[102]

---

102. Aristotle *Economics* 3.1 (Barnes 2:2146–47).

IV

ON THE CONCORD
OF MARRIED COUPLES

49. To rehearse the blessings of concord and how everything in the universe and the universe itself consists of peace and concord would be an endless task, which has no place here. We have proposed to speak of marriage. I say that the greatest tranquillity and a great part of happiness in marriage is concord, and the greatest disturbance and unhappiness comes from discord. The Pythagoreans often cited this saying of those handed down by their master, Pythagoras: "Sloth must be avoided and banished from the body, ignorance from the mind, indulgence from the belly, sedition from the city, discord from the home and, in general, intemperance from all things."[103] In Homer, Ulysses wishes for Nausicaa, daughter of Alcinoos, a husband and a home, and concord, which is the greatest and most sought-after good in life. For when man and wife live together in concord, they cause great sorrow to their enemies, great joy to their friends, and most of all to themselves.[104] How fortunate do we imagine the marriage of Albucius[105] must have been, who lived with his wife, Terentiana, for twenty years without the slightest displeasure? How much more fortunate the marriage of Publius Rubrius Celer, who lived with his wife, Ennia,[106] for forty-four years without a quarrel?

From discord arise dissension, wrangling, disputes, fighting. Most women are quarrelsome and difficult, and when they scold their husbands for the most trivial reasons, it ends up in hard feelings. There is nothing that

---

103. *Maxims of the Pythagoreans*, 111a, in *The Sentences of Sextus*, ed. Henry Chadwick (Cambridge, 1959), 93.

104. Homer *Odyssey* 6.180–85.

105. This person is probably C. Albucius Silus, a famous declaimer of the first century, much admired by Seneca the Elder. Of his wife, Terentiana, nothing is known.

106. I have found no ancient source that mentions this couple.

so alienates a husband from his wife as frequent altercations and a wife's bitter tongue, which Solomon compares to a leaky roof in winter,[107] since both things drive a man from his home. The same writer said that it was preferable to live in the desert than with a quarrelsome and irascible wife. A few insupportable women have conferred this benefit upon all women, so that no woman is thought to be tolerable. Whence came the interpretation of Gaius:[108] "Celibate is akin to celestial and in Greek *eïtheoi* is equal to *hemitheoi*, that is, celibates are demi-gods." A saying arose from this: "He who is without a wife is without strife," as if to say that all married couples quarreled.

50. This very thing deterred many peaceable natures, alien to quarreling, from taking a wife. Many invectives have been written against the female sex on account of this, undeservedly, to be sure, and at one time divorces were sought and harshly carried out. Even today they are desired by many among the Christian people because they say that their wives would be more agreeable if they knew that they could be driven out if they were not docile and tractable. In this matter, in my opinion, either men are deceived or women are very stupid not to see that they should be more obedient to their husbands so that they may live more pleasantly with those from whom they can in no way be separated. Otherwise, they turn a permanent necessity into a misery that they can never throw off.

Much depends on the woman to ensure concord in the home. For a man's character is less irritable than a woman's, not only among humans but in the whole animal world, as Aristotle said:

> Since males are more spirited and more fierce, they are also more simple and less cunning, endowed with a more noble spirit. Females, on the contrary, are more malicious and more inclined to suspicion and plotting. Therefore it comes about that they are influenced by the vaguest conjectures and their tender minds are hurt by the slightest blow and they frequently expostulate with their husbands and anger them by the importunity of their complaints. The male is quicker to be reconciled than the woman, and it is true also that among men

---

107. Prov. 19:13.

108. Quintilian *Education of the Orator* 1.6.36. Vives certainly must have believed this to be the famous second-century Roman jurisconsult, now best known for his *Institutes*, an elementary manual of Roman law. Erasmus discusses this same etymology in his *Refutation of Josse Clichtove* (*CWE* 83 [Toronto, 1998]:125). Modern editions of Quintilian print "Gavius" for "Gaius." Gavius Bassus was a grammarian during the time of Cicero.

those who have more feminine feelings and are less high-born retain the memory of offenses longer, seek revenge relentlessly and are not content with mere revenge.[109]

There was in Rome a tiny shrine on the Palatine dedicated to a certain goddess, in which if there was some domestic quarrel between spouses, they said what they wished and were reconciled. This goddess was called Viriplaca, a name that signified that it was not the wife who had to be appeased by the man but the man by the wife.[110] Even if the fault was your husband's and not yours, the initiative in winning back favor must be taken by you, since you are under his power and authority. How much more must your husband be mollified by submission, blandishments, and penitence if any of the fault resides with you. Although the most important part of what I have been saying has to do with concord, I shall add some further details.

51. The principal and most effective requirement to assure concord is that the wife love her husband. For it is the nature of love to elicit love in return. Certain women should not be astonished if they are not loved by their husbands, even if they affirm that they love their husbands. Let them see if they love them as much as they claim. Let them love truly, and they will be loved. Things that are feigned, simulated, and counterfeited give themselves away eventually and do not have the same efficacy as genuine and clearly defined things. If husband and wife love each other mutually, they will want and not want the same things, which in the last analysis is staunch friendship, as the great authority wrote.[111] There will be no discord or dissension among those who have one heart, which does not desire different things, and one mind, which does not think different things. I never saw my mother, Blanca, in fifteen years of marriage, arguing with my father or entertaining views contrary to his. They had one mind and identical feelings. But concerning my mother, there will be another opportunity to speak of her in more detail.[112]

52. Since some women love impetuously and are driven by impulse to destroy marital discord, I must exhort them to prudence by some little rules and calm their violent feelings. The most important thing is to control these impulses, that is, the passions and emotions that take hold of women's weak minds with greater violence and drag them along, since they offer less resis-

109. Aristotle *The History of Animals* 9.1, 608b (Barnes 1 : 948–49).

110. Valerius Maximus 2.1.6. Viriplaca was a Roman goddess who helped wives win back their husbands' favor after an estrangement.

111. Sallust *Catiline* 20.4.

112. See below, par. 140.

tance. There must be great restraint in a woman's mind, and she should manifest it in her actions. She must be continually warned not to act in a certain way only for the sake of appearance, for that is useless and ineffective. Let her be what she wishes to appear, and her appearance will be more natural, more authentic. She should not think that she can deceive everyone by her simulations. Men are not stumps or stones, who cannot distinguish the artificial and the feigned from the true and genuine. Furthermore, though they may deceive onlookers, they cannot deceive nature, which did not endow false and counterfeit things with the same energy and efficacy that it gave natural and real things. Let them make proof of it themselves, considering within themselves whether they think women to be modest who affect modesty, and whether they love in return those women who falsely claim to love them.

53. The counsel that the poet Horace gave to Lollius concerning a friend, that he should accommodate himself to his friend's character and activities, will be of use to the married woman. Horace advises, "If he wants to go hunting, do not set about composing poems, but, dismissing the Muses, follow in the train of the pack animals laden down with nets and dogs."[113] Amphion and Zethus, sons of Antiope, were brothers—in fact, twins. The first was very gifted in playing the lyre, the other had no training at all. Since the sound of the lyre did not please Zethus and this seemed to be a source of discord between them, Amphion laid aside the lyre.

So a wife should adapt herself to her husband's character and interests, and not hate or despise them. It is recorded that Andromache, the wife of Hector, fed Hector's horses hay and oats with her own hands because she saw what delight her husband took in them, and used every care in feeding them so that they would be good in battle.[114] Plinius Caecilius declares in many of his letters that he loved his wife singularly, and among these letters there is one that he sent to his wife's aunt, Hispulla, who had brought her up. In this letter he not only thanks her for having molded her character when she was a young girl, but also gives the reason why he loved her so much, in these words:

> She loves me, which is a sign of chastity. In addition to this she has an interest in literature, which she conceived out of affection for me. She has copies of my books, she reads them again and again and even

---

113. Horace *Epistles* 1.18.39–40. The story of Amphion and Zethus follows in the Horatian passage.
114. Homer *Iliad* 8.185–90.

learns them by heart. What concern she shows when I have to plead a case, how joyful she is when I have finished it. She posts people to report to her what approval and what applause I won and what was the outcome of the trial. Whenever I give a public recitation of my works, she sits nearby, her face discreetly veiled and listens to my praise with avid ears. She sings my verses and sets them to the cithara, not taught by any musician, but by love, which is the best of all teachers.[115]

54. Recently, when I was in Paris and visited Guillaume Budé[116] at his home, his wife passed through the vestibule where we were walking. She was a very beautiful woman and I was able to divine immediately from her countenance and her whole bearing, which was truly that of a heroine, that she was a woman of great virtue and a prudent mistress of the household. After she greeted her husband with due respect and me courteously and graciously, I asked him if that was his wife. "This is my wife," he said, "who is so attentive to my wishes that she treats my books with no less care than my children, for she sees that I am very dedicated to my studies." In this she merits even greater praise than the wife of Pliny, in my opinion, because she knows nothing of literature, while the other was well versed in it.

55. How much more prudent and honorable these women than those who hold their husbands back from the study of letters and from honorable pursuits and exhort and impel them to the acquisition of wealth, amusements, and pleasures so that they, too, may partake of this material gain (entertainment and luxuries), since they have no hope of being able to share their interests in study. In their stupidity, they do not recognize how much more true and substantial is the pleasure that comes from having wise rather than rich husbands or those given to fine living. Nor do they see how much more agreeable and pleasant it is to spend your life with wise men rather than with ignorant fools, who have not set the bridle of wisdom upon their passions, who are driven hither and thither by the passions awakened in their minds and drawn far away from the path of justice and moral rectitude.

A wife shall not only not show aversion to her husband's studies but to anything else by word, look, gesture, or any outward manifestation. She will

---

115. Pliny *Epistles* 4.19.

116. Guillaume Budé (1468–1540) was the most famous of the French humanists. He was awarded several important posts by Francis I, including master of requests and royal librarian. His wife, Roberte Lelieur, was a well-educated woman who perhaps assisted him in his research in addition to providing him with a large family. Vives met Budé while in Paris in 1519, and they exchanged numerous letters.

love all things in him, admire everything, show her respect and approval. She will put faith in his words even if he tells her things that seem improbable or incredible. She will take on his facial expressions, smile at him when he smiles, and be sad when he is sad, maintaining always the dignity of virtue and integrity befitting a married woman. She will make clear to her husband that her sympathy with his moods comes from a spirit of friendship, not adulation. She will not prefer herself to her husband in anything. She will think of him as father, master, greater, more powerful, and better than herself, and she will reveal this in her conduct and state it openly. How can friendship and love exist if being rich you despise your husband who is poor, or beautiful despise a husband who is ugly, or noble disdain one lowly born.

56. The satirist said, "Nothing is more intolerable than a rich woman."[117] Jerome said the same thing, writing against Jovinian. Theophrastus also said that it was a torment to suffer a rich wife,[118] but I do not believe this is so, unless they add that she is also wicked or foolish. What madness it is not to recognize how vain a thing money is, since it is the least of those things that can elevate men's spirits! But many people have shallow and empty minds that become inflated at the slightest breeze. Silly woman, does marriage not render all things common? If all things are common between friends,[119] how much more is that true of marriage, not only in matters concerning money, but friends, relatives, and everything else as well? "The Romans," as Plutarch said, "stated this in their laws, by which it was forbidden that anything could be given or received between spouses, so that nothing would seem to be the private property of either one of them."[120] In the ideal republic, as Plato teaches, "mine and thine must be eliminated."[121] How much more is this true of the ideal home, which is best and most perfect, and therefore happiest, when it has one body under one head? If it had several heads or several bodies, it would be a monster. Am I saying that nothing belongs to the wife, everything to the man? Just as, according to a simile of Plutarch, diluted wine, even if it contains more water than wine, is still called wine,[122] so no matter how much more the woman brings to the marriage than the man, it all belongs to him.

117. Juvenal, *Satires*, 6.460.
118. Jerome *Against Jovinianus* 1.47 (*NPNF*, 2d ser., 6:83).
119. Erasmus *Adages* I i 1 (*CWE* 31:29).
120. Plutarch, "Advice to Bride and Groom," *Moralia*, 143A.
121. Plato *Republic* 462C.
122. Plutarch, "Advice to Bride and Groom," *Moralia*, 140F.

57. Does not he who possesses the woman herself and who is her master possess everything that belongs to her? And what is more, you hear what God, Lord of all creation, says: "You will be under the power of a man, and he will have dominion over you."[123] Therefore, a husband must not be derided for his physical form. You have beauty in your body, woman, but your husband has your beauty and you in his possession. I am not going to discuss how trivial and insubstantial is the gift of beauty and how it depends solely on men's opinions. The same woman appears very beautiful to some and very ugly to others. How uncertain and fragile, fraught with danger, how fleeting! One fever, a single wart or hair could turn you from a fine beauty into a sight hideous to behold. And yet this unstable and perishable thing can swell and exalt foolish and vain minds to an astonishing degree, as the wind inflates a wineskin. For that reason the poet said, "Pride on beauty waits."[124] In men, no one looks for that grace of form, but in women, they think it to be appropriate. And yet you read the saying of the wise king: "Charm is deceitful and beauty is vain; the woman who fears the Lord will be praised."[125] Finally, if you and your husband are the same flesh, or, rather, the same person, then he cannot possibly be ugly if he has a beautiful wife. But what is the purpose of all this vaunting of beauty, as if we did not know that the body of a woman, however beautiful, is nothing but a dung heap, covered with a white and purple veil? If we could see into the beautiful body of Alcibiades, said a certain philosopher, how many foul and abominable things would appear![126]

58. "The only true nobility is virtue,"[127] according to the poet. I will hold my tongue concerning the stupid conception we have of nobility acquired and preserved by war, cruelty, robbery, fraud, and pillaging, an idea nurtured by the masses, that great teacher of error. No matter how noble you may be, if you marry a husband of lowly birth, you make yourself even lower than he. The wife is not nobler than the husband, nor will the human race be different in this respect than all other living things. Children trace their lineage to the father, according to the practice of all nations, since he is regarded as having the stronger claim. If you are of the highest nobility,

123. Gen. 3:16.

124. Ovid *Fasti* 1.5.419.

125. Prov. 1:30.

126. Boethius *Consolation of Philosophy* 3.8; Aristotle *Protrepticus*, frag. 10a, in *Aristotelis fragmenta selecta*, ed. W. D. Ross (Oxford, 1955), 40.

127. Juvenal *Satires* 8.20.

either your husband becomes noble through you or you lose your nobility through him. In civil law, husbands, not parents, confer nobility on women. Consequently, those who were born of noble parentage were no longer called noble if they married one of low degree. This was made clear when the patrician women of Rome expelled Verginia,[128] a daughter of noble parents, from the shrine of patrician chastity, saying that by her marriage to a plebeian she was no longer a patrician but a plebian. She did not deny it, nor did she consider it shameful to be a plebeian, nor did she spurn the plebeian class in comparison with the patrician, nor was she ashamed to be called Verginia, wife of Lucius Volumnius.

59. Cornelia, daughter of Scipio, entered into a household that was eminent and distinguished for the holding of many high political offices, but plebeian nonetheless, and not to be compared to her paternal household. She was of the Cornelian line: undeniably the leading family in all of Rome, and from the stock and preeminent family of the Scipios—daughter of Scipio, the conqueror of Africa, prince of the Senate, of the Roman people, and of all peoples; daughter of Tertia Aemilia, of the Aemilian line, celebrated in Rome and in the whole world, with such glorious distinctions of race in all her ancestors, paternal and maternal. Yet she still preferred to be called Cornelia, wife of Gracchus, rather than daughter of Scipio. She even became angry with some who, thinking to do her honor, called her by the name of Scipio.[129]

Marpessa, as Greek writers tell us, preferred her husband, Idas, a mortal man, to Apollo, whom they considered an immortal god.[130] Thesta, the sister of Dionysius I, tyrant of Syracuse, was married to Philoxenus. When he had set a plot in motion against Dionysius and was forced to flee from Sicily, Thesta was summoned by her brother and severely reproved for not having revealed the flight of her husband to him. She replied, "Did you think me such a degenerate and base wife that if I knew of my husband's flight, I would not have followed him and would have preferred to be known in any part of the world as the wife of the exile Philoxenus rather than the sister of

---

128. Livy 10.23.3–5. This Verginia is not to be confused with the more famous Verginia, whom her father killed in public rather than surrender her to the lust of the decemvir Appius Claudius.

129. Plutarch *Tiberius Gracchus* 8.5. Vives frequently cites Cornelia as a paragon of self-abnegation and devotion to her family. Plutarch tells us in his *Life of Cornelius Gracchus* that the Roman people erected a statue to her memory with the simple inscription "Cornelia, Mother of the Gracchi."

130. Plutarch, "Parallel Stories," *Moralia*, 315E–F; Homer *Iliad* 9.557–60.

Dionysius, the king, here in my native country?" In admiration of this holy and noble spirit, the Syracusans, after the expulsion of the tyrants, honored her in her lifetime and rendered her the greatest honors upon her death.[131]

60. Maria,[132] wife of the emperor Maximilian, inherited this region of Flanders from her father, Charles. The Flemish had little respect for the simple and meek character of Maximilian and referred all decisions concerning their governance to Maria, as if she were their leader. However, she never decided anything that was within her power without consulting her husband, whose will she regarded as law. And she had the authority to administer everything according to her own wishes without incurring the ill will of her husband, since Maximilian refused nothing to his beloved and prudent wife, owing both to his own mild disposition and her integrity of character. In this way, Maria in a short time added much to his authority, enhancing his power. That region became more obedient to its rulers, since respect for them was doubled: the sovereignty of the one supported and sustained by the other.

The prudent woman should not think that the dowry she brings with her into her husband's home consists of money, beauty, or splendor of lineage, but chastity, modesty, moral integrity, obedience to her husband's authority, and diligent care of her children and of the house. She who is so endowed is richly dowered. Otherwise, the woman who possesses wealth— which makes her overbearing, without virtue to guide her—brings wrangling, not wedlock, in her train. These are the words of Alcmena to Amphitryon in Plautus:

> I think not that a dowry which is dowry called,
> But chastity and shame and curbed desire,
> Fear of the gods, the love of parents,
> Peace with kin; a wife compliant to your will,
> Generous to the good, helpful to the virtuous.[133]

61. So much for the mind. Now the bridle must be put on the tongue, which is easily done if the mind is bridled. The reason why many women have no control of their tongue is that their mind is uncontrolled. Anger

---

131. Plutarch *Dio* 21.

132. Maria, daughter of Charles the Bold, was duchess of Burgundy. Through his marriage to Maria in 1477, Maximilian became the ruler of the Burgundian Netherlands. Maria helped him to adapt to her country, but after her death in 1482, the people of Bruges rebelled against Maximilian and even held him prisoner for a time in 1488.

133. Plautus *Amphitryon* 839–42.

takes hold of them, carries them away, and renders them powerless over themselves. As a result, there is no limit to their quarreling and no logic in their abusiveness, since there is no room for reason or judgment. The fire ignites and consumes everything, for it has found good kindling in a soft and yielding material ideal for burning. Then unrestrained rage of emotion and tongue bursts forth, which I have often marveled at in good women. And in those in whom chastity or propriety or holiness or other excellent virtues were not lacking, I was forced to find moderation and temperance lacking in their angry tongues. This made me quite ashamed even though their vituperations had nothing to do with me, but with people who were complete strangers to me, if what pertains to a Christian can be considered alien to any other Christian.

Therefore, though it be very difficult, it is a beautiful and outstanding virtue in a woman to control the tongue. This will not involve too much effort if she will gain control over herself, fortify and strengthen herself so that she will not allow herself to be carried away by violent emotions. When she is at rest, sane and sober and in control of herself, let her often reflect and resolve in her mind that if she should get into an argument with her husband, she should not hurl any grave insults against him concerning his family, body, mind, or manner of life, which she knows will offend him greatly. This should never be done, but especially not in the presence of those whom he strongly wishes not to know about it. Once he has been provoked by this insulting language, it will be difficult for him to make reconciliation; and even if he does become reconciled, every time he remembers that humiliation, he will not be able to look at his wife with a favorable eye. In the eyes of God, too, what displeasure it brings! The Lord said in the Gospel of Matthew, "Whoever becomes angry with his brother and utters the expression 'raca' (i.e., 'Why you . . . !') will be liable to the council; and whoever says 'You fool' will be liable to hell's fire."[134] Now consider what will happen to you if you utter a great injury not only against your brother, but your father, God's representative (as far as you are concerned), and all your relatives?

62. But if your husband insults you, do not let it remain in your memory. Bear up with it patiently, and by this tolerance you will gain great favor with him when he has calmed down. You will turn his furious temper to good thoughts and find him more docile and agreeable afterwards. Terence, who described human mores in his comedies, says of a chaste maiden:

134. Matt. 5:22.

> She, as befits a girl of decent birth,
> Modest and chaste, bears hurts and injuries
> From her spouse and hides his misdemeanors.[135]

In this way, a husband's affection is restored to his wife, from whom he had been estranged. This is the same advice given by the wise nurse in a play of Seneca to Octavia, wife of Nero: "Vanquish rather a cruel spouse with obedience."[136]

63. Women, you possess a tender and defenseless body. In addition, you are burdened with almost daily troubles resulting from your sex: the annoyances of menstrual discharge, the discomforts of the womb, the dangers of childbirth, a condition that merits your husband's sympathy. See to it that you do not drive away the pity your husband owes you by your importunity, that your misery does not make you miserable. Do not bring up as a reproach against your husband some good deed you have done him. This is a hateful thing even among strangers, and he who throws his benefice in the teeth of another loses all gratitude for it, driving it from the other's mind. Besides, if you reflect on it, it is not possible to do a good deed for your husband, since you owe him as much as you do your father and your own self. A modest woman will not make frequent reference to her lineage, her talent, or her dowry. This is annoying and can arouse aversion even in the most loving husband. Juvenal says he would prefer to marry a humble woman of low birth rather than Cornelia, the daughter of Africanus, of whose virtue we have already said many things, if her father's fame should make her haughty:

> I prefer a Venusine to you, Cornelia,
> Mother of the Gracchi, if with your lofty virtues
> You bring great haughtiness and reckon
> Triumphs as part of your trousseau.
> Take away your Hannibal, I pray,
> And Syphax vanquished in the camp.
> Away with you and all of Carthage too![137]

64. That sage writer, Plutarch, warns that at the beginning of a marriage any occasion for contention and argument must be avoided, since love has not yet adhered, and tender and fragile as it is, could be dissolved

---

135. Terence *The Mother-in-Law* 164–66.
136. Seneca *Octavia* 84–85.
137. Juvenal *Satires* 6.167–71.

on any pretext, as newly made vases break at the slightest touch.[138] There should be no quarreling in the marriage bed. For where will they lay aside their resentments if they make the place best suited for reconciliation hateful and hostile because of their quarrels, and spoil the medicine, as it were, that should have served to cure these troubles? There are certain little things that can strengthen or weaken love, which the wife should notice in her husband so that she may adapt herself to his temperament and wishes. I shall give a few examples, which will suffice for the understanding of all the rest.

Know what kind of foods he likes, how he likes them prepared and with what seasoning, and which ones he dislikes. Does he like his food highly seasoned or bland, hot or cold; this kind of meat, fish and drink, or some other; what hour does he prefer, what tablecloths and napkins, tables, trays, plates, bowls, kettles, saltcellars, cups; how does he like the table set, what guests does he prefer, what type of conversation? Then you must please him in the way you make the bed: the cushions, blankets, bedspread, sheets, and pillows you should use. The same goes for chairs, benches, furnishing, and all kinds of domestic appurtenances, which are entrusted and delegated to the woman.

65. These are little things in themselves, as I said, but of great importance to human beings, whose emotions are aroused not by the size of things but by the value they put on them. Is it not a small thing to cut a plum with a knife, to rip linen, to sharpen a saw, to hear a pig grunt and similar insignificant things? Yet how many people are profoundly disturbed and shudder at these things so that they would more readily be wounded than tolerate these sounds, by some strange quirk of nature, peculiar to each individual. How much Isaac appreciated the porridge offered to him by his son so that this act won him his father's blessing,[139] which was esteemed as the greatest inheritance in those days! Who has not heard of hatred between spouses arising from a late supper, or broth that was a bit cold, or a dirty tablecloth, which then developed into violent conflict and a bitter divorce? This is the essential rule to follow: A wife should observe her husband's ways carefully and discreetly and behave toward him as she would wish her servants to behave toward her if she had the same disposition. It must also be added that these repeated peccadilloes first shake the foundations of love, though they be firmly fixed, and then when it begins to totter, undermine it altogether.

66. Once it was the custom of kings to go about personally dispensing

138. Plutarch, "Advice to Bride and Groom," *Moralia*, 138E–F.
139. Gen. 27:4.

pleasant things and favors that would win them goodwill, such as acts of munificence, distribution of gifts and pardon; painful, hateful, and harsh things were executed by their ministers, such as exile, confiscations, capital punishment. The story is told that within the memory of our fathers there was a prominent woman of Sicily who carefully observed what her servants did that found pleasure with their master. Then she discharged those duties herself, leaving to them tasks that were ungrateful and annoying.

In this regard, I must severely castigate Flemish wives, who, when their husbands wish to relax their tired minds and indulge their fancy, perform their duties sluggishly and grudgingly and drive them out of the house, as if it were a desert. The husbands betake themselves to local beer or wine taverns and, finding willing companions there for their entertainment and an abundance of everything, give themselves over to every kind of vice: gluttony, drunkenness, gambling, whoring, and idleness. They leave their wives and small children at home starving, and they squander all their substance, even to their tunics and wallets, avoiding their home as if it were a cave in which a wild beast lurked, to wit, their shrewish wife.

Some of these wives are not unwilling to put up with this as long as they do not have to lay a hand on the furniture or the kitchen utensils. Such is their indolence and torpor, and at times their impudence and obstinacy that they would rather die, once they have taken offense, than show even the slightest forgiveness to their husbands. Thus, they bring about the corruption of their husbands' morals together with the loss of their possessions. You will see that many men who were frugal when they were bachelors become wicked and profligate husbands. But these same women, who are so slow and lethargic in their domestic duties, are marvelously quick and diligent in roaming about, dallying and gossiping, and show remarkable assiduity and alacrity in dressing and adorning themselves.

V

HOW SHE WILL CONDUCT
HERSELF PRIVATELY WITH
HER HUSBAND

67. It will not be inappropriate here to discuss how a wife should act with her husband in private, without other witnesses. She should know first of all that in ancient times those women who made sacrifice to Juno, the guardian and protectress of marriage, never left the gallbladder behind after the sacrifice was completed but removed it from the victim and threw it behind the altar, signifying by this that neither anger nor bitterness should exist between spouses. They also coupled Mercury and Venus in marriage,[140] that is, cleverness of language and the gratification of the senses, since a wife should unite herself to her husband and bind him to herself more closely day by day through the complaisance of her manner, the charm of her speech, and her ingratiating behavior.

There is nothing more efficacious in attracting someone to yourself than pleasantness of manners and conversation. What good is a woman's talent and intelligence unless it is accompanied by gentleness and mildness toward her husband? There is no one who would not prefer to converse with his dog rather than with an oppressive and surly wife. A prudent wife will have a store of fables, narratives, and anecdotes that are both pleasant and edifying to restore and revive her tired or sick husband. She will also regale him with wise precepts that exhort to virtue and deter from vice. Likewise, she will have on hand a selection of grave sayings against the attacks and assaults of both kinds of fortune, by which she will gradually bring her husband back to earth when he is too elated by prosperity or raise his spirits when he is cast down and prostrated by adversity—in both cases restoring him to equilibrium. If he is the victim of raging emotions, she will calm the storm through womanly, chaste, and prudent assuagements. That was the

---

140. Plutarch, "Advice to Bride and Groom," *Moralia*, 141F.

way Placidia,[141] daughter of Theodosius, calmed her husband, Athaulf, king of the Goths, when he was set on obliterating the Roman name from the face of the earth. She turned him from his cruel resolve by the sweetness of her eloquence and her manner and brought him back to sanity and humane feelings.

68. There is much on this subject in Saint John Chrysostom's writings on the Gospel of John, of which I give the following synopsis:

> It is of great importance for a wife to give good advice to her husband and to calm him when he is overcome by agitated emotions. A husband will not listen to his father or teacher as he does to a good wife. A wife's admonitions have a certain pleasure not to be ignored, since they seem to emanate from an unbounded good will. For a wife loves the man whom she is counseling and looks out for his prosperity no less than for her own. I could adduce many examples of this, of men tamed through their wives' help. A husband must be given advice by example and not by the empty sound of words. You will accomplish this if he sees you without defect, not dressed luxuriously, nor looking for superfluities but content with what is necessary. But if you philosophize with words and show yourself quite different in action, he will scorn your idle talk and refute your preaching with your actions. To give an example: if you do not seek out gold, jewels and costly attire, but adorn yourself with modesty and charity, and require the same of him, he will abide by your counsel. If you are anxious to please a man, you must adorn your soul, not corrupt your body. Gold does not make a wife loveable and desirable, but modesty and piety and affection, which would lead you to give your life for your husband, if it were necessary. Care of the body is costly and burdensome to a husband, but the soul is pleasing to him and costs nothing.[142]

69. The occasions for giving advice must be watched for; not all times are propitious. A friendly office performed at the wrong moment is an annoyance. You will imprint the seal on soft wax and impart counsel to a yielding spirit when his mind is not perturbed by some trouble, when he is alone without any witness. Use skillful and persuasive language and do not be

---

141. Galla Placidia, sister of Emperor Honorius, was captured by the Goths in 410 and married to the Visigothic chieftain Athaulf in 414. In deference to his bride, Athaulf wore Roman robes at the ceremony and allowed her to lead the procession. On his deathbed, he asked his brother to return Placidia and make peace with the Romans.

142. John Chrysostom *Homily on the Gospel of John* 61.3 (*NPNF*, 1st ser., 14:225–26).

exaggerated in your advice. Finish with your talking before producing satiety. Then give the reason why you are offering this advice. Like the first arrows that hit the target, this explanation will make the words of admonition reverberate more deeply in his heart.

Then you will turn the conversation to something more pleasant, which will mitigate and remove any previous harshness, if there was any. Tell him about all your cares and preoccupations, provided they are not frivolous and not unworthy of a man's hearing. Regard him as your sole associate, interlocutor, consultant, master, and lord. Confide your thoughts to his bosom and if anything distresses you, find comfort in him. These things contribute to reciprocal love and harmony, since we are naturally inclined to love those into whose heart we can pass on our cares and emotions like an unburdening of part of our woes, and in whom we can most trust. In turn, those love us who feel that they are loved and are so trusted that they are admitted into the inmost recesses of our heart, and that nothing remains secret or concealed to them.

Women should not think, however, that this law applies equally to them and to their husbands. They should not wish to probe into all the designs of their husbands. This kind of curiosity is often troublesome and looked upon as garrulity, which sometimes irritates their husbands' feelings. Likewise, husbands have some things that they do not wish to be known by their wives, and keep reserved for themselves. In Homer, Juno says to Jupiter, "Do not be wroth with me afterwards if I depart to the dwelling places of deep Ocean without your knowledge."[143] Jupiter replies, "Do not pry into all my plans or hope to know them."[144]

70. And yet the discreet woman with utmost vigilance and instinctive sagacity will ferret out whether her husband harbors any suspicions against her or any seeds of anger or hatred, some remnant of distrust. If such exist, she will devote her energies to dispel them before they take root. These increase for the slightest reason and become fatal. She will rid his mind of these gently and make amends to her husband. Undetected and hidden diseases gain strength and kill more quickly than those that manifest themselves externally. Let her not wrench it out or handle it roughly, lest she implant it more deeply in her attempt to tear it out; but rather, let her remove it without any sense of pain, that is, without protests and complaints. She should not think that either gods or men will be favorable to her if she does not appease her husband.

143. Homer *Iliad* 14.310–11.
144. Homer *Iliad* 1.545–46.

The Lord says in the gospel: "If you are offering your gift at the altar and there remember that some grievance with your brother still remains, leave your gift there and hasten immediately to be reconciled to your brother and then come and offer the gift you intended."[145] In vain do you implore peace of God if you have not made peace with your friend. How much more so with an angry spouse? Let the wife see to it again and again that whatever is said or done in the bedroom and in the sacred marriage bed is to be considered an inviolable secret and must be guarded with greater silence than the secrets of Ceres at Eleusis,[146] or, to put it more aptly, than what is confided to the priest by the penitent. What madness it is to reveal such intimate and private matters!

71. When the noble and well-bred people of Athens were engaged in a war with Philip, king of Macedon, they apprehended letters of his to his wife, Olympias. They refrained from opening them or reading them, however, considering the secrets of spouses as sacred (as indeed they are), and they did not permit them to be divulged or known by others. Thus, they sent them sealed and untouched to the queen in Macedonia.[147] They were a people worthy to have wives who would maintain silence and secrecy. If they did this to an armed enemy, how much more fitting that you should do the same for your husband? Porcia, the wife of Marcus Brutus, voluntarily tested her own constancy by inflicting a wound upon herself to see if she could keep important secrets, and when she was convinced that she could conceal her wound, she dared ask her husband what plans he was turning over in his troubled mind. The plot to murder Caesar that was confided to her by Brutus she guarded with as much tenacity as one of the conspirators.[148]

Nor shall a wife strive merely to be a friend to her husband always, but also not to make enemies of others and expose her husband to dangers through personal feuds. She must not use her husband as a go-between to avenge wrongs she thinks have been done to her unless her chastity is at risk, which is a woman's most prized possession. But this will not occur if she does not wish it and if she uses caution. If someone has said something disrespectful to her or done something that has offended her delicate sensitivity, she should not go rushing off to her husband and stir up his anger with fiery words (which anger is wont to supply) and have him take up arms.

---

145. Matt. 5:23–24.

146. Eleusis was a small town on the coast of Attica where the Mysteries in honor of Demeter, or Ceres, were celebrated.

147. Plutarch, "Precepts of Statecraft," *Moralia*, 799E.

148. Valerius Maximus 3.2.15.

A good woman will repress all this and consider herself safe and protected on all sides if her chastity is intact, without which nothing is pure. In the bedroom and the marriage bed there will be not only chastity but a sense of shame, so that she will remember she is a wife, in whom Plutarch wishes that the greatest love should be joined with the greatest modesty.

72. They say that the legitimate wives of the Persian kings feasted with them and behaved in a convivial manner, but that they were not admitted to the more lewd celebrations, which were reserved only for dancing-girls and concubines.[149] Such was the homage they paid to marriage. For as that prince was wont to say, "Wife is the name of dignity, not of sensual pleasure." So the title of husband is one of association, closeness, and union, not of lust, as we have stated above. It is fitting that men do not immerse themselves in immoderate pleasures or divert themselves with women other than their wives. But we are not teaching men here what their role should be. Let them be on their guard that they do not become teachers of lust and lasciviousness to their wives. They must bear in mind the saying of Sextus the Pythagorean:[150] "Every unchaste and excessively impassioned lover is an adulterer with his wife." They should also harken to Saint Paul's precepts: "Let them possess their wives like vessels of generation unto holiness, not for immoderate and illicit cupidity as the Gentiles do, who do not know God."[151] The spouse in the Canticle of Canticles calls his spouse his sister to signify that marital love is purer.[152] But let us return to women.

73. They must not contaminate the chaste and holy marriage bed by sordid and lustful acts. "Let the marriage between you be honorable," says Saint Paul, "and the marriage bed unspotted."[153] When the chaste Spartan woman was asked whether she had ever made the first advances to her husband, she answered, "No, but my husband did to me." This is to say that the chaste woman never roused her husband's desire or engaged in sex except to satisfy her husband. Trebellius Pollio[154] writes that Zenobia,[155] Queen of Palmyra, a very learned woman and wise in the governing of her kingdom,

---

149. Plutarch, "Advice to Bride and Groom" and "Table Talk," *Moralia*, 140B; 613A.

150. A collection of maxims, probably made in the second century, was attributed to a certain Xystus in the Syriac translation or to Sextus Pythagoreus, according to Saint Jerome. The original collection was probably non-Christian, to which Christian accretions were made. These sayings are collected in *The Sentences of Sextus*, ed. Henry Chadwick (Cambridge, 1959).

151. 1 Thess 4:4–5.

152. Song of Sol. 4:9.

153. Heb. 13:4.

154. Trebellius Pollio *The Thirty Pretenders* 30. He was one of the writers of the so-called *Historia Augusta*, a collection of biographies of Roman emperors who reigned from A.D. 117 to 284.

155. Cf. Book 1, n. 69.

was of such chastity that she did not lie with her husband until after she had ascertained whether she was pregnant or not. After having sexual relations with him, she would abstain from her husband until the time of her menstruation. If she had conceived, she slept alone until she had brought forth; but if not, she gave her husband the opportunity to create children. Who would think that this woman derived any lustful or even moderate pleasure from the sexual act? Worthy of admiration and esteem is this matron who was no more moved to lust by her sexual organs than by her hand or foot. She was worthy to have children without sexual intercourse, which she desired only for the purpose of bearing children, or without pain, since she was made pregnant without pleasure.

Even more exemplary is our Christian queen, Ethelfleda [156] of England, who after her first child no longer lay with her husband. And Etheldreda, [157] queen of that same nation, went even further, for in her two marriages she induced both of her husbands to practice perpetual chastity. There were many other couples who lived entirely without carnal relations, like Henry of Bavaria, [158] Roman emperor, with his wife, Cynegunda; Julian martyr [159] with Basilia. In the city of Alexandria there were Chrysanthus and Daria; [160] and there were Amos and his wife; Malchus the monk, also, with the woman who was his fellow slave, whose life was recounted by Jerome. [161]

74. These saintly persons understood all too well what has been handed down by wise men, that the pleasure of the body is not worthy of our preeminence as human beings, which we possess through the nature of the soul. Therefore, the closer one is to God and the more he has received of that

---

156. Ethelfleda, or Aethelflaed (d. 918), was the daughter of Alfred the Great, king of Wessex. She married Aethelred, ruler of Mercia, in 886 and ruled in her husband's place long before his death.

157. After a first short-lived marriage to a local ealdorman, in which she remained a virgin, Etheldreda wed Egfrith, the young king of Northumbria, for political reasons. He agreed that she should remain a virgin, as in her previous marriage, but after twelve years he wanted their marital relationship to be normal. Etheldreda refused, became a nun, and founded a double monastery at Ely. She died in 679.

158. Henry II, duke of Bavaria (973–1024), was the last Holy Roman Emperor. He was canonized by Pope Eugenius III in 1146.

159. Saints Julian and Basilissa married but by mutual consent lived in perpetual chastity. She founded a convent, and he was martyred under Diocletian. There is a very fanciful account of their lives in the *Acta Sanctorum* for January 9.

160. Chrysanthus, an Egyptian, and his Greek wife, Daria, lived together in virginal purity. They both openly professed Christianity and were put to death under the emperors Carinus and Numerianus in 282 C.E.

161. Jerome *The Life of Malchus* 6 (*NPNF*, 2d ser., 6:317).

excellence of the mind, the more sensual pleasure is spurned and repudiated. Only the less noble, humble, and lowly person, drawn to his baser and more loathsome nature, will make habitual use and exercise of sensual pleasure, and partake very little of that higher nature.

Wives, put off your shawls and put on modesty and always hold on to this decorous mantle of nature, by day and by night, with strangers, with your husband, in the light, and in the dark. May God and his angels and your own conscience never see you divested of the veil of modesty. Nothing can be imagined more ugly or more foul than if you are divested of that cover. The grave poet Hesiod does not want women to take off their chemise even at night inasmuch as the nights also belong to the immortal gods.[162] When Rebecca, the daughter of Bathuel, was brought to Isaac, whom she was to marry, and came upon him when he was walking in the field, she asked him who he was. When she learned that he was Isaac, her promised spouse, she immediately covered herself with her pallium.[163] This wise and well-brought-up-maiden taught all others that first and foremost deference is owed to one's husband. For to whom should we show greater deference than to the one to whom the greatest reverence is due?

162. Hesiod *Works and Days* 729–30.
163. Gen. 24:64–65.

VI

ON JEALOUSY

75. Cicero defines jealousy after the opinion of the Stoics as "A sickness that comes from the thought that another person may possess what one wished for oneself." [164] It is also defined as "The fear that someone may share with you what you wish to be yours alone." However it is defined, it is surely a ferocious vexation and a relentless and uncontrollable tyranny, which as long as it reigns and rages in the mind of the husband, precludes any hope of concord in the marriage. It would be better for both of them to die than that either of them should fall victim to jealousy, especially the husband. What torment and torture can be compared to it, both for the one afflicted by the excesses of jealousy and the one who causes this fear? From this come complaints, protests, shouting, hatred of oneself and of the other person, unceasing suspicion, wrangling, altercation, fighting, even death. For we read and hear tell of many wives slain by their husbands for the sole motive of jealousy. Some wild beasts are also affected by this passion. Aristotle writes that the lion tears the lioness to pieces if he catches her in adultery. [165] Many have seen the female swan killed by the male because she followed after another swan. Therefore, every effort must be made to prevent the husband from being seized by these furies, and if he is seized by them, to free him from their power. The wife will succeed in this only in one way, viz., if she says or does nothing that may make her husband suspicious. She must give even less opportunity if he is suspicious by nature.

76. Paul, [166] Jerome, Aristotle, and other great and wise writers say well

---

164. Cicero *Tusculan Disputations* 4.17–18.

165. This information is not found in the extant works of Aristotle, but is attributed to Aristotle in Pliny *Natural History* 8.17.

166. 1 Thess. 5:22.

that neither should evil be done nor that which has the appearance of evil. "This is a difficult task," you say, "for who can control suspicions?" You can, in many ways. First, if you live chastely, and this alone is the surest way. Time is the parent of truth. Time weakens and eliminates falsehood; it confirms and corroborates truth. If you are chaste and you have a jealous husband, hope that he will put away that disturbance of the mind in a short time. But if you are unchaste, know for certain that not only will it not be destroyed, but it will grow stronger with each passing day. In brief, if you are innocent and put up with a jealous husband, you are blessed; if guilty, you are wretched. You will love your husband and exert every effort to make him feel that he is loved, but make sure it is not feigned, for he will hate you the more bitterly as he sees your dissimulation more clearly. What is feigned not only does not achieve the desired effect but often the very opposite.

77. I warn women often, and they must be given this warning very often, more than men, not to be deceived into thinking that it does not matter whether you actually do something or seem to do something. They are inexperienced and stupid if they hope to change the way things are by resorting to their stratagems and pretenses. Let the woman show that not only does she not love anyone as much as her husband but loves no one but her husband. If she loves others, let it be for the sake of her husband, or let her not love them at all, however dear they are to her husband.

Most—indeed, one might say all men—allow and even enjoy having other things in common with their wives, but not friends. Wives are the same with regard to their maidservants and female friends. In public she must comport herself with great modesty and should not take pleasure in associating or conversing with other women's husbands or with women who do not have a good reputation for their chastity. She should not even abide the sight of a loose woman. She should neither send nor receive letters without the knowledge of her husband. She should talk very sparingly of other women's husbands and should not praise their beauty or any of their physical endowments; nor should she willingly listen to their being praised. She will not stare at them or do anything in their presence that could be construed as in the least improper. Avoid meeting or conversing with any man or woman your husband does not wish you to talk to, even if it be your mother, if that is his pleasure. If you know him to be of a suspicious nature, do not plead for any man's cause with him or with your brother or father or son or relative, unless he is a blood-relation or so closely related by marriage that it would not occasion any malicious interpretation. Otherwise, your husband will suspect that you had other motives than the desire to do good or show compassion, for suspicions always tend to see the worse side of things. You will be on surer grounds to show favor to groups of men, as a city, a people, or a province, in which case a malicious interpretation will have less credibility.

78. All these things had to be said because I am trying to demonstrate that not only must evil be avoided, but any semblance or appearance of it. Women must rid themselves of the erroneous conception that the affection and solicitude for their chastity shown by their husbands is a form of jealousy, since a wife's good reputation is a matter of paramount importance. There are some women who, if they are not granted the utmost liberty in everything, accuse their husbands of jealousy. In their incredible impudence and temerity, they brand their husbands with an indelible stigma in the talk of the town, from which he will get a bad reputation and become the object of scorn and derision. Are these women or vipers? wives or enemies? This is not Christian conduct, but a mark of uncontrolled and irrational stupidity. You would not know whether to be amused or indignant by the fact that women of this sort come and go, stay home, return, engage in conversations and banquets wherever, whenever, and with whom they wish, do everything they feel like doing, with their husband's consent, and then accuse him of jealousy.

79. Now I must say a word about female jealousy. If a woman suffers from this, I shall not suggest various remedies for her cure as long as it is not excessive and violent and does not upset the peace of the home and become an intolerable burden for her husband. If it is of that type, I think she must be given medical treatment. Above all, a woman should bear in mind that her husband is master of the household, and not all things permitted to him are permitted to her; human laws do not require the same chastity of the man as they do of the woman. In all aspects of life, the man is freer than the woman. Men have to look after many things; women are responsible only for their chastity. They must close their ears to those who wish to convey some adverse comments about their husbands, making it clear to them that their gossip inspires our ill favor. Hermione,[167] the wife of Cadmus who left her husband because of her jealousy, laments in the play of Euripides that she met her ruin through the insinuations of evil women, because she

---

167. Hermione was not the daughter of Cadmus, as Vives mistakenly states (confusing her perhaps with Harmonia), but the only daughter of Helen and Menelaus. In the *Andromache* of Euripides, v. 930, cited here, Hermione is jealous of her husband Neoptolemus's attentions to his slave-consort, Andromache, and plots to kill her. In a long digression, she blames gossipy women for instigating her to this action. This line became proverbial. It is cited in Plutarch, "Advice to Bride and Groom," *Moralia*, 143F; and Jerome *Against Jovinianus* 1.48 (*NPNF*, 2d ser., 6:385).

had lent credence to these calumniators. If a woman decides to denounce her husband or engage in a serious quarrel with him on account of a concubine, let her call to mind the story about a certain man who was pursuing a fugitive slave, and when the slave took refuge in a mill, he said, "Where else would I expect to find you?,"[168] that is to say, "than in the place where I would have thrown you if I had caught you." So she should reason, 'Where would the concubine rather see me or what would she rather see me doing than flee from my home and the marriage bed and in grave discord with my husband, so that then she can gain complete control of my husband with very little effort, since I have estranged and alienated him by my unreasonableness?' I shall not mention popular gossip, to which a virtuous lady should not expose herself or her husband no matter what wrongs and indignities she may have suffered from him.

80. The story is recorded of certain young women, recently married, who suspected that their husbands, who sometimes spent the night hunting, were having amorous associations with other women. They followed them out into the woods. There in the darkness they were transfixed by their husbands' javelins and torn to pieces by their dogs, since they thought they were wild animals. They paid a huge penalty for their prying jealousy. How much more moderation and prudence Aemilia Tertia, wife of Scipio Africanus the Elder, showed when she became aware that her husband was attracted to one of her maidservants. She pretended not to notice anything, lest she seem to condemn the conqueror of the world and leader of his people for incontinence and herself for impatience in not being able to tolerate a wrong done to her by her husband, the greatest man of his time. And to show that she nourished no ill feelings for this affront, when her husband died, she rewarded this maidservant, her husband's concubine, with a legitimate marriage to one of her freedmen, thinking that if there is any feeling beyond the grave for what goes on in this life, her husband's shades would find pleasure in this.[169] This wise woman was not unaware that she was wife and mistress of the household wherever her husband went. If she was envious of her husband's sleeping with another woman, that feeling was inspired by lust, not love.

81. Besides, if you become angry with your husband, you will irritate him the more, whereas if you put up with him, you will more quickly win him back, especially if he compares your pliant character to the obstinate insolence of a concubine. Terence, master of human emotions, writes in the

168. Plutarch, "Advice to Bride and Groom," *Moralia*, 144A.
169. Valerius Maximus 6.7.1.

The Mother-in-Law that Pamphilus was converted to his hated wife by his beloved concubine Bacchis after he came to know himself and Bacchis and the woman he had in his house. He compared the character of both of them in this way:

> She, as befits a girl of decent birth,
> Modest and chaste, bears hurts and injuries
> From her spouse and hides his misdemeanors.
> His heart, in part won over by his wife's compassion,
> In part worn down by the other's abuse,
> Slipped free of Bacchis and transferred his love
> To the one in whom he found a kindred spirit.[170]

82. Not to be passed over in silence is the deed of that noble matron who saw that her husband was snared in the toils of love by another married woman. He went to her house daily at great risk of his life, since the woman's husband and her brothers were lying in wait for him. Going up to him, she said, "My husband, you cannot tear yourself away from this illicit love, and I do not demand this of you. I ask but one thing, that you do not engage in this love affair at so much peril to your own life. She says that she wishes to be with you; take her to your own guarded dwelling. I will give her the best furnished part of the house, and I shall move to another part. I give you my word that I shall treat her no differently than I would my own sister. If you find that I act otherwise, you may drive me from the house and keep her."

She persuaded her husband, and one night he brought her into his castle, though she was trembling and afraid of her lover's wife. But she welcomed her most warmly and most courteously, lodged her in her own bedroom, always called her by the name of sister, visited her twice a day, and ordered that she be given more care and comfort than herself, without ever showing her any sign of hatred in word or in deed. "Now," she said, "my dear husband, you will love and enjoy her more safely."

For almost a year the husband did not have sexual relations with his tender, noble, and chaste wife, who was undeniably more beautiful than the concubine. Only God knows what the wife had in mind. As far as men were able to judge, she did not seem to take it badly, especially since she had delivered her husband from danger. She spent much time in church and in prayer. Everyone could easily see that she was afflicted, but none heard her complain or show indignation. After a year, the husband was reconciled completely to his wife and began to nurture a bitter hostility for his mistress.

170. Terence *The Mother-in-Law* 164–70.

He expelled her and accorded such love to his wife that he proclaimed that his mind, life, and spirit rested in her and that he would not be able to go on living if she died. I do not mention names because all parties are still living.

83. I have said all these things about persons who have a clear cause for jealousy. For there are those who have no sure reason yet act inappropriately and intolerably, procuring certain torment for themselves and their spouses for an uncertain offense. This is done by many women who love inordinately or indulge their passions to excess, or create fantasies for themselves or seize on weak conjectures as if they were proven facts. Is your husband exchanging pleasantries with someone? Do not immediately think that he is in love. A great part of your emotional state is based on what you believe. Feelings arise more from opinions than from facts. Do not be influenced by casual suspicions when you should not even be moved by tried and proven facts.

VII

ON ADORNMENTS

84. This, like everything else, should depend on the wishes and character of the husband. If he prefers simple adornment, that is what you should use. For if you seek more splendid adornment, you are decking yourself out not so much for your husband's eyes as for someone else, which is not the mark of a good woman. What does a woman who is, first of all, a Christian and, moreover, married to a husband who does not approve of such luxury, have to do with gold and silver? Do you refuse to adapt yourself to Christian ideals of adornment at the bidding of your husband when you should even put on diabolical adornment if he so wished? Ambrose writes about cosmetics in this way:

> From this come provocations to vice that make them paint their faces with elaborate colors for fear of not pleasing their husbands and from adulteration of their visage they rehearse themselves for the adulteration of their chastity. What madness it is to change one's natural appearance and seek out artificial embellishment! While they are afraid of their husband's judgment, they betray their own, for she first pronounces judgment on herself when she wishes to change the face she was born with. So by trying to please others she first displeases herself.[171]

This is the opinion of Ambrose when the husband has given no express command in this matter, and the prudent husband will not do so. But if he does or if you know that this is his wish, dissuade him politely at the right moment and in earnest. If you get nowhere, you will satisfy his wishes externally, but you will say with Esther, who was dressed and adorned with all

171. Ambrose *On Virgins* 1.6 (*NPNF*, 2d ser., 10: 367).

the devil's pomp, "Thou knowest my necessity, O Lord, that I loathe the symbol of my high position and my renown, which binds my brow when I appear at court. I loathe it like the menstrual cloth and will not wear it when I am alone in silence." [172] Even if a married woman has the liberty to choose her apparel and adornment as she wishes, let her reflect that she has no reason to seek out finery and fastidiousness of attire and has already caught what others say they are seeking with those nets.

85. Cyprian Martyr [173] advises brides to take heed that they do not delude themselves into thinking that their desire to please themselves is to satisfy their husbands, lest while using them as an excuse, they make them accomplices to the crime. I have already set out my own opinion on the subject of adornments. Now it is well to listen to Peter [174] and Paul, [175] who wish that the personal care of a Christian married woman be simple and easily obtainable, and that they stand out more for their sanctity of life than for gold and precious stones. The virtuous woman has found other truer adornments in chastity, as Sextus said, [176] and in the proper raising of children, as Cornelia said of her sons, the Gracchi, [177] and in the fame of her husband. The wife of Philo the philosopher went out in public without her gold crown when other women were wearing theirs, and was asked why she was not wearing it. She replied: "Sufficient adornment for a wife is the virtue and glory of her husband." Who did not have more esteem for the wife of Cato, who was not very wealthy, than for the wives of many tax collectors, who were inundated with riches? Is it not better to have been Xanthippe, wife of the poor Socrates, than wife of Scopas [178] or any other rich man of the period? "The adornment of a woman," said Democrates, [179] "is sparseness of speech and of ornament, and she who has an excellent husband is the most adorned."

86. Chrysostom in many passages persecutes with fire and sword this hydra of feminine adornment and suggests many remedies for this plague

---

172. Esther 14:16.

173. Cyprian *On the Dress of Young Women* 8 (PL 16:196). Saint Cyprian, bishop of Carthage (A.D. 249–58), was martyred under the emperor Valerian. Vives quotes often from this treatise, which prescribes a rather stern code of morals for unmarried young women.

174. 1 Peter 3:3–4.

175. 1 Tim. 2:9–10.

176. *The Sentences of Sextus* 235 (Chadwick p. 39).

177. Valerius Maximus 4.4.

178. Scopas of Crannon was a wealthy ruler who offered Socrates gifts and an invitation to his court, but the philosopher declined both offers. Diogenes Laertius, 2.25.

179. Cf. Book 1, p. 103.

that renews itself continually and in so many different forms. I will compress his diffuse treatment, which is his usual manner, into a few words, drawing on several of his works:

> This cult of clothing, jewelry and household furnishing is a kind of idolatry. So recherché, so painstaking is it that gold, jewelry and clothing become idols to you. You treat them and revere them just as that ancient error revered its images. What would you think if I said that this vice renders you a vile and contemptible wife in the eyes of your husband? Whom do we esteem less than those who are frequently in need of us? If a woman often importunes her husband concerning her adornment, she will become contemptible in his eyes and will inspire the suspicion that she does not love him because he is her legitimate spouse joined to her by God, but because he is diligent in procuring her riches and abetting her vanity and pride. The husband will know that he is truly loved when his wife makes little of material advantages and obeys him as her superior and as God's representative. When she demands very little and for things of little value, then he will know that she does not love him out of necessity but out of affection, as ordained by God. Indeed, when the greatest part of the husband's earnings are lavished on the wife's adornment, and the economic condition of the family are reduced to penury, what pleasure can there be in that marriage? Perhaps this female adornment was pleasing at the beginning of the marriage because of its novelty, but little by little it will lose its charm together with its novelty, just as the habitual contemplation of the heavens and the stars, the most beautiful spectacle that exists, loses its wonder. But if your husband is not interested in those things anymore, for whom do you adorn yourself? You wish to find external approval and to be praised by others, and that is the desire of a woman of little virtue.

87.

And is it not true that a modest woman of simple adornment finds more admirers and better men than an extravagant woman showing off her rich apparel? Men of wisdom and virtue will praise a woman of judicious taste while pleasure-loving and intemperate youths will praise the woman of lavish taste, although it is not so much a matter of admiration as desire. And yet, whatever the promptings of lust, they will still reproach the luxury and incontinence of a woman. One of them may say, 'What fault is it of mine if someone else has evil suspicions about me?' You give rise to this suspicion and fuel their passion in your style of dress, your walk, your appearance, every movement of your body. If the Apostle condemns so vehemently all signs of wealth, gold, pearls and sumptuous attire, how much more will he proscribe articles that are sought after so eagerly and with such wiles? I refer to such things as applying Tyrian purple pigment to the face, painting the eyes with antimony, walking affectedly, speaking in sweet tones, bestowing lascivious glances intended to enkindle the fires of lust, wearing the pallium and the tunic in a suggestive way, sporting an elaborately fashioned cincture, sandals that make noise and other incitements to lascivity. These things are totally opposed to chastity and are regarded as the essence of shame and indecency. If the Apostle forbids such things in those who are subject to a husband, live a pampered life and are overflowing with riches, what do we think he will say of unmarried women? While I do not wish to enter into discussion with pagan women in the matter of adornment, what will a Christian woman respond when she enters the church with such pomp and hears the apostles preaching the contrary from the pulpit? Does she come here to refute their words with her actions and to cry out, as it were, that no matter how often their words are repeated and inculcated into her she does not hear them and pays no heed to them? If a pagan assisted at one of our ceremonies and heard these words spoken by the apostles of Christ and then witnessed this follower of the apostles acting in this way, would he be able to contain his laughter and not prefer to walk out, offended by this useless farce?

This is all taken from Saint John Chrysostom.[180]

88. For the rest, just as we do not approve excessive finery, pomp, and precious apparel in a married woman, so we do not approve squalor and sloppiness or a careful and studied adornment in a simple and humble garment. There are some women on whom crude and coarse rags are becoming because of their natural attractiveness; there are others who know how to achieve this same effect by their clever ingenuity. "One must allow for the place, time, manner of life, and received custom of a city," they say. Yes, some concessions must be made when nothing can be obtained otherwise, but not too much and much less than what is demanded. Aristotle in the

---

180. John Chrysostom *Homily on the Gospel of John* 61.4 (*NPNF*, 1st ser., 14:226); *Homily 10 on the Epistle to the Philippians* (*NPNF*, 1st ser., 13:232); *Homily 8 on 1 Timothy 2.9* (*NPNF*, 1st ser., 13:433); *Homily on Psalm 48* (*PG* 55:507).

Economics, books filled with traditional wisdom, is of the opinion that a woman should employ less adornment and display than the laws and customs of a city prescribe. "For she should consider," he said, "that neither elegance of vesture nor excellence of beauty nor abundance of gold ensure a woman's praise so much as modesty of possessions and the desire to live honorably and with dignity."[181]

Therefore, more importance must always be given to reason, to holiness, and to piety than to vain judgments and corrupt morals introduced by men of infamous life and accepted and confirmed by the depraved sentiments of the crowd. A group of holy matrons should conspire together to make an assault on these customs so that, clothed in their humble ordinary apparel, they may give an example of what is appropriate and lead the way for others to follow. How much greater merit there is to get rid of an evil custom rather than to follow it! And we should not give up hope that a few women can eradicate what a few women have instituted. Likewise, we must not so despair of the human spirit as to think that it can accept evil, but not good, especially since the natural condition of the mind is to be inclined toward good. The consensus of good women should prevail as much for good as the consensus of evil women has accomplished for evil. They should begin to engage in the contest with integrity, modesty, and chastity and think it honorable to win victory by these virtues rather than by ostentation of wealth, which drives frivolous minds to great rivalries and contentions.

89. All women approve and commend honesty, patience, love, and obedience to the husband; few envy others to the extent of imitating them, but all without exception envy and covet adornment—clothing, necklaces, brooches, jewels, earrings, rings, engraved vessels. O proud and foolish creatures, made for vanity and ostentation! Hence arise contentions which enflame the mind to the point that, as Cato[182] wisely says in Livy's history, "Rich women wish to have what no other woman can have, and poor women stretch themselves beyond their means in order not to be derided for their poverty. It thus comes about that since they are ashamed of what they should not be ashamed of, they will not be ashamed of what should shame them." They despoil their husbands and their children so that they may be clothed. There is hunger and need at home so that they may parade in public clad in gold and silk. They compel their husbands with their lamentations

---

181. Aristotle *Economics* 3.1 (Barnes 2:2146).

182. Livy 34.4.15–16. In 195 B.C.E., Cato the Elder gave a speech against the proposed repeal of the Oppian Law, which had been passed in the critical time of the Second Punic War. Despite Cato's efforts, the law, which severely restricted women's luxuries and expenses, was repealed.

to ill-gotten gains and lowly deeds so that no neighbor, blood relation, or relation by marriage can show herself richer or better adorned. And these grave and outrageous acts would be tolerable if they did not also sell their chastity to acquire what their husbands would not or could not give them.

90. Some remedy must be devised for these great evils, either through the agreement and conspiracy of rich matrons, who by their example could recall others to a better mentality; or by some law or restraint like the ancient Lex Oppia, which set a limit on female adornment. Christian preachers should emulate not only holy examples of Christian piety but the pagan Pythagoras and surpass him in this glorious struggle. Justinus writes of him as follows: "Pythagoras taught married women chastity and obedience to their husbands, and he inculcated frugality into them as the mother of these virtues, and by the assiduity of his preaching he brought it about that noble matrons put aside their gold vestments and other accouterments of their high position as if they were instruments of luxury, saying that the true adornment of matrons was chastity, not fine raiment."[183] Will they not find this same sentiment expressed more clearly and more copiously in our own writers? Cyprian, Jerome, Chrysostom, Ambrose, Augustine, Fulgentius, and Tertullian are full of this advice.

91. Tertullian exhorts women as follows: "Go forth now adorned with the cosmetics and embellishments of the apostles, assuming the whiteness of simplicity, the red blush of chastity, your eyes painted with modesty and your spirit with silence, inserting in your ears the word of God, fastening to your necks the yoke of Christ. Bow your head to your husbands, and you will be sufficiently adorned. Occupy your hands with the working of wool, fix your feet at home and they will be more pleasing than if they were shod in gold. Dress yourselves in the silk of a good life, in the brocade of sanctity, in the purple of chastity. Painted in this way, you will have God as your lover."[184] I should like to add a few words to that, which seem to me to contain the same exhortation. All corporal things are signs of the incorporeal. In the spirit lie efficacy and truth, in the body shadow and vain appearance. The head of man is God; the head of woman is man. Do you seek a greater or more outstanding adornment than the excellence and honor of your husband? If you cover your head with obedience, you will be wearing a most elegant headdress.

92. It is not fitting that a man cover his head, since he is the image of

183. Justinus 29.4.8–11. Justinus, or Justin, who lived sometime between the second and fourth centuries, wrote an epitome of a lost treatise of Pompeius Trogus on Hellenistic history. His own comments are usually moralizing, as in this case.
184. Tertullian *On Female Adornment* 2.13 (*PL* 1 : 1448).

God in the world. It does behoove a woman, since she is subject to the man. Every woman who has uncovered her head has shaken off the law of her husband. If your head gleams with gold and precious stones, you set yourself against your husband. If you are covered in silk and brocade, you are not subject to your husband's authority. What good is an ineffectual sign without the reality to which it corresponds? You walk about without a head-covering, and you repudiate the command of the apostle. The ardor of conjugal love is a carbuncle. Firmness in a holy resolve, resistant and indestructible, is a diamond. These are said to be the qualities of that stone. An emerald represents exhilaration in the Lord, of which the apostle says, "Rejoice in the Lord always."[185] The ring is an adornment of the hands in the performance of good works, of which Solomon said, "She worked with the wisdom of her hands."[186] The easy and sweet yoke of the Lord[187] is a gold necklace, set with precious stones. The cincture is that girding up of the loins[188] that the Lord bids us to do as we press on in expectation of his coming. The shawl is modesty and chastity, with which the whole body of a woman is covered. Is there any garb more resplendent than the rich variety of virtues, with which the spouse, daughter of the king, is adorned in Psalm 44? She attends the spouse on his right side, dressed in many-colored robes with gold fringes.[189] Her glory is all turned within herself, where the gaze of her spouse is fixed, most beautiful among the sons of men, on whose lips grace is diffused.[190] Unhappy women, why do you pursue vain shadows? These are true and substantial adornments that will bring you glory both in death and in life, that will win you great renown among men and abundant and eternal gratitude with God.

185. Phil. 4:4.
186. Prov. 31:13.
187. Matt. 11:30.
188. Luke 12:35.
189. Ps. 45:14–15.
190. Ps. 44:3.

VIII

ON BEHAVIOR IN PUBLIC

93. Married women should be seen more rarely in public than unmarried women. For what the latter seem to be seeking, the former have already obtained. Therefore, all their attention should be directed to preserving what they have found and striving to please him alone. The Spartan legislator ordered that wives appear in public with their faces veiled, because it was fitting that they should neither look at others nor be looked at by others, since they had at home one whom they should wish to look at and by whom they should wish to be looked at.[191] This custom was observed by the Persians and practically all peoples of the East and many of the Greeks. But they did not go about with their heads covered, as they do nowadays in some European cities, in order to remain unknown and unseen, while they see and recognize others. In this custom, one is tempted to admire not so much the elegant manner of these women (Did I say elegant manner? I should say the gross impudence in a face covered with a thin veil) as the stupidity of their husbands, who do not see what an occasion for shameful acts this affords. "They will not do anything," their husbands will say. Would to God they had not!

In any case, a window must not be left open to the occasion of sin. Therefore, let women's faces be free of veils, but veiled with modesty. The ancient custom of wearing a veil was not so much for the purpose of not being seen by men as not seeing men. Fauna,[192] the wife of Faunus, king of

---

191. Plutarch, "Sayings of Spartans," *Moralia*, 232C.

192. Macrobius *Saturnalia* 1.12.21–28. Fauna was the wife of the sylvan Italic deity Faunus. She was often identified with the Bona Dea. According to Varro, an encyclopedic writer on Roman antiquities, she never emerged from her home and never saw or was seen by men.

the indigenous tribes of Italy, never laid eyes on any man save Faunus as long as she lived. In death she was venerated under the name of the *Bona Dea*, and not only were all men excluded from her worship, but not even the image of a male animal was allowed to be seen. I do not say this because I prescribe that women should always be cloistered and covered up, but that they should be seen rarely in public and even less among men, which will be greatly appreciated by their husbands. How pleasing it must have been to Tigranes—who had invited Cyrus, king of Persia, to a banquet—when, in the ensuing discussion of Cyrus's beauty (for he was extremely handsome), he asked his wife what she thought of his appearance, and she answered, "I cannot say, for as the gods love me, I never took my eyes off you during the whole banquet to look at any other man." [193]

94. A holy matron will not willingly listen to strange men or talk about them or their appearance. What importance does other men's beauty have to do with her, since she should regard all men, handsome or ugly, as the same to her except for her husband? He should be more beautiful, more attractive than all others, as an only son is to his mother. To the spouse in the Canticle of Canticles, his bride is the fairest of all women, and reciprocally she thinks of him as surpassing all men in beauty and charm. [194] No less pleasing to Duilius [195] was the simplicity of his wife. I shall use Jerome's own words:

Duilius, who was the first to have a triumph in Rome for a naval battle, married Bilia, a maiden of such chastity that she was an example to her age, when unchastity was regarded not as a vice, but as a thing of ill omen. When he was a palsied old man, he overheard in a conversation the accusation that he had stinking breath. He went home sad and when he complained to his wife that she had never told him of this so that he could remedy this defect, she replied: "I would have done so except that I thought all men's breath smelled that way." [196]

This chaste and noble woman is worthy of praise on both accounts: whether she was unaware of it or whether she bore it patiently, and because her husband discovered this physical defect not through his wife's disgust, but through the insult of an enemy. They say the same thing happened to Hiero, king of Syracuse. [197] Certainly this could not be said by

---

193. Xenophon *The Education of Cyrus* 3.1.41.

194. Song of Sol. 1 : 15–16.

195. In 260 B.C., Gaius Duilius won a naval battle and destroyed the Carthaginian fleet off the coast of the town of Mylae in northeastern Sicily.

196. Jerome *Against Jovinianus* 1.46 (*NPNF,* 2d ser., 6 : 382).

197. Plutarch, "Sayings of Kings and Commanders," *Moralia,* 175C.

those women who have kissed many men before marriage and many while they were married.

95. How much modesty a woman should demonstrate in public can be deduced from what I have said about keeping secret what happens at home and in the bedroom alone with her husband at night.[198] What is the good of my censuring that barbaric custom whereby among certain peoples husbands and wives wash themselves promiscuously in the same public baths? Such a custom, more bestial than human, should not even be mentioned. I would have a woman hear few things, especially when men are speaking, and say even less. If she thinks she may hear or see something unseemly, let her withdraw immediately. A certain secular public speaker says wisely of women, "A married woman should keep her eyes cast on the ground, and she should herself be more discourteous than demure toward those who greet her impolitely. She should rebuke his shamelessness first in her facial expression and then in word."[199] Hiero, whom I mentioned earlier, fined the poet Epicharmus[200] a great sum of money because he had made reference to an indecorous story in the presence of the queen.[201] Augustus Caesar forbade women by edict to attend athletic spectacles because the contestants were naked.[202] This is not surprising, since the same emperor promulgated laws on adultery and chastity.[203] For this same reason and also to avoid mixing with the great throngs of men who were present, all women left Olympia and Pisa during the celebration of the Olympic games.

96. Therefore, she will not speak, save when it would be harmful to keep silent; she will not listen to or give heed to things that do not pertain to upright morals. The titillation of the flesh is a dangerous thing, which we always carry around with us, and it does not obey judgment or reason. Saint Augustine took note that the apostle Paul, in speaking of other vices, said "Resist," but of lust he said, "Flee."[204]

---

198. Cf. par. 70.

199. Seneca the Elder *Controversies* 2.7.3.

200. Epicharmus was a Sicilian writer of comedy who was active during the first quarter of the fifth century B.C.

201. Plutarch, "Sayings of Kings and Commanders," *Moralia*, 175C.

202. Suetonius *Augustus* 44.

203. In A.D. 18 Augustus instituted stricter marriage laws, including the *Lex Julia de maritandis ordinibus,* making marriage compulsory for men between the ages of 25 and 60, and the *Lex Julia de adulteriis coercendis* that prescribed harsh punishments for adultery and other extramarital liaisons.

204. 1 Cor. 6:18.

For (says St. Augustine) we must resist the other vices on the spot with the help of God, but lust we must overcome by flight. Against the attacks of lust take flight if you wish to gain the victory. Do not be ashamed to flee, if you desire to obtain the palm of chastity. You must flee because chastity has inherited a formidable enemy, which it must resist and fear every day. Truly to be pitied and bewailed is the condition in which the pleasure passes quickly but the torment remains without end. The onslaught of lust passes in a moment but the dishonor of an unhappy soul lasts forever.[205]

Where are those ladies of the court who find it is death to be alone without their entourage of young men to talk to day and night? What would they answer to Augustine or, rather, to the apostle of Christ? They say they do this with pure intentions and without any suspicion of evil. This is not believable to me nor to the wise man who asks, "How will anyone contain fire in his bosom without being burned?"[206] But let us say that they converse without any thought of obscene things. The same wise man says that he who seeks danger will perish in it.[207] But if you assert that nothing evil will enter your mind, which is difficult to believe, can you say the same for the men as you do for yourself? You do wrong either in deed or in exposing yourself to danger or in instigation.

97. Juvenal castigates those women who know

> 'What the Chinese or the Thracians do,
> Or what goes on throughout the world.'[208]

In his oration on women, Cato wishes that the virtuous woman know nothing at all about what laws are passed or abrogated in their city, what goes on in the forum or the senate-house.[209] Hence the popular Greek saying: "Woman's work is the loom, not the assembly." Aristotle thinks it is less unseemly for the man to know what is done in the kitchen than for the woman to know what takes place outside the home. Therefore, he prohibits her from speaking or hearing about the conduct of the state.[210] Seneca writes that his aunt was never seen in public for sixteen years while her husband was ruler of Egypt, never admitted into her house anyone from the prov-

---

205. The sermon from which this passage is taken was falsely ascribed to Augustine. It actually comes from Caesarius of Arles *Homily* 41 1.8; *Corpus Christianorum* 108 : 180–81.

206. Prov. 6 : 27.

207. Sirach 3 : 27.

208. Juvenal *Satires* 402–3.

209. Livy 34.2.10–11

210. Aristotle *Economics* 3.1 (Barnes 1 : 2147).

inces, never asked anything of any man, and never suffered anything to be asked of her.

> And so that province, which was so given to gossip and so ingenious in slandering its prefects, in which even if one escaped blame he did not escape a bad name, looked up to her as a unique example of integrity. And (a difficult task for those who enjoy piquant wit) they curbed their freedom of speech and to this day they wish for another like her, although it is not to be hoped for. It would have been a great thing if that province had approved of her for sixteen years, but more marvelous is the fact that it never knew her.[211]

Obviously, this wise woman knew that contact with men would be detrimental to the integrity of her name, and that fine flaxen cloth should not be handled by many hands. Numa,[212] king of Rome, as Plutarch tells us, accustomed women to be silent and completely abstemious and not to speak even of necessary matters in the absence of their husbands.[213] It is related that when a woman once pleaded her case in the forum, the Senate consulted the gods to ask what this prodigy portended.

98. It behooves newlywed women to stay at home for several months after they have lost their virginity. Thus Elizabeth, wife of Zacharias, remained in the house for a little while after she had conceived.[214] She did so because as an old woman, she had lain with a man; newlywed women, because they were virgins. In both cases, it behooved them to be ashamed of their deed, even though it was not illegitimate.

There are some women who take on airs because of honors accruing to others, such as to their husband, brother, neighbor, relative, or even, God forbid! a friend or a neighbor of slight acquaintance. What folly it is to act in such a way that another is made good and worthy of honor through his own virtue while you become wicked and unworthy of honor because of someone else's virtue! There are not lacking those who so abuse their relatives' prestige that they make them unpopular, like the wife of the brother of Emperor Vitellius,[215] who arrogated more power to herself from her brother-in-law's rule than did the empress herself. The imperious domina-

---

211. Seneca *Consolation to Helvia* 19.6.

212. Numa Pompilius, legendary second king of Rome, is credited with having established the religious institutions of Rome.

213. Plutarch *Numa* 3.5–6.

214. Luke 1:24–5.

215. Tacitus *Histories* 2.63 partly attributes the emperor's increasing arrogance to the political machinations of his sister-in-law, Triaria and contrasts Triaria's behavior with that of the emperor's modest wife, Galeria.

tion of the sisters of Hieronymus,[216] king of Syracuse, drove the people to rebellion, in which he and all his family were annihilated. There was a certain nobleman of our own time who had a most haughty wife, and when he was divested of his wealth, it was universally thought that he deserved it, since his wife had so cruelly abused her husband's power.[217] Thucydides does not even allow that a good woman be praised in the conversations of the crowd, much less criticized, but he wishes that she be completely unknown to strangers and not be the subject of rumor.[218]

99. It is not a proof of chastity for a woman to be too well known, celebrated, and sung of and to be on people's lips under some name they have given her, as to be called beautiful, or squint-eyed, or red-haired, or lame, or obese, or pale, or skinny. These are characteristics that should not be publicly known in the case of a good woman, as we pointed out in the previous book.[219] There are some women, however, whose manner of life requires that they have public dealings, such as those who buy and sell. I should prefer, if possible, that women did not engage in these affairs, but it depends on the country in which they live and their state of life. If it cannot be avoided, then let old women be employed or married women past middle age. But if it is absolutely necessary that young women be occupied in these activities, let them be courteous without flattery and modest without arrogance and sooner suffer a loss in their sales than in their chastity. I say this on account of some women who entice the buyer with too much coaxing. "It is not the duty of matrons, but of prostitutes, to fawn on strange men," said Plautus.[220] Buyers are quick to learn their wiles, and they avoid them like the Siren's song. A reserved woman will make greater profit, since the buyers will judge from her face and her manner that she will not lie or deceive.

A rich merchant takes pleasure sometimes in flattery and joking, but rare is the person who pays money for it. And when it comes to serious bargaining, they will put no faith in a wanton woman. If it works sometimes with young clients who are deceived by their emotions, it does not succeed with old men, mature persons, and the rich, in whom the desire for gain

---

216. Hieronymus was the grandson of Hiero II, tyrant of Syracuse, and succeeded him at his death in 216 B.C. Since he was only fifteen years old at the time, he was left in the charge of guardians. It was his aunts rather than his sisters who exercised an evil influence over him.

217. Livy 24.4.25–26.

218. Thucydides 2.45; Plutarch, "Bravery of Women," *Moralia*, 242E.

219. Cf. Book 1, par. 94.

220. Plautus *Casina* 586.

overrides all feelings. But no matter what the case, a woman should always have in mind that the most certain and stable treasure is chastity joined with modesty.

100. Seeing that I would have women confined to their homes, one may well imagine what I would allow her in waging war and the use of arms. I would ordain that she never mention these things by name, and would to God that they could be taken away from Christian men as well! The widow Judith is dead and gone, who was merely a figure of things to come, and who by her continence and holiness cut off the head of Holofernes, that is, the devil. Deborah, who was a judge of Israel, has made way for the gospel of Christ, and yet even she did not so much help the people of God at war with warlike counsels and stratagems as with fasting, prayers, and prophecy. When Saint Ambrose speaks of these two women in his book, *On Widows*, he addresses himself to Christian women in these words: "The Church does not conquer enemy powers with secular arms but with spiritual arms, which have strength from God to destroy fortifications and the heights of spiritual wickedness. The armor of the Church is faith; the armor of the Church is prayer, which vanquishes the adversary."[221]

101. A woman should give no sign in public of arrogance or disdain or affected manners either by voice, word, gesture, or walk. All will be simple and plain, tempered and seasoned with modesty and propriety. In all places, gravity and severity in speech, in countenance, and in every gesture become the married woman. Toward younger men of licentious habits, she should show even a fierce and haughty exterior, and most of all toward women of uncertain reputation, lest by her ingratiating behavior and kindness she seem to approve of their morals. She should give evidence in her facial expression of her opinion of them. Livy writes that Hispala, a well-known Roman courtesan, summoned by Sulpicia, almost fainted at the thought of meeting such a dignified woman.[222] So married women should preserve their sense of dignity so that loose women will be ashamed even to look at them.

A woman should not think that because she is married she can hear or say whatever she pleases. When she was unmarried, she could have the excuse of ignorance if she heard or said anything obscene without blushing. Now as a married woman with carnal experience of a man, she will not be exempt from the charge of licentiousness and disgrace if that sort of thing should arise.

102. And since some shallow-minded women are easily influenced by

221. Ambrose *On Widows* 1.49 (*NPNF*, 2d ser., 10:399).
222. Livy 39.9.11–14.

the slightest breeze of a paltry honor, they must be admonished to be more serious-minded than to be swayed by such light gusts of wind and prudent enough to know what a ridiculous and despicable thing worldly esteem is. What difference does it make whether you are called Cornelia or Lady Cornelia, Madame or Mademoiselle or Demidame? For these distinctions are observed in France. What an empty mind if it can be affected by the faint sound of a word! Foolish woman, don't you see that you are not a lady simply because you are called by that title? Do those who call women queens and empresses immediately make them so by giving them this name? The angel Gabriel called his queen and mistress by the simple name of Mary,[223] and do you deem it unworthy to be called by your proper name by your husband, who is superior to you? How ignorant you are of your true desires. No one can call a woman mistress except it be the one he loves, for she in the end is his mistress and tyrant, to whom he is a base and ignoble slave. But if no woman is worthy of honor unless she has the word "Lady" prefixed to her name, then all those Roman women in all of Italy, Greece, and Africa lived in dishonor and misery, for no woman was called "Lady" then, and no man was called "Sir."

Come now, how much difference do you think there is whether you have the first place or the last either in sitting or walking? Among some peoples, to be first is the place of honor; among others, it is to be last; among others still, to be in the middle. This is all based on men's opinion, not on nature. Therefore, if you wish to satisfy opinion, when you are in the first place, think that you are among those who give preeminence to the first place; when in the middle, as if you were among those who honor that position; and similarly if you are in the last place. In that way, you will always have the place of honor in your own opinion. And conversely, so that you will not be too exalted when you are given the place of honor, imagine that you are among those who regard it as the lowest.

103. As for people giving place to you in the street, is it not the stronger yielding to the weaker, the sturdy-limbed to the lame, the strong to the infirm, the unencumbered to the one laden down, the swift to the slow? And do you think there is any other reason why men address women so charmingly and hold them in such esteem and even veneration but that the stronger sex handles the weaker with delicacy like thin and fragile glass, and because the slightest offenses wound them and leave a deep mark?

Therefore, it is not your virtue that wins you honor, but the politeness of others; nor are you honored because you deserve honor, but because you

223. Luke 1 : 30.

are greedy for honor. When they see that you wish it so avidly and are won over by it, it is a small thing for them to gratify your wishes. They call you "Lady," they smile at you, talk to you persuasively. What does a word cost? They make way for you in the street. This, too, costs them just a little going out of their way, and in the meantime they catch their breath. They place you first at table, for they do not mind sitting below you. They give you the better appointed part of the house, softer garments, gold, silver, precious stones. They do the same thing for children so that they will not cry, and think you no wiser than children, as indeed you are not if you are influenced by such things. They leave you those things which, if taken away, cause you great pain, while for them it is a matter of pride and boastfulness to show their disdain for them and to have you cultivate and keep things for which they have no time. And since they know what you are like, no one will think that you are more respected because you are respected by men, but will rather think that they are well bred and polite to show respect to those who they know will take it ill if they are without a semblance of honor.

104. I am a man, but since I have taken it upon myself to educate you through paternal affection, I will not hide or dissimulate anything that pertains to your education. I will even reveal our secrets, although I do not know if men will appreciate my doing so. So I want you to know that you are laughed at and deluded by us with that empty appearance of honor, and the more desirous you are of honors, the more you are an object of derision and slanderous talk. We generously lavish on you those absurdities that you call honors, but not without compensation, for you in turn provide us no small pleasure through the foolishness of your emotions and fancies.

You do not know at all where true honor is to be found. Honor must be merited, not sought after, and it must come in due course, not be courted. The proof that you deserve honor is when you are not offended at being treated with contempt. It is of such a perverse nature that, as the natural historians write of the crocodile, it pursues those that flee it and flees those who pursue it, fierce to those who are kind to it and gentle with those who are cruel to it. "There is no quicker way to fame," said Socrates, "than through virtue, which is the only thing that does not seek glory, yet finds it."[224] Sallust writes that Cato the Younger preferred to be good rather than appear good.[225] Therefore, the less he sought after glory, the more he attained it.

The surest road to true honors is virtue, which, just as it cannot be

224. Seneca *Letters to Lucilius* 79.13.
225. Sallust *Catiline* 54.6.

without honor, so it does not resent being despised. If you wish to know the true definition of honor, it is the respect for and testimony, so to speak, of outstanding virtue. Virtue is content with itself. It does not seek out honor, and the more outstanding it is, the less it does so. We bestow honor when we wish to carry out a duty. There is a popular saying that honor is owed to women, and women, who are not unfair judges in their own regard, readily acknowledge and gladly welcome it. But this is an ignorant and uninformed statement, as is often the case with the common people. For if it is agreed that the male sex is superior in every kind of virtue, honor is owed to them by women and not vice versa.

105. In setting man over woman, God also, as author and originator of all things, indicates that man is more worthy of honor. It must be rendered to him, unless we have become so absurdly perverse as to think that kings and princes owe honor to their subjects rather than the subject to his lord. If a king were to uncover his head before a farmer and yield place to him, that would not be honor, but pure foolishness and mockery. So it is not honor that a man shows a woman, but a farce and a travesty. How much more accurate that maxim would be if instead of saying that women are to be held in honor, it should be changed to say that we must make concessions to the weakness of women; women must be put up with and tolerated as the weaker sex by the stronger, the blind person by one who has sight, the sick by the healthy.

The woman who thinks that flattery, adulation, and blandishments are honors deserves no other honors and praise. And yet there are some women who are so out of their mind that although they know they are being flattered, they still think they are being praised. Poor wretches, don't you know how greatly flattery differs from praise? Do you consider it praise when he who gives the praise does not express his true feelings, yet all the while you know that it is false and that he is not speaking sincerely, but merely for the sake of ridicule and deception? You should believe no one more than yourselves concerning your own worth.

A woman who has examined herself sees clearly that there is nothing in her that deserves praise except a mind that deems itself unworthy of all praise. If there is any good in her, it is the gift of God—it is owed to him, to him is due all praise, all thanksgiving. If there is any evil, it is owed to our wickedness. All reprehension and remonstrance rightfully belong to us, all praise to another. Although I am recommending that honor should be spurned, I do not wish that dishonor done to chastity should be considered a matter of no importance. It is very close to unchastity. "She who does not fear the suspicion of adultery, does not fear adultery itself,"[226] said Porcius Latro.[227] Since there is such worthlessness in human honors, dignity, and praise, it is the quality of a lowly mind to abase itself to such an extent that it envies anyone for any human thing.

106. But if it is a vile thing to envy honor and praise, it is much worse to envy money or clothes or possessions, for this is to confer honor on these things. It is not fitting, either, to envy beauty or health or fecundity. These are gifts of God, as we said of all good things that fall to the lot of mortals. It would seem as if we do not envy the one who has received these gifts, but that we blame and reproach God, who distributes these blessings. I won't mention that these are no more to be envied of their possessor than we would envy the heavy baggage of one about to set out on a long journey. For what else are these blessings of fortune than troublesome burdens in life? And, worst of all, by their weight they force the mind down to earth as it strives after heavenly things.

If envy is absent, then it will be easy to avoid other vices that usually come of envy, such as quarreling, scolding, reviling, curiosity about what goes on in another household, prying into what they do, what they say, how they live, and by what means. A good woman will never do such things, but only a shameless one, deserving of scathing rebuke, unless you wish to come to the aid of the indigent. The poor have been left in your care, and you will give help to the orphan. Blessed are you if yours is the mind of which the psalmist says, "Blessed is he who gives thought to the poor and the needy. In the day of evil the Lord will deliver him. May the Lord preserve him and give him life, and make him blessed upon earth and not hand him over to the will of his enemies. May the Lord bring him succor on his bed of sorrow; you have changed his bed-covering in his illness."[228]

---

226. Seneca the Elder *Controversies* 7.9.

227. Porcius Latro was a native of Spain and friend of Seneca the Elder, a writer on Roman declamation. He was one of the greatest speakers of the Augustan period.

228. Ps. 41:1–3.

IX

HOW SHE SHOULD
BEHAVE AT HOME

107. If to the two virtues of chastity and great love for one's husband there is added skill in governing a household, then marriages become happier and more harmonious. Without the third there is no family prosperity; without the other two there is no marriage, but harsh, unending torment. Paul joins to prudence and chastity in women the care of the household, and commenting on this passage Saint John Chrysostom has this to say: "Notice, I pray you, the unspeakable diligence of Paul. He who leaves nothing untouched of all that could remove us from the tempests of worldly occupations gives great attention to domestic affairs. Where those matters are duly regulated, there is ample room for divine grace to find a peaceful welcome. If not, everything collapses at once. The woman who zealously takes care of her home must necessarily guard her chastity with equal zeal, for when she is devoted to the management of these tasks she will not easily occupy herself with luxurious habits, banquets and untimely and vain pastimes."[229]

108. A Spartan woman captured in war was asked by her conqueror what she knew how to do. She answered, "I know how to keep house."[230] Regarding the management of the household, Aristotle said that men should be the earners and women the custodians of the earnings.[231] Nature seems to have made them meticulous in this regard, not to waste what has been acquired and to be ever anxious and concerned that it not be lacking. But if a woman is prodigal, a man will never be able to earn enough without her dissipating it in a short time. In that way, the family possessions would quickly go to ruin and would not last. Therefore, a good mistress of the

---

229. John Chrysostom *Homily 4 on the Epistle to Titus* 2:5 (*NPNF*, 1st ser., 13:532).

230. Plutarch, "Sayings of Spartan Women," *Moralia*, 242C.

231. Aristotle *Politics* 3.4, 1277b; (Barnes 2:2027).

household will not be extravagant. Those who are free with money will be equally liberal with their chastity, as Sallust relates of Sempronia: [232] "Everything else was dearer to her than honor or money so that it was hard to distinguish whether she regarded money or her good name less." [233] I do not say that I approve that she hold on tenaciously and unreasonably to what has been acquired or forbid her husband from using the money for good works, or that once the money has entered her strongbox it will never find its way out, as from the Cretan labyrinth or the tower of Danaë. [234] Some women are guilty of this, ignorant of how much they should save or hold on to.

109. For that reason, the Essenes [235] did not admit women into their sacred way of life because they said they were not suited to a sharing of goods in common. [236] When once a woman has seen something in her possession, she does not allow it to pass on to another free of charge. So a woman will accustom her family to parsimony and frugality, for this is the role of women rather than of men. She will do this in such a way, however, that shows she knows the difference between parsimony and avarice, frugality and squalor, and that living frugally is not the same as going hungry. She will see to it that nothing is lacking to the family in food or clothing. In this regard, we should harken to the opinion of Aristotle: "There are three things—work, food, and punishment. Food without work and punishment makes them insolent. Work and punishment without food is cruel and makes the servant weak. It follows therefore that the mistress of the household shall apportion the work to be done by the servants and will provide sufficient food, which is the servant's reward." [237]

110. She will administer everything according to the will and command of her husband, or certainly in a way that she knows he will not disapprove. She will not be harsh with the servants or stern, but mild-mannered and benevolent, so that they will look upon her more as a mother than a mistress, as Jerome said. [238] She will require respect of them through mildness rather than severity, and the shortest road to this is through virtue. Quarrels,

232. Cf. Book 1, par. 22.

233. Sallust *Catiline* 25.3.

234. Danaë was shut up in a tower by her father, but Zeus came to her in a shower of gold. From their union the hero Perseus was born.

235. The Essenes were members of a religious sect that flourished in Palestine from the second century B.C.E. to the end of the first century C.E. They were strict observers of the Law of Moses and lived ascetic lives of seclusion.

236. Pliny *Natural History* 5.73.

237. Aristotle *Economics* 1.5, 1344b (Barnes 2:2132).

238. Jerome *Letters* 148.25 (PL 22:1216).

chiding, abuse, clamor, and blows do not add to authority and respect, but rather detract from them. You can achieve whatever you wish more quickly and more opportunely by discretion, reason, seriousness of purpose, words, and advice than through hostility and violence. We respect prudent persons more than angry ones. A quiet command is more persuasive than a vehement one. Calm has more authority than agitation. I do not mean that matrons should be sluggish or inert, but I advise them to inspire respect and not be so tranquil that they appear to be asleep. They should not give orders in such a way that they are despised. Let them be alert and attentive, severe without being cruel, strict without harshness, exacting without being too rigorous. They are not to hate anyone among the servants, especially if he is not bad. If a servant has had long service with you, he should be regarded more like a brother or a son. We love dogs and cats that we have nurtured for many years. How much more deserving of affection is a human being!

111. Among maidservants, domestic servants, female attendants, and, in general, all those who act as servants, constrained by necessity or induced by financial rewards—ignorance is the cause of many acts of imprudence and dishonesty, as often happens among the masses of unskilled workers. And so they must be instructed and advised to remember the precept not of any ordinary mortal, but of Saint Paul, that they accomplish their tasks with alacrity and tranquillity,[239] in a friendly and even joyful spirit, without criticism or defiance or murmuring, not sullen or ill-tempered, lest their work lose favor both with God and with men. Let them keep their hands unsullied by theft or rapacity, in which respect brute beasts show more gratitude than many men.

What wild beast is so savage that it would repay the kindness of nourishment and rearing by causing harm to the one from whom it received so many benefits? But this is usually done only by men of lowly spirit, well deserving of servitude; those possessed of such qualities are slaves of their gullet, voracious, gluttonous, light-fingered, and they grumble that everything is not open to them. They engage in idle and dangerous talk and are offended if they are not privy to every secret; they beg shamelessly and are never satisfied; they do not consider the ample wages they receive but think only of satisfying their own boundless cupidity. They bring the wicked and impudent upbringing received in the mean circumstances of their paternal home into honorable households and then accuse their mistresses of impatience. Intent on their own advantages, they hate their mistresses and yet demand love from them. They think they are ill-treated if they do not

239. Eph. 6:6–7.

receive what they have not deserved. In addition to these vices, if everything does not go according to their wishes, they denounce that house violently, where they were given exemplary treatment but were not given the opportunity to cultivate their vices.

112. Therefore, let those who act in this way know that they are human beings who have been dipped in that sacred water and will one day stand before the tribunal of Christ, who will demand of them an account of their ministry and duties just as he does of the rule of great princes. In every man it is the soul and the mind that Christ examines, not greatness or social position or fortune, since God does not look at a man's face; and he bids his judges not to regard the person of the poor man in their judgment[240] or to judge him on the grounds of his being poor. And as the poor man who is meek, just, and like unto Christ is pleasing to God, so he who has joined vices to poverty is hated and abominable.

113. Therefore, maidservants must check their own evil impulses and treat things that belong to others with no less care and loyalty than they do their own, persuaded that what gives them sustenance is not something alien to them. They should love their masters and mistresses no differently than their fathers and mothers, since one who nourishes and rears you is like a father. The name itself declares it: Masters and mistresses are called fathers and mothers of the household. Moreover, according to Roman custom, freed slaves used the names of their masters, as if they were their parents.

Whatever they hear or see in the house they should consider as secrets that cannot be revealed without incurring the gravest guilt. This should be observed not only while they are still dwelling there but even after they have moved away. Of what use are walls and doors if the servants divulge everything? Would it not be better to raise a viper in the house than such unreliable people, whose loquacity and often malicious interpretations, which arise from stupidity or lying, hate and anger, are the source of calamities for innocent and upright persons? How or when will they ever make amends for such damages or expiate such a crime?

114. An architect promised Marcus Livius Drusus[241] that he would build him a house into which no other house would have a view. "Rather build me a house," he said, "in which the whole Roman people can see whatever I do."[242] Drusus spoke with great assurance. And in truth, so it is: All

240. Deut. 1:17.

241. Marcus Livius Drusus was the eldest of a circle of ambitious nobles around the orator L. Licinius Crassus. A political reformer and tribune of the people, he lived from 124 to 91 BC.

242. Plutarch, "Precepts of Statecraft," *Moralia*, 800F; Velleius Paterculus 14.1.

good men should live in private just as they would wish to live in public, and we should conduct ourselves within the walls of our house in such a way that if others were suddenly to see us, there would be no cause for shame. But such is the weakness of body and soul that besets the human race that many things are kept concealed through custom. Many things are tolerated at home that, when exposed to public view, are judged to be foolish and ridiculous. This is especially true of things for which we all demand pardon for ourselves but are not willing to grant it to others. Such is our unfairness, and while a person may do certain things in sober earnest every day, if he catches someone else at them but once, he makes fun of him and even calumniates him.

115. Everyone knows by experience what rivalries and enmities take rise throughout the city from these revelations, since we are all eager and curious to pry into other people's affairs but become vexed if our own affairs are known or adversely construed. The tranquillity of the city is disturbed because of these reports. Malevolence breeds wrath, and thence come quarrels and fights and factions among the powerful; and among the lower classes, accusations and calumnies about a person's life, fortune, and reputation. There was an old saying: "The guilty one fears punishment, the innocent fears chance."[243] It would be truer to say, "The guilty one fears punishment, the innocent fears calumny." The cause for all these evils is the garrulity of female servants, who, in their resentment, unbosom their feelings freely, reporting not what they saw, but what their vengeful spirit suggests to them. If their mistresses withhold one farthing from their stipulated wages, they are monsters of injustice and will never find pardon with God. How much public protest! What turmoil! What execrations! They think it a game to confound and embroil the peaceful state of things and to overturn or injure families of good standing. The reason why they live this way is their mental torpor and ignorance, which never did anyone any good. It never occurs to them that all our actions, words, and thoughts are seen by that eternal judge, who gives retribution to everyone according to his works.

116. Mistresses of the household should entrust matters that must be concealed only to servants of proven loyalty. Maidservants should show themselves of such reticence and loyalty as to be trusted no less than daughters. They should not say or do anything that could be taken by their mistress or their children as an example or incentive to do wrong. Often, one sins more by example than by deed. If they live in this way, not only will they render their existence more agreeable, but their life will be more honorable, pleasing both to God and to men, and a sure step toward a better

243. Publilius Syrus 629.

fortune. If not, they will consume their lives in the misery of servitude, hated and despised by all. This is the principal lesson female servants should learn. Then they should read now and then something that will improve their mind and their morals. If they cannot read, they can listen attentively to others who read to them. When they have time, they should assist at sermons; when they are occupied, in their moments of rest their mistress or her daughters may tell them things they have heard or read so that they may come away more sensible and morally better. I have said enough about maidservants. Let us return to married women.

117. A service obtained by love is more loyal and more satisfying than one extracted by fear. It is good that fear be absent, but not respect. Do not be too kind or obliging or indulgent or sociable with male servants, and do not associate with them too much. Let none of them dare joke or banter with you. Be loved by them, but not so much loved as revered. You do not wish to be feared as a mistress, but demand the veneration due to a mother. The servant class hungers after freedom, and if it is offered to them, they seize upon it and add to it.

I would not direct the male head of the household to observe the same lack of familiarity that I prescribe for the women, whom I do not wish to associate too freely with the servants. She should not generally have transactions with them or reprimand them or punish them herself, leaving this duty to her husband. Let her spend time with those of her maidservants and waiting-women who are of upright character and proven chastity. At the same time, she will help them by example, admonitions, precepts, incentives, and vigilant care so that no aspect of their life is hidden from her and so that she may apply remedies to vice just as antidotes are prescribed for diseases.

118. If one is discovered whose moral integrity is less than acceptable or is believed to be so, and if she does not profit by scolding and correction, she must be dismissed from the house. Poison easily contaminates everything around it, and the suspicious crowd believes that servants are like their mistresses.

How often do we encounter the saying in Jerome that mistresses are judged by their servants?[244] This is not surprising, since, according to the Greek proverb, "Even lap-dogs are said to mirror the character of their mistresses."[245] And those young men in Terence's comedy[246] judge the chastity

---

244. Jerome *Commentary on Isaias* 8.24 (PL 24:290).

245. Plato *Republic* 563C.

246. In Terence's play *The Self-Tormentor*, vv. 292–99, the two young men, Clitipho and Clinia, learn from the slave Syrus that Bacchis, Clitipho's mistress, lives modestly at home in the company of a shabby, ill-kempt little maid—a sign that the mistress is beyond reproach.

of the mistress from the squalor and unkemptness of her handmaid. Homer writes that the wise Ulysses on his return home killed those maidservants who had lain with the suitors, because not only had they brought disgrace to the house, but they had endangered the chastity of Penelope. After the defeat of his son, Absalom, King David sequestered indefinitely those of his concubines whom Absalom had defiled on the advice of Achitophel,[247] and they were never released from this confinement.

The mistress of the household will occupy herself in those skills that we mentioned in the previous book[248] and will keep her servants at their duties, like the chaste Lucretia, whom the king's son and his companions found working with her handmaids and apportioning them their tasks.[249] She will accomplish this duty the more diligently and carefully if part of the household must be supported by this labor.

119. Solomon, in his praise of holy women, said, "She seeks wool and flax, and works with the diligence and skill of her hands."[250] When Theano[251] of Metapontum was asked who was the best matron, she answered with a verse of Homer: "She who plies the loom and attends to her husband's bed."[252] Through such industry, the wise king continues, "She has become like a merchant's ship, bringing her bread from afar."[253] And to show that she did not indulge too much time in sleep, he says, "She rose up at night and gave food in due measure to her servants."[254] From there she met with her servants and instructed them on what was to be done.

It is the job of a diligent wife to prepare the food for the entire household and apportion tasks only for the female servants. The husband will assign work to the male servants, as we shall see. Concerning the night vigils of the woman, there are some charming and elegant verses of Virgil:

> When night had run the middle of its course
> And driven sleep away, when first to rise
> The faithful wife, whose task it is to ply
> The distaff and pursue her humble spinning,
> Stirs the ashes of the slumbering fire,

---

247. 2 Sam. 20:3.
248. Cf. Book 1, paragraphs 15–17.
249. Livy 1.57.9.
250. Prov. 31:13.
251. Cf. Book 1, par. 23 n.
252. Homer *Iliad* 1.31.
253. Prov. 31:14.
254. Prov. 31:15.

> Adding night to the labors of the day
> And sets her servants to their long day's work
> To keep the nuptial bed inviolate
> And bring her progeny to manhood.[255]

After taking care of the household, she dedicates what is left over to alms-giving. "She has opened her hand to the needy and extended her hands to the poor."[256]

120. The holy woman should not so devote her energies to the accumulation of wealth that she does not distribute to the poor and come to the aid of the indigent, and that not sparingly but without stint, convinced that she gives this on loan in this world and that she will receive more and better in the next. He adds: "She will not be afraid of the colds of snow for her household."[257] She will not be afraid even if in addition to offering a coin to the poor, squeezed from her fingers, she opens and reaches out her hand with generosity. She will not fear, since by her diligence and wool-making nothing is lacking to her house in the time of need. "And all her servants are clothed in double garments."[258] There is nothing more expedient in domestic affairs than to be fed and clothed well, not for the sake of pleasure, but as needed; not luxuriously, but practically.

It is difficult to maintain virtue that is harassed by bad example existing close by. Therefore, the mistress of the household, first of all, will teach frugality by her own life and thus will easily inculcate it into her servants. Otherwise, they will think that you are requiring of them what you yourself do not exemplify, and you will have to suffer their reluctance and grumbling in the fulfillment of your commands. Therefore, you must always be abstemious and sober, not solely for the sake of your domestic staff but for your own sake. What a foul thing are drunkenness and gluttony, mortal enemies of modesty and chastity, and inimical to a good name! There is no one who does not abhor a drunken and gluttonous woman as a bird of ill omen. Everyone knows that chastity is in peril when eating is immoderate and there is no longer any distinction between head and groin.

121. Solomon goes on to say that there is nothing in her house that she does not know, but she regularly looks into everything and knows where everything is, so that when the need arises, she will not be at a loss or waste

255. Virgil *Aeneid* 8.407–13.
256. Prov. 31:20.
257. Prov. 31:21.
258. Prov. 31:21.

time in looking for some object. She should know the financial status of the household, how much should be spent, how much saved, how to provide for the feeding and clothing of those in her care. Solomon said, "She has examined every nook and cranny of her house."²⁵⁹ That is to say that in whatever corner of the house she finds herself, whether she be spinning, sewing, weaving, or employed in some other task in which she can give free rein to her thoughts, she will review in her mind the bedrooms, closets, wardrobes, and every part of the house to discover what is lacking, what is superfluous, what has to be bought, sold, or repaired. This kind of attentiveness will protect and maintain family possessions.

She will supervise her maidservants at their work, whether they are cooking, spinning, weaving, sewing, or sweeping the floor. All these things are done more accurately and more thriftily when the mistress is present. "The master's face is better than his back," said Cato.²⁶⁰ And that wise saying, "Nothing fattens the horse or fertilizes the field so much as the eye of the master,"²⁶¹ can well be applied to the mistress of the household and the management of domestic affairs. There is nothing that preserves family possessions longer, more intact, cleaner, or more orderly than the prudent and watchful eye of the mistress. Doing these things and busying herself with her own work at all times, "She does not eat her bread idly"²⁶² and obeys God who does not wish that we eat our bread without the sweat of our brow. She also follows the example and precept of Saint Paul, who in the midst of those to whom he announced the mystery of the Lord, did not eat his bread in idleness, but in labor and fatigue day and night.²⁶³ For as long as he had time from his divine ministry, he used his hands in the performance of work, so that he would not be a burden to anyone, frequently giving the advice that he who refuses to work does not deserve to eat.²⁶⁴

122. A woman will not allow anyone to enter the house without the orders of her husband, as it was enjoined by Aristotle.²⁶⁵ The house will be kept much more closed when her husband goes away on a long trip, at which time, as Plautus said, it is right that good women should think of their

259. Prov. 31:27.

260. Cato *On Agriculture* 4.1.

261. Aristotle *Economics* 1.6, 1345a (Barnes 2:2133). The Spanish form of this proverb is "Ojo del amo engorda el caballo."

262. Prov. 31:27.

263. 2 Thess. 3:8.

264. 2 Thess. 3:10.

265. Aristotle *Economics* 3.1 (Barnes 2:2146).

absent husbands as present.[266] And since the care of the inhabitants of the house falls upon the woman, she will keep remedies on hand for common and almost daily maladies and will have them ready in a larder so that she may attend to her husband, small children, and the servants when required and will not have to send for the doctor often and buy everything from the apothecary. I should not wish that a woman dedicate herself to the art of medicine or have too much confidence in it. I advise her to be familiar with the remedies for frequent and everyday illnesses, like coughs, catarrhs, itching, colic, loose bowels or constipation, intestinal worms, headache or aching eyes, slight fevers, dislocations, burns, slight cuts, and similar ailments that occur almost daily for trivial reasons. Add to this the regulation of the daily diet, of greatest importance for the maintenance of good health, what should be consumed, what avoided, when and in what amount. She can learn this skill from the experience of other prudent matrons rather than from the advice of some nearby physician, or some simple handbook on that subject rather than from big, detailed medical tomes.

123. The virtuous woman, when she is free of domestic cares, will choose for herself—daily, if possible, but if not, on feast days—a secluded part of the house, apart from the noise and bustling. There, laying aside for a while the worries of the house and recollecting her thoughts, she will meditate on the contempt of these worldly things, since they are frivolous and unstable, insubstantial and quick to perish, and on how the brevity of our lives goes by with such speed that it seems not to pass but to be carried along, not to go by, but to flee. Then, with the help of some divine reading, she will raise herself to the thoughts and contemplation of divine things. Finally, having confessed her sins to God, she will suppliantly beg for pardon and peace from him and will pray first for herself. Then, having found more favor with God, she will pray for her husband, her children, and, finally, her whole household, so that the Lord Jesus will inspire a better mind in all of them.

Paul, the messenger of the divine commands, teaching the nascent church in Corinth, said, "If any brother in Christ has a wife who is an unbeliever, and she consents to live with him, he should not divorce her. And if any woman has a husband who is an unbeliever, and he consents to live with her, she should not leave him. For the unbelieving husband is sanctified through the believing wife and the unbelieving wife is sanctified through the believing husband."[267] Wife, how do you know whether you will save

266. Plautus *Stichus* 99.
267. 1 Cor. 7:12–14, 16.

your husband, or husband, how do you know whether you will save your wife? It is accomplished partly by prayer ("The assiduous prayer of the just man has much efficacy," says Saint James),[268] and partly by example of life, which the apostle Peter explains, saying, "Likewise let wives be subject to their husbands, so that if there are some who do not believe in the word, they may be won without a word through the behavior of their wives, seeing your behavior in holy fear."[269] We read of many Christian women who by their works led their husbands to the practice of religion, like Flavius Clemens, a close relative of Emperor Domitian, by Domitia;[270] Clovis, king of France, by Clotild;[271] and Hermenegild,[272] king of the Goths, by Ingund, and many others by other women.

268. James 5:16.

269. 1 Peter 3:1–2.

270. Suetonius *Domitian* 16. Usually known as Flavia Domitilla, Domitia was the wife of Flavius Clemens, cousin of the emperor Domitian. She was banished to the island of Ponza near Naples in A.D. 96 because of her Christian faith.

271. Gregory of Tours *The History of the Franks* 2.29–31. Clotild implored her husband for many years to become a Christian, but he did so only when he won a battle over the Alamanni after calling upon the name of Christ.

272. Gregory of Tours *The History of the Franks* 5.38; Paul the Deacon *History of the Goths* 3.10. Hermenegild was made king of the Visigoths in 580. He was brought up as an Arian but was converted to orthodox Christianity by his wife, Ingund, daughter of Sigebert I.

X

ON CHILDREN AND
THE CARE THAT MUST BE
TAKEN OF THEM

124. In the first place, if you bear no children, suffer it with resignation and an even mind, and, to a certain degree, even with joy, because you have been exempted from an incredible burden and fatigue. This is not the place to give an account of the miseries the pregnant woman must undergo during the period of gestation, what pain and what danger when she brings forth, and later in nourishing and bringing up her children what troubles and anxiety that they may turn out wicked and unprincipled, or that some misfortune may befall them! What unending fear about where they are going, what they are doing, that they may do evil or suffer some evil! For my part, I cannot understand the reason for this ardent desire for children. Do you want to be a mother? For what reason? To increase the world's population? As if it would be sparsely populated unless you brought forth one or more little creatures and added one ear of wheat or at most two to the harvests of Sicily and Egypt. As if God did not how to raise up children to Abraham from these stones,[273] if he so wished. Do not be worried about the house of God being filled. He will see to his house.

125. But you dread the stigma of sterility. That vanished with the law of Moses in the radiance of the grace of Christ. Now you live under a law in which you see that virginity is deservedly preferred to marriage. What of the fact that through Isaiah the Lord promises to saintly sterile women a much larger and more honorable place in his city than if they had left numerous progeny? And so that woman in Flanders should be criticized who was married until her fiftieth year without any offspring, and when her husband died, married another man with this sole purpose, to find out whose fault it was, hers or her husband's, that they had no children.[274] This desire

273. Matt. 3:9; Luke 3:8.
274. Isa. 54:1.

was worthy of an old woman, but one who had lost her senses. And yet I don't know if there is any other reason for a second marriage. She gave that as her excuse, which seemed rather honorable to the ignorant crowd. But the marriage did not bring her much happiness, for she bore a son the like of which no woman would wish to have.

But you wish to see children born of you. Will they be any different from the rest? You have children of the city, all of them baptized, whom you may embrace with maternal affection and think they were born of you. The law of mankind recommends this; religion commands it. And besides, your husband, if he is a good man, is the equivalent of many children, as Elkanah said to his wife, Hannah, "You are concerned about having children and you do not find tranquillity in your husband, who loves you more than ten children that might be born to you." [275] Indeed, women, whether you be pregnant or empty, you are victims of those immoderate and absurd appetites that are called "cravings." [276] "What terrible desire for children has invaded these unhappy souls," as the poet said. [277] If the troubles and afflictions that children cause for their mothers were painted for you on a panel, there would be no woman so eager for children who would not fear them like death, or one who already had them who would not hate them like ferocious animals or venomous serpents.

126. What joy, what reason for rejoicing is there in children? While they are small, it is nothing but tediousness; when they are a little older, there is continual fear of what direction they will take: if they turn out bad, everlasting grief; if good, you are constantly preoccupied that they may die, that something will happen to them, that they may go away or change. What need is there to adduce the example of Octavia, [278] the sister of Augustus? Would that there were not so many examples of those women, who from the happiest of mothers were suddenly stricken with affliction, wasted away in unceasing grief, and died. Then, if you have many children, there is greater anxiety and the vices of one not only diminish but destroy the joy you received from the others. I have been speaking of male children. In

---

275. 1 Sam. 1:8.

276. Vives uses the word *piccationes* (more commonly spelled *picationes*). The medical term *picae* is still used for the eating disorders that sometimes occur during pregnancy.

277. Virgil *Aeneid* 6.721.

278. Octavia is the classic example of a woman of misfortune. After the death of her husband in 40 B.C., her son, Marcellus, destined to succeed Augustus, died at the age of nineteen. She never ceased her mourning, retired from the world, and forbade any mention of her son in her presence, according to Seneca. She later suffered the repudiation of Mark Antony, her second husband, but brought up all his surviving children by Fulvia and Cleopatra.

watching over daughters, what torture and anxiety! What a host of cares in finding matches for them!

Furthermore, parents rarely see their children behaving properly, for true goodness, accompanied by wisdom, comes only at a more mature age and almost at the end of one's life. "When we begin to be wise, we die,"[279] said a certain sage. And Plato said, "Happy is the man to whom it is given to achieve wisdom and to order his life aright even in old age."[280] But when children have reached that age, their parents have returned to dust. What of the fact that very few children show or even feel gratitude to their parents for all their troubles? On the contrary, they neglect those by whom they were brought up with so much care. They hate those from whom they received more tender love than they had for themselves. They were treated kindly and indulgently by their parents, and they show harshness and surliness in return.

127. O ungrateful woman, that you do not recognize how great a benefit you have received from God in not having borne children or having lost them before they brought you grief. How appositely Euripides put it: "She who lacks children is happy in her misfortune."[281] I could have expounded on this subject more copiously, except it is not necessary at this point. If you do not bear children, be careful that you do not cast the blame on your husband. Perhaps the defect lies in you because you were condemned to sterility either by nature or by the will of God. I see in the writings of the greatest philosophers a consensus that women fail to bear offspring more through their own deficiency than through that of their husbands. Nature produced few sterile men, but many women, according to a wise plan of creation, because male sterility is a greater harm than female, since the power of propagation lies more in the man than in the woman.

But if you are cursed with infecundity, my dear woman, it is useless to behave like a madwoman. Whatever wicked deeds you may conceive in your mind, you will never conceive offspring in your womb. Oftentimes, through the secret designs of God, just in themselves but unknown to us, there is no offspring in a marriage. For it is a gift of God that good children or any children at all are forthcoming. Therefore, it is a waste of time to have recourse to any other remedies than to God. We must ask for offspring, and good offspring, from God, for if you produce bad offspring, it would be better to have given birth to a viper or a wolf.

279. Seneca *Letters to Lucilius* 23.10.
280. Plato *Republic* 331A; *Laws* 653A.
281. Euripides *Medea* 1092.

128. Therefore, ask for a son as did Hannah, the wife of Elkanah, who, by her prayers, tears, and sanctity of life, was granted not only a son, but a prophet and judge of Israel.[282] Or imitate the other Anna,[283] wife of Joachim, who, placing her whole trust in God, gave birth to Mary, queen of the world, for the salvation of mankind. Or Elizabeth, wife of Zachary, who, though sterile, gave birth to John,[284] precursor of the Lord, who brought forth many children for Christ, the greatest man ever born to woman. To Sarah, who endured her sterility with even mind at a time when sterility was regarded as a great disgrace, the Lord gave a son in her old age, Isaac, the image of Christ.[285] And this same Isaac prayed to the Lord for his barren wife, Rebecca, and obtained from him two champions of two mighty peoples.[286] To the sterile wife of Manoah, a modest and chaste woman, the angel of the Lord announced that Samson would be born, judge and liberator of Israel. That is what is given to those who ask in this way. The words of the angel to the mother of Samson are these: "You are barren and without children, but you will conceive and bear a son. Beware that you drink no wine or strong drink and eat nothing unclean for you will conceive and bear a son whose head no razor will touch. For he shall be a Nazarite of God from birth and from his mother's womb and he shall begin to liberate Israel from the hand of the Philistines."[287]

129. These words remind me to warn those that are pregnant that as long as they are carrying their child, they do not indulge in excessive drinking and drunkenness. Many children have inherited for a whole lifetime the vices their mothers engaged in during the period of gestation. And since the power of the imagination is incalculable in the human body, pregnant mothers should take care not to entertain violent thoughts of anything monstrous, foul, or obscene. Let them avoid any dangerous occasions in which some ugly sight may come before their eyes. And if they are exposed to such dangers, let them think beforehand of what they may encounter so that no harm may befall the child in their womb from some unexpected sight.

---

282. 1 Sam. 1:11. Elkanah had two wives, Hannah and Peninnah. Peninnah had children, but Hannah did not. After praying to the Lord, Hannah conceived and bore a son, whom she named Samuel.

283. The parents of the Blessed Virgin are never mentioned in the sacred Scriptures, but they are identified as Anna and Joachim in the apocryphal gospel, the *Protoevangelium of James*, widely circulated in the early centuries of Christianity. This gospel also records a number of events from Mary's early life.

284. Luke 7:28.

285. Gen. 17:5.

286. Gen. 25:21–22.

287. Judg. 13:3–5.

130. Once the children have been born, the discussion of the care that must be devoted to their upbringing would go beyond the limits that I proposed for myself in this work, if I were to examine each aspect singly in any detail. On this subject, many things have been written by ancient and modern writers in entire books dedicated to that study. I shall touch upon a few things that seem to me to be the duty of a wise matron. Above all, a mother shall consider that all her treasure lies in her children. A certain wealthy woman from Campania came to Rome and was welcomed into the home of Cornelia, the wife of Gracchus, and she spread out all her feminine adornments, for she was rich in precious metals, wardrobe, and jewelry. When Cornelia had congratulated her on her splendor, the Campanian woman asked if Cornelia would mind showing her her precious jewels. The two young Gracchi had gone off to school. She answered that she would do so in the evening. When the children returned, she said, "These are my only treasures."[288] When an Ionian woman was boasting to a Spartan woman about a woven fabric, richly and artfully made, the latter replied, "But I have four sons endowed with every virtue and they are my fabric and prize and wealth."[289] Therefore, in preserving and caring for this treasure, no effort should be spared. Love will render everything easy and light.

131. She will nurse them with her own milk if she can and harken to the voice of nature, which gave her breasts and a supply of milk for the newly born and seems to cry out, "Let her nurse what she has borne as other living things do." The wise and generous parent of all things that supplied blood for the formation of the fetus in the womb transfers it after birth into the white milk of the breasts, which are like a reservoir of abundant and wholesome nourishment for the sustenance of the child. She does not forsake the tender offspring that has issued from her womb but nourishes it with the same food with which she created it.[290] Nature returns no small thanks to the nurturer for her contribution and compensates her by giving her a more healthy body for cooperating in the work of nature, while those who refuse this hardship of nursing run great risks in drying up their milk.

Moreover, a mother's milk is more beneficial to the child than that of a wet nurse. Since it is most fitting that we are nourished from the same source from which we are made, there is nothing more adapted to the infant than that same substance from which it is formed. Besides, it is not uncommon that the wet nurse suckles the child reluctantly and with some feeling of

288. Valerius Maximus 4.4.
289. Plutarch, "Sayings of Spartan Women," *Moralia,* 241D.
290. Aulus Gellius *Attic Nights* 12.1.13.

annoyance, whereas the mother is always willing and happy. The very sight of her child dispels any clouds of sadness, and with gladness and cheerfulness she smiles happily to see her child sucking eagerly at her breast. And if it begins to laugh or lisp, she is filled with incredible enthusiasm and happiness.

It is unbelievable what advantages to health are procured from a mother's milk, not only in the human race but in the realm of all living things. Concerning dogs, to give one example of many, Columella[291] writes, "We will never allow pups to be nourished by another mother, if we wish them to retain their superior breeding, since a mother's milk and spirit foster their physical growth and their temperament." There are some, however, who have good reason to be exempted. I do not wish to make prescriptions without exception, and I have spoken of this matter in the previous volume.[292]

132. If the mother knows literature, she should teach her children when they are small so that they have the same person as mother, nurse, and teacher. They will love her more and learn more readily with the help of the love they have for their teacher. As for her daughters, in addition to letters, she will instruct them in the skills proper to their sex: how to work wool and flax, to spin, to weave, to sew, and the care and administration of domestic affairs. A pious mother will not think it a burden to consecrate some moments of leisure to literature or to the reading of wise and holy books, if not for her own sake, at least for the sake of her children, so that she may teach them and make them better. When Eurydice[293] reached a certain age, she devoted herself to literature and moral teachings solely so that she might pass these on to her children, which she did.[294]

The infant hears its mother first, and tries to imitate her speech in its first stammerings, since that age can do nothing but imitate and is skillful only in this. Its first sense perceptions and first information of the mind it takes from what it hears or sees from the mother. Therefore, much more depends on the mother in the formation of the children's character than one would think. She can make them either very good or very bad. I will give a

---

291. Columella *On Agriculture* 7.12.12. Columella was born in Cadiz, Spain; fl. A.D. 50. His work is the most comprehensive remaining treatise on agriculture from ancient Rome.

292. Cf. Book 1, paragraphs 8–9.

293. Plutarch, "Education of Children," *Moralia,* 14B. This is not the mythical Eurydice, wife of Orpheus, but a woman of Hierapolis in Illyria. Although a barbarian, she devoted herself to study late in life so that she could educate her children. Plutarch quotes an inscription she wrote dedicating a votive offering to the Muses in thanksgiving for her newly acquired knowledge.

294. Plutarch, "Education of Children," *Moralia,* 14B.

few precepts in brief on how to make them good. Let her take care not to speak in an uncouth manner, at least for the sake of her children, lest that type of speech remain fixed in the tender minds of children and increase with age, and be hard to unlearn once it has taken root. Children learn no speech better or more retentively than that learned from their mother. They reproduce it with whatever defects and virtues it may have.

133. When James,[295] king of Aragon, had freed my city of Valencia from the defilement of the Moors[296] (for which his memory will be forever blessed), he had many men from Aragon and women from Lérida immigrate to this city to repopulate it. The children born from these matches retained the language of their mothers, which is what we have been speaking for two hundred and fifty years. Tiberius and Gaius Gracchus were regarded as very eloquent speakers, and their language was formed by their mother, Cornelia,[297] whose letters, filled with eloquence, were read in earlier times. The Istrian woman, queen of the Scythians,[298] wife of Ariapithes, personally taught her son, Scyles, Greek.[299]

Plato forbids nurses from telling idle old wives' tales to their charges.[300] The same should be prescribed for mothers, for it is from this source that some children from this early upbringing still retain childish and capricious minds in later years and cannot bear to hear serious and sensible discourse, preferring books of foolish tales that do not contain a particle of truth or anything that resembles it. Parents, therefore, will have on hand pleasant stories and edifying tales that lead to the commendation of virtue and the deploring of vice. The child will hear these stories first of all, and before understanding what vice and virtue are, he will still come to love the latter and hate the former. He will grow up with these mental attitudes and will try to emulate those examples that his mother will approve for his imitation. He also will try to be unlike those examples that she denounces as immoral. The mother will heap praise upon virtue and express her hatred of vice,

---

295. Jaime I, king of Aragon, liberated the city of Valencia from the Moors on 9 October 1238.

296. Vives uses the term *Agareni*, a medieval Latin word that signifies descendants of Hagar and Ishmael.

297. Cicero *Brutus* 104. Cicero expresses his admiration for the letters of Cornelia in this same treatise, 211.

298. Actually, she was not the queen of the Scythians, but the concubine of Ariapithes. She came from Istria, a coastal city in the estuary of the Danube, and secretly taught her son oral and written Greek and Greek customs.

299. Herodotus *The Histories* 4.78.

300. Plato *Republic* 377C.

doing this repeatedly so that it will sink into his impressionable mind. She should have a stock of pious sayings and rules of life, which from frequent repetition will be inculcated into the child's memory, even if he is occupied with something else.

134. Children run to their mother, ask her advice about everything, ask her all sorts of questions, and whatever she answers they believe, admire, and consider as the gospel truth. Mothers, how many opportunities you have to make your children good or bad! At this age, high moral principles and pure Christian ideals must be infused: to despise the vain foolishness of wealth, power, worldly honors, fame, nobility, and beauty; to hold as beautiful and worthy of admiration and imitation and as the only true and substantial good justice, piety, fortitude, temperance, learning, clemency, mercy, and love of humankind.

No praise should be given to those who possess those former qualities, but only to those who are conspicuous for the latter. Whenever mention is made of someone having acted wisely, intelligently, or honorably, let her be prodigal in her praise. Whatever is done wickedly, cunningly, deceitfully, insolently, dishonestly, or impiously will receive her severe reprehension. When she embraces the child, kisses him, and prays for him, let her not pray in this wise: "May greater riches come to you than those of Croesus[301] or Crassus[302] or Cosimo de' Medici[303] or Fugger,[304] greater honors than were given to Pompey or Caesar. May you be more fortunate than Augustus and Alexander." But pray thus: "May Christ grant that you be just, temperate, contemptuous of fortune, pious, a follower of his, an imitator of Saint Paul, more upright than the two Catos, better than Socrates or Seneca, more just than Aristides,[305] more learned than Plato or Aristotle, more eloquent than Demosthenes or Cicero."

135. He will consider the petitions made in his behalf by those to whom he is most dear to be his most important goals; these he will seek after

---

301. Croesus was king of Lydia in Asia Minor (560–546 BC). His conquests and gold mines brought him proverbial wealth.

302. Marcus Licinius Crassus, nicknamed Dives (the Wealthy), was a member of the first triumvirate together with Caesar and Pompey. Like Croesus, he was proverbial for his riches.

303. Cosimo de' Medici (1384–1464) was the founder of the Medici family that ruled Florence from 1434 to 1537. He was thought to be one of the richest men of his time.

304. This is probably Jakob Fugger (1459–1525), called "the Rich," scion of a rich family of bankers and merchants that established itself at Augsburg about 1368. The family reached the peak of their fortunes under Emperor Charles V.

305. Aristides, surnamed the Just, was the great rival of Themistocles; he drew up the laws of the Delian Confederacy.

and strongly desire. The wise mother will never give an approving look or smile at something said or done by the child that was naughty, impudent, wicked, willful, or unruly. When children become used to seeing that these actions are approved by their parents and are pleasing to them, they will not put them aside when they are young or even mature men. She must punish him and show him that they are not to be done and that she is not pleased with them. On the other hand, she should reward him with embraces and kisses if he gives any sign of better tendencies.

There are certain little fires within us which are, as it were, the seeds of virtue implanted by nature,[306] as the Stoic philosophers observed. Christians call it by the Greek word *synteresis*,[307] a kind of survival or spark of that justice bestowed by God on the first parent of our race. If that little fire were permitted to grow, according to the Stoics, it would lead us to great virtue. But it is overwhelmed by depraved judgments and opinions, and when it begins to glow and burst into flames, not only is it not aided by any fuel, but it is smothered by adverse winds and rain and extinguished. Parents, nurses, guardians, masters of learning, relatives, close friends, acquaintances, the common people, great teacher of error—all of these try to pluck out these seeds of virtues by the root and stifle this flickering fire with the stupidity of their opinions, as if beneath a collapsed building

136. All without exception give great importance to riches, pay homage to nobility, adore honors, seek power, praise beauty, admire distinction, follow after pleasure, trod on poverty, esteem no curse to be greater than neediness, deride simplicity of heart, hold religion suspect and learning in abhorrence, and call any form of virtue madness or fraud. Those former things are the object of their prayers, and if anyone makes mention of the latter more virtuous qualities, they shrink from them as if they were unlucky or of evil omen. As a result, virtues are neglected and despised and no one cultivates them, while worldly ideals are held in honor and esteem and all aspire to them. For this reason, there is such a great supply of stupid and dishonest men and a dearth of good and wise men, although the nobler nature of man is more inclined to virtue than to vice.

The dutiful mother will counteract these corrupt opinions with other

---

306. Cicero *On Good and Evil* 5.18.

307. The Greek word *synteresis* was first used by Saint Jerome in his commentary on Ezekiel (1,10) to mean the spark of conscience represented by the eagle, one of four living creatures mentioned by the prophet. The term is usually spelled *synderesis* in Christian theology, imitating the Byzantine Greek pronunciation of the word. Scholastic philosophers, notably Thomas Aquinas, distinguish between *synteresis* as a habit of mind and *conscientia* as a single act of judgment.

more high-minded ones worthy of a Christian woman. She will nurture in her child that little fire we just spoke of by instilling good precepts and advice and will water the seed so that the fire will grow into a great light and the seed into a fruitful crop. She will not enervate the child's physical and mental powers by a pampered and indulgent upbringing, nor will she dull his energies with excessive nourishment or allow him to spend too much time in sleep and pleasant pastimes. These things retard the alertness of the mind. There are some mothers who, in their zealous care, think their children never have enough to eat or drink, or enough hours of sleep or sufficient clothing. Let them transfer this solicitude to the care of the mind, which provides for the health and vigor of mind and body. I have little remembrance of seeing great men who excelled either in learning and intelligence or in virtue, who were brought up indulgently by their parents.

137. Need I say that bodies weakened by delicate living do not attain to their proper strength? While these mothers think they are looking after the welfare of their children, they are ruining them. In their efforts to have them live a healthier and sounder life, they impair their health and shorten their days. Let them love their children, by all means, as they ought to be loved, more than all else. Who would try to abrogate or object to the law of nature, and who is so cruel as not to love those to whom she has given birth? But let them hide their love so that their children will not take advantage of it to do as they please.

Do not let love hinder you from keeping your children free of vice through blows, tears, and weeping. Through severity of diet and upbringing, both mind and body are made stronger. Concerning the rod and punishment, these counsels are found in the Book of Wisdom, which each of us ought to obey: "Folly is bound up in the heart of a child, but the rod of discipline will drive it from him." [308] "Do not withhold discipline from a child; if you beat him with a rod, he will not die. You shall beat him with a rod and save his soul from hell." [309] "The rod and reproof give wisdom, but a child left to his own will bring shame to his mother." [310] Indeed, the sinful flesh, [311] inclined to evil from its origins, has become a wicked servant that can be corrected only by blows. Therefore, the Lord declares that he loves the one whom he corrects and reproves. [312] In this it behooves parents of

---

308. Prov. 22:15.

309. Prov. 23:13–14.

310. Prov. 29:15.

311. Rom. 8:3. The phrase in Latin is *caro peccati*, which is interpreted in various ways by scriptural exegetes.

312. Heb. 12:6.

good sense to imitate God's manner of indulgence. He who refrains from the correction and punishment of his son does not love him. As the wise man said, "He who spares the rod hates his son, but he who loves him disciplines him diligently."[313]

138. Mothers, I do not wish you to be unaware that it is your responsibility, for the most part, that evil men exist, which will make you conscious of what kind of gratitude your sons owe you. Through your stupidity you fill them with wrong notions and continue to foster them; you even smile at their sins, crimes, and wrongdoings. When they are striving after the most noble virtues, shunning the world's riches and the pomps of the devil, you summon them back to the devil's snares through your tears and bitter reproofs, since you prefer to see them rich and honored rather than good.

When Agrippina, the mother of Nero, consulted soothsayers concerning her son, they answered, "He will be emperor, but he will kill his mother." "Let him kill me," she said, "as long as he is emperor."[314] Both prophecies were fulfilled: he was emperor and he killed her, but by then Agrippina did not wish to be killed, and she regretted that she had been instrumental in making him emperor.

You wish your sons to learn virtue through your indulgent upbringing rather than through toil, and you are happy to see them overcome by vice in the midst of worldly comforts. Therefore, many of you (for I speak not of all) mourn and weep, and you pay the deserved penalty for your madness in this life, pained to see how you have formed them. And you are not loved by them in return, since they feel that they are unlovable to everyone because of your love for them.

Everyone knows the story of the young man, who, when he was being led to torture, asked to speak to his mother. Moving his mouth to her ear as if he were going to whisper something to her in secret, he bit it off. When the bystanders reproached him for this act, that not only was he a thief but impious toward his mother, he replied that this was the reward for his upbringing. He said, "If she had punished me when as a boy I stole my companion's book, which was my first theft, I would not have reached this criminal state. But she was lenient and welcomed the thief with a kiss."

139. While I was writing this treatise, there was a woman in Bruges who had brought up her two sons with extreme leniency, and, as a result, in a depraved manner, against the wishes of their father. She secretly supplied them with money to gamble, drink, and go whoring. She saw one of them hanged, the other decapitated. The wise old saying tells us, "Better children

313. Prov. 13:24.
314. Tacitus *Annals* 14.9.

weep than old men." What can I say of the madness of those mothers who often show more love for children that are ugly, deformed, ignorant, dull-witted, lazy, drunk, insolent, and stupid than for those who are handsome, upright, learned, sharp-witted, clever, sober, well-behaved, quiet, and prudent? How is this to be interpreted: as an aberration of the human mind or a merited punishment for our sins that we love what is least to be loved? Mute animals fawn on the most beautiful of their young, and when the mother shows them particular affection, it is a sign of their noble stock. Hunters know beforehand that the best dog is the one which the mother cares for most among her offspring, the one to which she shows most attention and which she first carries back to her whelping-box.[315] But among mankind, as a rule, the one to whom the mother shows most affection is the most worthless and contemptible of all.

140. Do you wish to be truly loved by your children at an age when they know what true and holy love is? Then be sure not to have them love you when they do not yet know what love is, and prefer cakes, honey, or sugar to their parents. No mother loved her son more dearly than my mother loved me. But no son felt less loved by his mother than I. She practically never smiled at me, was never lenient toward me, and yet when I was away from home for three or four days and she did not know where I was, she almost fell into a grave illness. When I returned, I did not know how much she had missed me. There was no one I avoided more or shunned more as a child than my mother, but as a young man, no one was more constantly in my thoughts than she. Her memory is most sacred to me even now, and whenever she comes to mind, I embrace her if not physically, in mind and in thought.

I had as a schoolmate in Paris a very learned man, who counted among the numerous blessings he had received from God the fact that he had lost a very indulgent mother, saying, "If she were still living, I would not have come to Paris to study, and I would have grown old at home, devoting my life to gambling, whores, entertainments, and pleasures, as I had begun." How could he have loved his mother if he was happy that she was dead? The prudent mother will not prefer comforts for her son rather than virtue, wealth rather than learning and a good name, an inglorious life rather than an honorable death.

141. Spartan women preferred that their children should die honorably for their country rather than save their lives in flight. Wherefore it is recorded that many of them slew their cowardly children with their own hands, adding this as a funeral inscription: "He was never my son, nor a

---

315. Pliny *Natural History* 8.151.

true Spartan."[316] In the reign of Hadrian, Saint Sophia[317] had three daughters, whom she named after the three theological virtues: Faith, Hope, and Charity. She looked on with spiritual joy when they were strangled for the greater glory of Christ, and buried them with her own hand, not far from Rome.

Parents will not teach their children the arts of making financial profit, but the arts of sanctity. They will not propose as models those who have accumulated great wealth in a short time, but those who have attained to the highest virtue. The Megarians are deservedly reprehended for teaching their children sordid frugality and avarice, for they converted them into thrifty slaves rather than children.[318] This ancient reproach of the Megarians might well be leveled at many peoples of Europe today: Florence and Genoa in Italy, Burgos in Spain, London in England, Rouen in France. Thus, we see the common occurrence that those who have been continually urged to acquire wealth, make profit, increase their possessions, and procure riches at any cost resort to grievous crimes, punishable by death; and no small part of the blame is to be attributed to their parents, the instigators and promoters of these actions.

And what is most fitting of all is that when other paths to riches are not available, children despoil their own parents. When they see that all avenues to wealth are closed to them, they begin to hate their parents, and this hatred makes them desire their death and find a way to get rid of them. In fact, they tell that many parents were poisoned by their own children, who were tired of waiting for them to die. And so those parents who taught their children that the accumulation of riches was to be put before all else end up experiencing themselves the effect of their own teaching. Children prefer money to their parents and often blame their parents for their own vices as if they were corrupted by their example and negligence. The prodigal young man born of a prodigal father makes this lament in the textbooks of elocution: "I shall blame my prodigality on my father. I was not brought up with stern discipline, under the regime of a well-governed household which could form a young man's character and withdraw him from the vices of that time of life."[319]

142. But while those first years must be subjected to severe discipline—

316. Plutarch, "Sayings of Spartan Women," *Moralia*, 241A; 242A.

317. Saint Sophia was a legendary Roman matron who was converted to Christianity during the reign of Hadrian. The tombs of her daughters are located on the Appian Way and in the Catacomb of Calixtus.

318. Diogenes Laertius 6.41.

319. Seneca the Elder *Controversies* 2.6.2.

lest the child fall into vices from which he will not easily recover later on—
and there should be no sparing of the rod with boys, young girls especially
should not be treated with too much leniency. Indulgence corrupts boys,
but it is the utter ruin of girls. We men become worse through permissive-
ness, but women become wicked, since once their nature is set free for
pleasures and passions, it will plunge headlong into a multitude of vices
unless it is reined in. Jesus, son of Sirach,[320] gives this admonition: "If you
have daughters, look after their physical welfare, but do not show them a
cheerful countenance." Concerning how a daughter should be brought up, I
have given instruction in the previous book.[321] A mother should read it because there are many things there that are instructive for married women,
and it is a mother's duty to ensure that daughters put what I have taught into
practice.

As far as possible, parents should see to it that no lowly, foul, obscene,
dangerous, or wicked word be planted in a child's mind, and they shall do
this more by example than by word so that the child will not see anything
whose imitation would be to its detriment. And besides, as I have said, that
age is one of apish imitation and produces nothing of its own. Certainly,
it has nothing of its own, but imitates everything. Parents perhaps may be
able to extirpate from young minds examples taken from others by their
authority and love, and, one may add, by good advice. But they will not be
able to reprimand them for things of which they themselves are culpable,
and even if they tried to do so, the child is moved more by what it sees than
by what it hears. Juvenal is right in proclaiming that the example of parents
has more weight with children than the advice and precepts of many learned
men. Consequently, they will do more serious harm by a single misdeed
than they profited them with many holy counsels. In the fourteenth satire,
he gives this wise advice:

> Let no vile word or sight befoul
> The house where dwells a child.
> Far from his door all ladies of the night,
> And the chant of the prowling parasite.
> The greatest reverence is owed the child,
> If you plan some wickedness, do not
> Despise his tender years, but rather
> May a guileless child forestall your sinful act.[322]

---

320. See Book 1, n. 340.
321. Cf. Book 1, paragraphs 10–12.
322. Juvenal *Satires* 14.44–49.

143. Pliny censures Numidia Quadratilla for showing more enthusiasm for pantomimes than was befitting a woman of high standing. At the same time, he praises the wisdom of the old woman for not allowing her young grandson Quadratus to watch pantomimes either at her house or in the theater. When she was going to see them or felt like relaxing in a game of draughts, she would order her nephew to go somewhere to study.[323] The same author gives warm thanks to Hispulla, his wife's aunt, because in bringing up his wife, she gave her an upright and honorable training through her own word and example and ensured that she saw nothing in that house but what was blameless and worthy of imitation.[324] And surely greater vigilance must be exercised in the case of daughters so that nothing will stain their chastity, honesty, and modesty, which are more strictly required of a woman than of a man. The female of all species is more clever at imitation. In the aptitude for vice, which is common to both sexes, they show more quickness and ability. If authority is added to example, there is no stopping them, as when they are to imitate their mother or some woman whom the common crowd approves.

144. It thus comes about that in cities where women of gentle upbringing are bad, it is rare to find any lowly born women to be good. And those who are brought up by evil women rarely turn out otherwise. There is great truth in the old proverb: "The daughter is like the mother." But the daughter is not so much like the mother as she is like the one who brought her up, so that there are many bastard daughters who grew up with their paternal grandmothers, who were virtuous women, and deviating from their mother's character, took on the virtuous way of life of their grandmothers.

Cato the Censor removed Gaius Manlius from the Senate because he kissed his wife in the presence of his daughter.[325] The age of innocence does not know why things are done, but reproduces the same actions as a mirror reflects images, but not for the same ends. The wise and saintly Eleazar understood this. He was ordered by a decree from Antioch to eat pork, and his Gentile friends tried to persuade him at least to pretend to eat it, so that in appearance he would be considered to have obeyed the king. His answer was that he would rather die than do something that might be taken as a bad example by youth. These are his words:

> "It is not fitting at our time of life to make pretense; many young men would suppose that at the age of ninety years Eleazar had gone over

323. Pliny *Letters* 7.24.
324. Pliny *Letters* 4.19.
325. Plutarch, "Advice to Bride and Groom," *Moralia*, 139E.

to the foreigners' way of life, and might themselves be led astray because of my playing this part for the sake of a few paltry years of this corruptible life, and through this action I would bring disgrace and execration upon my old age. Even if I were to be delivered from the punishments of men for the present moment, I could not escape the hand of the Almighty, dead or alive. Therefore, by departing this life courageously, I shall prove myself worthy of old age, and perhaps I shall leave an example to young men if I die an honorable death with a ready and courageous spirit in defense of venerable and holy laws." With these words he was immediately dragged off to the torture. Those who escorted him, who had previously been more well-disposed toward him, were turned to rage because of these words, which they thought were spoken out of arrogance. But as his life was ebbing out under the force of their blows, he uttered a groan and said: "Lord, in your holy wisdom you know clearly that although I could have escaped death, I endure these harsh physical pains. Yet in my soul I suffer them gladly because of the awe I feel toward you." And so he died, and by his death he left a noble example and memorial of virtue and courage not only for the young but for all people.[326]

145. Therefore, children should be instructed through the example of their parents, and they must not be shown anything that might easily be turned into vice. Otherwise, they will more easily adapt themselves to that course of action because of ignorance of what is better or through man's nature, which is inclined toward the worse. The Lord punished Eli, judge and priest of Israel, not because he himself had been a bad example to his sons, Hophni and Phinehas, but because he did not punish them for their wickedness and depravity.[327] So he died by falling from a chair,[328] and the priesthood was transferred to another family. How much more severely will he punish those parents who by their own encouragement and example have taught their children to lead a wicked life!

146. But if punishment for the sins of grown children was visited upon the parent because he did not discipline them to the best of his ability, what will be done to those who by word and deed incited their children at a tender age to lust, pleasure, cupidity, and wicked behavior? By contrast, the teacher of the Gentiles, speaking of a woman who accustomed her children

326. 2 Macc. 6:24–31.
327. 1 Sam. 2:34; 3:13.
328. 1 Sam. 4:18.

to virtue, says, "The woman was seduced by deception but she will be saved through bearing children if she will persevere in faith, charity and holiness with modesty." [329]

If children die, we must consider this to be nothing more than the restitution of a trust. How much has been written by Plato, Cicero, Xenocrates, [330] and Seneca concerning the consolation of death! How celebrated is that saying devised by those who reflected on the unending woes that encumber this brief life of ours: "Best not to be born, and next best to die quickly." [331] This saying was endorsed by those who pursued wisdom; it is said to have originated with a certain Silenus, [332] who lived at the time of Croesus and Cyrus with the seven sages of Greece, but was really first pronounced by Solomon, who lived long before all of them. Solomon was alluded to by Job [333] from the land of Uz, who was a petty king of Arabia [334] before the time of Moses.

Whence it is that certain peoples, like the Thracians [335] and the Druids [336] among the Gauls, both from the tedium of this life and the hope of a better life to come, escorted with joy and singing those who met their end. But the most certain and most faithful consolation is that which is based on truth, namely, the consideration of a future life. Death is not an evil in itself; it is judged only on the manner of and circumstances of its occurrence. Happy are those whose exit from this life occurred when they enjoyed the friendship of Christ! Unhappy are those for whom it was otherwise! The former are transposed to immense happiness; the latter to the extremes of suffering and misery. Therefore, you must take care that you so instruct and form your

---

329. 1 Tim. 2:14–15.

330. Xenocrates was a Greek philosopher and disciple of Plato born in 400 B.C.

331. Erasmus *Adages* II iii 49 (*CWE* 33:160–62).

332. According to one legend, King Midas (of the golden touch) is said to have captured the wild nature spirit, Silenus, and asked him the secret of life. Silenus replied that the best thing for humanity was never to have been born; otherwise, people ought to leave the world as soon as possible. The story is told in the pseudo-Plutarchian *Consolation to Apollonius*. For this wise response, Silenus was sometimes associated with the Seven Sages.

333. Job 3:3.

334. The first verse of the Book of Job says that Job was from the land of Uz. This region was perhaps situated in Idumea, an area of Palestine south of Judea. Scholars have detected some Arabic coloring in the language of the book.

335. Thrace was a vast territory to the northeast of Greece occupying most of modern Bulgaria. The Thracians were a tribal people, usually depicted as cruel and rapacious by ancient writers.

336. The Druids were priests among the Gauls and Britons. Their practices were described by Julius Caesar in his *Commentaries on the Gallic Wars*, Book 6, chapters 13 and 14.

children that whenever the supreme commander commands them to leave this life, as they would a sentry's post, they leave in his good favor, with his approbation of their industry and goodwill.

147. Since this is so, with what great joy the death of infants should be welcomed—who without experiencing the toils and preoccupations of this life, ambition, envy, arrogance, and necessity; before the onslaught of sickness, with body intact, with only the slightest sensation of death, exchange this horrible prison for a blissful beatitude. What greater happiness can be wished for them than that in this loathsome pilgrimage filled with dangers and cares, they are suddenly transferred as if in rapid flight to their dwelling place? Or that while others must undergo a long and exhausting campaign, they should obtain the same reward with so much less effort?

We should pray for no greater blessing for them than that through the merits and mercy of him who cleansed us of our sins and rescued us from the servitude of the devil they be purged of their offenses and transported, pure and jubilant, from the darkness of this life before wickedness vitiate their hearts; and that they may fly back to that homeland in which everlasting bliss is to be found. To what comparable realm would parents wish their offspring to be borne away? Certainly to no other place, unless they are more influenced by their own interests than those of their children.

It is not right that they should resent their children's happiness because of their own empty joys or illusions of joy, or pretend that they are bewailing their children's fate when in reality they are lamenting their own. On the contrary, they should be joyous and cheerful for having produced citizens of that city of which God is the ruler and the angels the citizen body, and of which they themselves are worthy for having generated and brought up such offspring. It is in this way and because of this merit, I think, that Paul teaches that the woman will be saved.[337]

Therefore, it will be more well-advised and more pious to rejoice for this reason rather than be consumed with grief that what was not given but merely lent is now reclaimed. We must not by our mourning and laments condemn the judgment of God, who demands what is rightfully his. Instead, we should be thankful for the use of it that we have enjoyed for however brief a time. We must not imitate those who, forgetful of the advantage they have enjoyed, deem it an injustice if they cannot possess forever to their heart's content a benefit that is freely given.

337. 1 Cor. 7:16.

XI

ON THE TWICE-MARRIED
AND STEPMOTHERS

148. For those who have married again after the death of their first husband,
I shall give the following additional recommendations. Let them be careful
not to offend their present husband by making too-frequent reference to
their previous husband. It is the usual experience of mankind that the past
always seems better than the present because no happiness exists that does
not bring with it a great deal of disadvantages and admixture of bitterness.
When this is present, it brings intense pain; when it is absent, it does not
leave a significant trace of itself. It thus comes about that we are less affected
by past evils than we are by present ills.

Age moves forward at such a relentless pace that with each passing day,
the accumulation of woes becomes worse and our ability to support them
more enfeebled. Remembering a more vigorous time of life and compar-
ing it with that which weighs on us brings weariness with our present state
and a longing for the past. But Solomon does not wish that it should pass
through the mind of the wise man that former years were better than the
present.[338] Nor will it seem so to the prudent woman, and she will not think
that her dead husband was better or more agreeable than her present spouse.
For they often deceive themselves if, when they are annoyed by some trait
in their present husband, they remember only the pleasant things of their
former spouse. They make this comparison all the more invidious if they
find their present husband lacking in some quality in which their dead husband gave them more satisfaction. Without taking other things into account, they base everything on this one comparison. This breeds sadness,
unending complaints, and words that are grievous to the husband. While

338. Sirach 7:11.

they lament their dead husband and give tearful testimony of their longing for him, they lose both.

149. In general, stepmothers have a bad reputation as being prejudiced against their stepchildren. This is attested to by many examples, and their whole race is attacked in a Greek epigram, which recounts that while a certain stepson was paying homage at his stepmother's tomb, a pillar collapsed and took his life.[339]

Again and again, women are exhorted to make every effort to keep their emotions and passions under control. This is the source and origin of all good and of all evil. If you allow your feelings to dominate you, they will let in a great throng of calamities and miseries that you will not be able to cast out; but if you gain control over them, you will live a holy and happy life. We will achieve this if, in peace and tranquillity of mind, we meditate on how we are to conduct ourselves when we are assailed by these agitations and disturbances. Stepmothers, therefore, are not unjust and harsh except those who are tyrannized by their emotions, who do not exercise control over their feelings but rather are slaves to them.

A woman who is guided by reason and judgment will think of herself as one person with her husband, and will consider the children of each of them as common to both. For if friendship makes us hold all things in common[340]—so much so that many people love, cherish, and assist the children of their friends just as they do their own—how much more scrupulously should this be observed in matrimony, which is the culmination not only of friendships, but of all kinships and relationships? The cousins, brothers, and parents of a husband are regarded and addressed as such by a wife. How much more should this be true with respect to children!

150. A woman will take pity on their tender and defenseless age and, remembering her own children (if she has any), will love those of others. She will be mindful of the common lot of all mankind, and that her own children will find that others will treat them as she treated others, whether she is dead or alive. In a word, a good woman will be a mother to her stepchildren, as she will often hear herself called. What woman is so devoid of any feeling of human kindness that she would not be moved and softened by the name of mother—no matter who pronounced it, but especially in the mouths of children who do not know how to flatter, who call on them in the simplicity of their hearts with the same feeling as they would their true mother, who gave them birth?

339. *Greek Anthology* 9.67.
340. Erasmus *Adages* I i 1 (CWE 31:29).

How sweet is the name of friendship! How many feelings of anger it assuages! How much hatred it dispels! What can be found more effective than the name of mother, a name overflowing with incredible affection? Is it not true that even when you are enraged, you are appeased when you hear yourself called mother? You are fiercer than any beast if that name does not soften your feelings.

There is no wild animal so ferocious and untamed that if a tiny creature of its own kind fawns upon it, it does not immediately become gentle. Yet children of your husband cannot soften your spirit with their demonstrations of affection. You are called mother, and you respond with hostility. You turn preconceived hatred, often without cause, upon a defenseless and innocent age. Whereas it is the divine will that all should be brothers in goodwill and charity, you hate those joined to you by family ties, the brothers of your own children. Does not the spirit of their dead mother frighten, persecute, and harass you? Be aware, you stepmothers who live up to the name, that your uncontrolled wrath took rise solely from dreams proceeding from your own mad frenzy.

151. Why is it that stepfathers do not hate their stepchildren? Rare is the stepfather who does not love his stepson as his own son. I would be lying if my words were not confirmed by the annals of history, which relate that great kingdoms were left to stepsons by their stepfathers no differently than if they had been born to them. Augustus[341] left the Roman empire to Tiberius, and Claudius[342] left it to Nero, even though the former had a grandson and great-grandson and the latter a son. It is not that they did not know that they were not their natural sons, but that they understood by reason and judgment that there was no cause for hatred between stepfathers and stepsons, unless they had created it themselves through their own behavior.

What blame can stepfathers lay on stepchildren for not having been born their natural offspring? This is not in the power of men but of God. But

---

341. Augustus made Tiberius his successor only when forced to do so. Two of his grandsons by his daughter Julia, Gaius and Lucius Caesar, had died within two years of each other. The third, Agrippa Postumus, was of a violent nature and had to be banished. His great-grandson, Gaius (later to be called Caligula), was two years old when Augustus died.

342. Vives neglects to mention the intrigue that led to Nero's accession to power. Urged on by her lover, Antonius Pallas, Claudius's financial secretary, Claudius's wife, Agrippina, schemed to have her son Domitius adopted by the emperor. Thus, Domitius became Tiberius Claudius Nero Caesar. Agrippina also contrived to have him marry Claudius's daughter, Octavia. Pushed aside in this power struggle was Claudius's own son, Britannicus, only three years younger than Nero. To ensure Nero's succession, Agrippina had Claudius poisoned, according to Tacitus and Suetonius.

stepfathers do not coddle their stepsons or play with them as their mothers would wish. By that argument, natural fathers do not love their children either. Did I say that stepfathers do not love their stepchildren? Some mothers are so mentally deranged that they think their husbands have little love for the children born to them because they do not play foolish games with them night and day. The male sex cannot play childish games as women can. The nobility of the man's spirit restrains and conceals love; he commands it, and is not its slave.

But you stepmothers, why do you not kiss your stepchildren always, comb their hair, teach them good manners, as if they were your own? Such thick darkness settles upon your minds from the clouds of your passions! You think that what you love deserves everyone's love, and no one shows enough love as far as you are concerned. Whatever you hate you think is worthy of everyone's hatred and loved too much by others. There are not lacking those stepmothers who, while hating their stepchildren with a deadly hatred, swear that they love them. They are mad if they themselves believe it or hope that others will believe it. They are even more insane if they presume that they can deceive God. And you ask that Christ, whom you call father, will hear you when you detest your stepchildren, by whom you are called mother? The apostle John does not believe that God, who is invisible, is loved by one who hates his brother, whom he sees.[343]

343. 1 John 4:20.

XII

HOW SHE WILL BEHAVE
WITH HER RELATIVES AND
IN-LAWS

152. Nigidius Figulus[344] writes that the word *soror* (sister) comes from *seorsum* (apart) because she goes to live apart,[345] passing into another house and family. For this reason, a married woman will begin to be more dutiful toward her in-laws than toward her own blood relations. This is proper for many reasons: Because she has been transplanted, as it were, into that family, for whom she will generate children and will make more numerous through her fertility, then for the reason that she has already procured the benevolence of her own kinsmen and must now seek the love of her husband's relatives. In addition, so that her children, if she has any, will be more beloved of their father's family and kinsmen, supported by their love not only toward their father but also toward their mother. Finally, it is of great advantage both in marriage and in widowhood if you are loved by your husband's relatives, and it is a great disadvantage if you are hated by them. This was the aim of those who first transferred marriage from within the family to external relationships so that love and friendship would be more widely diffused and propagated. Therefore, it is expedient to gain fully the love of one's in-laws and, once gained, to preserve and cherish it.

153. They say that mothers-in-law have a stepmother's hatred for their daughters-in-law, and that daughters-in-law in turn have no great love or respect for their mothers-in-law. Terence voiced the common sentiment in this regard: "All mothers-in-law hate their daughters-in-law."[346] One woman

---

344. Nigidius Figulus was a scholar, grammarian, and friend of Cicero who died in exile in 45 B.C. In the passage of Aulus Gellius in which this etymology is given, the writer is not Nigidius Figulus, but another grammarian, Antistius Labeo. Nigidius is mentioned a few lines later in this source, which may explain Vives' erroneous attribution.

345. Aulus Gellius *Attic Nights* 13.10.3.

346. Terence *The Mother-in-Law* 201.

said wittily that even a likeness of a mother-in-law made of sugar is bitter. Plutarch of Chaeronea and, after him, Jerome in his polemic against Jovinian,[347] say there was an ancient custom in Leptis Magna in Africa, according to which the new bride on the day after the wedding would ask her mother-in-law to lend her a pot. The mother-in-law would say that she had none. Thus, immediately after the wedding, the bride would be made aware of the mother-in-law's stepmotherly character and would be less offended if, in the future, something more acrimonious should occur between them. When I reflect on the reason for this enmity, the jealousy of both parties seems foolish to me.

154. A man is placed in the middle between mother and wife, and each of them persecutes the other as if she were a mistress. The mother is discontent because all the son's love is transferred to the daughter-in-law. The wife cannot suffer that any other woman be loved besides herself. As a consequence, rivalries, hatred, and quarrels arise as between two dogs when someone strokes one of them in the presence of the other. The Pythagoreans were of the opinion that friendship is not diminished by the addition of friends but increased and strengthened.[348] So a mother should not think she is less a mother when her son marries, nor a wife think herself less a wife if she has a mother-in-law; but, rather, the one should reconcile the man to the other if some little difference arises. Foolish mother-in-law, do you not wish your son to love his wife, friend, and inseparable companion? Would you have tolerated not being loved by your husband? What greater unhappiness can you wish for your son than that he live with a hateful and hostile woman? Foolish daughter-in-law, do you not wish that a son love his mother? Do you not love your mother? You will be loved by your husband as a companion and a sweet wife, while your husband will love his mother as one to whom he owes his life and sustenance and upbringing and, consequently, a debt of filial piety. Since the daughter-in-law is not unaware that she and her husband are one, she will consider her husband's mother her own and will love and respect her no less than her true mother and indeed will be more dutiful toward her so that she will please her the more and win her favor.

155. A good and virtuous woman will not take it ill if her husband loves his mother; but, rather, if she notices that he is not attentive enough toward his mother, she will urge and entreat him to conduct himself as a true son

347. Plutarch "Advice to Bride and Groom," *Moralia* 143A; Jerome *Against Jovinianus* 1.48 (*NPNF,* 2d ser., 6:385).
348. Cicero *On Duties* 1.56.

should. Agrippina, the granddaughter of Augustus, who had married Germanicus, Livia's grandson through her son Drusus, was hated by Livia both as daughter-in-law and as stepdaughter.[349] She herself was of a harsh and violent nature but of such chastity and so loving toward her husband that by these two virtues, she turned the indomitable pride of Livia into feelings of benevolence.

Daughters-in-law should support and sustain their mothers-in-law in their time of need with the same devotion true daughters would show. Ruth, the Moabite, rejected her native land and all her kin for the sake of her mother-in-law, not wishing to desert the wretched and afflicted old woman in her sea of troubles.[350] She comforted her with words, cheered her by her labor, and fulfilled the role of daughter in every way. Nor did that piety go unrewarded, for aided by the counsel of her mother-in-law, Ruth found a husband, Boaz,[351] a rich man, and bore Obed.[352] She was the great-grandmother of King David, from whose lineage Christ the Lord was born.

156. I perceive another cause for this hatred. Often, mothers-in-law are oppressive and bothersome to daughters-in-law because of their criticism; they become censorious and assume the role of teachers of morals, while in turn daughters-in-law interfere with the running of the household, and in either case there is a lack of moderation. Remonstrances and admonitions should not be harsh and inappropriate, but the right moment must be chosen and the words used must not be acrimonious, but helpful. Nor is it fitting that the older matron should do nothing in the house, sitting there idle and carefree like a guest. On the contrary, the advice of older people is not only useful to the young but necessary as well. One who avoids this gives proof of defect of character. You can be assured that one who is recalcitrant to advice has many things that are worthy of reprehension. Among the sayings of the wise king we read. "He who obstinately despises reproof will suddenly meet his doom, and healing will not save him."[353]

Criticism is never unprofitable, even when it comes from an enemy, even when it is false, as long as it serves to make us more careful not to do anything that would justly deserve rebuke. Moreover, in the case of the household, it is especially expedient that a young woman without practice

349. Tacitus *Annals* 1.33. Tacitus gives no intimation that Livia ever relented in her animosity toward Agrippina.
350. Ruth 1:16ff.
351. Ruth 4:13.
352. Ruth 4:17.
353. Prov. 29:1.

and experience, and even after she has had much practice, should listen to one older than she. An old dog does not bark without reason. You will be the wiser if you add an older person's wisdom to your own. Therefore, let each one yield some of her rights to the other so that they may achieve harmony. The mother-in-law should admonish, encourage, discourage, and, if necessary, reprimand at the appropriate time, always out of true love and affection without any trace of bitterness or hatred. The daughter-in-law in turn should listen with an attentive, alert, and eager spirit in order to improve herself and apprehend the rules of virtue that come from age and experience. The mother-in-law will instruct the daughter-in-law in domestic affairs but in such a way as to be a good counselor and guide for a future mistress of a household. The daughter-in-law will obey her as the mother of her lord and master, or, rather, as her own mother, since through the bond of matrimony all relationships are made one, especially those fundamental ones of parents and brothers and sisters.

XIII

HOW SHE IS TO BEHAVE
WITH HER MARRIED SON OR DAUGHTER,
WITH HER SON-IN-LAW AND
DAUGHTER-IN-LAW

157. As she should adapt herself to her husband's will and judgment in all other things, so also in the matter of the marriage of their children. It is prescribed by Aristotle in the second book[354] of his *Economics* and by reason itself that the greatest authority over the children should reside with the father. So in Roman law children were under the power of the father, not the mother, as long as he lived, even after they were married and grown up, unless they were released from his power.[355] How much power fathers should have over their own sons if God willed that even Joseph should have some power over Christ! When the angel of the Lord announced to Joseph in a dream that that which was in Mary's womb was not conceived of a man's seed but by the power and working of the Holy Spirit, he said, "Mary will bring forth a son and you will call him by the name of Jesus."[356] He did not say, "She will bear you a son," which is what is usually said to true fathers, for women bring forth children for men. Yet he added, "You will call," to signify the right and authority of the one thought to be his father, while he said to the Virgin, "His name shall be called Jesus."

158. In marrying a daughter, I would advise that she be at least seventeen years old. That is the opinion of Plato, Aristotle, and Hesiod.[357] Nature, too, concurs in this, since it engenders great feelings of sexual desire at the beginning of puberty. We must allow these feelings to be allayed spontaneously so that they will be less given to carnal lust in the future. At that age

354. This passage is not in the second book, but the third. Aristotle *Economics* 3.1 (Barnes 2: 2147).

355. Justinian *Institutes* 1.9.

356. Matt. 1:21.

357. Plato *Laws* 785B; Aristotle *Politics* 7.16, 1335a (Barnes, 2:2118); Hesiod *Works and Days* 698.

they have strength to carry children in the womb, provide nourishment for the fetus, and further its development. If marriage is a sacrament, a chaste and pure action, at which we know that God is present to give his good auspices, and we see the church bearing the torch in the role of the *pronuba*, what is the meaning of all these occasions of sin and wrongdoing? Promiscuous banquets of men and women, groups of people dancing under the influence of wine and drunkenness, tickling, touching, talking nonsense— all are calculated to inflame lustful desires, with everyone vaunting their best finery. Nor is there lacking that tireless intermediary and broker of pernicious unions, the devil.

159. On a day of such mystery when nothing but what is pure and holy should be said and done, the celebrations encourage lust, aided by the cunning of beauty. The wine excites you, the occasion is inviting, the lavish surroundings puff up pride, the time of life stirs up violent feelings. Assignments at table and certain inane honors move some to arrogance, others to hatred, others to envy. One day is not enough for the nuptials; preliminary ceremonies must be celebrated and postnuptials, while in the meantime a good part of the family patrimony is squandered on the banquet and the take-home gifts and other donations. What is more, the patrimony is bestowed upon those to whom it will be of no benefit and who will return no gratitude, but rather will demand it as their right. And all of this is a concession to female vanity, to indulge their palate, their pride, their desire for amusement, and their fickle vanity. They are eager either to amuse themselves in uninhibited pleasure or show off their wealth, even that which they do not possess.

But when the wedding is over, the prudent woman will not maltreat her daughter-in-law, nor think that by her dislike she will win over her love or even that of her son, if he loves her. If, on the other hand, she gives her good advice, if she instructs her, if she says and does things in her presence that the daughter-in-law will accept as examples of chastity and frugality, if she does not sow discord between the two spouses but eliminates those that have sprung up from some other source and strives with every effort to effect harmony between them and manifests her motherly love for her daughter-in-law, then she will easily earn her son's affection and the great love and respect of her daughter-in-law. How much more fervently her son will love her through whose instrumentality he has a more chaste and frugal wife and one more like-minded, so that he will not only feel indebted to her as the author of his being, but as the teacher of his wife and the one responsible for no small part of his happiness.

160. The daughter-in-law will act no differently toward her mother-

in-law than she would toward her own mother, since through her she has learned more skills, improves herself, and enjoys the greater love and favor of her husband. The exact opposite occurs in the case of a harsh mother-in-law. A mother will not claim the same rights to her married daughter as when she was single. She will consider that she has gone off to another household, as to a foreign colony, to raise up offspring there. She will give her better advice or recall to the mind of the married girl recommendations she had given her before she was married. She will not discuss things with her that she thinks may offend her husband. She will not take her to church, will not take her from her house, and will not even speak to her if she thinks this would be contrary to the will of her son in law. And do not say to me resentfully, "Can I not speak to my own daughter?" She is your daughter, yes, but not your wife. What jurisdiction you have over her you transferred to your son-in-law.

Rather, if you love your daughter and desire to see her happy, that is, living in harmony with her husband, be her counselor and advise her to be obedient to her husband in all things and not even talk to you if he does not wish it. Whoever wishes more control over another man's wife than a husband would permit is an adulterer. Whoever touches the property of another without the owner's permission is a thief. She will love her son-in-law as she loves her own son and will have more respect for him than for her son. A mother-in-law will not presume to have the same power over a son-in-law as she does over her son, except that she will desire his welfare in equal measure and will advise and encourage him equally, but more in the way of persuasion and suggestion than giving orders. Since he is joined by an indissoluble bond to your daughter, whoever he is, he must not only be tolerated but approved. You must praise him before your daughter to prevent any semblance of discord from creeping in, for it is the seedbed of the greatest unhappiness. A wife will live more happily if she is completely ignorant of her husband's defects rather than trying to resign herself to them. What shall we say, then, of mothers-in-law who accuse their sons-in-law in front of their daughters—do they not condemn their own judgment in having chosen them, such as they are?

XIV

ON A MARRIED WOMAN
OF ADVANCED YEARS

161. Married women advanced in years will inherit the fate of the ibis,[358] the famous bird of Egypt. Those who have concerned themselves with the study of natural history tell us that when it comes to the end of its days, it purges its body of all foul humors using an aroma from nearby Arabia and emits a passing sweet breath from its mouth.[359] When a woman is free of all carnal desire and has fulfilled her duties of bearing and bringing up children, she will emanate an odor that is more heavenly than earthly. She shall say and do nothing but what is of great sanctity, and may serve as an example to those younger than she. "Then her name will begin to be known," as Gorgias[360] said, "when her face is unknown."[361] Then the holy actions of her past life will come to light. Then the truly good woman, through obedience to her husband, will hold sway, and she who always lived in obedience to her husband will command great authority over him.

Archippa,[362] wife of Themistocles, through her unswerving obedience to her husband, so won over his love and loyalty that this very wise man and spirited leader obeyed his wife in practically everything. This gave rise to a chain of command the Greeks used to refer to humorously: "Whatever this boy (Cleophantus, who was the darling of his mother) wants, the Greeks want. For whatever he wants, the mother wants; whatever his mother wants,

---

358. The ibis was worshipped by the Egyptians as the avatar of the god Toth. It was celebrated for its purity, and its flesh was regarded as incorruptible.

359. Cicero *On the Nature of the Gods* 1.81.

360. Gorgias (c. 485–c. 380 B.C.E.) was one of the most influential of the ancient sophists. One of Plato's dialogues is named after him.

361. Plutarch, *Moralia*, 242F.

362. Plutarch, *Themistocles*, 32.

Themistocles wants; and whatever Themistocles wants, so do the Athenians, and whatever the Athenians want, all Greeks want."[363] The Lord bade Abraham to listen to what Sarah told him, since she was now an old woman free of all carnal desires[364] and would not counsel him anything that was childish or shameful, under the instigation of lust.

162. But of whatever age she is, let her not think that she is exempt from the law and has license to do whatever she wishes. She must always be subject to her husband, spend her days under his protection and guardianship, and adorn herself with chastity. But when she arrives at this age, with her children all married, freed from earthly cares, she turns the eyes of her body to the earth to which she must render her body. Then, with the eyes of her soul looking to heaven, where she is to go to take up residence, she will raise all her senses, her mind, and her soul to the Lord, and, girding herself for that departure, she will meditate on nothing that is not suited to that impending journey. Let her take care, however, not to slip from true religious feelings into superstition through ignorance, a vice that often affects that age. Let her be intent on pious actions[365] but trust more to the mercy and kindness of God. Let her not be too confident in herself, as if by her works she can arrive at her fixed goal rather than by the goodness and gift of Christ. And since the soul still retains more vigor than the body, let her omit physical labors and increase those of the soul. She will pray more frequently and with more attention. She will think more often and more fervently of God. She will fast less often and will tire herself less in visiting churches. There is no necessity to deny her inner spirit or wear out her aged body. Let her profit others by her good advice; let her do good by the example of her life, as she will receive no small reward in return.

363. Plutarch, "Bravery of Women," *Moralia*, 185D.
364. Gen. 21:12.
365. James 5:16.

BOOK III

ON WIDOWS

I

ON THE MOURNING
OF WIDOWS

1. The holy woman should know that when her husband has died, she has suffered a most grievous loss. A loving heart, full of warmth and affection, has been taken from her; not only has half her soul perished (for that is how certain learned men referred to those whom they loved intensely),[1] but her whole self has been wrested forcefully from her and annihilated. This is cause for honest tears, justifiable sorrow, and irreproachable grief. The greatest proof of a shameless and cruel mind is not to weep over a husband who has died.

There are two types of women equally guilty, though in opposite ways, in the matter of mourning a lost husband: those who mourn too much and those who mourn too little. I have seen here in the Low Countries and in Britain women who were no more stricken by their husband's death than if some casual acquaintance had died; this is sure indication of a cold conjugal love, than which there is nothing more wicked and more detestable. When they are reproved for this, their answer is that it is the nature of the region in which they live, a common excuse of those who blame the influence of the stars or the weather or the soil for their vices. The nature of a region does not produce moral failings. If it were so, then wrongdoers should not be punished, but their place of origin. We do not acquire vices from the air or the sky but from our manner of life. One can lead a good or a bad life in any climate.

There is no region on earth so cursed that it does not produce good men, nor one so blessed that it is without evil men. Then again, I have seen many women who would gladly have paid for their husbands' health with their own lives. One cannot ascribe vices to the nature of a certain locality.

1. Horace *Odes* 1.3.8.

The climate of northern Thrace is bitterly cold, but Pomponius Mela[2] writes this of its inhabitants: "There is no lack of spirit in the women either; their fondest wish is to be killed and buried together with their dead spouses and since many women are married to one husband at the same time, they hotly contend for this privilege before those assigned to give judgment. The decision is based on moral conduct and it is a great cause of joy to win in these contests."

2. Authoritative writers have recorded that Indian women[3] used to vie with one another in this same manner. Among the ancient Germans, from whom almost all Belgians are descended, "Only virgins marry and their hope and aspiration to be a wife is satisfied but once in a lifetime. They take one husband as one body and one life and have no further thought or desire than to love not so much their husbands as matrimony itself."[4] You can see from this how customs change with the introduction of pleasures and riches and how the ardent desire for wealth has extinguished the holy aspirations of love. The whole law of Christ gives expression to nothing else but charity, love, fervor. "I have come to set fire to the earth," says the Lord, "and what greater wish have I but that it be kindled."[5]

But when we joined the affluence of the devil to the poverty of Christ, and luxury and drunkenness to abstemious piety, shameless self-indulgence to chaste austerity, paganism to Christianity, the devil to God—then Christ, spurning that kind of partnership, took away his gifts and left those of the devil. But perhaps nowadays these women have such strength of character that they will find comfort as soon as possible in their own wisdom and, though beaten and prostrate, will raise themselves up immediately. I should find this praiseworthy in a man, that is to say, a wise man, but in the weaker sex this unexpected wisdom is suspect.

3. We know that great and wise men mourned the death of friends whom they scarcely knew, and even shed copious tears over them. Solon, the Athenian lawgiver, one of the seven ancient sages, ordered his funeral to be solemnized with tears and lamentations so that his friends could manifest the great longing they felt for him.[6] When Lucretia was killed in Rome,

---

2. Pomponius Mela *Description of Places* 2.19. Pomponius Mela was a Spaniard from Tingentera, near the modern Gibraltar, who wrote his *De Chorographia* during the reign of Claudius. He shows great interest in ethnography and in the description of remote regions.

3. Plutarch, "Whether Vice Be Sufficient to Cause Unhappiness," *Moralia*, 499C; Valerius Maximus 2.6.14; Jerome *Against Jovinianus* 1.44 (*NPNF*, 2d ser., 6:381).

4. Tacitus *Germania* 19.

5. Luke 12:49.

6. Plutarch *Solon* 21.

Junius Brutus, avenging her death and the violation of her chastity by the king's son, drove the kings from Rome. In retaliation the kings started a war, and Brutus was killed in the first armed clash. The matrons of Rome mourned the death of this defender of chastity for a year.[7] If they showed such grief at the death of another woman's husband because he had defended another woman's chastity, how much more reasonable is it that you mourn not only the avenger, but the protector of your chastity; the defender of your body; the father of your children; the support, master, and defender of your family, home, and all your possessions?

4. Shall I put it more clearly? You would weep if you did not come away from that union richer than when you entered into it; now the joy that money brings soothes and alleviates your feelings of sorrow. You would mourn him when he is dead if you had loved him when he was alive; you do not mourn him now that he is gone because you never had any affection for him. There are some women who rejoice at their husband's death as if they had shaken off some cruel yoke, as if liberated from the fetters of a despot, almost exulting in a new-found freedom. What blindness of heart! A ship without a rudder is not free, but abandoned, and a child without a teacher is not free, but directionless, without rule or law. So a woman bereft of her husband is, in the true meaning of the word, widowed—that is, destitute and deserted. She is at the mercy of the winds like a ship without a rudder, and is carried along hither and thither without plan or purpose, like a child deprived of its tutor.

Certain women may say, "My husband was the kind of person that it was easier to live without than with." No good woman ever said such a thing, and no bad woman ever failed to say it. If your husband had been as dear to you as the laws of marriage that come from God dictate, which require that you think of him as another self, you would suffer his death as if it were your own. To a bad woman, if her husband does not grant her the freedom to indulge in all kinds of misbehavior, he is intolerable. For a virtuous woman, no husband is so troublesome that she would prefer him dead rather than alive. But what is the use of discussing these matters? I have made it abundantly clear in the previous book that a woman who does not love her husband with all her heart as she does herself is worthy neither of the name of good woman nor that of wife.

5. O provident nature! Or rather, O God, most wise teacher of a good life! There is no virtue for which he has not created an exemplar in some living thing to refute justifiably those who scorn virtue. What shame and

---

7. Livy 2.7.4.

humiliation bees inspire in the slothful! And ants in those who are indolent!
The fidelity of dogs is proof that unfaithful men are inferior to them; and
are not doves and sheep a living condemnation of fraud and cunning?

Doves and turtledoves are an example to us of the loyalty and affection
of marriage and are almost a reproach to us. As Aristotle recounts,[8] these
birds are content to live with one male and do not accept another. When it
has lost its mate, the turtledove does not drink water or perch on the leafy
boughs or join in the pleasures and frolicking of the other birds of its species. It is this chaste and holy love to which Solomon refers when he invites
the spouse to come to him in these words: "The voice of the turtledove is
heard in our land."[9] And he compares the spouse now to a dove, now to a
turtledove.

Difficult and quarrelsome wives should listen to what Pliny says of
doves: "Chastity is uppermost with them and adultery unknown. They do
not violate their mutual fidelity and they watch over their home together.
Unless she is without a mate or has lost her mate, she does not leave the nest
and she puts up with domineering and even abusive males. If they suspect
adultery, although this is not in their nature, then they complain loudly and
peck fiercely with their beaks."[10]

For that reason, the Lord wishes that doves or turtledoves be offered in
the purification of a woman who has borne a child[11] to signify that the infant
that is placed in the sight of the Lord was born of a chaste and loving marriage. These little birds are a symbol and example to those persons who have
so deviated from the norms of human conduct that they must be taught what
is right and holy by tiny creatures. I can add a quotation from Aelian on this
matter: "Crows," he said, "are united to each other by a certain love and
fidelity. They love each other in an extraordinary way when they first become mates, nor do they indulge in random promiscuity. Experts in the
study of these birds relate that when one of them dies the other does not
join itself to another mate, but lives out the rest of its existence in sad solitude. It is recorded that in ancient weddings after the hymn to Hymen[12] this
bird was invoked as a symbol of the concord between the two spouses."[13]

6. But those women who cannot put an end to their tears and mourning

---

8. Aristotle *History of Animals* 9.7 613a (Barnes 1:955).

9. Song of Sol. 2:12.

10. Pliny *Natural History* 10.104.

11. Luke 2:24.

12. Hymen was the Greek god of marriage.

13. Aelian *On the Nature of Animals* 3.9. Claudius Aelianus (c 170–235) was a Roman author and
teacher of rhetoric who wrote in Greek.

are no less guilty. They fill the air with unceasing laments over their recent bereavement and throw all into confusion, tearing their hair, beating their breast, lacerating their cheeks, striking their head against the wall, dashing themselves upon the ground, and prolonging their grief to great lengths, as in Sicily, Greece, Asia Minor, and in Rome—to such an extent that in the laws of the Twelve Tables [14] and in decrees of the Senate a limit had to be set to the expression of mourning. Accordingly, when the apostle wrote to these people, he had to console them, saying, "I do not wish, brethren, that you be ignorant concerning those who have fallen asleep, so that you may not be saddened, as others do who have no hope. For if we believe that Jesus died and rose again, even so God will bring with him those who have fallen asleep in Jesus." [15]

Let a widow mourn her dead husband with true affection, but not cry out or afflict herself by beating her hands together or with blows to her limbs or her body. In her grief, she should observe modesty and moderation and not make such show of her distress that others will see it. When the first shock of sorrow subsides, she should begin to take thought of consolation. I do not wish to cite the reasons for consolation, as explained by philosophers in lengthy tomes. I am teaching the Christian woman and believe that the remedy is to be found in Christian philosophy, in comparison to which all other human wisdom is mere folly. Let us call to mind what I just quoted from the apostle: those who have fallen asleep in Jesus will be led to eternal beatitude with the same Jesus. And so we should be of good hope. [16]

7. The wise woman will therefore reflect that all mortals were born and live under this law, that they must render their debt to nature as to a creditor whenever it shall demand it back. Some sooner, some later, we are all bound by a common lot of being born, living, and dying. Our souls are immortal, and this life is a point of departure for that other eternal and blissful existence for those who have spent this temporary life in a holy and pious manner. This is made very easy by the Christian religion, not through our merits, but through the goodness and justice of him who loosed us from the bonds of death by his death. . He nullified with his blood the decree of the Father by which the whole human race was condemned to death unless he had come to its rescue.

Death is the entrance into the port from a voyage at sea. Those who

---

14. Cicero *On Laws* 2.59; Seneca the Elder *Controversies* 4.11; Seneca *Letters to Lucilius* 63.13. The Twelve Tables were the earliest written form of Roman law. Adopted about 450 B.C., they remained the foundation of Roman civil law until Justinian's codification about A.D. 530.

15. 1 Thess. 4:12–13.

16. 1 Thess. 4:13, 17.

die precede us, who are soon to follow. Liberated from our bodies, we will lead a life in heaven until we will again be clothed with those same bodies. Not weighed down and oppressed as now, but as if clad in light garments, exchanging mortality for immortality,[17] we will enjoy everlasting happiness. With these words, Paul bids us to console one another. This is genuine and lasting Christian consolation: when those who survive the death of their friends will not think that they have been taken away, but that they have been sent ahead to that place where they shall soon be happily reunited with them, if they but apply themselves by the exercise of virtue to arrive where they believe and hope their friends have arrived.

This is what Christian priests should preach to those who have recently become widows. With such consolations they should restore their sinking spirits—not as some others do, who toast the widow at the funeral banquet and bid her be of good cheer, assuring her that she will not lack suitors and that they already have someone in mind as her future spouse. But what else do you expect those who have drunk and eaten their fill at a banquet to disgorge?

17. 1 Cor. 15:53.

II

ON THE
HUSBAND'S FUNERAL

8. As in so many other things, so in the great pomp attending funeral celebrations vestiges of paganism have remained in the church. The pagans su-
perstitiously believed that the souls of those whose bodies were unburied
would suffer great torment in the underworld, and they thought that by the
pomp of the funeral procession they could acquire glory for the dead man
and his posterity. But even among them, there were not lacking those who
did not conceal their belief that such practices were of no avail. Virgil in the
person of Anchises, a wise man, as Virgil depicts him, said the loss of a burial
was a small thing.[18] And Lucan said:

> Nature receives all into her great lap;[19]
> The sky covers those who have no grave.[20]

Moreover, the great advocates of wisdom—Diogenes,[21] Theodorus,[22] Seneca,[23] Cicero,[24] but especially Socrates[25]—taught with convincing argu-

---

18. Virgil *Aeneid* 2.646.

19. Lucan *Pharsalia* 810–11.

20. Lucan *Pharsalia* 819.

21. Diogenes, called "the Cynic" (c. 412–c. 423 B.C.), flouted all human conventions by his
life and teachings. To show his disregard for death, he left instructions to cast him out without
burial to be devoured by wild beasts, place him in a ditch and throw a handful of earth over
him, or throw him into the Ilissus. Cf. Diogenes Laertius 6.79.

22. Theodorus of Cyrene, born about 340 B.C., called "the Atheist," was forced to leave Athens
because of his religious and moral views. Cicero and others tell the story that when he was
threatened with crucifixion by Lysimachus, king of Thrace, he replied that it made no difference whether he rotted on the ground or in the air. Cicero *Tusculan Disputations* 1.102; Diogenes
Laertius 2.97–103; Valerius Maximus 6.2. ext. 3.

23. Seneca *On Leisure* 14.3.

24. Cicero *Tusculan Disputations* 1.102; *On the Nature of the Gods* 1.2.

25. Plato *Phaedrus* 115C.

ments that it makes no difference where the corpse rotted. M. Aemilius Lepidus,[26] who was elected leader of the Senate on six occasions, instructed his children a short time before he died to carry out his body on a bier not spread with sheets or purple, and that they should not spend more than ten sesterces on the rest of the funeral. He said that the funerals of great men were ennobled by their fame, not by lavish expenses.[27] Valerius Publicola[28] and Menenius Agrippa,[29] one the expeller of the kings and champion of liberty, the other the spokesman and arbiter of public peace, and many other outstanding men so disdained the honor of burial that though invested with great power and rich in resources, never took thought in their lifetimes about the preparations for their interment. Surely they would have done so if they had believed that burial was so important, as the common people did. I come now to our own times.

9. The martyrs of the Christian religion did not think it was important where their lifeless body lay as long as they had made ample provision for their soul. They were confident that when Christ would restore their souls to their bodies, he would easily find even the finest ashes of their bodies in his home, which he knows from top to bottom. Augustine, in the first book of the *City of God,* says: "All these things, viz., the care of the body, burial arrangements, the pomp of the funeral procession, are more a consolation to the living than any advantage to the dead. If an expensive funeral is of any benefit to the impious, then a cheap funeral or none at all will do harm to the pious."[30]

And yet we see that such is not the case. The funeral preparations did not alleviate the torment of the profligate rich man[31] in the gospel, nor was

26. This is not the triumvir but one of his ancestors. He became pontifex maximus in 180 B.C.E. and censor in the following year, and was *princeps senatus* from his censorship until his death in 152 B.C.E.

27. Livy *Periochae* 48.11–16. The *periochae* are summaries of missing books of Livy compiled in the fourth century.

28. Livy 2.16.7; Valerius Maximus 4.4.2. Livy tells us that as consul together with Junius Brutus, in 509 B.C. Valerius Publicola overthrew Tarquinius Superbus, last king of Rome. In spite of his great renown, he was so poor that he was buried at public expense.

29. Livy 2.33.22 When he was consul in 503 B.C., Menenius Agrippa convinced the *plebs* of the futility of secession from Rome by using a parable about the limbs and the belly. He, too, died so poor that his estate could not bear the expenses of his funeral. He was buried by the common people, who each contributed a few pence for the purpose.

30. Augustine *City of God* 1.16–19.

31. Vives uses an unusual proper adjective for the rich man, *Azotus,* that is not found in the gospel account. Vives may have confused the story of Dives and Lazarus with the parable of the prodigal son in the preceding chapter of Luke's gospel, where the Greek adverb *asotos,* which means "lewdly" or "prodigally," is used. In addition, he may have been thinking of the definition of *asotos* given in Cicero *On Good and Evil* 2.23.

it a disgrace to Lazarus that his body was left unburied upon the ground. The former suffers torment in hell for the evil life he led, while Lazarus is restored in the bosom of Abraham and receives the reward of a pious and innocent life.[32] This is not to say that the practices of burial should be done away with altogether, for the holy fathers Abraham,[33] Isaac,[34] Jacob[35] and Joseph[36] gave instructions about their burial as they were dying, and Tobias is commended by the angel of the Lord because he had buried the dead.[37]

But the provisions for burial should be directed to the good of the dead, not the living. The dead man has to deal with God alone, who recognizes in those who have died the merits gained in their former existence, as he does the pure and chaste mind of those who are living. He is not pleased by pageantry and ostentation but by holy faith and trust in him, and love for one's fellow man. If you give alms, you will receive them, and being merciful, you will obtain mercy.[38] Make friends for yourself and for your deceased at the expense of the wicked mammon[39] of iniquity so that in the next life, you may find those who will welcome you into eternal dwellings.[40]

The Lord in the gospel promises paradise to those who perform works of charity and denies it to those who do not. On the method of giving alms, he instructs you not to share your fortunes with your neighbors or with the powerful, who will repay you if the need arises.[41] This would be like lending money at interest, which a certain secular writer[42] justly called "gifts with hooks attached." Rather, give generously to the poor and needy, who cannot return your favor in equal measure; and thus you will receive in the end a rich reward from God.

10. How much better it is to clothe poor strangers than rich relatives, to feed hungry strangers rather than wealthy priests, and to distribute to poor widows and orphans the great expenditures devoted to candles and magnificent tombs! How much more certain and more copious the interest to be gained on this investment! In the time of your mourning, remember

32. Luke 16:20–25.

33. Gen. 25:9.

34. Gen. 35:29.

35. Gen. 49:29.

36. Gen. 24:25.

37. Tob. 12:12.

38. Tob. 4:7–8.

39. The word *mammonas* used in the Greek New Testament and in the Vulgate is a transcription of an Aramaic word meaning wealth regarded as an object of worship.

40. Luke 16:9.

41. Luke 14:13.

42. Pliny *Natural History* 9.30.

those under the yoke of necessity who are always in tears. Their tears will accompany yours; their joy will cheer you. Your deceased will find in them advocates and patrons to plead his cause who enjoy much favor before that eternal judge, and be as present to him in his day of peril as they were in their own.

From what I have said, it is sufficiently apparent what I think of those widows who, in order to give a splendid funeral to their husband, defraud creditors or do not fulfill testamentary legacies, although this should be their first care. I need not discourse here about how men are bound by debts and how important is the sacrosanctity of testaments. The real and enduring honor of funerals resides in men's hearts, not in the pomp of funeral ceremonies, nor in tombs of marble or of bronze or more precious metals. All pray at the tomb, no matter how humble, of a good man; they curse the magnificent mausoleums of the wicked, with all the more bitterness and hatred if they know it was built with ill-gotten gain. And what if it was their own money extorted by violence or retained by fraudulent means? Then there would be no end of curses and just imprecations. The debts of the deceased are passed on to the one who was aggrandized by his inheritance. Personal debts that the husband contracted are by divine and natural law incumbent on wife and husband. The woman who is solvent and does not discharge her debts is a thief. She does injustice to the will of her husband, to the love and covenants of marriage, and to the laws of God, and is not yet free of her legal obligations.

III

ON THE MEMORY
OF ONE'S HUSBAND

11. The widow should remember and have it ever before her eyes that our souls do not perish with the body but are released from the burden of the body and freed from the fetters of this bodily weight. Death is a parting and a physical separation of body and soul, but the soul does not migrate into another life in such a way that it completely renounces all earthly things. They are sometimes heard by the living, and they know many of our actions and events either through the privilege of their beatitude or through the intermediacy of angels, who frequently communicate between them and us. Therefore, the pious widow should consider that her husband has not been altogether taken away from her, but that he is still alive with the life of the soul, which is the true and real life, and also in her constant remembrance of him.

Friends who are absent from us or free of their bodies still live with us if their image is impressed on our mind and is daily renewed and continually present in our thoughts, living and thriving within us. They have completely died when they have been consigned to death, that is, oblivion. Valeria Messalina,[43] the wife of Sulpicius, was asked by her brothers after her husband's death whether she wished to marry again, since she was still youthful, healthy of body, and a woman of refined beauty. She answered, "Indeed not, for Sulpicius will always be alive for me."[44] These were the sentiments of a pagan woman who had no certainty about the immortality of the soul. What is to be expected of a Christian woman?

43. Valeria Messalina was the sister of Valerius Messala Corvinus. She was married to the famous Roman lawyer Servius Sulpicius Rufus; a number of his legal opinions are preserved in Justinian's *Digest.* This story about her is found only in Jerome.
44. Jerome *Against Jovinianus* 1.46 (*NPNF*, 2d ser., 6:382).

Therefore a widow, shall cultivate the memory of her husband, not as if he were dead, but absent, with more veneration and piety than weeping. It will be a great oath for her to swear by her husband's departed spirit. Let her so live and act in the knowledge that she will please her husband, no longer a man, but a pure and simple spirit, almost a divine presence. Let her place him as an observer and guardian not only of her external actions, as he was when confined by the body; but now relieved of this burden, a free and pure spirit, he will become the guardian of her conscience as well. Let her so deal with her family, so administer the household, so bring up her children that her spouse will rejoice and feel that he has been fortunate to have left such a wife behind him. Let her not conduct herself in such a way that his angry spirit will take vengeance on a wicked, unprincipled woman.

12. In Xenophon[45] we read that Cyrus the Great, as he was dying, ordered his sons to preserve his memory piously and inviolably for the sake of the immortality of his soul and for the honor and reverence due to the gods. Let there be an end to tears and weeping, lest we seem to be mourning our dead ones as if they were completely annihilated rather than merely absent to us. If it is fitting that a widow preserve such a revered and holy memory of her husband, what punishment will they deserve who pursue their husband's dead spirit with curses and bitter abuse and who declare openly that they never loved them while they were alive and would never love any others whom they might marry in the future? No one is exempt from faults or some unpleasant qualities. Whoever hears them, unless he is completely out of his mind, cannot but think that they will behave in the same way with a second husband as they did with the first. From a previous friendship, we gain experience for the next one. These demented women do not see that such evil talk will make it all the more difficult to find a prospective partner, and if they do marry again, their husbands will be led to suspect that they will be no less hated than were their predecessors. For if they had really loved their husbands, they would never have been able to bring themselves to feel and speak of them in such a way, when in fact their love and piety should have increased by their longing for them.

45. Xenophon *The Education of Cyrus* 8.7.22.

IV

ON THE CHASTITY AND
MORAL RECTITUDE OF A WIDOW

13. In treating of the laws of widowhood, where could I better begin than with the words of Paul, who, writing to the Corinthians, said, "Unmarried women are occupied with things that pertain to the Lord, how they may please him; married women are concerned with the things of the world, how to please their spouse."[46] Therefore, it behooves the married woman to be totally dependent on the dispositions and wishes of her husband, but when she no longer has a husband, she should turn to the holy spouse of all women, Jesus Christ. All that adornment and personal care should now be gone, which, while the husband was living, might have been seen as a desire to please him. Now that he is gone, all display and all of her life should be adjusted to the will of him who succeeded her husband, an immortal in the place of a mortal, God in the place of man. For him it is the mind alone that must be adorned and embellished, for it is this that Christ espouses for himself alone and in which he finds delight and satisfaction.

"But those who intend to marry look after their appearance," someone may say. What I said of virgins is applicable here. A widow should adorn herself much less, since she should not be seeking a match and should not readily accept it when it is offered. A good woman approaches a second marriage unwillingly and reluctantly, compelled by unavoidable necessity. Besides, in a virgin, personal adornment is tolerated; in a widow, it is repugnant. Who would not feel aversion for a woman who, after having one husband, still yearns to remarry and proclaims openly that she is looking for another, and in repudiation of her spouse, Christ, marries first the devil, then a man—thus becoming widow, wife, and adulteress all at once? How much more easily those women who express their widowhood in their bearing, dress, and demeanor find a new match. Even depraved and dishonorable men are attracted by good morals, and virtue is pleasing even to malice. From what they see, they conjecture that if they were to marry them and had the ill fortune to die first, what kind of widow they would leave behind them. There is no husband who does not wish his death to be mourned by his wife and that he be missed.

14. But since we have the sayings of the philosophers and the teachings of the apostles on married women, it is reasonable to hear what their feelings are about widows. Of them Paul writes to Timothy, "She who is a real widow, left alone, has put her hope in God and perseveres in prayer night and day, whereas she who is self-indulgent is dead even though she lives. Give these commands so that they may be above reproach."[47] Those who see them walking, eating, drinking, and talking and performing the other external functions of life think they are alive. But if one could fix his gaze on their inmost organs or, rather, peer into the secrets of their mind, he would see a sinful soul estranged from God, lying there lifeless. Ambrose, Jerome, Augustine, and all the saints reiterate this same thought: that tears, mourning, solitude, fasts are the adornments of the pious widow. Paul himself made it sufficiently clear what banquets, diversions, and dances a widow should frequent when he said that she should persevere in prayer day and night.[48] When her mortal husband has been taken away, the widow should have more time to pass at leisure with her immortal spouse, to speak to him more frequently and more intimately. To make myself clear, the widow should pray more frequently and with greater devotion, fast longer, attend mass and sacred functions, read more diligently, and turn her thoughts to those things that improve life and morals.

15. Anna, the daughter of Phanuel of the tribe of Aser, who had lived seven years with her husband, was found by Christ the Lord in the temple after eighty-four years of widowhood. She never departed from there, diligently intent on prayer and fasting day and night.[49] We require more and greater virtues of a widow than we do of a married woman. The latter must adapt herself to the will of a mortal man to whom she is married, and she is divided between God and man. The former has received Christ as her immortal spouse, and therefore everything must be of a higher order befitting such a spouse. She is not divided, but she can and must devote herself entirely to him. Her words must be more chaste and more modest inasmuch as

47. 1 Tim. 5:5–6.
48. 1 Tim. 5:5.
49. Luke 2:36–38.

speech is the mirror of the soul and character of every person. The old saying has it: "As is your life, so is your speech." Filthy words are detrimental to our thoughts. "Evil conversations corrupt good morals," as Saint Paul quotes from Menander.[50]

16. I wish not only that a widow's words express her meaning chastely and honestly, but that they instruct and correct those who hear them by their learning and example, for there is a certain type of speech that men utter that joins great wisdom with great goodness. Though it seems only to express the concepts of the mind, it also instills learning at the same time and reforms morals. A woman widowed of her husband should not think that she is exempt from the laws of human marriage and may do whatever she pleases. Often, widows show what they were like when married and in the freedom of widowhood reveal what they concealed from fear of their husband, as birds freed from the cage immediately return to their true nature. The apostle teaches that such widows should be avoided, since they publicize their own guilt, rendering their first vows void.[51] Many women give free vent in a sudden outpour to the vices dissembled during their marriage, now that the obstacle posed by their husband has been removed. A woman can be seen for what she is by nature and in character when she is free to do whatever she pleases. As Jerome said, "The truly chaste woman is the one who could have sinned if she wished. But the one to whom only the opportunity was lacking is always prepared for unchastity."[52] As a widow, a woman must act more circumspectly, since all vices are imputed to her, just as all praise of virtue remains solely with her; for while her husband was alive, a great part of the responsibility for both vice and virtue was attributed to him.

17. In widowhood, Christ the spouse will give his help to one who wishes to live a holy life, and to him must be attributed any good that is produced and to us any evil. And just as a man places all his joy in a good wife, so it can hardly be imagined how dear and agreeable to Christ is the woman who shows herself a true widow, that is, one who, left alone in this life, puts all her hope and confidence, all her joys and pleasures in Christ. Of such a woman Paul teaches that she is held in much esteem even by bishops,[53] for the church obtains many things from Christ through their prayers. Such a woman merited to be among the first to see Christ in the

---

50. 1 Cor. 15:33; Menander *Sententiae* 803, ed. Siegfried Jaekel (Leipzig, 1964), 79.

51. 1 Tim. 5:11–12.

52. Jerome *Against Jovinianus* 1.47 (*NPNF*, new 2d ser., 6:383).

53. 1 Tim. 5:5.

temple and to make prophecies about him to those who were present.[54] Such a woman is praised by the testimony of God and is commended to us by his command, for he said through Isaiah, "Seek justice for the orphan, and defend the widow."[55] Again in the psalm, concerning Christ the Lord: "He will shelter the orphan and the widow."[56] And in Exodus: "You shall not harm a widow or an orphan. If you do harm to them, they will cry out to me, and I shall hear their cry. And my wrath will be kindled and I shall strike you with the sword, and your wives shall become widows and your children orphans."[57]

54. Luke 2:36–38.
55. Isa. 1:17.
56. Ps. 146:9.
57. Ex. 22:22–24.

V

HOW THEY SHOULD
CONDUCT THEMSELVES
AT HOME

18. Although saintly men have wished that the widow visit the church frequently and be assiduous in prayer, they did not exempt her from practical
concerns. The Doctor of the Church, speaking to Timothy about widows,
said, "If a widow has children or grandchildren, let her first teach them their
religious duty to their own family and to make some return to their parents."[58] The widow should teach these lessons, and her children and grandchildren should learn to behave modestly and show loyalty to their parents.
We often see it happen that those brought up by a widow are less obedient
than they should be to those to whom they owe obedience, spoiled by the
excessive indulgence of the widow. Thus, the expression "a widow's child"[59]
has become a proverb among many peoples, especially our own. It is used
of young men who are badly brought up, of corrupt, insolent youths who
lead a morally depraved life.

I should counsel a widow to place the care of the upbringing of her
children upon some virtuous and sensible man, for, out of blind love, she
thinks she is treating her children too severely, even when she is far too
lenient with them. Not that there were not some very wise widows who
brought up their children very well and wisely, such as Cornelia with the
Gracchi and Veturia with Marcius Coriolanus,[60] who, in all his glorious

58. 1 Tim. 5:4.

59. This proverb is cited in Francesc Eiximenis *Lo llibre de les dones*, ed. Frank Naccarato, rev.
Curt Wittlin (Barcelona, 1981), vol. 1, ch. 100, p. 153: "Mas les viudes solen mal nudrir lus
infants, en tant que infant mal nudrit es apellat nodrit de viuda comunament."

60. Valerius Maximus 5.4.1. Coriolanus received this cognomen for his capture of the Volscian
town of Corioli. He later turned against Rome and, at the head of a Volscian army, besieged
the city about 490 B.C. It was only at the entreaty of his mother, Veturia, and his wife, Volum-
nia, that he returned to Rome.

deeds for the republic, at home or abroad, was goaded and inspired by the incentive to win the approval of his mother and the one who brought him up.

19. I have spoken in the previous book of how children should be instructed. The widow may seek there what she should do in this regard. Concerning the family, the apostle said, "If anyone (and consequently any widow) does not take care of his own, especially those of his family, he has renounced the faith and is worse than an unbeliever."[61] But she should not, especially if she is still of a comely age, mix too freely with the members of her household, harkening to the words of Saint Jerome to Salvina:[62]

> The reputation of chastity is a delicate matter with women, and like a beautiful flower it quickly withers at the slightest breeze and is damaged by the slightest breath of wind. This is especially true when the woman is at an age prone to vice and the husband's authority is absent, whose shadow is a wife's protection. What business has she in the midst of a crowded household and flocks of servants? I do not wish that she look down upon them as servants but that she feel shame in their presence since they are men. In any event, if her pretentious house requires these services, let her put an elderly man of good morals in charge of them, one who bases his honor on the esteem of his mistress. I know that many women, even though the doors of their house were closed to the public, have suffered from the bad reputation of their male servants, who aroused suspicion either by the immoderate care they took of themselves or the sleekness of their plump bodies or their age prone to lust or a carefree haughtiness that comes from the knowledge of a secret love. Even if well concealed this self-confidence frequently bursts out into the open and he despises his fellow servants as if they were his slaves.[63]

20. I add to these recommendations that a widow should decrease her domestic staff, especially the men, and should hire an older woman, one who is upright and prudent, under whose regime she will live and whom she will consult in things pertaining to womanly responsibilities. If she herself is already well advanced in years, then let her take to herself an old kinsman of

---

61. 1 Tim. 5:8.

62. Salvina was a lady at the imperial court whose husband, Nebridius, prefect of Gaul, had died. Jerome wrote her a rather stern and outspoken letter in which he warns her of the dangers of widowhood and counsels her to watch over her son and daughter.

63. Jerome *Letters* 79.8 (*NPNF,* 2d ser., 6:166).

the family in whom to confide. Finally, let her always avail herself of the advice of someone whom she knows to be a man of good sense, who will look after her interests and is a man of proven reliability. The ancient Romans wished their women to be always under the control of men, whether they be fathers, husbands, brothers, or close relatives.[64]

She should prefer to live with her mother-in-law rather than with her mother or her own relatives, both in memory of her husband, to whom it will be seen as a tribute in that she prefers his family and race to her own, and because she transferred herself into that family, for which she bore or at least would have borne children. In addition, respect for chastity is considered to be more severe among the relatives of the spouse than among the immediate family, since love is less strong there, and hence tolerance is almost nonexistent and freedom more restricted. But a holy woman will not be motivated so much by these considerations, although these will also influence her, as by the memory of her husband and her devotion to him. So the younger Antonia,[65] daughter of Octavia and Mark Antony the triumvir, the wife of Drusus, spent her last years with her mother-in-law, Livia.[66] So Ruth preferred the country and home of her mother-in-law, Naomi, to her own.[67] That is my advice, unless living with the mother-in-law or in-laws there are some licentious and wayward young men who can harm her good name or even put her chastity in jeopardy, or if some of the female relatives have a tainted reputation. In that case, it would be wiser to return to your own relatives.

64. Livy 34.2.11; Justinian *Institutes* 1.8ff.
65. Antonia Minor's husband, Nero Claudius Drusus, died at the age of thirty. His father, Tiberius Claudius Nero, was the first husband of Livia, whom Augustus later married.
66. Valerius Maximus 4.3.3.
67. Ruth 1:16.

VI

HOW SHE SHOULD BEHAVE
IN PUBLIC

21. Widows will have to go out into public occasionally. Let them do this with their heads covered and showing in their whole demeanor what they profess in name. For the word "widow" in Greek and Latin means "abandoned" or "left alone." There is a great difference between a woman who is alone and one accompanied by a husband. If we required such severity of character and dress from a wife, what shall we expect from a widow? They must be an example of chastity, frugality, and modesty. If they are to be an example, how will it be fitting that they issue forth adorned and attired with the armor of the devil, vaunting their proud spirit and laying the snares of Satan instead of the example of Christ? Saint Ambrose said very well: "Mourning garments and a severe, sad countenance inhibit lewd glances and extinguish lustful desires."[68] It will be safest to go out into public rarely and then with a good, respectable woman and to go directly to your destination. Do not seek out churches where there are crowds of men, but where there is solitude, in which there is no opportunity to sin but ample opportunity to pray.

You need not frequent the company of priests and monks. The devil is shrewd, and, through long experience, he has learned in what manner each one can be seduced. He easily obtains what he desires when he has found the right moment, because this is his sole occupation. If a widow wishes to consult someone about religious matters, let her choose an old man whose lust is already spent and has not been replaced by new vices, one who is not after his own advantage and does not use flattery through hope of gain, a man of solid and serious learning, who has acquired wisdom through native intelligence and experience. Such a man will not put excessive constraints upon the woman's spirit, nor will he relax the reins that curb freedom, and

68. Ambrose *On Widows* 51 (*NPNF*, 2d ser., 10:399).

will deem nothing more important or worthy of more esteem than truth and piety. Let the widow have recourse to such a person if she has doubts, and ignore others. Jerome gives this advice to Eustochium:[69] "If you be ignorant of something or have doubts about something in Scripture, ask one whose way of life commends him, whose age absolves him from blame, whose reputation does not condemn him, who can say, 'I have espoused you to one man, to show yourself a chaste virgin to Christ.'[70] If you cannot find such a man to instruct you, it would be wiser to remain ignorant in safety than to learn at your own peril."[71]

A widow does not belong in the marketplace, in male gatherings, or in crowds. In those places, there is great danger for the virtues that are most honored in a widow—chastity, modesty, good reputation and holiness.

22. A widow must behave in such a way as to consult the best interests of others as well her own. In public, exposed to men's eyes, in contact with many people, little by little she assumes a bold air; chastity and shame waver and are exposed to danger. If she is not defeated in the battle, she is surely under attack. And as far as being under the assault of the enemy is concerned, everyone speaks of it not as it really is, but as he likes. The cares of this world make cool our fervor for heavenly things, and as the Lord bears witness in the gospel, if the seed falls among thorns and is suffocated by the cares and anxieties of this life, it cannot grow to fruition.[72]

And as the sea that has been stirred up by the winds is still in agitation after they have subsided and the storm is passed, so the human mind, freed from the affairs of this world, returns to it in feeling and thought. The mind is still breathless after its labors and cannot return immediately to its usual tranquillity. When it is disturbed, you see what kind of supplications it will make—anxious, confused, smelling of the mud of this world, just as one cannot draw clear and limpid water from a turbid spring. Peace of mind is that which elevates us to colloquies with the divine, as it did with Mary Magdalen, who put aside worldly things and sat at the Lord's feet, intent on his words.[73] For that reason, she received Christ's praise, that she had chosen the best part, and it would not be taken away from her.[74]

---

69. Eustochium (368–418), together with her mother, Paula, a Roman noblewoman, was given spiritual guidance by Saint Jerome. The two women followed him to the East and directed several convents in Bethlehem. Jerome's letter to her is a long treatise on virginity.

70. 2 Cor. 11:2.

71. Jerome *Letters* 22.29 (*NPNF*, 2d ser., 6:34).

72. Luke 8:14.

73. Luke 10:39.

74. Luke 10:42.

But some woman may object: "My patrimony is at risk; a suit is being brought against me." Listen to Ambrose on this point: "Do not say, 'I am alone.' Chastity seeks solitude; the modest woman seeks seclusion, the unchaste one seeks company. If you have a lawsuit pending and fear your adversary's attorney, the Lord intervenes with the judge, saying, 'Seek justice for the orphan and defend the widow.'[75] If you wish to protect your patrimony, the heritage of chastity is greater and a widow keeps it better than a married woman. If your servant erred, forgive him. It is better to bear up with another's fault than lay bare your own."[76]

23. What of the fact that we see that judges are so disposed by natural inclination to favor the cause of the one who has weak advocates or none at all? In those cases, judges take the place of advocates, since they often oppose the most cunning defenders and advocates. This is because we have a natural aversion to great power and wealth and help those with little resources and try to abase and humble those who exalt themselves and raise up the lowly. In fact, it is the common belief (as a wise man once said) that in every contest he who is more powerful, even if he is the victim of injustice, seems to be the one who does wrong, simply because he is more powerful. What I have said of judges you may consider to apply also to advocates. To all of them the case of the widow will be a stronger one when they see that she is impeded and inhibited by her modesty from giving convincing arguments herself. The less she recommends her own cause, the more approval she receives. The cause of a woman vowed to a life of holiness is more worthy of belief, since they do not believe that such a person would retain possession of or seek after what is not her own. Thus, a good woman does not bring the arguments of a litigant into court but the authority of testimony and the weight of a previous favorable opinion.

24. The loquacious, importunate busybody will inevitably pester and annoy her hearers and deprive herself of the protection I mentioned. I have spoken of good judges and advocates or those whom the widowed woman does not judge to be evil. But there are some who are so corrupt and dishonorable that they render their decisions not according to fairness but motivated by shameless lust. The severity of public good order would exact punishment for these abuses except that, as a wise man said, laws are like spiderwebs that entrap tiny insects, but are broken by bigger prey.[77] But if a virtuous widow knows them to be such (their public reputation will reveal

75. Isa. 1:23.

76. Ambrose *On Widows* 57 (*NPNF*, 2d ser., 10:400).

77. Plutarch *Solon* 5.2.

them for what they are), she will avoid them at all cost, even to the detriment of her possessions and at the risk of her own life. The same goes for all lecherous and libertine individuals.

As for running about from one house to another, Paul teaches that widows who idly gad about from house to house should be ostracized as dishonorable.[78] Not only are they idle but garrulous and inquisitive, blurting out things they should not. For there are some widows who, when they think they have performed all their own domestic tasks, insolently meddle in the affairs of others and like wise counselors give advice, encouragement, instructions, reprimands, and criticisms; they are remarkably sharp-eyed outside their home but blind when at home.

---

78. 1 Tim. 5:13.

VII

ON SECOND MARRIAGES

25. It is heretical to say that second marriages should be totally rejected and condemned. That it is better to abstain than marry again is not only a counsel of Christian purity, that is, of divine wisdom, but also a recommendation of pagan, that is, human wisdom. Cornelius Tacitus writes, as I have mentioned before, that among German women only virgins married.[79] There have been women who were widowed in their early youth but refused to marry again, especially women of great renown: Valeria, the sister of the Messalae, and Porcia, the younger daughter of Cato, of whom it is told that once when a woman of very good morals, who had a second husband, was being praised in her presence, she replied that a happy and chaste woman would never marry twice.[80] Cornelia, the mother of the Gracchi, refused marriage to Ptolemy, king of Egypt, after the death of Gracchus. Although she was wooed with great promises, she preferred to remain Cornelia, wife of Gracchus, rather than queen of wealthy Egypt.[81]

In popular representations and in the theater, second marriages are satirized even in the songs of mimes: "Frequent marriages give rise to ill report;"[82] "The woman who marries many men is pleasing to many men."[83] Valerius Maximus, with reference to ancient practices, says, "Those who were content with one marriage were honored with a crown of chastity, for they were of the opinion that the mind of a true noblewoman remained uncontaminated in its essential purity if after losing her virginity in the mar-

---

79. Cf. par. 2.
80. Jerome *Against Jovinianus* 1.46 (*NPNF*, 2d ser., 6:382).
81. Plutarch *Tiberius Gracchus* 1.4.
82. Publilius Syrus 311.

83. Publilius Syrus 524.

riage bed she would no longer show herself in public. They thought that the experience of many marriages was an indication of a kind of legitimate intemperance."[84]

26. Many reasons are adduced by widows, which they put forward as a pretext for their desire to remarry. This is what Saint Jerome says of them, writing to Furia:[85]

> Young widows, some of whom have turned back to follow Satan after indulging their sensual desires in their marriage under the law of Christ say: 'My meager patrimony is diminishing daily, my ancestral inheritance is being dissipated, a servant spoke to me insultingly, my maid servant ignored my orders. Who will handle my public affairs? Who will be responsible for the rents of my estates? Who will see to the education of my children? Who will bring up my children and my house-slaves?' And—for shame!—they adduce, as a reason for remarriage the very thing which of itself should have prevented their marriage. A mother does not bring home a foster-father for her children but an enemy, not a parent but a tyrant. Enflamed by her passions, she forgets the fruit of her womb and before her own children, who are ignorant of their unhappy fate, she puts aside her recent mourning and arrays herself as a new bride. Why do you use your patrimony as an excuse, or the arrogance of your servants? Confess to your moral turpitude. No woman takes a husband in order *not* to sleep with him. Or if lust is not the stimulant, what madness is it to prostitute your chastity like a whore so that you can add to your wealth, and that for a worthless and perishable thing a precious and permanent possession, your chastity, is defiled? If you have children, why do you seek to marry? If you do not have any, why do you not fear sterility, which you have already experienced, and prefer something uncertain to the certain loss of your chastity? Betrothal papers are being drawn up for you now so that later you will be compelled to make a will. Your husband will feign illness, and what he wants you to do when you are on the point of death he will do himself, confident that he will survive you. If it should happen that you have children of this second husband, then domestic strife and internal contention will result. You will not be allowed to love your own children or regard them with equal affection. You will have to bring them food in secret; he

---

84. Valerius Maximus 2.1.3.

85. Furia was a friend of Jerome to whom he wrote a long letter on the duties of a widow.

will be jealous of your dead husband and if you do not hate your own children, he will think that you still love their father. But if he has offspring by another wife when he takes you into his home, even if you have a heart of gold, you will be portrayed as the cruel step-mother, the butt of all writers of comedy and mimes and every rhetorical commonplace. If your stepson is ill or has a headache, you will be defamed as a poisoner. If you do not feed him, you are cruel; if you do, you will be called a witch. I beseech you, what great blessing can there be in a second marriage to outweigh all these evils?[86]

27. What can I add of my own concerning the praises of continence and dissuasion of a second marriage after the torrential eloquence of Jerome or the sweet ambrosia of Ambrose? She who wishes can seek it there. It is not for me to cite these passages here, since it is not my purpose to give exhortations to a certain manner of life but rules concerning it, whatever it may be. Nevertheless, I would encourage the chaste woman to persevere in holy widowhood, all the more so if she has children, which is the goal and fruit of marriage. But if a woman is not confident that in leading this type of life she will be able to overcome the stimulations of lust or the talkativeness of evil tongues always ready to find fault, let her heed the words of the apostle Paul to the Corinthians: "I say to widows and to the unmarried that it is well for them to remain single as I do. But if they cannot exercise self-control, they should marry. For it better to marry than to burn."[87] And to Timothy he says, "Do not accept young widows, for when their natural desires make them unfaithful to Christ, they want to marry again, and so they incur condemnation for having violated their first pledge. Besides, they learn to become idle and go around from house to house, and they are not merely idlers, but gossips and busybodies, saying what they should not say. Therefore, I would have younger widows re-marry again, bear children, manage their households and not give the adversary any opportunity to revile us. For there are some who have already turned away to follow after Satan."[88]

28. Some do not wish to marry, alleging freedom as an excuse. If it is freedom of the spirit you desire in order to dedicate yourself entirely to God more freely without having to care for a husband, who would not approve of it? But if it is so that you may do whatever you please without anyone to reprehend or admonish you, then that is freedom of the flesh, and the occasion not of freedom, but of death. It is not the token of an upright and

---

86. Jerome *Letters* 54.15 (*NPNF,* 2d ser., 6:107).

87. 1 Cor 7:8–10.

88. 1 Tim. 5:11–15.

wise woman to ask that the inexperienced and weak sex be subject to no power or authority when human and divine laws have always made it subject to the power and rule of men.

Some refuse second marriages not for love of purity and chastity, but out of vainglory. They will hear from Christ what he said to the foolish virgins, "I know you not,"[89] and what he said to the hypocrites, "You have received your reward."[90] These women, widowed of their husbands, have not become brides of a vain and fruitless stupidity but, rather, its unfortunate and toiling slaves.

But as for those who remarry, let it not be immediately or shortly after their husband's death. That would be a sign that they did not love them when they were alive, since they so quickly put aside their sorrow, grief, and mourning. And if they must make provision for their house or their children, let them take care of it before the turmoil of the wedding and before coming under the control of the new husband. And if they have parents, they should not deprive them of the right they have over them, and they should give them great power, even total discretion, in arranging the new marriage. For the fact of losing a husband does not mean they have also lost their father, and although they are freed from the laws of their husband, this is not true in the case of their parents, to whom they owe no less now that they are widows than when they were unmarried women.

29. We have the opinion of the Saint Ambrose on this subject, found in his first book on the patriarch Abraham: "If a woman loses her husband while she is still young and is in fear of falling victim to her weakness, let her marry in the Lord, if she so wishes, leaving the choice of a spouse to her parents so that she will not seem to be driven by desire, if she were to arrogate this right to herself. It should be made to seem that she was sought after by the husband rather than the contrary."[91] In place of parents, older blood relatives or relatives through marriage should be called upon. Widows who find husbands for themselves without consulting those to whom they owe the respect due to parents, or do so against their advice and objections, are worthy of rebuke. They make it quite clear that they are doing this not so much to counter the impulses of the flesh without committing sin as to satisfy their lustful desires, and would do so without marrying if it were possible without incurring disgrace. Therefore, the marriage is contracted out of respect for men, not for God, so that no one will dare reprehend as a vice that which has the protection of a sacrament. God, however, will rep-

---

89. Matt. 25:12.
90. Matt. 2:5.
91. Ambrose *On Abraham* 1.91 (*PL* 14:154).

rehend and punish it, since nothing is veiled from his eyes. Rather, he sees the vice naked and exposed, as all things are visible to him. If it is only through pious motives and the desire to escape guilt and for no other reason that marriage is sought, they should not be concerned about who the husband is, as long as he frees them from any fault through marriage. And they owe this honor to those whom they are ordered to obey by a divine oracle, that the desire should come from the woman but the choice from the parent. The woman signifies that she wishes to marry; the father decides whom she will marry. Besides, when the mind is seized by feelings of passion, it does not see what is beneficial to it, for the nature of all passion is to stir up, excite, and confound everything, to obscure the light of what is good and true so that it is not discernible.

30. But there are some widows who are more free, who are not in the care of their relatives. These women live contrary to the established practice of the people of ancient Rome, among whom no woman was allowed to perform even a private action without a person of authority and who wished the woman to be in the power of parents, brothers, or husbands. But it is granted to certain women by their guardians to choose a husband at their own discretion. They should seek husbands proper for widows to marry— not lascivious, carefree, imprudent, complaisant young men, who are not able to govern either themselves or a wife or a household.

They should look, rather, for a man past middle age, serious, severe, respected, experienced, judicious. By his tact, he keeps the whole household attentive to their duty, and by his wisdom so regulates and directs everything that a sober good humor reigns in the house. Thus, there is obedience without defiance, the members of the household persevere in their task without trouble, and everything is clean and intact, since they know that they find acceptance with the one person whom they wish to please more than the whole city.

But if the widow is forced into another match against her will, it would be best to conceal the wedding, the desire for which is loathsome to her, lest she reveal to the people something for which she fears censure. Therefore, second marriages should be celebrated in silence, almost in secret, without fuss and dancing. The spouses, satisfied that the wedding is known to their relatives, will avoid strangers, so that people will hear of the fact of their marriage rather than of their plans to be married. No one with a foul disease asks publicly that medicine be administered to him; and no one, unless perhaps he is insane, proclaims that he has attained something for which he will be criticized for having desired.

APPENDIX:
ON MARRIAGE[1]

1. This is not the place to discuss the praise or blame of marriage or to touch on inveterate questions, such as whether a wise man should take a wife; or those topics treated by our own Christian authors concerning marriage, celibacy, and virginity; and other questions discussed by Saint Augustine and the other writers of our holy religion. I know there have not been lacking those who vehemently attacked the institution of marriage—not only heretics, such as the Manichaeans,[2] who required total abstinence from marriage, whose error was condemned and rejected; but also pagans, who pronounced judgment on the entire female sex from some evil examples in accordance with that all too common practice of judging a whole nation from knowledge of only a few individuals. Thus, the Carthaginians[3] became notorious for their treachery, the Cilicians[4] as brigands, the Romans for their avarice, the Greeks for their fickleness.

Respectable matrons ought to hold in hatred and vent their hostility upon dishonorable women as a disgrace and shame upon their whole sex.

1. In the first edition (Antwerp, 1524), the second book begins with a chapter entitled *De coniugio* ("On Marriage"), which is omitted in the revised version and consequently did not belong to the definitive text as far as Vives was concerned. This chapter does not appear in the two Basel editions (1538 and 1540) nor in the *Opera omnia* in two folio volumes published by Nicolaus Episcopius (Basel, 1155). It was included, however, in the Spanish edition of Mayáns y Siscar (Valencia, 1782–90), and, since this is available in a modern reprint (London: Gregg Press, 1964), I have thought it opportune to provide a translation of it in an appendix.

2. The Manichaeans, once considered a Christian heresy but more of a religion in its own right, was founded by Mani or Manichaeus (216–74). It taught that life in this world is radically evil. While the elect of the religion abstained from all sexual contact, the catechumens were allowed to marry but not to conceive.

3. In Latin the ironic phrase *Punica fides*, literally "Punic" or "Carthaginian" faith, was commonly used to refer to their proverbial craft and deceit.

4. The Cilicians inhabited a region in southeast Asia Minor. They were notorious for their piracy on the high seas.

Yet no one has dared to pour blame upon the female sex without having to admit that a good woman is the best of possessions, bearer of good fortune, and a favorable omen. As Xenophon says in his *Oeconomicus,* "She is the greatest cause for a man's happiness."[5] "There is nothing sweeter than a good wife,"[6] said the wise Theognis. Sextus in his *Sentences* calls her a man's glory.[7] The tragedian Euripides, who was exasperated by two unvirtuous wives[8] and filled his tragedies with invectives and maledictions against women and was called a misogynist in Greek,[9] still does not hesitate to say that there is no greater pleasure than that which two good spouses enjoy.[10] Hesiod, a poet hostile to women, said that just as there is nothing more unfortunate for a man than to find a bad wife, so there is nothing more fortunate than to happen upon a good one.[11]

2. Solomon, who lost his mind because of women and from a wise man became the most foolish of men, as if cursing his own misdeeds, is often carried away with great passion in his castigation of women, but in such a way that he often states clearly what kind of women he means. In Proverbs he writes that a foolish and bold woman will be without bread and that a man is consumed by a bad wife as wood is by a ship-worm.[12] But in the same work, how splendid and marvelous is his encomium of the good woman, of whom he says, "Noble is her husband at the city gates, as he takes his seat among the elders of the land. Fortitude and dignity are the vesture of a holy woman and she will laugh in the last day. She has opened her mouth unto wisdom and the law of kindness is upon her tongue. Her children have risen up and called her blessed and her husband has commended her. Many women have amassed riches, but you have surpassed them all."[13]

These and other things the wise king said, which I see meet with the universal approval of all wise men. I do not strive to enter into what men of

5. Xenophon *Oeconomicus* 7.11–12.

6. Theognis 1225. West, *Greek Lyric Poetry* (Oxford, 1993), 73.

7. *The Sentences of Sextus,* ed. Henry Chadwick (Cambridge, 1959), 237, p. 39.

8. Their names were Melito and Choerile, according to ancient lives of the poet. Cf. *Euripide,* ed. Louis Meridier, vol. 1, *genos Euripidou kai bios (The Life and Family of Euripides)* (Paris, 1970), 2–3.

9. Aulus Gellius *Attic Nights* 15.20.5.

10. From Euripides' lost play, *Andromeda,* in *Tragicorum graecorum fragmenta,* ed. Augustus Nauck. Supplementum addidit Bruno Snell (Hildesheim, 1964), 400. Vives probably would have derived this quotation from the collection of Stobaeus, *Ioannis Stobaei Anthologium,* ed. Wachsmuth and Hense (Leipzig, 1884–1912), 63.22.

11. Hesiod *Works and Days* 702.

12. Prov. 5:4.

13. Prov. 31:23–29.

great discernment have discussed or rather declaimed; nevertheless, learned men have taught that one should marry, as they themselves did. To begin with, the seven sages of Greece married; after them Pythagoras, Socrates, Aristotle, Theophrastus, the two Catos, Cicero, Seneca—no doubt because they saw that there was nothing more natural than the union of man and woman, whereby the human race, which is mortal in its individual members, is perpetuated in its totality. In this way, you render to posterity what you received from your forebears and return thanks, as it were, to nature. Aristotle in his moral writings [14] exhorts the citizen to marry not only for the sake of having children but also for living together, since that is the first and most important union that exists.

3. I shall explain why this is so. Beginning with that association and friendship by which all men are joined together like brothers, descended from God, the father of all things—by which nature itself, which is much the same in all men, binds us together with a certain bond of love—the one that exists among those who share the same sacraments is closer, and it is made closer still through human institutions and civil law. We are more prone to establish relations with our fellow citizens rather than with strangers. Among citizens, our special friends are dearer to us; and among these, our kinsfolk are more beloved; and of those joined by blood, none is closer than the wife, [15] whom that first progenitor of the human race, upon first seeing her, immediately proclaimed she was bone of his bone and flesh of his flesh. [16] And when there were not yet fathers or mothers, he formulated a law as if it were a law of nature: "For her sake a man shall leave father and mother and shall cling to his wife, and they shall be two in one flesh." [17] Who will deny that marriage is a most sacred thing, which God instituted in Paradise, when mankind was yet pure and untouched and defiled with no stain? He chose it in his mother. He approved it by his presence at the marriage feast, and he wished to perform the first of his miracles on that occasion, [18] to give an example of his divinity and declare that he had come to save both those who were lost through such unions and those who were born to them. [19] But we are not writing here of the praise of marriage, which men of great eloquence have often done in long discourses; we are only instructing the virtuous woman.

14. Aristotle *Economics* 1.3 1343b (Barnes 2:2131); *Ethics* 8.12, 1162a (Barnes 2:1836).
15. This section is based on Cicero *On Good and Evil* 5.65.
16. Gen. 2:23.
17. Gen. 2:24.
18. John 2:1–11.
19. Matt. 18:11; Luke 19:10.

BIBLICAL REFERENCES INDEX

GENERAL INDEX

Paris and Vienna, 75
Pasiphaë, 20, 160
Paul, Saint, 18, 21, 47, 69, 72, 71, 81,
    88, 89, 92, 94, 96, 127, 137, 155,
    159, 164, 176, 181, 195, 199, 227,
    230, 245, 254, 256, 262, 263, 272,
    304, 311, 312, 313, 315, 321, 324
Paul III, 12
Paula (friend of Saint Jerome), 59,
    69, 73
Paulina (wife of Seneca), 68, 189
Paulinus, Saint, 18, 178
Paynell, Thomas, 16
Penelope, 61, 127, 160, 193, 260
Perseus, 189
Peter, Saint, 47, 94, 166, 195, 237,
    263
Petrarch: *On the Remedies of Good and Evil
    Fortune*, 30
Phanuel, 312
Phaon, 65
Phemonoe, 65
Philetas, 76
Philip of Macedon, 139, 226
Philo, wife of, 237
Philoxenus, 217
Phinehas, 280
Phryne, 90
Piccolomini, Alessandro, 27
Pierre of Provence, 75
Pindar, 67
Pisistratus, sons of, 136
Pittacus of Mytilene, 158
Pizan, Christine de, xxiv–xxvi; *Book of
    the City of Ladies*, xv, xviii–xix, xxii;
    querelle des femmes, xx; *The Treasure of
    the City of Ladies*, xxii
Placidia, Galla, 224
Plantin, Christopher, 32
Plato, 16, 18, 46, 48, 67, 77, 78, 117,
    139, 164, 196, 207, 208, 237, 267,
    272, 281, 291; *Apology of Socrates*, 5;
    Laws, 90; *Phaedrus*, 119
Plautus, 101, 218, 248, 262
Pliny the Elder, 23, 128, 193, 302
Pliny the Younger, 177, 213, 279
Plutarch, 16, 27, 33, 53, 71, 103, 131,

144, 145, 162, 188, 191, 215, 220,
    247, 288
Poggio Braccioline: *Facetiae*, 35
Pompey the Great, 190, 196, 197, 272
Ponthus and Sidonia, 75
Porcia, 18, 66, 190, 226, 322
Postumia, 131
Proba, Valeria, 69
Propertius, 76
Prosper of Aquitaine, 78
Protesilaus, 189
Prudentius, 18, 78
psychology of women, Greek view,
    xi–xii
Ptolemy, 322
Publicola, Valerius, 305
Publilius Syrus, 113; *Mimes*, 13
Pyramus and Thisbe, 75
Pyrrhus, 102
Pythagoras, 48, 66, 108, 210, 241,
    329
Pythian priestess at Delphi, 67, 82

querelle des femmes (the woman question),
    xix–xx
Quintilian, 17, 22, 23, 53, 54, 58, 71,
    86, 101, 139

Raguel, 156
Rebecca, 136, 165, 229, 268
Redgrave, Robert, 31
Rémy, Nicholas, xxi
Ribero, Pietro Paolo de, xix
Roig, Jaime: *The Mirror*, 26
Robert, King (of England), 188
Rodrigo, King (of Spain), 145
Rodrigo Jiménez de Rada, 188
Rodríguez de la Cámara, Juan: *Triumph
    of Women*, xx, 24
Roman law: *Corpus of Civil Law*, xii; *Lex
    Oppia*, 102, 241; marriage, xii–xiii;
    Twelve Tables, xii, 303
Roper, Margaret, 33
Ruth, 166, 317

Sallust, 65, 139, 251, 255
Salonia, 196